DEATH *of* THE DAILY NEWS

DEATH *of* THE DAILY NEWS

How Citizen Gatekeepers Can Save Local Journalism

ANDREW CONTE

University of Pittsburgh Press

Published by the University of Pittsburgh Press, Pittsburgh, Pa., 15260
Copyright © 2022, University of Pittsburgh Press
All rights reserved
Manufactured in the United States of America
Printed on acid-free paper
10 9 8 7 6 5 4 3 2 1

Cataloging-in-Publication data is available from the Library of Congress

ISBN 13: 978-0-8229-4719-6
ISBN 10: 0-8229-4719-6

Cover design: Alex Wolfe

Dedicated to the people of McKeesport, Pennsylvania,
and to people everywhere telling their own story.

CONTENTS

DEATH *of*
THE DAILY
NEWS

PART I
Postmortem

1

Place of Death

I am very sad. Technology is great but I like to hold my newspaper in my hand. It's handy and you don't need a password. It's just there and I will miss not having that.

Two first-term members of Congress, John F. Kennedy and Richard M. Nixon, boarded the Capitol Limited train at Washington's Union Station on the Monday morning of April 21, 1947, headed to McKeesport, Pennsylvania, the economic and spiritual center of the Monongahela River valley and home to one hundred thousand unionized industrial workers. As the two newest members of the House Labor and Education Committee, the lawmakers were scheduled to appear that night at the Penn-McKee Hotel before more than one hundred people at an event sponsored by the local Junto Forum, a business-minded civic group. The men planned to debate the Hartley labor bill, which would eventually become the Taft-Hartley Act and set new rules for organized workers at a time of widespread labor strikes and heightened fears over communism.

Nixon, then thirty-four, spoke rigidly that night as he defended the rights of business owners to set limits on striking laborers; Kennedy, a boyish twenty-nine, maintained a more casual manner and talked about how unions needed to protect industrial workplaces from turning into sweatshops. Both kept up an evenhanded conversation despite some union members in the audience who turned agitated. "Naturally, I was slightly prejudiced because I am Republican, but at the same time, I was impressed by Kennedy," moderator William C. Baird later recalled.[1] "Both of them were excellent speakers and handled themselves well. They were very personable, and it was hard to tell which one had come from a wealthy family and which had worked his way up." McKeesport's local newspaper, the *Daily News*, chronicled the event in the next day's edition under the headline "Congressmen debate merits of House-passed labor bill; Nixon sees rights protected, Kennedy fears civil strife."[2]

For the two Navy veterans at the center of the debate, the visit to southwestern Pennsylvania helped them form a bond: after the presentation, six Junto members took the lawmakers to the Star Restaurant across the street from the Baltimore and Ohio Railroad station for coffee and sandwiches while they waited for the midnight train back to Washington. On the long ride back, the men stayed up late talking about how to handle communist threats in the United States and overseas. "Of one thing I am absolutely sure," Nixon later wrote. "Neither he nor I had even the vaguest notion at the time that either of us would be a candidate for president thirteen years later."[3] When the two men famously met again in 1960 for the United States' first televised presidential debate, McKeesport's newspaper reminded residents the candidates had met before, right there in the city's Penn-McKee Hotel.[4]

For McKeesport, the original event in 1947 underscored the industrial community's political and economic relevance. At one time, residents of the city had imagined that they might build a steel empire to rival that of larger, more established Pittsburgh, twelve miles downriver. That dream never came to fruition, but McKeesport, which sits at another confluence, of the Monongahela and Youghiogheny rivers, did dominate the Mon Valley with its manufacturing and blue-collar workers. National Tube Works opened a factory in 1872 to turn out pipes made from iron sheets rolled into tubes and welded.[5] By the end of the nineteenth century, the company had started making its own iron and then steel for seamless pipes, and it manufactured about 70 percent of all steel tubing in the United States. Within another few years, National Tube Works merged into the newly formed U.S. Steel, its factories occupying nearly all the riverfront through McKeesport, and the company gave the city its moniker of "Tube City."

Around the same time that National Tube Works started out, in 1884, three local men—Edward B. Clark, Harry S. Dravo, and William B. Dravo—decided to start their own newspaper, the *Daily News*, to compete with the existing *McKeesport Times*, where the Dravos had been working.[6] Their newspaper, originally based out of a small wooden building, made its mark on the city over the years with several significant civic developments: it had the first structure illuminated by private electric light in 1889, and later, when the *Daily News* opened an iconic art deco building at the heart of the city in 1938, it had the city's first air conditioning. Purchased in 1925 by four local men, including a prominent local politician, State Senator William D. Mansfield, who served as publisher for the rest of his life, the newspaper eventually grew to have 46,836 subscribers in the early 1970s, with about 130 employees. As a reminder to readers of its place in their lives, the newspaper carried a slogan beneath the nameplate at the top of every front page: "More than a newspaper, a community institution."

All of McKeesport's manufacturing production, in turn, supported a thriving community with some fifty-five thousand residents at its peak in the 1940s. McKeesport had been home to the first G. C. Murphy five-and-ten-cent store, and the city served as the company's headquarters, with 560 outlets spread across twenty-four states.[7] McKeesport boasted a half dozen movie theaters, several furniture stores and jewelry shops, and more than seven hundred retail stores, including three big department stores—Cox's, Jaison's, and Imel's.

The city retained so much importance that Kennedy returned as president on October 13, 1962, just days before the Cuban Missile Crisis unfolded, and spoke to a crowd of twenty-five thousand people. He stood on a wooden stage with red, white, and blue bunting hanging from it and a tent erected overhead. The dais sat at the spiritual center of the city in a small grassy parklet between the municipal building and the art deco home of the local newspaper, the *Daily News*. Some people had slept overnight to be near the front of the crowd, and afterward the audience thronged so close to the stage that its railing collapsed. "The first time I came to this city was in 1947, when Mr. Richard Nixon and I engaged in our first debate," Kennedy said to laughter and cheers that day.[8] "He won that one, and we went on to other things." A year later when an assassin killed Kennedy, McKeesport's residents quickly started a fundraising drive for a memorial. The nine-foot statue stands on an eight-foot granite base, marking the place where the president spoke; it's believed to be the first Kennedy statue ever built.[9]

Like Pittsburgh and river towns throughout southwestern Pennsylvania, McKeesport fell on hard times in the 1970s and 1980s as foreign steel imports undercut American manufacturers and the steel industry collapsed under the weight of out-of-control spending and out-of-date infrastructure. McKeesport's population shrank to less than twenty thousand, and its famed business district withered away under the dual pressures of economic decline and the growth of suburban shopping malls. Workers boarded up two multistory parking garages near the city center, and blocks of retail shops and offices around City Hall were left to sit empty behind dusty plate-glass windows. G. C. Murphy merged with Ames Department Stores in 1985, which moved away the retail company's head-quarters and laid off nine hundred local employees. The Penn-McKee Hotel, where the future presidents had debated, turned first into a retirement home and then a homeless shelter before owners abandoned it in the early 1990s. Criminals have since looted and vandalized the building, setting fire to it twice.[10]

Then at the end of 2015, the city suffered another major blow: the McKeesport *Daily News*, the newspaper that had been operating for 131 years at the center of the city, near the site where the Kennedy statue stands, rolled the last of its forty thousand-plus editions off the presses in the basement of its art deco home and closed.

"We grew up knowing that our personal life-changing events—graduations, weddings, births and deaths—were all recorded in the newspaper," State Senator Jim Brewster, who delivered the newspaper as a boy and later worked at a newspaper before going into politics, said at the time.[11] "The Daily News was on-the-scene when elections were won or lost; when projects succeeded or failed. It reliably reported school happenings, sporting events, crimes, fires, burglaries, and robberies."

Ernie Harkless, who had worked at the *Daily News* for more than forty-four years, summed up the feelings of many when he lamented the loss of the printed newspaper: "I am very sad. Technology is great but I like to hold my newspaper in my hand. It's handy and you don't need a password. It's just there and I will miss not having that."[12]

Overnight, with the death of the *Daily News*, McKeesport joined a growing number of small and midsize American cities that might be called "news deserts," or places that face an emerging crisis as citizens struggle to find out what happens around them. The consequences of losing their source of local news might come as a surprise to many people, even to the most loyal readers and civic leaders, but it threatens not only the ways they discover local news and information but also their very self-identity and the ties that bind them together as members of a community. The death of the *Daily News*—the singular loss of a relatively inex-pensive, easy-to-access source of local information—represents a larger threat to American democracy, upon which citizens have depended for more than two and a half centuries.

2

Time of Death

Newspapers therefore become more necessary in proportion as men become more equal, and individualism more to be feared. To suppose that they only serve to protect freedom would be to diminish their importance: They maintain civilization. . . . If there were no newspapers there would be no common activity.

On the morning of January 1, 2016, for the first time in exactly 131 years and 6 months, residents of McKeesport woke up without a local daily newspaper of their own: the final edition of the *Daily News* had rolled off the presses inside the newspaper's art deco building early the previous morning with a boldface headline reading, "Thanks, Mon Valley." Trib Total Media, the company that owned the newspaper, decided to close it as part of a consolidation of assets that included selling two other daily newspapers, selling a group of weekly newspapers, and closing one other newspaper in Monessen, nineteen miles south of McKeesport. Reporter Patrick Cloonen, who had become a household name to many readers over the previous fifteen years, started his last day on the job by covering a board of supervisors' budget meeting in a nearby community; he then came back to the newsroom to file his story and stayed a little past dinnertime to clear out his desk. "God will provide," Cloonan said. "He's provided for me up till now; he will provide for me in the future."[1]

For McKeesport's residents, the newspaper had existed so long—for more than a century, or for more than four or five generations of some families— that many had taken it for granted and few knew what to expect after it closed. Ordinary citizens and community leaders alike expressed a great sense of loss not only from the lack of information but also, perhaps even more significantly, from a loss of identity tied to the newspaper and the community.[2] For many, connections to the *Daily News* stretched back through their family history: "My dad faithfully read it; my grandfather faithfully read it," Colleen Denne, director of the Carnegie Free Library of McKeesport, said in an interview.[3] "Then we got it when we moved back. It was just what you did; you got the *Daily News*."

Community leaders in McKeesport experienced an additional sense of loss from not only the death of a community institution but also the end of their main way of reaching constituents. Even though the public officials did not always agree with the newspaper's coverage, they relied on the *Daily News* more than they realized to share information about the work they did for the community. While they had focused most on the newspaper's accountability reporting that often challenged those in power, these community leaders had not paid as much attention to the daily coverage that kept their names in print. State Senator Jim Brewster described an almost religious devotion to reading the *Daily News*: "It was like reading the Bible," he said. Mayor Michael Cherepko said he tried to look at the newspaper's closing from a glass-half-full perspective by noting that its reporters at least would no longer be telling any more negative stories about him and the city: "I said, 'Well, you know, I guess, we don't got to worry about all the negative stories.' That was being the glass half full, even though back then, I definitely knew that we were going to lose the good publicity, the good stories that were being told."

Others just saw the closure as further evidence of McKeesport's decline from an industrial center, once nationally famous for the steel pipe it produced, to an economically depressed city in the otherwise down-on-its-luck industrial Monongahela River valley. The newspaper's closure followed losses of factories, retail stores, and major businesses such as the headquarters of the G. C. Murphy retail chain with outlets across half of the United States. For evidence of the decline, residents had only to pass through downtown to see the rows of boarded-up storefronts across from city hall or drive through residential neighborhoods to see some houses with broken windows, weeds taking over the yard, and other signs of abandonment. "It's just another sad, unfortunate situation for us as a community, to try to pick up the pieces after," said Mark Holtzman Jr., superintendent of the McKeesport Area School District and a lifelong resident. Even amid staggering losses, the newspaper's closure still represented another significant, and distinct, blow to local morale. "It's sad," the mother of a toddler said. "To me it is, because the *Daily News* was such a big part of my life growing up. I've been in McKeesport for thirty-seven years, so I saw the decline of

McKeesport. . . . It's like I live in a ghost town. People died to come to McK-eesport; now people wouldn't be caught dead in McKeesport."

Few residents of McKeesport seemed to fully realize in that moment, on the morning of New Year's Day 2016, exactly what they were losing when the *Daily News* closed. They would come to discover the depths of that loss over the coming years not only as they started to feel less informed about the events happening in their community but also as they acknowledged growing distances among each other, and, perhaps most surprising of all, a lost sense of who they are. The newspaper not only chronicled daily life in McKeesport but, as a common touchstone for everyone from the poorest resident to the most powerful leaders of the community, created a shared conversation among everyone and ultimately came to define what it meant to be part of the community. When the newspaper's presses stopped running, an uncomfortable silence suddenly draped over everything, leaving residents scrambling to hear word of what was happening around them. "I would definitely say it wasn't until well after they were gone that I can honestly say, 'Man [the *Daily News*] covered everything,'" Cherepko, the mayor, said. "They were just out there. They covered everything going on in McKeesport."

Massive Disruption

Similar stories have repeated thousands of times all across the United States since the Great Recession of the mid-2000s, when massive technological change ran head-on into an economic crisis that threatened the newspaper industry. This disruption across the journalism industry has created significant changes in the way journalists gather and disseminate local news—and in the ways that citizens engage with information. More people access news via free online networks rather than subscribing to a printed daily newspaper or scheduling time to watch local television newscasts, creating financial distress within the news business and causing local newspapers, especially, to shrink or disappear entirely. More than a quarter of all US newspapers, or 2,100 of them, have closed since 2004,[4] while the number of journalists has fallen by half to 36,500 positions since 2006.[5] "The age of linear, analogue, top-down, elite-mass journalism has ended, as measured in declining newspaper circulations, journalistic redundancies and closures of titles, and fragmenting broadcast news audiences," Brian McNair, a media researcher at Australia's Queensland Technology University, wrote in 2013.[6]

The problems for local news only have continued to worsen since gaining speed during the Great Recession, and printed newspapers have been hit especially hard. The two years from 2007 to 2009 proved to be pivotal for the collapse of newspapers across the United States: more than one hundred newspapers closed, revenues declined by nearly one-third to $37 billion, and twelve thousand journalists left the business, shrinking the overall workforce by 17.5 percent.[7] Daily circulation of print newspapers peaked at sixty-three million subscribers in 1973, started declining in the early 1990s, and began to fall rapidly in the twenty-first century.[8] The losses have continued: after 2006, weekday print circulation decreased 40 percent to an estimated twenty-nine million subscribers in 2018, and as readers left advertisers abandoned newspapers too: advertising revenues alone, without counting circulation income, collapsed to $14 billion from a high of $49 billion.[9]

As a result, many communities have lost newspapers. Some closed newspapers were located in cities that had more than one daily newspaper, such as Denver, Seattle, and Honolulu, but most were in smaller areas and were the last surviving daily newspaper in their community. "Cuts in funding beget shortcuts in production," media researchers Marcel Broersma and Chris Peters write, "and the worry is that a lack of resources for proper reporting leads to a decline in the overall quality of news, which quickly descends in a downward spiral."[10]

Journalists for more than a century have rallied around the banner that they "afflict the comfortable and comfort the afflicted," meaning that they hold powerful groups such as politicians and corporations accountable while also sticking up for people who do not have a voice of their own. Classic examples of this occur when reporters search public records to find politicians wasting tax dollars or write about people being evicted from their homes without legal remedies. The full quote that inspired the journalists' mantra comes from the satirical and fictional bartender in the 1902 book *Observations by Mr. Dooley*, which goes much further to explain the all-encompassing role of news outlets in the daily lives of readers: "Th' newspaper does ivrything f'r us. It runs th' polis foorce an' th' banks, commands th' milishy, controls th' ligislachure, baptizes th' young, marries th' foolish, comforts th' afflicted, afflicts th' comfortable, buries th' dead an' roasts thim afterward."[11]

Many traditional newspaper journalists likely would embrace that broader notion of what they do as well, romanticizing their role in the communities they cover. Many see themselves as having a significant purpose in community life, upholding newspapers as a civic institution on par with libraries, churches, schools, and government itself. By fulfilling a larger, seemingly indispensable community service, journalists carved out a role for themselves that could be supported by both readers who subscribed to the newspaper to find out all the many things happening around them and by the advertisers who sought to place their own messages in front of this rapt audience. This unspoken agreement among journalists, readers, and advertisers allowed the industry to enjoy a lengthy period of relative financial success and calm throughout much of the twentieth century. With strong financial backing, news outlets of varying sizes could provide blanket coverage of local events from school board meetings to church festivals, write in-depth stories about public officials and community leaders, and cover even the minutia of daily life in many communities. Literally, the newspaper told about the lives of its readers from birth announcement to obituary.

The newspapers' business model, from the largest national media outlet down to the local community newsroom, depended on mass communication, or what the Harvard University media economist Robert G. Picard described in 2014 as "high market power over distribution platforms, mass audience, and mass advertisers."[12] Newspapers sometimes lost money on subscriptions that did not generate enough money to cover the cost of printing and delivery, but they more than made up the difference by charging advertisers for access to those subscribers. If a large enough audience in a given community subscribed to the newspaper to read about local events and information, advertisers would be eager to place advertisements in these publications at a high cost, generating income for the media outlet and its employees.

Media outlets, in turn, provided middle-class jobs for journalists who came to see themselves as professionals with jobs that allowed them to determine the news of the day, acting on behalf of the public to attend meetings, interview elected officials and celebrities, visit crime scenes, review restaurants and movies, and more. In the pre-internet age, the many untold decisions journalists made each day informed what information their readers would receive, a process known as "gatekeeping," determining what information passes through the gates of publishing to consumers and what gets ignored or discarded. In large cities with more than one newspaper, competing outlets might present alternate perspectives on the stories of the day, highlighting one point of view over another. But in many small towns, the newspaper singularly informed the public about what happened in the community—and if a certain publisher, editor, or journalist liked one idea over another, they could control who heard about it. Journalists make decisions every day about what events to cover, what sources to interview, what quotes to use and facts to cite, where to run the story—on the front page or buried inside—and the headlines and photographs to place around it.

Then the internet began to shift this role that newspapers and journalists had carved out uniquely for themselves. New technologies broke up the traditional business model by giving consumers more options for discovering information, and often without them having to pay for it. The changes snowballed by 2007 with the introduction of Apple's iPhone, the advancement of other smartphone technologies, and the advent of innovative delivery methods for information. Suddenly, readers could make up their own minds about what information to consume—and what they shared with others around them. Anyone with a smartphone or laptop could publish a story, photograph, video, graphic, or audio clip and share it, literally, with the rest of the world. "Moments can be captured by anyone on the typical cell phone, uploaded to YouTube, possibly altered in programs like Photoshop, and passed in ever-widening ripples through Facebook and Myspace pages—all without passing through a single journalistic filter where assessments can be made about credibility, context, relevance, and even fair play," Tom Fiedler, former dean of the College of Communication at Boston University, wrote in 2009.[13]

People not only were sharing information via the internet but looking for it there too. The increased use of technology over the internet, in particular, has altered journalists' gatekeeping role by making it possible for consumers to decide for themselves what sources of information to access and absorb. Journalists might offer a unique, enterprising perspective on the news, but even in the smallest towns, readers had other options for competing perspectives, even if only from their neighbors posting to social media. As soon as consumers started looking away from traditional media outlets, advertisers (who also suddenly had other options) no longer were willing to pay large sums to place their messages where they always had before, draining media outlets of both subscription revenue and the much more significant advertising dollars. Suddenly, newspapers lacked the distinct value that they once had as these emerging forces contributed to declines in subscriptions, advertising revenue, and, ultimately, stability. Many journalists, in turn, saw their own value plummeting, and while many were kicked out, others simply opted to leave the industry, citing instability, pay cuts, increased stress, burnout, and other symptoms of serving a failing business model.

But what about the internet? Yes, most print publications also have a robust online presence, but the internet does not generate revenues like print advertising does, paying publishers fractions of a penny for each reader who views a story. That shift contributes to a downward spiral in which online news outlets chase after smaller amounts of money. When news outlets make little bits of money with each consumer's internet click on a story, they need to generate more sensational short stories that will bait consumers into clicking. Enticed to create more short, clickable stories—either through incentives that pay them by the click or through punitive measures that punish them for failing to meet quotas—journalists start producing faster, bite-size content that draws in eyeballs and can be shared quickly and easily. That does not always leave enough space to tell the full story with depth. More news coverage over time has come to closely correspond with news releases from government, businesses, and nonprofits as journalists quickly take the information they are hand-fed and pass it along with few alterations to the public. At the same time, fewer news outlets can afford to produce the enterprise or in-depth investigative stories for which readers might pay. Instead, readers have come to expect news content for free, and fewer people will pay for light, inconsequential news coverage, further diminishing news outlets' resources, leading to even less hard-hitting, original reporting.

Online-only news outlets have fared better with business models designed to support smaller staffs in targeted geographic or niche areas, yet most of the money generated by news on the internet ends up with just a few companies. The number of visitors to digital-native online news outlets—those that originally started on the internet—peaked in 2016 around 22 million and has remained relatively level since then.[14] Digital advertising revenue continues to grow, topping $100 billion for the first time in 2018, but much of that money goes into a few pockets: Facebook alone collected more than half of the mobile digital display advertising revenue and 40 percent of the digital display advertising revenue.[15]

All the massive disruption caused by the internet has liberated citizens to find information on their own. Previously, readers might have settled for inadequate or one-sided stories from the only printed source they easily could access, particularly for news and information about their local community. Now they may seek out sources of information from multiple sources, judging its worth not necessarily from the quality of the fact-checking but based on something more subjective such as the writer's point of view. The same patterns that have been established at the national level showing consumers drifting to certain news sources for their conservative or liberal slant play out in smaller communities as citizens align with one faction or another: if you agree with the mayor, you will seek out information that validates the actions of city hall, and if you see failures in local government, you will look for perspectives that reinforce that thought.

Expanding News Deserts

Hundreds of orange and blue dots appear scattered across a map of the United States, clustered in high-density places such as the northeast, the Midwest, Florida, Texas, and California, with each one representing a weekly or daily newspaper that has gone out of business. Since 2004, the United States has lost more than 2,100 of them, leaving areas that have little or no sources for professionally generated news.[16]

Another map shows the areas left behind, the counties with one newspaper marked in orange and those with no newspaper in red. Again, like maps showing an emerging virus, the colors cut across wide swaths of the country, bisecting the United States from Montana and the Dakotas in the north through Nebraska, Colorado, Kansas, Oklahoma, New Mexico, and Texas in the south. Other clusters emerge out of the southeast, stretching from Florida through Georgia, north through the Carolinas into Virginia and west toward Alabama, Mississippi, Tennessee, and Kentucky.

Together, these two maps, created by researchers at the University of North Carolina, reveal a portrait of America with emerging news deserts that consume wide swaths of the country: residents of 225 counties have no newspaper at all, while those in 1,528 counties have just one, and it's usually a weekly.[17]

The term "news desert" first appeared in 2011, when the Chicago-based columnist Laura Washington wrote in the magazine *In These Times* about how journalists had failed to adequately cover poor urban communities, which she called a "communications desert."[18] She considered the paradox of how media seems to be everywhere, with the growth of internet news and social media sharing, and yet also nowhere in local urban communities that "are parched for information and news coverage with context and quality."[19] Washington called out journalists for looking out across the communities they claim to cover within Chicago, which she pointed out is a majority-minority city, and failing to see large groups of people of color: "In urban America, most news decision-makers are still white males with scant ties to or knowledge of the people they purport to cover. Reporters parachute into black and Latino neighborhoods to cover violent crime and community conflict. They are quick to interview the vagrant on the corner with the rag on his head, but not so much the hardworking neighborhood entrepreneur."[20]

Within days, the local blog *Chicago Is the World* shortened the concept while inviting readers to "visit the news desert we live in."[21] Steve Franklin, the site's ethnic media project director, wrote that Washington finally had articulated what he had been feeling about the media's lack of interest in local neighborhoods: "The mainstream media is shrunk and shrinking. Folks want to know what's happening in their neighborhoods. But they get zip instead. Zip magnified. They get stories from the media with the largest clout and pocketbooks, if they read or hear them, that make them feel about their neighborhoods, or tell them nothing good is happening or is going to happen."[22]

Tom Stites, a media researcher and former journalist at the *Chicago Tribune* and the *New York Times*, had been serving at the time as a media fellow at Harvard University's Berkman Klein Center for Internet & Society. He had appeared at a conference alongside Washington, where she had explained her concept. The idea of news deserts resonated with him, so he started using it in presentations and papers: "Elites and the affluent are awash in information designed to serve them, but everyday people, who often grapple with significantly different concerns, are hungry for credible information they need to make their best life and citizenship decisions. Sadly, in many communities there's just no oasis, no sustenance to be found—communities where the 'new news ecosystem' is not a cliché but a desert."[23]

Michelle Ferrier, another media researcher, later defined these places more broadly as "media deserts," or communities where residents lack easy access to "fresh, local news and information to inform and educate the public."[24] She used the term "media" rather than "news" to describe these deserts as places that not only have experienced the loss of news outlets but also experience other deficiencies such as a limited access to broadband internet or to technology such as mobile devices, or that suffer from negative implications caused by coding algorithms such as those used by internet search engines.[25] In 2016 research, Ferrier and her colleagues used mapping data to show the extent of these media contractions. Fewer than half of adults subscribe to a newspaper in two-thirds of the nation's zip codes.[26]

No matter how one defines these deserts, gaps in local news coverage create problems related to not only informing the public but also engaging citizens overall in conversations about what goes on around them. Local newspapers fulfill the basic functions of keeping people connected, such as providing original reporting, defining public agendas, supporting economic growth, fostering geographic communities, helping voters make choices, and holding public officials accountable. Many local publications use more space to focus on the ordinary functions of daily life than to dig into investigations of public officials, but in the process of chronicling the mundane, they knit community together through the moments that otherwise might be overlooked. Perhaps unwittingly, Columbia University researchers echoed the words of Mr. Dooley back at the turn of the twentieth century when they wrote in 2012 about the roles of newspapers in the lives of citizens: "Journalism exposes corruption, draws attention to injustice, holds politicians and businesses accountable for their promises and duties. It informs citizens and consumers, helps organize public opinion, explains complex issues and clarifies essential disagreements. Journalism plays an irreplaceable role in both democratic politics and market economies."[27]

But while newspapers once provided comprehensive coverage across broad sectors of community activity—news about local government, sports, and business; reviews of the arts and restaurants; comics and crossword puzzles—the internet has broken up that information into many little places, if anyone shares it at all. As fragmented as community news coverage has gotten, the Columbia researchers predicted that coverage likely will continue to worsen before it improves, and in some places such as midsize and small cities with no daily newspaper, coverage "will get markedly worse."[28]

Oases might appear in places across the American news desert, but it seems likely that the market forces behind the disruption will continue to expand into more and larger communities, gobbling up more local news operations just as Africa's Sahara Desert continues to expand by acquiring more of the green vegetation around it.

Citizens as Journalists

The old saying that you should "never start a fight with someone who buys ink by the barrel" really hits home whenever you stand in a newspaper pressroom and see the giant containers of ink, sometimes standing as tall as a grown man and rounder than a group of them standing together. The phrase was intended as a warning, particularly among politicians, that it makes little sense to take on the local newspaper, which can use all that ink to seemingly write endless stories about any topic the publisher wants. A politician who wants to win over the public can hardly afford to fight against someone who can print story after story in opposition.

Now, in the internet age, every person with access to a smartphone, tablet, laptop, or computer has more electronic "ink" at their disposal than any print publisher could ever buy. Growing more readily available since the late 1990s, technology has allowed each one of us to take an active role in creating and shaping the news, whether we realize it or not. In that way, amateur citizens who create and share the information—or news—they gather have unwittingly become what are known as "citizen journalists," whether professional journalists like it or not (and, spoiler alert, they most often do not).

Jay Rosen, a journalism professor at New York University, was among the first people to recognize this phenomenon, and he coined this definition in 2008 to explain what was happening: "When the people formerly known as the audience employ the press tools they have in their possession to inform one another, that's citizen journalism."[29] Critics since then have pointed out two significant shortcomings about Rosen's depiction: First, it neglects the fact that professional journalists also are citizens. Journalists commonly point out this distinction— that journalists are people too—when they are trying to gain access to any public realm where the community gathers. City officials might attempt to bar journalists from council chambers, but they can only do so by banning everyone from the public as well. If ordinary citizens can enter a meeting space, journalists can be there as well. Second, Rosen's definition equates the storytelling of amateurs to the journalism produced by trained professionals in terms of quality. While that might be true in some cases, citizens often lack the expertise that working journalists have to quickly triage a situation, glean the most salient points, verify them from multiple perspectives, and then communicate them to others in ways that are easy to understand.

Regardless of how one feels about the advent of citizen journalists—or the quality of their work—they exist and are growing in numbers as more people around the world gain access to the technologies that allow them to reach others with their words, images, and thoughts. The practice of creating user-generated content became so commonplace by the early 2000s that some media watchers had started referring to a "Generation C" (for "content"), recognizing the group of people who for the first time possessed the ability to create their own stories and who were being embraced by websites and applications that wanted to collect and disseminate that information.[30] The *Huffington Post*, for example, gained online prominence after its founding in 2005 by allowing anyone, from the already famous to the completely unknown, to contribute their own content and publish it on the media outlet's platform.[31] More than one hundred thousand people took them up on the offer, including many prominent names such as Barack Obama, Jennifer Aniston, and Oprah Winfrey. The "real achievement" of this idea, the publishers said, "was giving a spotlight to a huge number of people who weren't previously afforded one. In a time before the ubiquity of social media, the HuffPost platform was a public square where Americans of all walks of life could have a voice on matters both political and personal."[32] The experiment lasted for more than a decade, until 2018, when the *Huffington Post* shook up the world of citizen journalism once more by turning off the option for anyone to create a post and share it. By then, the cacophony of voices had reached such a confounding and overlapping decibel that the words of so many ordinary citizens became difficult to discern. The publishers wrote then, "One of the biggest challenges we all face, in an era where everyone has a platform, is figuring out whom to listen to. Open platforms that once seemed radically democratizing now threaten, with the tsunami of false information we all face daily, to undermine democracy. When everyone has a megaphone, no one can be heard."[33]

On the positive side, citizen journalism leads to a democratization of information by bringing more voices into public discourse and stimulating users to become more active in democracy. People who have high levels of trust in citizen journalism, for instance, also tend to get more involved in politics.[34] McNair, the media researcher in Australia, points out that "the decentralization of news has opened the media to an unprecedented diversity of voices and perspectives."[35] Media researchers Jane B. Singer and Ian Ashman have put the sentiment this way: "When journalists control the product and the discourse surrounding it, relations with users are destined to be held at a distance. Yet in a seamless network, with its flattened or even obliterated hierarchies, all are in close proximity, a click of a mouse away."[36] This idea of citizen journalism then goes a long way toward addressing the concerns raised about news deserts, that a few professional journalists—white men sitting at some distance in a board room, in the parlance of columnist Laura Washington about media coverage in Chicago—make decisions that disregard the realities of life in the communities they are supposed to be covering. When citizens are given the electronic ink to tell their own story, they can report what truly matters to them with an authenticity born out of their unique experience.

On the flip side, early experiments with citizen journalism also unearthed the challenges that untrained amateurs often encounter when they attempt to gather and report information about everything that goes on around them. Advance Publications—a newspaper chain owned by the family of founder Sam Newhouse, who had purchased the *Staten Island Advance* newspaper in 1922—owned Michigan's *Ann Arbor News* when it decided to shut down the newspaper in 2009 after 174 years of publication.[37] With a digital-first mission, the company created the AnnArbor.com website with half as many journalists and started putting out a twice-weekly print newspaper. Advance's executives said at the time that they believed residents of the college town, home of the University of Michigan, had higher-than-normal comfort with using the internet. With a "stated goal of being of, by and for the community," the newsroom promoted a "welcoming and interactive atmosphere" with free wireless internet as well as "comfortable couches and chairs to foster a relaxed environment where local folks can gather to discuss news and events, or simply surf the Web."[38] In response, several citizen journalists created online blogs and websites to provide local coverage by covering school board meetings and live-tweeting city council meetings.[39] The Online News Association and Poynter responded to the challenge by providing training for citizens who wanted to take up the work of gathering and telling local news. Despite all of these efforts, the quality of local reporting plummeted, residents started to question the veracity of information appearing on the local blogs, and gaps widened between the community and the remaining professional journalists.[40] A local resident and lawyer summed up the public's concern by telling a media researcher that the citizen journalists were not able to replace the professional journalists: "'They aren't accountable for what they say,' he says. And when it comes to governments, 'the lack of accountability is missing there, too.'"[41] Advance ultimately relented after four years, shutting down AnnArbor.com and rebranding the twice-weekly newspaper with the original name, *Ann Arbor News*.[42]

Most often, the concept of citizen journalism has been considered in the context of traditional journalism, with academics and professionals asking whether amateur newsmakers can create reliable, meaningful, original content. The entrepreneur and former journalist J. D. Lasica once famously referred to amateurs committing "random acts of journalism," which sounds derisive when taken out of context.[43] What he meant was that while few amateur bloggers create content on the level of professional journalists, these nonprofessionals can play a meaningful role in conjunction with traditional media: "Many readers have begun to turn to gifted amateurs or impassioned experts with a deep understanding of niche subjects, rather than to journalists who are generalists and cover topics a mile wide but an inch deep."[44] Compared to a traditional model in which journalists control the product and keep relations with users at a distance, this shift results in greater community engagement by asking citizens to cultivate news information and to share it with the public. This involvement by ordinary people breaks down barriers separating those who create news from those who consume it.

On another level, amateurs' contributions to local storytelling have gained credibility among professional journalists in moments of crisis, when citizens are close to the action and can record what they are witnessing in real time. Professional media outlets now regularly incorporate information from social media posts, especially videos and photographs, into their reports. This phenomenon has roots in the 2010 Arab Spring protests across the Middle East, and it became so commonplace over the following decade that it seemed completely normal when protesters inspired by former President Donald Trump stormed the US Capitol Building in January 2021. Individuals witnessing these events and participating in them posted images and information to social media sites such as Twitter and Instagram, often getting out the word faster than traditional outlets could report and disseminate the information. In these cases, Harvard's Picard has gone as far as to argue that the "citizens have become the primary providers of breaking news."[45] On the day of the Capitol attack, images recorded by the protesters themselves and by bloggers traveling with them filled television stories, online news sites, and even printed newspapers. That work by ordinary people who were witnessing a historical moment firsthand created the narrative that people came to understand amid a bewildering situation with conflicting reports. While citizens provided the images, however, professional journalists played a significant role in sifting through the firehose of information on the internet to discern what seemed accurate and how it could be formed to tell a linear and easily understood narrative.

Beyond these moments of crisis when citizens play a clearly defined role in gathering and sharing firsthand accounts, however, traditional professional journalists often have been unkind about the role that amateurs can play in the generation of quality news content. In the British-American author Andrew Keen's book *The Cult of the Amateur* (2007), he derisively blames user-generated free content for threatening traditional media such as newspapers and magazines, as well as culture itself.[46]

Faced with the potential for consumers to take a more active role in creating content, some editors simply have rejected the idea as impractical and unethical, saying few ways exist to verify the veracity of the information.[47] Typical of this thinking, the editor of one Texas community newspaper told researchers, "It does not make any sense. News is meant to be reported professionally, not through some random citizen. . . . Journalism is a profession and it cannot be done by anyone."[48] Similarly, European journalists questioned the abilities of nonprofessionals to sort through complicated information, consider all perspectives on a particular issue, and present an unbiased, ethical, fact-based account.[49] One mid-career Swedish journalist suggested to a researcher that professionals bring a level of "news sense" that the public does not always comprehend: "If someone is walking along the street and sees a dog poop on the grass, takes a picture with his mobile phone and puts it on his blog, there's not a lot of news value in that."[50]

The professional journalists fail to grasp in these criticisms that they, alone, no longer get to decide what information the public sees, and that they have no control over what media outlets the public values. If enough individuals want to see a photo of a dog pooping on the grass, they decide its value by clicking on the image, sharing the image with people in their circles of online friends, and even potentially generating income in the process. The balance of power for determining what has news value has shifted inexorably toward the people—citizen journalists—and away from professional journalists.

But although the people have power to collect information, share it, and determine its value, the work of citizen journalists does not exist without flaws. In fact, the work of untrained amateurs often results in the dissemination of inaccurate, unverified, and deeply biased information. Amateurs often contribute content sporadically and only on selected topics, they tend to focus only on their own perspective, and they often report information from biased points of view, even if that's something as simple as opposing a local public official.[51] Editors also worry about how to ensure the accuracy of information submitted by the public, and about avoiding libel situations. Typical of this thinking, one editor told media researchers, "My principal concern is that I see a lot of the citizen but not a lot of journalism. There's a lot of slander and personal anger or bitterness, but not news."[52] Some outlets have attempted to address these shortcomings with standards for citizen journalists that evoke the unofficial rules that many professional journalists have adopted for themselves. For the run of its experiment, the *Huffington Post* posted its Citizen Journalism Publishing Standards, a concise list that basically encapsulates many key principles from a Journalism 101 college course for how to be an ethical and responsible storyteller. Some highlights include

Stick to what you directly observe when reporting a story—never invent details or embellish facts.

Be very careful to avoid hearsay in your reporting, no matter how trustworthy the source may be. If someone tells you that their landlord refuses to turn on the heat, you need to make sure that you don't repeat that information as if it was a fact. You have to emphasize that the interviewee is making that claim either by paraphrasing their comments or through a direct quote.

Stick to the facts. Though you may sympathize with the people you are interviewing, do not take a position.

Never plagiarize—it is the hallmark of a lazy journalist.

Do not misrepresent yourself when you interact with a source.

Fact-check your sources, many of whom may be prone to exaggeration or have an agenda when talking to a reporter.

Always strive to verify any information from sources, either through your own interviews, through trusted news outlets, or through legal documents.[53]

Beyond reasons of ego and practicality, journalists feel self-interest in safeguarding their unique role as gatekeepers to information and as the sole disseminators of reliable news. In the traditional model that existed through much of the twentieth century, news outlets organized themselves around distinct geographic areas and created an economic model based on their unique ability to deliver information within that community. This, in turn, led journalists to create professional standards for themselves, which set parameters for their work while also elevating them as people who could be counted upon to make sense of complex situations. The Society of Professional Journalists maintains a code of ethics that includes four principles—"seek truth and report it," "minimize harm," "act independently," and "be accountable and transparent"—along with nearly three dozen bullet points beneath them.[54] News outlets and journalists set up these systems and standards with seemingly pure motives to set guiderails for anyone who would attempt to tell the stories of their community in a journalistic way, separating the work of professionals who follow the rules from amateurs who are ignorant of them. More cynically, the rules also allowed professionals to justify their ability to derive financial profits from reporting information and delivering it to the public. Naturally, journalists and traditional media outlets feel threatened by citizens reporting and disseminating information on their own, undermining the potential for making money from the practice.

Used as a tool to separate professionals and amateurs, the rules journalists create also have the potential to drive a wedge between them and the communities they cover. As media outlets have consolidated into larger corporate entities focused primarily on wringing profits out of disseminating the news, journalists have gotten further removed from the people they seek to serve. Owners of newspapers and radio and television stations once came from the communities they covered, but in the twentieth century many were replaced by large conglomerations or by corporate shareholders who had little interest in local affairs beyond the ability to make money from reporting about them. At the same time, most American adults say they have lost trust in the news media, worrying about accuracy, bias, and lack of transparency.[55] This growing separation allows the professional journalists to lose touch; they look out across their coverage areas and miss many people and perspectives because of the blind spots that every person has. Each one of us is an expert on our own experience, and we must work hard at truly understanding that of others.

Social Capital (or Why Local News Really Matters)

Traveling throughout the United States in the early 1830s, the French social scientist Alexis de Tocqueville detected a unique aspect of American life that separated it from what he previously had witnessed in European monarchies. He equated the strength of American democracy with the proliferation of newspapers at the time. In his estimation, engaged citizens needed a way to share and receive news about topics of public concern both in their local communities and in the nation's affairs, allowing them to not only know contemporary issues but also hold public officials accountable for their actions. Impressed by the role of the media, de Tocqueville could not envision the survival of a robust American democracy without newspapers: "Thus hardly any democratic association can do without newspapers. There is consequently a necessary connection between public associations and newspapers: newspapers make associations, and associations make newspapers .... Thus it is in America that we find at the same time the greatest number of associations and of newspapers.."[56]

From this perspective, the local newspaper not only informs citizens but also helps build community among its readers. Conversely, in places where local newspapers have died, local residents lose touch with each other and eventually become less engaged in civic life. This phenomenon revolves around the concept of "social capital," or the idea that the connections among people in a group—such as a place where they live or an organization to which they belong—have value.

L. J. Hanifan, an educator who grew up in a West Virginia timber camp and ended up earning an advanced degree from Harvard University, originated this idea of social capital in the early twentieth century while writing about how community involvement adds to the success of public schools. After earning a master's degree, Hanifan returned to West Virginia, where he worked with the school districts in Elkins and Belington, among other places, and he noticed that areas where parents were more involved in their children's studies seemed to do a better job of educating them. He wrote in 1916 that schools must first build up value within the connections among residents before they can build a successful education system:

> In the use of the phrase *social capital* I make no reference to the usual acceptation of the term capital, except in a figurative sense. I do not refer to real estate, or to personal property or to cold cash, but rather to that in life which tends to make these tangible substances count for most in the daily lives of a people, namely, goodwill, fellowship, mutual sympathy and social intercourse among a group of individuals and families who make up a social unit, the rural community, whose logical center is the school. In community building as in business organization and expansion there must be an accumulation of capital before constructive work can be done.[57]

Within this idea, neighbors who come into contact with each other begin to build worth among each other through their connections and interactions, and the value they develop can then be used by the members of that community for their own personal benefit—but, more important, for the overall aggregate gain of the group as well. "The community as a whole will benefit by the cooperation of all its parts, while the individual will find in his associations the advantages of the help, the sympathy, and the fellowship of his neighbors," Hanifan wrote.[58]

Social scientists in the latter part of the century picked up on this theme, elevating Hanifan's work and adding to it. French sociologist Pierre Bourdieu wrote decades later, in 1986, that one could identify social capital accumulating among the members of any particular social group that may be defined by "institutional relationships of mutual acquaintance and recognition—or in other words, to membership in a group."[59] The group may be defined in various ways, such as by a shared family structure, class, school, or political party, or simply by proximity in a geographical, economic, or social space. Each person may determine their own volume of social capital based on their number of connections and the access to economic, cultural, or symbolic capital those connections yield.

Newspapers, as a means for quickly and relatively inexpensively informing large groups of people, play a key role in helping people of a community learn about opportunities for interacting and gathering—or moments in which they can start building social capital. Local journalism at its best plays a watchdog role and provides an essential community service for democratic societies and market economies. Just as significantly, newspapers simply let residents know what goes on around them—advising about opportunities to get involved in local cultural events and kids' sports leagues, about employment openings and events at senior centers, about volunteer programs when groups of residents form around some civic issue, and, yes, about the activities of the local bowling clubs. Nearly two hundred years after de Tocqueville roamed America, social scientist Robert Putnam wrote at the turn of the twenty-first century in his seminal work, *Bowling Alone,* about how social capital seems to be declining across the United States as people spend more time on their own rather than connecting with others. Putnam drew a direct line between newspaper consumption and civic engagement, noting that people who read a local newspaper are more likely to be involved in their communities. He even put an emphasis on those who *read* the news over those who simply watch it on television or the internet: "Compared to demographically identical nonreaders, regular newspaper readers belong to more organizations, participate more actively in clubs and civic associations, attend local meetings more frequently, vote more regularly, volunteer and work on community projects more often, and even visit with friends more frequently and trust their neighbors more."[60]

The stakes are especially high in small and midsize communities, where residents rely on the local newspaper as a primary, if not only the only, source of reliable and credible third-party information. Penny Abernathy, who headed up a news desert research center at the University of North Carolina, noted that "the fates of newspapers and their communities are inherently linked" so that when the publication fails, the community also suffers.[61] Writing in 2016, investigators at the Pew Research Center confirmed what de Tocqueville had sensed in early American life and what Putnam had observed as people chose to spend more time focused inwardly: people who are civically engaged—by voting, volunteering, and connecting with those around them—also happen to be more likely to use and value local news.[62]

Why should this matter to more people, whether they read the news or not? As it turns out, places where residents lack easy access to local news sources also are more likely to be places where people struggle to find work and other basic

goods such as fresh, healthy food options.[63] The concept of news deserts draws
on the idea of food deserts, which the US Department of Agriculture defines as
places with limited access to healthy, affordable food, based on factors such as
distance, income, and transportation access.[64] Abernathy points out that these
two frames overlap: nearly half of the Americans who live in a county without
a newspaper also live in a food desert. Residents of counties considered news
deserts are generally poorer, older, and less educated than average Americans: 18
percent live in poverty, compared the national average of 13 percent; the average
median income is $45,000 per year, compared to $59,000; the average median age
is forty-two versus thirty-eight; and the average percentage of residents with at
least a bachelor's degree is 19 percent rather than 33 percent. As newspapers play
a key role in the creation of social capital, that intangible value that exists among
people who get together and know each other, it seems possible that they also
contribute to the creation of real capital too. Just as school districts where parents
and community leaders get involved do better, communities that have resources
for developing and maintaining social connections tend to have healthier environments for their citizens too. The places that most need to develop real value
for their residents tend to be the ones that lack access to local news outlets that
will help them develop social capital.

Writing in his native Portuguese in the late 1960s, Brazilian educator Paolo
Freire wrote about the need for humans to speak with honest, true words in a
multidirectional conversation rather than from a monarchical or dictatorial position: "Human existence cannot be silent, nor can it be nourished by false words,
but only by true words, with which men and women transform the world."[65] Local
newspapers play a key role in helping citizens access and share these true words
so that they may make educated decisions about the ways they want to govern
their communities and maintain a quality of life they value.

For that process to work, citizens also must play a key role in using news and
information to create opportunities for building social value. The conversation
must be interactive and multidirectional rather than from an all-knowing journalist to a passive audience, as happened in the twentieth century when CBS
news anchor Walter Cronkite and others like him had nearly monopolistic
control over what qualified as newsworthy. The lucrative financial model that
supported large news organizations and tens of thousands of journalists through
much of the twentieth century with stability has eroded and shows no signs of
returning. At the same time, the practice of journalism as a relatively closed
system has shifted to one of openness, in which professional journalists, citizen

journalists, and consumers have options. Local news has been democratized, giving ordinary citizens greater access to information, as well as more responsibility in how they use and share it with others around them.

As communities look to build social capital through the exchange of information, journalists and citizens—professionals and amateurs—must now work alongside each other in a common pursuit of the truth by seeking discovery with and through each other. For professional journalists, that means opening newsrooms and turning to the public for story ideas, canvassing residents for what they know about the places where they live, and expecting readers and viewers to be involved in asking difficult questions of public officials, government entities, business interests, and community groups. In that scenario, the journalist then becomes a guide to information, allowing citizens to take ownership of and accountability for the news. In an ideal scenario, individuals would value this service so much that they would pay for it, much in the way that a climber scaling Everest would hire guides to clear the path, carry supplies, and ensure the success of the mission, knowing that value exists in having someone who knows the way. It also would mean that as journalists look out across the coverage areas they aim to serve, there would be no way for them to overlook groups of people and their problems because those citizens would be just as involved in the creation of the news as they are.

Increased community engagement by professional journalists, on their own, will not solve the problem of making the news more relevant to everyone because traditional news organizations already have abandoned many communities, leaving behind news deserts. In those places, citizens must take up the responsibility for discovering information, holding the powerful accountable, and telling the news for themselves and their neighbors. The democratization of information—through the disruptions caused by computers and the internet—allows citizens to retake control of local news in ways that never have existed before, and it calls them to take greater care in the gathering and dissemination of what they discover or think they know. Journalism, perhaps like never before, belongs to the people rather than to professional journalists, wealthy publishers, or even corporate shareholders. The same technology that has shifted the balance of power toward the people gives them the tools to act as broadcasters and publishers of information essential to their immediate community—and, more critically, to serve as gatekeepers to information for other people around them.

To come back to de Tocqueville and his observations from nearly two centuries ago, he recognized then the role of sharing news to support American democracy and (although he would not have used these words) build social capital among the citizens of any community: "Newspapers therefore become more necessary in proportion as men become more equal, and individualism more to be feared. To suppose that they only serve to protect freedom would be to diminish their importance: They maintain civilization. . . . If there were no newspapers there would be no common activity."[66]

De Tocqueville wrote about the role of newspapers because he could not imagine something so powerful and pervasive as the internet, connecting people within their local community but also with individuals across the vast distances of the world. Even today, with easy access to information enabled by smartphones and broadband connections, the principles that de Tocqueville identified remain true: the sharing of information maintains civilization by bringing people together to understand each other better, developing relationships that create real value, and helping citizens hold each other accountable to the common good. The internet raises the question of whether people will share information of real value, however, and whether the dissemination of inaccurate, unverified, and biased information leads instead to social decay.

3

Cause of Death

If we understand the revolutionary transformations caused by new media, we can anticipate and control them; but if we continue in our self-induced subliminal trance, we will be their slaves.

The media researcher David Manning White set out in 1949 from Boston University, where he chaired the School of Public Communication, to find out whether a single person in the mid-twentieth century could control the flow of information reaching thousands of citizens in a community. He visited the newsroom of a newspaper with thirty thousand subscribers in an industrial Midwestern city of one hundred thousand people.[1] White focused on the decisions made by a single wire-copy editor, a man in his mid-forties who had twenty-five years of experience in the journalism industry. This "Mr. Gates," as White called him, had the job of sifting through the wire copy from the Associated Press, United Press, and International News Service to determine what stories would make it into the morning newspaper. For one week, Mr. Gates saved every piece of wire copy that came across his desk, putting all the discarded stories into a large box and passing all the acceptable ones through to publication.

At 1:00 a.m. every day after he had finished making up that day's pages, Mr. Gates then spent a couple of hours or so on the tedious job of going through the box of discarded stories and writing notes in the margin about why he had rejected each one, if he could remember. White then added up all the total column inches that came in through the wire services (with about five lines of wire copy making up a single inch), and the amount that actually made it into print. Mr. Gates ended up using only about 10 percent of the 12,400 inches of wire copy that came into the newsroom. So what did he reject, and why?

Like anyone, Mr. Gates used his own judgment—highly subjective and reliant on his own values—to decide what stories should appear in the newspaper. On one wire story, he wrote in the margin, "He's too Red," or communist. On another, he wrote, "Never use this."[2] And when it came to the national conversation about a plan for providing benefits to elderly citizens, the editor said he felt the plan's merits were dubious; he concluded that the chances of stories about that subject making it into the newspaper were negligible. Mr. Gates marked eighteen wire stories with "B.S." and another sixteen with the word "propaganda." On one story, Mr. Gates wrote, "Don't care for suicides." He favored political stories while rejecting ones about crime. In every instance when he had a choice, Mr. Gates chose the story that seemed the most "conservative" in political leanings and in style, setting aside anything he judged to be sensational. Stories with many facts and figures were passed over for those that seemed interpretive and easygoing.

During the high-profile trial that week of a Catholic priest who was convicted in Hungary for speaking out against communism, Mr. Gates refused to run the comments of an American cardinal who pointed out that Hungarian officials had prevented Western wire services from having full access to the proceedings: "It is very unfortunate that our news agencies are not giving their sources of information in their day-by-day reports on the trial of Cardinal Mindzenty. It should be made clear that 'restrictions' have been made on the few American correspondents who have been present at the trial."[3] Mr. Gates apparently didn't like the insinuation that the American reporters were somehow not doing their jobs, and so he wrote in the margins, "pure propaganda," and he rejected three wire stories with the comment in them.

At the end of the week, White asked Mr. Gates whether he had any prejudices that might jaundice his reading of the news. He responded in a self-aware way that he most certainly did:

> I have few prejudices, built-in or otherwise, and there is little I can do about them. I dislike [President] Truman's economics, daylight saving time and warm beer, but I go ahead using stories on them and other matters if I feel there is nothing more important to give space to. I am also prejudiced against a publicity-seeking minority with headquarters in Rome, and I don't help them a lot. As far as preferences are

concerned, I go for human interest stories in a big way. My other preferences are for stories well-wrapped up and tailored to suit our needs (or ones slanted to conform to our editorial policies).[4]

At the end of the research project, White concluded that this one wire-copy editor did, indeed, serve as a gatekeeper to information, at least among the subscribers of that newspaper, who represented a sizeable percentage of the community: "It begins to appear (if Mr. Gates is a fair representative of his class) that in his position as 'gate keeper' the newspaper editor sees to it (even though he may never be consciously aware of it) that the community shall hear as a fact only those events which the newsman, as the representative of his culture, believes to be true."[5] White conceded that his study focused on the actions and thoughts of just one editor, but he reasoned that these kinds of decisions are repeated all the time throughout news organizations with one journalist, or several of them at most, making broad decisions that shape the public's understanding of a particular issue or what they even hear about what goes on each moment. "From reporter to rewrite man, through bureau chief to 'state' file editors at various press association offices, the process of choosing and discarding is continuously taking place," White reasoned.[6]

In the pre-internet age, when people relied on just a few accessible news sources to learn about the world and their community, the decisions by these gatekeepers shaped what they knew.

Gates and Channels

Writing a few years before White, just after World War II, German-American experimental psychologist Kurt Lewin first articulated this concept of gates and channels as he considered the most-efficient ways to bring about social change.[7] For instance, if one wants to encourage more people to drink milk, does it make sense to launch an expensive propaganda campaign with posters, lectures, and media advertisements? Or would it make more sense to focus on convincing a few "key" people such as housewives, who, in Lewin's estimation, make critical decisions about what food enters homes? Similarly, if someone wanted to reduce racial discrimination, he argued, they could be more effective by focusing on social workers, business leaders, and politicians. In either situation, a few people serve as gatekeepers who make decisions about what items to pass through and what ones to reject.

In Lewin's concept, which was published in 1947, after he died, he describes how food starts out in certain channels, such as the farm, the family garden, or the grocery store. At each step, people make choices that shape the availability of certain types of food. The farmer, for instance, decides what items to grow, and the grocery store owner chooses from among all the available types of produce and vegetables to determine what to carry. Shoppers then make decisions about what of all those items in the store to purchase and bring into their home. Ultimately, people in the household decide what items to serve at mealtime or to eat out of the refrigerator and pantry.

Along the way, forces exert themselves on the gates to influence the choices that people make, such as the cost of the food item, its nutrients, and its taste: "A certain area within a channel may function as a 'gate'; the constellation of the forces before and after the gate region is decisively different in such a way that the passing or not passing of the unit through the whole channel depends to a high degree upon what happens in the gate region."[8] Then, just as he talks about the flow of food from farm to table and about the choices that gatekeepers make, Lewin offers one line about the way people think about the news business: "This holds not only for food channels but also for the travelling of a news item through certain communication channels in a group, for movement of goods, and the social locomotion of individuals in many organizations."[9] Lewin's sentence here, in the larger context of his overall findings, almost seems like an afterthought, but that one line inspired a whole new understanding of the journalistic decision-making process.

Lewin was the first to talk about the gatekeeping phenomenon in a theoretical sense, but others before him had considered the outsize role the media plays in determining what information reaches the public. Upton Sinclair, in *The Brass Check* (1919), harangued the media for aligning with elites in society to prevent working-class perspectives and concerns from reaching the general public: "Politics, Journalism, and Big Business work hand in hand for the hoodwinking of the public and the plundering of labor."[10] Publishers refused to produce the book, so Sinclair self-published, and then many newspapers refused to review it or even carry advertisements about it.[11] Walter Lippmann, in his seminal book *Public Opinion* (1922), analyzed the role of public relations workers and marketers who attempt to influence the public, and he spent considerable time describing the ways in which editors and reporters make decisions about what information to include: "Every newspaper when it reaches the reader is the result of a whole series of selections as to what items shall be printed, in what position they shall be printed, how much space each shall occupy, what emphasis each shall have. There are no objective standards here."[12] Lewin's articulation of the phenomenon through gates, however, captured the imagination of media researchers and gained almost folkloric status in the second half of the twentieth century. Researchers focused on how a newsroom gatekeeper, such as a reporter or editor, makes subjective decisions, often unconsciously, that impact what information gets passed along to readers and consumers.

This concept resonates with so many people because the real-world ramifications are easy to see. The *New York Times*, for instance, never boasted that it prints all the news, but instead promises at the upper left-hand corner of every front page to give readers "all the news that's fit to print." Gatekeepers along the way at every news organization make decisions about what seems "fit," from the reporters who decide whom to interview, what questions to ask them, and what details or quotes to include; to the editors who decide what information seems "newsworthy" enough to include, where and when to run it, and how to present it; to the publisher, who shapes the newsroom by deciding what types of people to hire and how to reward them. If a few white men make these decisions, as often happens, for a readership that includes a diverse audience, it makes sense that they will overlook perspectives that they not only do not appreciate or understand, but do not even see.

Similarly, consider the role of African American newspapers during the pre-internet period of the twentieth century in informing their readers about key moments in the civil rights struggle. Black people living in a predominantly white community, in which white publishers controlled the local flow of information and made the decisions about what sorts of stories to put in the community newspaper, had few ways of learning about the outside world from a Black perspective. National newspapers such as the *Pittsburgh Courier* and the *Chicago Defender* disrupted this censorship by having reporters across the United States who would discover information and report it back to the main bureau. Editors there would compile the information into a publication that would be printed in the hub city and then shipped out across the country by rail car, with conductors dropping off bundles of newspapers at designated spots. The *Courier* ended up with more than a dozen bureaus nationwide, providing an alternate perspective on the news for hundreds of thousands of mostly Black readers. During World War II, the *Courier* informed its readers about how a Black seaman named Doris Miller manned an anti-aircraft gun during the Japanese attack on Pearl Harbor, ignoring rules that forbade Black men from firing weapons. The *Courier* also told about and championed the Double V campaign, insisting that as Americans fought against fascism across Europe and Asia, they also needed to oppose racism at home. Then, after the war, the *Courier* played a key role in informing Black readers about civil rights developments across the United States, exposing stories of racist attacks and discrimination that white-owned media outlets ignored or underplayed.

The relationship among gatekeepers and news consumers always has been complex, with newsroom editors making decisions about what they think readers will want, and readers showing their approval or dislike for those decisions by making their own decisions about whether to buy a newspaper or subscription. The rise of the internet, which gives consumers seemingly endless choices for finding information, further complicates these arrangements, but it does not eliminate the interface of gatekeeper and consumer; instead, gatekeeping continues to evolve as a theory for understanding the role of journalists in informing the public. The journalism educators Pamela Shoemaker and Timothy Vos wrote in 2009 about how gatekeepers may determine a "person's social reality" by setting the parameters for their understanding of the world around them: "Gatekeeping is the process of culling and crafting countless bits of information into the limited number of messages that reach people each day, and it is the center of the media's role in modern public life."[13] Rather than gatekeepers simply serving a one-way role with the public, however, the researchers envision gatekeepers who pay even more attention to the feedback from the public to determine what items to pass through. Gatekeepers in modern newsrooms frequently track internet measures such as page views, click rates, and time on page to determine what sorts of information consumers want. If readers click more often on stories about car crashes and house fires, for instance, alert editors will notice this activity and consider that knowledge when making decisions about how often to deploy reporters to cover breaking news events.

The Medium Is the Message

Wearing an ill-fitting brown tweed suit, black shoes, and a clip-on necktie, Marshall McLuhan sat near a crackling fireplace inside his home in a wealthy Toronto suburb in 1969 to meet with a reporter from *Playboy* magazine. The reporter later described McLuhan as "tall, gray and gangly, with a thin but mobile mouth and an otherwise eminently forgettable face."[14] The fact that a reporter from the racy magazine would even show up at the home of a media professor might seem unusual, except that by the late 1960s, when the article came out, McLuhan was making himself a household name with bold pronouncements about how technology was ending the era of the printed word. It was the sort of thinking that first drew the interests of beatniks and leading figures of the 1960s counterculture, and that then seeped into mainstream consciousness. After John Lennon and Yoko Ono launched a global Christmas campaign against the Vietnam War in 1969 with billboards saying, "War is over! If you want it. Happy Christmas from John & Yoko," they were interviewed by McLuhan for the Canadian Broadcast Corporation:

> **McLuhan:** "Can you tell me? I just sort of wonder how the 'War Is Over,' the wording . . . The whole thinking. What happened?"
> **John:** "I think the basic idea of the poster event was Yoko's. She used to do things like that in the avant-garde circle, you know. Poster was a sort of medium, media, whatever."
> **Yoko:** "Medium."[15]

McLuhan's name even became half of a nonsensical rhyming couplet on the television variety show *Rowan & Martin's Laugh-In* as comedian Henry Gibson would look into the camera and say, "Marshall McLuhan, what are you doin'?" Eventually, filmmaker Woody Allen gave McLuhan a cameo in the movie *Annie Hall*, pulling him out from behind a signboard to scold a man standing in line at the movies for getting his theories all wrong.

With the *Playboy* interview, the journalist was trying to help more average people understand McLuhan by having him explain his radical ideas in plain language. In an era when many people were still getting used to the power of television to transmit images, McLuhan's ideas often seemed so far out that they were indecipherable. He famously said things like, "The medium is the message." Sitting inside his home, McLuhan tried to explain the nature of his research and how he would probe new ideas like a safecracker waiting to find the right combination that would make the tumblers inside fall open: "There's really nothing inherently startling or radical about this study—except that for some reason few have had the vision to undertake it. For the past 3500 years of the Western world, the effects of media—whether it's speech, writing, printing, photography, radio or television—have been systematically overlooked by social observers."[16] McLuhan worried that few people were paying attention to how television was changing their lives. The new medium had the power to transform the culture by bringing people together instantaneously to share moments such as the moon landing and presidential debates, and it was changing people's habits so that they spent more time inside watching rather than sitting outside talking. McLuhan was trying to wake them up to at least see the transformation happening: "But most people, from truck drivers to the literary Brahmins, are still blissfully ignorant of what the media do to them; unaware that because of their pervasive effects on man, it is the medium itself that is the message, not the content, and unaware that the medium is also the message."[17] The stakes involved in figuring out what the changes meant, McLuhan warned, were extremely high, with the potential to affect nearly every aspect of a way of life that most people took for granted:

> Today, in the electronic age of instantaneous communication, I believe that our survival, and at the very least our comfort and happiness, is predicated on understanding the nature of our new environment, because unlike previous environmental changes, the electric media constitute a total and near-instantaneous transformation of culture, values and attitudes. This upheaval generates great pain and identity loss, which can be ameliorated only through a conscious awareness of its dynamics. If we understand the revolutionary transformations caused by new media, we can anticipate and control them; but if we continue in our self-induced subliminal trance, we will be their slaves.[18]

Wake up, McLuhan was saying, because humans could bend technology to their will to accomplish what they wanted to make their lives easier and more fulfilling; if they did nothing, the technological changes would simply happen and haphazardly change their way of life, for better and for worse.

McLuhan died in 1980 on New Year's Eve at age sixty-nine—about a half decade after the invention of the first personal computer and three years before the birth of the internet. Many of the things he said seemed to make little sense when he was alive, but they now sound particularly prescient. In his book *Understanding Media* (1964), McLuhan floated the idea that "electric light is pure information." It seems at first like nonsense, except that he goes on to explain that electric light is a medium that can be used to deliver content when it is used, for instance, in a sign to make a message. As people become more aware of how different media shape messages, they can then start to use technology to accomplish their desires, rather than be used by it. McLuhan wrote about how some companies were starting to figure this out: "It is only today that industries have become aware of the various kinds of business in which they are engaged. When IBM discovered that it was not in the business of making office equipment or business machines, but that it was in the business of processing information, then it began to navigate with clear vision. The General Electric Company makes a considerable portion of its profits from electric light bulbs and lighting systems. It has not yet discovered that, quite as much as AT&T, it is in the business of moving information."[19] From our modern vantage point, McLuhan seems like a soothsayer as well as a savant. The General Electric company ended up owning the NBC television network from 1986 to 2013, using electricity to fill Americans' homes with all manner of content from comedy shows to news about the world. AT&T, meanwhile, became the world's largest telecommunications company, using fiber technology to send messages by light signals into millions of consumers' homes and owning WarnerMedia, with ten thousand hours' worth of viewing on its HBO Max entertainment service alone (at least until it announced plans in May 2021 to spin off the subsidiary).[20]

The medium really is the message, man. Can you dig it?

When it comes to newspapers, then, the forces behind McLuhan's theories have had a devastating impact as consumers have drifted away from printed products delivered to their home and have moved toward electronic content—words, images, and sounds—transmitted through their smartphones and computers. After all, it was McLuhan who warned in 1964 that even though people were still taking the newspaper, fewer of them were reading it: "People don't actually read newspapers—they get into them every morning like a hot bath."

McLuhan understood that changes brought about by electronic technology alter the ways in which people communicate news and information, and that, in turn, reshapes society, culture, and life as well. In early twenty-first century culture, the internet, social media, and connected devices such as personal computers, laptop computers, tablets, and smartphones have accelerated the pace of change. Throughout history, as new technologies have been introduced—writing implements, the printing press, the light bulb, radio, television, the internet—their impact can be measured by how humans adopt them, and how that, in turn, affects contemporary culture. From the earliest times, changes in communication tools greatly have impacted civilizations; notable examples include the stylus, papyrus, parchment and pen, printing press, telegraph, cinema, and broadcast radio. Computers and the internet are no different: humans determine the value of each medium by how they use it, and we have adopted computers and the internet in ways that have transformed every aspect of modern life.

Long before the invention of the smartphone and social media in the 2000s, McLuhan realized that humans have an intrinsic love of technological gadgets that appear as a narcissistic extension of themselves. He recognized the earliest moments of an emerging age of anxiety, when new technologies compel human engagement even when the person lacks something particular to say and when information continues to flow more quickly than it can be processed. The rapid availability of information from multiple sources creates a state of "allatonceness" in which time and space vanish. "Information pours upon us, instantaneously and continuously. As soon as information is acquired, it is very rapidly replaced by still newer information."[21]

Anxiety also stems from attempting to do modern work with outdated tools and concepts, leading to cataclysmic clashes. Feelings of uncertainty create bias toward adopting new media technologies, even at the peril of the older ones and even though users have not innovated the work they seek to accomplish. The media theorist Neil Postman wrote in *Technopoly* (1992) that this phenomenon of constantly leaning forward might be particularly true in the United States, where it seems everyone lusts for the latest invention: "New technologies alter the structure of our interests: the things we think *about*. They alter the character of our symbols: the things we think *with*. And they alter the nature of community: the arena in which thoughts develop."[22]

For our internet age, then, this transformation in media ecology means that while many people say they still enjoy newspapers, magazines, and books, they actually turn to the internet for most of their information—and journalists meet them there. While journalists and consumers have readily embraced new tools for storytelling, the news industry has struggled to accomplish the old, traditional tasks of delivering printed information in new ways that allow them to make money from the news. Consumers' shift to the internet for information has upturned the financial model that supported the news industry for much of the twentieth century by undermining the systems that made printed media—newspapers, in particular—profitable. Media companies that adapt to these changes are the ones that are succeeding, while those that bump up against emerging technology with outdated methods grow frustrated at their inability to keep up. At many local news outlets, the content has moved ahead to keep pace with the speed of change, while the methods for monetizing that information to pay for journalists has not.

Rise of the Citizen Gatekeeper

Despite the obvious challenges of standing still as new technologies remake the surrounding culture, not everyone in traditional media embraces change. Even with vast technological changes and their impacts on the traditional models for local news gathering and delivery, some journalists still view local news coverage from an outdated perspective with a one-way, top-down model in which a professional gatekeeper makes decisions about what the public should know. The technology around the gathering and disseminating of information has evolved so rapidly and so comprehensively that journalists have had a hard time even seeing how the changes have altered what they do, how they do it, and who they do it for. Worse, many journalists have lost touch with the communities they serve, even as they continue to argue that user-generated content does not meet professional standards for credibility. This type of thinking ignores the reality that citizens already are creating their own content every moment, without waiting for someone to give them permission.

Traditional journalism suffers when practitioners remain wedded to outdated methods and thinking. Echoing the insights of McLuhan a generation earlier, the European media researchers Marcel Broersma and Chris Peters warned in 2013 that journalists still were not doing enough to adapt to the new realities brought about technological innovation: "A major problem for journalism is thus that it tries to tackle the technological and social transformations of today with the logic of yesterday."[23] That sounds an awful lot like McLuhan, who was writing nearly fifty years earlier, "In the name of 'progress,' our official culture is striving to force the new media to do the work of the old."[24] Given the challenges facing residents of news deserts in terms of searching for local news and information, one easily could extend these warnings to the public too: communities suffer from using outdated methods and thinking to address the technological and social transformations of today. Old models—such as the traditional printed newspaper weighed down with legacy costs—die for a reason, and it does not make sense to keep repeating the same mistakes. Instead, communities must be looking at ways of innovating how they acquire and share information. Even in places where printed newspapers continue to make money (and many of them still do), they must operate with newfound efficiencies, with smarter decisions about the allocation of reporters and resources, and with an eye to rapidly approaching changes.

Much of the research around Lewin's theory about gatekeepers has focused on the role of those individuals in the middle, like Mr. Gates in White's study, who decide what information passes through to the public. From a contemporary perspective in which newspapers have died and left behind whole communities wondering how to make sense of what goes on around them, a broader interpretation of Lewin's theory leads to a sharper understanding. It helps to consider the gatekeeper role while keeping in mind McLuhan's observation that rapid technological change also reshapes culture. Changes to the media ecology have encouraged consumers to adopt new technologies and to use emerging ways of information gathering, leading to the collapse of local news environments.

Within the arid atmosphere of a news desert, then, it makes sense that while myriad channels of local information transmission continue to exist, the journalist's gatekeeper role has been removed along with the journalism jobs and newspapers that have disappeared. Instead, curious citizens are forced to seek their own news and local information amid what can seem like an overwhelming number of sources that often include politicians, public safety agencies, schools, churches, family members, neighbors, and gossipmongers. When journalists become overwhelmed with information, they use frames to determine what seems newsworthy and to triage information into manageable pieces.[25] Members of the public typically lack any sort of professional training, and they must instead develop their own methods for sorting information and making sense of their local community. They do this instinctively, assuming information-gathering roles without considering that they are seeking to complete the tasks that professional journalists once performed. Even if they do this work poorly or incompletely, citizens fall into the task naturally as they attempt to figure out what happens in their community so they can make decisions that affect their quality of life.

Amateur news gatherers rarely call themselves journalists or even think of themselves in that way, but whether they realize it or not, individuals frequently generate original content about the news happening around them, and they make judgments, often with little thought, about what pieces of information to pass along to the people around them. These are the essential tasks of gatekeeping. The media researcher Ken Doctor wrote about the emergence of this phenomenon in his book *Newsonomics* (2010) just as social media sites such as Facebook and Twitter were coming into use and Instagram was being born: "In the age of Darwinian content, you are your own editor. We have now become our own gatekeepers; we no longer see the news world as a gated community."[26] Doctor continued, "While traditional command-and-control media, like daily newspapers and broadcast news, certainly maintain strong, if diminished, gatekeeping functions, think of the other gates, though, that have opened for all of us. Among them: blogs, podcasts, Twitter feeds, Facebook scrawls, LinkedIn messages..."[27] As he looked around at the still-emerging ways for individuals to consider information and share it with others around them, Doctor set up the idea for a

Conceptual Framework:
Ecology of News Desert Affects Gatekeepers

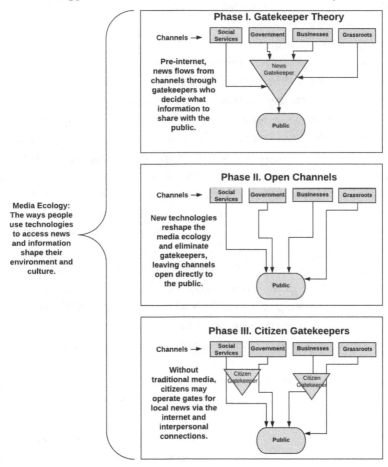

FIGURE 1. New technologies give power to citizen gatekeepers to shape local news and information. Created by the author.

new phenomenon that took form over the following decade-plus: if social media platforms serve as informal gates to information, the people who share content via these places are then, by logic, gatekeepers.

Beyond the arrival of accidental gatekeepers, many individual citizens have looked upon new technologies and made deliberate, conscious decisions to involve themselves in the task of considering all the available information in their community and attempting to make sense of it. Often, they do this work without training or significant resources, but they take on the responsibility because they realize no one else will do the work; the traditional news outlets that once served the community have hollowed out so much that they no longer provide robust coverage, or they have disappeared altogether.

In many cases, volunteer Facebook group administrators fulfill a gatekeeping role where they live. The Facebook Journalism Project provides direct grants and social media training for professional journalists, and it offers paths for volunteer administrators to make money through video advertising, subscriptions, and events.[28] The social media platform rarely, if ever, gives direct payments or journalistic training to individual citizens who attempt to do the work on their own. Still, amateur gatekeepers take on the responsibility for discovering and channeling information about their community. An anecdotal example reported by NBC News in 2021 involves a Facebook administrator in Beaver County, Pennsylvania, forty-five miles northwest of McKeesport on the other side of Pittsburgh: "The group isn't just a side project for its sole administrator, lifetime Beaver Falls resident Deanna Romigh; it gives her a sense of purpose. . . . Romigh, who is deaf, said the group is her way of getting information and bonding with her neighbors. 'I need to know everything, too,' she said. 'I'm not invisible. So I just made my own group. I never thought it would grow this big. I mean, I'm shocked myself.'"[29] This person has taken on the role of the traditional news gatekeeper: looking at her community, considering information, choosing what information to share with others, and making decisions about what other people post as well. Unlike traditional gatekeepers, she has no training and does not get paid. She is not alone, however. By its own estimate in 2020, Facebook reported the existence of "tens of millions of active communities on Facebook where people come together to talk about their interests, learn new things, be entertained and make connections."[30]

In other, rarer, instances, citizens have turned to more traditional methods to assume journalistic gatekeeping roles. The *Suburban Gazette*, a family-owned newspaper in Stowe Township, seven miles northwest of Pittsburgh (and twenty miles from McKeesport), went out of business in 2017 after 125 years of operation.[31] Local businessman Sonny Jani had grown up listening to his father read the newspaper while they worked in their Blue Eagle Market; later, the *Suburban Gazette* had marked the births of his two children, and it had run his father's obituary when he died. Jani decided to start his own newspaper after the *Suburban Gazette* collapsed. He staked a $50,000 tax write-off to the experiment, hired one full-time employee, and called on other local citizens for their help, agreeing to pay freelancers and a part-time editor for their contributions. Dozens of people responded, with some only filing a single story and others becoming regular writers. One citizen, for instance, owns a moving company in the community and agreed to cover local government meetings for fifty dollars per story. Only one person, the part-time editor, had any formal training as a journalist: Sonja Reis had attended Penn State University and then had written for the *Pittsburgh Post-Gazette* and *Tribune-Review* and other local newspapers. The new biweekly newspaper, *Gazette 2.0*, typically consists of eight pages and runs about 4,400 copies every other week, with nearly four hundred going to paid subscribers and the rest given away at local stores. The newspaper sells advertising, with a full-page ad costing $300, and local communities pay to run legal notices. The formula has worked by keeping overhead costs low: *Gazette 2.0* had $95,000 in revenue for 2020, and it would have turned a small profit except that Jani invested the additional income into creating more content. In March 2021, Jani gifted the newspaper to Reis, and she became publisher while holding on to her full-time job as the communications and marketing director for a local community development corporation.

Rather than abandoning gatekeeper theory in an age when consumers have many choices for discovering information, we can reimagine it for the contemporary media ecology of the twenty-first century. Technological changes have democratized information by shifting privilege away from a few media insiders who could use their own values to control the flow of information. At the same time, this democratization has given new resources to ordinary citizens so that they, like professional journalists, may create their own content and make decisions about what pieces of information to share with others in their informal networks. "Citizens are no longer passive receivers but rather are actively engaged in (re) creating, challenging, questioning, correcting and personalizing news media," the English media professor Todd Graham points out.[32] Now that individual citizens can acquire and share information on their own, traditional media such as newspapers, magazines, and broadcast radio and television no longer serve as gatekeepers to limit what the public can read, see, and know. Instead of living with a top-down model in which information flows from sources through media gatekeepers to the public, each citizen exists in a horizontal model among an information flow from multiple channels, trying to determine what to consume or seek to comprehend.

The media researchers Shoemaker and Vos described how consumers of information have an influence over the traditional gatekeepers, reshaping the decisions they make about what to publish or broadcast.[33] People who read stories and share them via social media and other channels ultimately have an impact on the traditional news gatekeepers as they decide what types of information to pass along: if the audience consumes more cat videos, gatekeepers will notice that and start looking for more cat videos to pass through their gates for people to watch. "In the audience channel, we see that the Internet now allows anyone to become a gatekeeper by passing along news items and commenting on them in many web sites, such as digg.com, reddit.com, YouTube and Facebook," they wrote in 2009.[34] Readers in this paradigm make choices about what they like, consuming content for themselves and sharing it with others via social media; in this way, they inform the decisions of the traditional gatekeepers who are making choices about what people want. Once journalists select a topic for coverage based on their judgment of its newsworthiness, readers take over by voting for the content they like with their online clicks and shares. The traditional gatekeepers may then choose to heed these choices or ignore them in favor of their own judgment about what they feel people should be getting.

The situation of news deserts requires an even broader reimagining of citizens' role in places where traditional news outlets—and their professional gatekeepers—no longer exist. If no Mr. Gates stays up into the early morning making choices about what articles to publish in that day's newspaper, citizens no longer have the luxury of leaning on his expertise, as subjective and flawed as it might be. Before, each person could pay some nominal amount of money to receive a daily printed summary of what had happened the previous day. Subscribers might have thought they were paying for just the news. Ultimately, they were paying for a small group of journalists to consider everything happening both in their local community and across the world, to decide what seemed most important or newsworthy, and to provide short synopses of those things they deemed worthwhile.

When that system breaks down, citizens must start to make those decisions on their own to determine what pieces of information have value because of their immediacy, accuracy, relevance, and lack of bias. In these cases, journalists aren't available to use their professional training to triage raw information and break it down into digestible, bite-size pieces based on traditional standards of newsworthiness. Because they lack that sort of training, however, citizens on their own, not surprisingly, often make questionable choices about what pieces of information have meaning in their lives, can be trusted, and should be shared with others.

At the same time, a lack of formal journalistic sorting also can lead to an erosion of social capital as people fail to make sense of their community and lose sight of opportunities to gather, make decisions, and take steps to understand their neighbors. Residents become more disconnected, leading to lower levels of public conversation and civic engagement, undermining their whole sense of community and belonging. When residents are more closely connected, Putnam wrote in *Bowling Alone*, they become "more tolerant, less cynical and more empathetic to the misfortune of others," and when they are less connected, it can lead to opposite changes: "When people lack connections to others, they are unable to test the veracity of their own views, whether in the give-and-take of casual conversations or in more formal deliberation. Without such an opportunity, people are more likely to be swayed by their worst impulses."[35] Citizens left on their own find themselves with potential access to overwhelming amounts of information coming from various unfiltered sources, and, paradoxically, they are often unable to make sense of all the data without a professional journalist to sort it out and tell them what pieces are worthy of their attention.

Inevitably, individuals on their own—frequently in unpaid, amateur ways— assume the role of a new kind of citizen gatekeeper who decides what raw information to digest and then pass along to the people within their spheres of influence. As in White's determination of traditional gatekeepers, citizen gatekeepers might take many forms, such as those who merely pass along information, those who highlight key parts of the information, and those who conduct their own independent analysis of the information. This process may take place through traditional models such as printed newspapers or newsletters, or, more likely, through online sharing. Most often this sort of citizen sorting takes place on social media platforms, where individuals create, share, like, and retweet information that seems relevant and important, sometimes without taking even a moment to contemplate what the information says or why it should be shared. At the same time, many citizen gatekeepers also share information as they always have, through direct person-to-person interactions and gossip.

This shift in paradigm to the model of citizen gatekeeping has the potential to reverse the lack of community engagement that occurs when traditional media withdraw or leave, allowing social capital to rebuild through meaningful networks. The decentralization of news also opens media infrastructure to a new and unprecedented diversity of voices and perspectives from ordinary citizens who previously lacked the mechanisms to afford a public voice.

By bringing together Lewin's gatekeeping theory and McLuhan's radical thinking on the ways technology shapes culture, it becomes possible to see how technological changes in the computer and internet age have shaped the media ecology—and how, as a result, the role of traditional media gatekeepers has diminished, or even disappeared in the case of news deserts. That does not represent the end of the story, however. If people take the time to recognize the technological and cultural changes happening around them, they can make choices that help them navigate the phenomena and use innovations to their advantage. In the absence of traditional journalistic gatekeepers, citizens must instead take an active role in reimagining their own place in the media ecosystem as they shift from being passive recipients of information under the old paradigm.

Individuals become the gatekeepers of the information around them. This newfound opportunity also brings a responsibility to take the job seriously, to be aware of what information they consume, and, most important, like Mr. Gates, to develop systems—with their acknowledged flaws and biases—to decide what they will share with others. They must first see that they play a serious, critical role in setting the discourse of their community, and then they must work at doing a better job of it.

PART II

Stages of Grief

4

Losing

We went to [the *Daily News*] for everything. Just to know what was going on in the community and the neighboring communities—people, fairs, churches, checking who won the games, anything local, obituaries, everything.

Loss of Identity

Visitors driving into the city of McKeesport from the west cross over the Monongahela River by passing over a four-lane bridge named for William D. Mansfield, a former state senator (1923 to 1934) and the former publisher of the *Daily News*, the city's former newspaper. The Mansfield family owned the *Daily News* from 1925 to 2004, when it sold the publication to the publisher of another local newspaper. Just when some journalists were expecting to lose their jobs, that owner sold the newspaper again in 2007 to Richard Scaife, the billionaire publisher of the *Pittsburgh Tribune-Review*, who purchased it for his regional media conglomerate known as Trib Total Media.

Scaife had inherited most of his fortune as the offspring of wealthy families—the Mellons and Scaifes—who had made their money from banking, oil, coal, aluminum, and other big industries, and he used his resources to pursue his passion for newspapers. He had purchased a midsize regional newspaper, the *Tribune-Review*, in Greensburg, Pennsylvania, twenty miles east of McKeesport, in 1970. Then, during a newspaper strike that shut down Pittsburgh's two daily newspapers in the early 1990s, he started the *Pittsburgh Tribune-Review* in the city. Scaife had developed an affection for newspapers, he often told his employees, during a year of bed rest after a horse fractured his skull when he was nine years old; he then collected newspapers from around the world and spent endless hours reading them.

In private life, Scaife had long supported conservative causes, going back to his enthusiasm for Arizona senator Barry M. Goldwater, the 1964 presidential candidate; building through his substantial financial support for the Heritage Foundation, the conservative Washington think-tank; and continuing through his efforts to discredit Democratic president Bill Clinton in the 1990s.[1] Scaife had used his wealth and his Pittsburgh newspaper to search for evidence of fraud, or worse, in the Clinton White House by hiring former *New York Post* reporter Christopher Ruddy to write about the death of Vince W. Foster Jr., a deputy White House counsel who died by suicide seven months after Clinton came into office. Foster had been a law partner to Hillary Clinton, but the *Tribune-Review*'s reporting found little more than unproven conspiracy theories about his death. Ruddy went on in later life to found NewsMax, the conservative news site, with Scaife's financial support. Scaife, meanwhile, in a plot twist, ended up befriending the Clintons: his newspaper endorsed Hillary Clinton for president during the Pennsylvania primary in 2008 after she met with Scaife and the Trib's editorial board; when Scaife died, President Clinton eulogized him in a memorial service attended by the newspaper's employees.

Scaife's purchase of the *Daily News* had little to do with politics and instead grew out of the publisher's admiration for local newspapers and desire to expand the Trib's circulation. With his significant financial support, Scaife maintained the *Pittsburgh Tribune-Review* as an award-winning newspaper with a full-time bureau in Cairo, Egypt, and he bought up and marketed enough regional publications that, together, they briefly grew into the region's largest daily news outlet.[2] His purchase of the *Daily News* added a small amount to the overall subscription tally—about fifteen thousand subscribers when he took over—but the newspaper meant more than numbers to Scaife. He kept a second-floor office—with plush carpeting, wood paneling, and a private bathroom and kitchen—just steps away from the newsroom, though he rarely used it. His financial support, meanwhile, covered annual losses at his newspapers, including the *Daily News*, even beyond his death in 2014. Shortly after he passed away, managers of Trib Total Media, the parent company, moved over to a consolidation plan to stop hemorrhaging money over the following two years. That included selling off McKeesport's newspaper; when no buyers could be found, it was shut down.

That the *Daily News* owed its continued existence to the offspring of industrialists who made their wealth from natural resources and steel should not have surprised anyone. To appreciate the community's attachment to its newspaper, it helps to know a little about McKeesport's history and its ties to American manufacturing. Before European settlers arrived in what would become western Pennsylvania, the Delaware Tribe, led by Queen Alliquippa, controlled the swampy lands near the confluence of the Monongahela and Youghiogheny Rivers.[3] David McKee, a Scottish immigrant and protestant Presbyterian, arrived at that spot in 1755, seeking religious freedom and building a log cabin along the riverbank. As more European settlers came into the area, McKee established a skiff ferry to carry travelers across the water. His son, John, later laid out plots for development in 1795 and named the area McKees' Port. The land around McKeesport also served as a witness to history as General George Washington visited, first in 1753 to meet with Queen Alliquippa and again two years later during General Edward Braddock's unsuccessful attempt to claim Fort Duquesne at the confluence of the Monongahela and Allegheny rivers to the west, at the site of present-day Pittsburgh.[4]

McKeesport's first coal mines opened in 1830, supplying resources to the iron-manufacturing industry, and twenty-one years later the city's first foundry opened.[5] National Tube Works Company opened in McKeesport in 1872 to take advantage of nearby steel production, giving rise to the moniker "Tube City."[6] Over time, competitors arose to make steel pipe nearby, and in 1901 U.S. Steel purchased and combined ten steel and pipe manufacturing companies to form U.S. Steel National Tube Works, the world's first billion-dollar company, valued at $1.4 billion.[7]

McKeesport's factories reached peak production after World War II, and the manufacturing production, in turn, supported a thriving community. McKeesport boasted a half dozen movie theaters, several furniture stores and jewelry shops, and more than seven hundred retail stores, including three big department stores.[8]

The collapse of industry in the 1980s, likewise, resulted in the decline of the local economy, with workers losing jobs and McKeesport's thriving downtown giving way to empty storefronts and abandoned buildings. The community's retail sales dropped 65 percent in the half century after 1960 (adjusted for inflation); an entire block across from city hall sat empty even though it once housed a department store, a jeweler, a men's clothing shop, a photography supply store, a veteran's club, an armed forces recruiting center, a branch of the post office, and the headquarters of the G. C. Murphy retail chain.[9] As one ethnographer put it in a research project looking back at the collapse, "Without an income, people had diminishing resources with which to maintain their former lifestyle and small businesses as a result lost their source of profit. Socially, families were fractured as relatives were forced to move away in search of employment in other regions of the country."[10] McKeesport, like similar communities across the region, lost residents, retail businesses, and revenues from property and income taxes. Today, many buildings in the city's central business district sit empty and boarded up; part of the facade of the four-story Executive Building fell off in January 2018, and the city tore down a three-story office building near city hall when debris started falling from the roof.[11]

The city's physical condition serves as a reminder of many residents' own poverty. The city has fewer than 20,000 residents (19,731), according to US census estimates, and a demographic mix that is 60 percent white and 34 percent Black; the median age is 43.8. Nearly half (48.3 percent) of the housing dates to before 1939, more than one-fifth (21.4%) of the housing units sit vacant, the median home value is $46,000, and renters occupy nearly half (48.7 percent) of all housing units. A third of the population (33.1 percent) lives in poverty, reaching as high as 59 percent of children under the age of five, and the median family income is $42,926. The unemployment rate is 15.7 percent, and 43.6 percent of people who are sixteen or older are not in the workforce.[12]

Politically, McKeesport leans heavily Democratic; the mayor and all seven council members belong to the party. Even when Republican president Donald Trump successfully created many inroads among Democratic areas outside of Pittsburgh in the 2016 presidential race, Democratic candidate Hillary Clinton won 64 percent of the vote in McKeesport.[13] In the 2020 presidential vote, Democrat Joe Biden again won 64 percent of the McKeesport vote, while Trump's standing dipped by two percentage points to 32 percent.

Throughout it all, the up and the down, the *Daily News* wove itself into the life of McKeesport by telling the stories that defined the region and its people. While it's easy to idealize the role of any local newspaper in the community it serves, the *Daily News* mostly told the routine stories of daily life in the city, and occasionally it dug into more serious investigations or in-depth profiles. The year before the *Daily News* closed, the Press Club of Western Pennsylvania recognized the staff as finalists in the investigative and enterprise category for newspapers with fewer than forty-five thousand subscribers in its annual Golden Quills contest; the newspaper had covered stories of illegal gambling in the Mon Valley and prosecutors' attempts to convict the people behind the bookmaking and slot machines.[14] That same year, the Pennsylvania NewsMedia Association awarded two reporters from the *Daily News* with second place for features writing among newspapers with fewer than twenty thousand subscribers.[15] After Trib Total Media closed both the *Daily News* and the *Valley Independent* in nearby Monessen in 2015, the Press Club honored both publications for their century-plus of service each:

> December 31, 2015, not only marked the close of the year, but also the end of an era when two of Western Pennsylvania's longest serving newspapers—*The Valley Independent* in Monessen and *The Daily News* in McKeesport—printed their final editions.
>
> *The Valley Independent*, founded in 1903, and *The Daily News*, founded in 1885, served the Mon Valley for generations, chronicling the story of its people and communities, which included one of the biggest stories in America's economic history—the rise and fall of the steel industry. Just as importantly, the newspapers served as the training ground for countless journalists working both locally and nationally.[16]

For readers, the *Daily News* helped residents of the city and the surrounding areas make sense of their community's ambitions and eventual decline while threading themselves together into one identity with a common, shared narrative. Many former readers said they could see themselves and their neighbors reflected in the newspaper's daily stories about what happened, notices about upcoming events, and features on the people living there. People read the newspaper not only to find out the news but also to belong to something larger than themselves. "I feel like the *Daily News* kept this whole area feeling like they were the community, you know like the sense of community between all the areas it served," Colleen Denne, the local librarian, said. "We were all the focus of the *Daily News*, and I think we all felt like we were one area. It wasn't divided. We were just all one because we shared that."

Speaking nearly five years after the newspaper closed, community leaders and residents talked about their shared sense of loss.[17] Yes, they no longer had that source for finding out information, but for many the newspaper's death seemed to hit closer than that. People felt a sense of civic connection and pride that came from reading the newspaper and being part of a story that stretched far into the past—and that seemed like it would go long into the future. When the newspaper's presses stopped running, it seemed like the community's story

FIGURE 2. A map hanging on the wall inside the *Daily News*'s main lobby displays McKeesport in the eastern time zone, along with the cities Chicago, Denver, and Los Angeles in the other time zones. Photo by the author.

had derailed too. "What you're talking about is a paper that reflected the entire community, everything from the communions and the graduations," said a retired newspaper journalist, seventy, who had once worked for the *Daily News* early in his career. The citizens of McKeesport saw the *Daily News* chronicling their lives as evidence for nearly every aspect of their existence—from birth announcements to obituaries—to the point that, in many minds, the publication came to represent the community itself. "It was the informant or the crier for the entire valley," said the mother of a toddler at a library event. "Not only did it keep us up on what was going on, but there were different parts of the paper that people actually looked forward to, like wedding announcements, obituaries. . . . [The newspaper] was just something that I looked forward to, and I didn't realize how important it was until it wasn't here. . . . There were so many things that they provided that you just took for granted because it was just there." Yet another person, a male retired print shop operator, seventy-five, simply called the newspaper "the heart of the valley."

The publishers of the newspaper embraced this idea that the identities of their product and the areas they covered could not be separated. The *Daily News* carried a tag line on its front page that said, "More than a newspaper—a community institution." Later, Scaife used his personal wealth and personality to reinforce those connections by serving as grand marshal in the annual holiday parade and by making donations to tear down abandoned buildings and build recreation facilities. When a local after-school group needed help building a deck-hockey rink, Scaife wrote a check. For many people in the working-class community, it seemed eccentric that someone with so much money would take an interest in the minutia of their daily lives.

Even the *Daily News*'s location in a high-profile, art deco building along a busy street across from the headquarters of McKeesport's main civic building represented the newspaper's primary spot as a community institution at the heart of everything. The building has a large first-floor lobby with high ceilings, tan tiles, and a long desk that wraps around the room with lighted signs along its black countertops, telling customers where to go for help with subscriptions, classifieds, advertising, and other services. A neon-lit map of the United States hangs along the lobby's back wall with a clock showing McKeesport in the eastern time zone—next to clocks identifying Chicago, Denver, and Los Angeles in the other time zones—placing the local community on par with some of the nation's leading cities. Outside of the newspaper building, the statue of President John F. Kennedy stands on the spot where he spoke in 1964.

When the *Daily News* closed, all these markers of community pride suddenly turned to symbols of the community's losses. Trib Total Media hung plywood over the first-floor windows of the newspaper building, protecting the glass and structure inside from damage but also sending the unmistakable message that the building, sitting at the center of the city, no longer had any use, at least for the moment. Not only did residents experience the physical loss but the closure left residents feeling a deep, unexpected wave of defeat as they realized how much the newspaper had tied together the place they lived. "I just think it left a hole," Fire Chief Jeffrey Tomovcsik said to describe the sense of civic failure. "They referred to themselves as a community institution. I mean they really were. They were around for so long, and a lot of people relied on them so heavily for their news." Jennifer Vertullo, the mayor's assistant, worked as a reporter, editor, and photographer for the *Daily News* right out of college and left just before the newspaper closed; she was one of ten reporters when she started in

2000 and just one of four when she left. "I think that, culturally, people miss the *Daily News* being the *Daily News*," she said.

> You know that whole slogan that it had, that it was more than a newspaper, it was a community institution.... They miss that aspect of it, and people who complained about it for the last twenty years of its existence still miss it. That's a strange phenomenon that you have with these people where they're like, "I miss my Daily News, I miss my Daily News," but they were the first people to call us and complain when we didn't lay it out exactly the way they wanted or have the exact content that they expected to see.

Many residents of McKeesport described even a personal sense of detachment from the newspaper closing because it had meant something to them in their own history or that of their family. Several people could recall exactly the first moment their name or photograph appeared in the newspaper, often as the result of success in school, the arts, or sports. The newspaper's journalists had been present in these people's lives at key moments to chronicle what they had accomplished and to add their piece to the community's story. It meant something to see one's name and photograph in the newspaper, especially with the article clipped out and hanging on a refrigerator or bulletin board at home and serving as a physical connection to the region, its present, and its past. "If you won in the art show in your elementary school, you got to line up and have your picture taken," a forty-five-year-old marketing director said. "Or if your sports team won a championship or something like that, you would always check the sports section to see if you got your picture in. . . . I remember anticipations of events at school or at the game the next day to see if your picture was in the paper." A former local congressman would get stacks of newspapers delivered to his office so he could cut out stories about constituents and send them laminated copies with the words "Compliments of Congressman Gaydos."

Mark Holtzman Jr., the school superintendent, grew up in McKeesport and played football for the high school when the team won a state championship, and he recalled how the newspaper promoted the young men on the team, helping some of them win the attention of college recruiters. After every Friday night game, readers could turn to the newspaper to relive big moments from the game, and the players gained some sense of fame from having these moments replayed in photos and stories. "To get your picture in there or to be written about was a huge deal," Holtzman said. A grown adult with a major position of leadership in the community, Holtzman, like many others, said he still has a box filled with yellowed news clippings along with other memorabilia. Tomovcsik, the fire chief, remembered the name of the newspaper photographer, Elmer, who would come out to take pictures of his Little League baseball and soccer teams in nearby Port Vue. Cherepko, the mayor, talked about playing baseball in the Daily News League, a local semi-pro summer series of games for men who had graduated from high school and still wanted to play; in another attempt to connect with readers, the newspaper had sponsored the entire annual season, and the name stuck even after the publication disappeared. "I don't know if they officially changed the name, but even to this day, everyone still refers to it as the Daily News League," the mayor said.

State Representative Austin Davis said the newspaper had started covering him when he was still in high school and served as chairman of the mayor's Youth Advisory Council, with the title of "junior mayor." The youth council that year conducted a series of community events with local leaders and residents, and the newspaper covered all of them, giving Davis a start in politics at an early age. Like the athletes, Davis looked eagerly to the newspaper to see how it covered his activities. "I was an odd kid because I was interested in the news, so I read the *Daily News*," he said.

For many people, the *Daily News* also provided their first job. Both the mayor and the state senator said they delivered the newspaper as boys, and the fire chief said his brother had a route. Colleen Denne, the librarian, remembered substituting on a delivery route for a friend whenever she went away for band camp. The newspaper boys and girls not only distributed the newspapers but also collected payments from subscribers and connected with the people on their route. "Mrs. Wiggins always gave us cookies on collection day," Denne said. "It was a part of our life. It was a big part of our lives, delivering the paper, and you got to know all your neighbors."

The *Daily News* represented more than just a source of information for the residents of McKeesport and its surrounding communities: the newspaper wove its way into their shared sense of identity and, in many ways, into their actual lives and memories of growing up in the region. The newspaper's owners promoted this idea of it being a "community institution" by communicating that message to readers, contributing money to civic interests, and playing up the newspaper's physical location at the center of the city. When the newspaper closed, residents not only felt the loss of local news but also experienced a fracture within their community, undermining what it means to belong to

McKeesport and the region. They also understood that the death of the newspaper represented another challenge, among many, facing the region, including
manufacturing facilities closing, people moving away, and large sections of the
downtown area falling into disuse, combining for a feeling of civic despair. The
overall sense of loss that accompanied the newspaper's failure has deep roots in
the residents' personal lives and in their own understanding of themselves and
their place in the community.

Loss of Awareness

Diane Elias, a school board member who runs a restaurant called Di's Kornerstone Diner, keeps a newspaper box from the *Daily News* inside the front door of
her restaurant, displaying a copy of the last issue. When the newspaper came out
every day, people would buy a copy from the box to read while eating their breakfast or lunch, and now the newspaper box serves as a nostalgic reminder of that
time. "We went to [the *Daily News*] for everything," Elias said. "Just to know what
was going on in the community and the neighboring communities—people,
fairs, churches, checking who won the games, anything local, obituaries, everything. . . . It was really missed." Now, because the *Daily News* closed, residents of
McKeesport do not know where to turn for the kind of information that makes
up the regular life of any community.

The death of the newspaper also meant a loss of civic awareness for residents
and community leaders, as they lacked an institution committed to chronicling
city meetings, police and fire incidents, and civic events such as annual festivals, church gatherings, and school pageants. The newspaper told the minutia
of daily life—the negative things that happened with the economic collapse and
increase in crime but also the moments that helped people see how their actions
fit together into a larger narrative. Public officials put little value in those simple
stories because they seem so basic, and only once they disappeared did people
realize how much they relied on that kind of information to find out what happens and learn about events that bring people together. "The motto here, or in
that newsroom, was, 'It didn't happen unless you read it in the *Daily News*,'" a
former reporter said. "And the truth of the matter was, we did a pretty good job
of it. You know, arrests and deaths and fires. I chased a lot of ambulances and
fire trucks here." It seemed the newspaper covered almost everything, he added:
"It's impossible to describe the amount of information that was in this newspaper
about the community. It is absolutely impossible—births, deaths, car accidents,

fires, robberies, crime, that sort of stuff." Vertullo, the mayor's assistant who previously worked at the *Daily News*, recalled that when she started in 2000, the newspaper had separate reporters for the McKeesport police department, the school board, and the city, and that the city reporter covered other meetings by the sewage authority, the redevelopment authority, the planning commission, and the zoning commission. "Every time somebody sneezed, somebody was there to cover it," she said.

While the newspaper's closure meant less information sharing, it also fractured residents' connections among each other, limited the public's access into community conversations and governance, and ultimately undermined the sense of shared narrative. Holtzman, the superintendent, said that without a newspaper, the community has a harder time holding together, especially with many transient residents who no longer have a toehold for quickly and easily learning about the local conversations taking place; about half of the students in the district start the school year somewhere else or leave before the school year ends, illustrating how their families are moving into and out of the community. "To be honest, I don't think we do a great job of being connected," he said. When the newspaper existed, residents could quickly and affordably dial into the conversations about everything from the police blotter and government projects, to features about interesting people, to local sports and activities. Churches advertised Sunday services and summer fairs, schools shared information about performances and events, and annual celebrations such as the holiday parade at Thanksgiving received prominent placement. Each of those moments has the potential to help residents make connections that strengthen overall civic life. When the information disappeared, fewer of those connections happened and the ties among people started fraying.

Vertullo saw the loss of awareness as a lack of connectivity too: "There's no way for people to get that community aspect." The consequences of poor access to information also mean that people do not know about opportunities, events, and information that impact their lives. "When that shut down," Vertullo said, "people didn't know who passed away, they didn't know who was hiring, they didn't know any of the events that were happening." Many reporters hate writing story obituaries because they involve talking with survivors and have little of the glamour of a front-page article, but readers rely on death notices both to find out about their friends who have passed and to discover how others have lived. When the printed newspaper went away, senior citizens said that they often no longer knew about people who had passed until weeks later when they already had been memorialized and buried. Denne, the librarian, agreed that the lack of information extends to missed opportunities for people in need; she expressed frustration that people who come to the library looking for help, as many now do, rarely know about ways to access available resources for housing, food, employment, tax preparation, and more. Even if the newspaper did not serve as a directory for social services, it would tell stories about government agencies and nonprofits that provide assistance in ways that allowed readers to learn about what exists. At the most basic level, people just don't know as much about their community as they did when the newspaper existed. "Even to this day, I probably hear, 'Well, without the *Daily News*, we don't know this, we don't know that,'" Mayor Cherepko said. "I would say that I hear that, without question, on a weekly basis."

For many residents, especially older and poorer ones with limited ability or access to technology, the newspaper represented an easy, relatively inexpensive way to stay connected with community conversations. A group of senior citizens talked about how they know an online obituary now exists for the community, but they do not have any way to easily access it without smartphones or computers of their own. These seniors live in a high-rise housing building, and the common room does not have a computer. One woman, age eighty-five, said she has a computer but does not regularly use it, waiting instead for her daughter to print out stories for her to read. When the *Daily News* was alive, the printed newspaper just showed up every day, and people with no technology skills, and few financial resources, could simply read what happened and who had died. At the library on a typical Thursday morning, people of all ages sat at computer terminals on the main floor of the building and in the basement children's area. Denne said many residents come in simply for access to technology, and the people there that morning surfed the internet for information and worked on personal projects such as filing taxes. "We have a lot of people who come in here every day to use the computer, so I'm assuming they don't have Wi-Fi at home," the librarian said. "And then there's homebound people, and you wonder, how do they ever even find out what's going on? They probably don't."

Many people said they worry that senior citizens, residents with limited means, and others who lack access to technology end up getting left out of the community's shared narrative now that the newspaper has closed. They have few resources for learning about what happens around them. "We just have that older generation now who just never had that internet," Tomovcsik said. "They never learned." Elias, the diner owner, agreed that many people in the community have not kept up with technology: "I try to tell them to go online, and go on to this site, but they're completely lost."

Elected officials, in particular, said they feel the loss of awareness among their constituents because people can no longer rely on the *Daily News* to share stories about government and politics. Several community leaders said that before the newspaper closed, they worried about its negative stories; later, they realized the newspaper also told stories of governmental meetings, of civic work such as helping new businesses, and of elected officials delivering money and assistance to their communities. Without the *Daily News*, elected officials said that although they may share information directly with constituents, it does not have the same validity as the newspaper, which could be expected to tell the whole story, the bad with the good. Even as someone immersed in public life and with easy access to technology, Rep. Davis said he does not feel as connected to information about city council or as aware of city actions as he did before. It's hard for him to keep up with what happens in local government, even though he serves the community in the statehouse. "Every month, it was like clockwork that there was going to be a long story about what happened at the city council meeting," Davis said. "Now, I don't really hear what goes on, [even though] I'm really informed." That loss of access to local news and information, he said, negatively impacts residents' ability to be aware of changes that affect their lives. Vertullo, the former newspaper employee, offered a similar perspective: "You had people who really looked forward to seeing what happened at the McKeesport council meeting, and they would go and get their paper on purpose the next day, if they weren't a subscriber, just to find out what happened."

While it might seem that elected officials would welcome the loss of local news coverage as a freedom to do whatever they want with less accountability and public oversight, politicians in McKeesport said they miss having a dedicated local platform telling stories about the work they do. "It's a double-edged sword," Davis said. "While I'm sure some elected officials look at media and journalists as a pain, in some ways they are our friends in this business." Politicians might have worried about the newspaper's stories that challenged their authority, but even the critical articles kept the elected leaders' names in front of voters. That kind of public exposure also keeps politicians honest, Davis said. Elected officials often act differently in private if they know the public has no idea what they are doing and no one is watching. "There are a lot of things sometimes that we know in political circles that would not necessarily end in the same result if they ended up on the front page of a newspaper," Davis said. In other words, public accountability through the news forces politicians to make sure their actions meet what constituents want.

Mayor Cherepko said he particularly misses having the *Daily News* serve as a microphone for disseminating information about actions of local government, saying he saw the newspaper as a way to "really get the positive information out to people." Even if the *Daily News* often wrote stories the mayor didn't like, it also told the public about the groundbreakings, the new initiatives, and the decisions about tax cuts and spending that he wanted them to know. Brewster, the state senator and former mayor, shared a similar frustration, saying that without the newspaper chronicling the actions of government, constituents do not know all of the work—such as demolition of abandoned buildings—he has done to help them. "I mean, they can see a building is torn down, but they have no idea how you got the funding, and what you had to go through to get it down," he said. Government cannot be as transparent as it needs to be, he added: "If you talk to people, regional people, they will say, 'We had no idea.'"

It seems obvious that the closure of a local newspaper will result in a loss of awareness for the people who relied on that news outlet for information, but residents of McKeesport did not fully realize how much they counted on the *Daily News* for both basic information about their lives and for stories that kept them knitted together. Political leaders, meanwhile, did not appreciate how much they needed the newspaper to tell stories about their governmental actions to constituents.

Loss of Control

As a retired advertising salesman, one sixty-seven-year-old man talked about how he still likes traveling around southwestern Pennsylvania and meeting new people, but when he tells them where he lives, in the Mon Valley, they often have a reaction that makes him shake his head in disbelief. "When I talk to people from outside of right here in the Mon Valley, and I say, 'Yeah, I live near McKeesport,' [they say], 'Oh, man, they're shooting people there all the time. There has to be bodies lying on the street,'" he said. "And that's the impression because of TV news—what's on there is if it bleeds, it leads."

Until the *Daily News* died, residents of McKeesport felt they had at least some control over the stories told about their community. The editors and reporters came into the newspaper building every day, and many of them lived in the city or nearby. People saw them on a regular basis at local meetings and events and in coffee shops and restaurants. Citizens knew they could get the journalists on the phone or simply walk into the newspaper's lobby at the center of the city and ask to speak with someone. Public officials had an even closer connection, seeing or hearing from journalists almost every day. If an elected official had a serious concern, they even could contact the publisher directly. Brewster, the state senator, remembers fondly a day when Richard Scaife, the billionaire owner, shared lunch with him at Tillie's Restaurant and how they both had the lasagna because it was the best thing on the menu. Meetings like that solidified their relationship, and if Brewster needed something, he could reach out and expect the publisher to get back to him.

When the local newspaper went away, nearly all the community's influence over its own story—real and perceived—disappeared too. Larger regional newspapers and the three local TV broadcast network affiliates still do occasional stories about McKeesport, but residents no longer see the reporters on a regular basis, they don't run into them at Little League baseball games or concerts in the park, and not even the mayor can reliably reach many of the editors, producers, and reporters making decisions about what stories to tell about McKeesport. Also, because these larger news outlets have fewer resources for covering local news, the people running them must make difficult decisions every day about where to send reporters as they attempt to cover the entire region of southwestern Pennsylvania. Most often, they focus on the biggest stories, which tend to be murders, other truly heinous crimes, and high-profile incidents such as house fires. None of these bigger outlets have enough journalists to cover the small stories and minutia of daily life, even though those are the events that make up the substance of any community.

As an aggregate result of the editorial decisions made every day, McKeesport's story seems overly negative and filled with mayhem—certainly to people from the outside, but even to the people who live there. "The impression that is given of my hometown is the exact opposite of what it really is," one woman said. "And it's because we don't have the proper exposure. The things that are televised or that are coming on the news are always bad things because they don't talk about the good things on the news. The information that needs to get out to the masses doesn't. It makes us appear to be a desolate town and we're not that. We're not that. McKeesport is a great place. It really is. Nobody gets to see the other side of things because we don't have a voice." Another woman, the marketing director, said she used to look forward to reading the *Daily News* to see positive stories about her community, and she misses that when she watches television news:

"It was like good news and happy things in the newspaper that you were looking forward to. However, on the [TV] news, it's all like death and disaster and shootings, and everybody's being robbed, and everybody has footage of somebody, you know, this person called the police."

Public officials who have a vested interest in portraying McKeesport as a safe and prosperous place said they feel an even bigger loss of control over the community's stories as the news has shifted from a balance of positive and negative stories to now more of a focus among regional media outlets on just the bad news. These leaders talked about how when the *Daily News* existed, they could develop relationships with reporters and editors to exert some leverage over how the newspaper covered stories. Holtzman, the superintendent, described how his family members worked in public jobs that required them to develop and maintain contacts with the newspaper: "My father was the chief of police here quite a few years, and my grandfather was a fireman, and my brother currently is a fireman here in the community, so we're basically a family of public service. And a lot of times that newspaper was very important to reporting; some of that could be positive or could be negative. Building a good relationship with the *Daily News* was very, very important for my family, I think in retrospect." Davis, the state representative, acknowledged how much elected officials miss the type of nuanced coverage the *Daily News* provided. "It really just did a great job kind of championing not only, you know, the negative things that happened in the community but really trying to be a champion for the positive things that happened," he said. "With their demise, we've seen a lot of the media coverage of McKeesport is negative, and there are a lot of positive things that happen, but they don't get covered."

Mayor Cherepko, who first thought the death of the *Daily News* would mean fewer negative stories, came to see that the newspaper also told many positive stories that depicted a balanced view of the community, and that it explained— often in detail—the work he does to promote McKeesport. The mayor has launched an initiative called McKeesport Rising, which is the sort of topic that the local newspaper would have covered with a lot of ink but that regional television stations will not carry over the air or larger newspapers in print. When the *Daily News* closed, Cherepko lost the ability to place positive stories with local reporters; at the same time, he cannot stop regional news outlets from covering major negative stories. As a result of that lost feeling of control, the mayor said it seems like negative stories dominate the narrative about McKeesport. "If you had five of six good stories in a day [in the *Daily News*], one negative story wasn't the end of the world," he said. "That's what I really opened my eyes to: for [the *Daily News*], yeah, they covered the bad story, but there were four or five good ones in there. That was, I would say, the biggest thing that I missed once they were gone."

People outside of local government also have less influence over the community conversation, particularly as they attempt to challenge those in power or provide alternative perspectives. Fawn Walker-Montgomery once served on McKeesport's city council, later ran for mayor, and now works as a community activist against what she describes as "all forms of violence," which includes crimes, police brutality, racism, and governmental decisions that favor one part of the city and leave others neglected. She used to look at the *Daily News* as a means for connecting with residents who might join her efforts or who would at least appreciate the work being done. She could call upon the newspaper to cover her activities, and she could encourage the reporters to write about what she was doing. "It was a way to get the word out to people about all of the community activities I was doing," she said. "It was a way to help shift the narrative about McKeesport because it was, you know, it was just such a bad rap sometimes." Similarly, the newspaper gave Walker-Montgomery a forum to challenge the mayor and other public officials to address McKeesport's blight and crime rate. Often the media outlet seemed to favor the perspectives of people in power, she said, but at least she could raise questions and expect to see the newspaper address them. Without the newspaper reporting on the community, she finds it harder to be heard. "A newspaper just helps with that; it helps with the narrative," she said. "Even though I felt the paper could be used a little bit more for accountability and advocacy, at least when we had it, people knew about what was going on, and they felt good when they saw a good story."

Few people in McKeesport seemed to appreciate how much they relied on the *Daily News* until it disappeared. Suddenly they no longer saw themselves reflected in the community's ongoing story, they missed opportunities to connect with neighbors and make friends, and they realized that they just did not know what happens all around them. Organizations that once relied on the newspaper to get out the word about their events had to find alternative ways of reaching people, and public officials found out that the negative stories they disliked were a small price for all the attention they received the rest of the time. Local newspapers—like libraries, hospitals, churches, schools, and other long-term institutions—play an important role in community life, but one that can be easy to take for granted. The death of the *Daily News* serves as a warning for places that still have local news outlets, even if they have been diminished by cutbacks and circulation losses: the local newspaper not only informs the public; it also brings people together in ways that create community.

5

Searching

They want more details because they didn't read it through the paper, the stories that would be covered through the *Daily News*. . . . Right now, it's just like, "Hey, I heard this; I heard that."

E ven as they come to terms with what their community has lost, the residents of a newly formed news desert also must start to figure out what happens all around them without the assistance of professional journalists. Surrounded by an overwhelming amount of raw data, people must on their own start to identify what pieces are accurate and meaningful to their lives, or what journalists would call "newsworthy." Much of the information that flows through a community every day has little value to most people because it does not involve them, it's not based in reality, or it has been twisted by a partisan in some way to reveal only a portion of the actual truth.

In a traditional newsroom setting, professional gatekeepers such as editors, producers, and reporters—like David Manning White's "Mr. Gates" in his 1950s research study—sort through all the available information to determine what seems worth keeping and what can be discarded. While this remains a highly subjective process, influenced by each gatekeeper's own perspective, professional journalists typically have undergone training on how to triage information, and they employ frames to sort out what seems important to large numbers of people, what has been verified for accuracy, and what comes from a particular point of view that might influence the quality of the information. Journalists make countless decisions based on these sorts of judgments every day, determining what meetings to cover, what questions to ask, and what topics to report out to the public. With limited resources, they must decide what seems worthy of their effort and attention, and what can be downplayed or ignored. A proposed utility tax on every home that uses water or that receives garbage pickup, for instance, will have more impact than an assessment for street repairs that affects only one portion of the community.

When professional journalists disappear from a particular community, citizens must make these decisions on their own, first figuring out where to look for raw information and then making sense of what they find. Without any formal training, these people typically do what humans have done from the beginning of time: they look around, they ask questions, and they listen to what people are saying. They do this by simply talking with the people around them; by using the technologies that connect them, such as social media; by looking to people in leadership positions for their guidance; and by seeking alternative sources of professional journalism, even if they do not provide the level of attention or detail that the local newspaper once did.

After the death of the *Daily News*, the residents of McKeesport said they find out about what happens in the community by talking with others at church, the grocery store, the barber shop, or basically anywhere that people gather. Even as they do this, many participants said they realize it can be difficult to separate actual news from gossip. Several of them described the information-gathering process like a giant game of telephone, in which each person, often unintentionally, twists the details just enough that the original message gets completely obscured after passing through several exchanges. While technology makes it easier for residents to connect with each other to share information, it also means that false rumors and misinformation, too, can move more quickly and have greater impact. It also becomes clear that not everyone enjoys the same level of access to information, with public officials and community leaders typically gaining greater access to primary sources of information, giving them an advantage over ordinary citizens.

Word of Mouth

Di's Kornerstone Diner brings new life to a building that once housed a fast food restaurant and that sits near one entrance of the Olympia Shopping Center, a strip mall with a grocery store, a payday loan outlet, a laundromat, and a rent-to-own furniture and appliance store. Boxes holding regional newspapers—the

Post-Gazette from Pittsburgh, eighteen miles to the west, and the *Tribune-Review*, based in Greensburg, nineteen miles to the east—sit outside the front door. The red-and-white checkerboard pattern painted on the outside of the restaurant carries through to the inside, appearing on many of the laminated tabletops and matching the red carpet that runs throughout. Several televisions tuned to local broadcast stations hang on the walls, along with black-and-white historical photographs of McKeesport. A shelf with knickknacks such as antique bottles and old-fashioned cooking utensils sits along a wall above an open window that looks into the kitchen, where a cook stands over the grill. A big yellow arrow with the name of a local amusement park, Kennywood, sits on the shelf.

The owner, Diane Elias, often can be found there, standing behind the diner counter and near the window where cooks pass dishes out from the kitchen. Because of back pain, Elias stands and moves around. She manages the waitresses who are walking around taking orders and delivering meals, and she tends to the computerized cash register. She greets almost every diner, recognizing many of them, and fills them in on the latest information about who has been in recently. Voters in McKeesport recently placed Elias onto the board of directors for the McKeesport Area School District based almost solely on her reputation from the diner; she did not spend any money on yard signs, advertisements, or flyers. "Honestly, I didn't really push it," she said. "My name is known. So, yeah, to be honest with you, when I ran for school board, it was all word of mouth. People coming in here."

Since the *Daily News* closed, Elias said, more people have been coming to her restaurant looking for confirmation about the rumors they hear. "I see it with the older generation, the seniors," she said. "They're lost. I feel like they got lost. They'll ask me, they'll come in and say, 'Hey, Di, have you seen so and so? Did you hear this happened?' Or 'Is that true?' Or, you know, they're always trying to clarify." People feel like they can turn to Elias and her diner for information because she hears a lot and because the network of people who come into the diner includes police officers and firefighters, government workers, elected offi-cials, and other local leaders. Basically, many of the people who run McKeesport seem to also eat regularly at Di's because of its good, affordable food, and because other people go there too.

Elias and her waitresses know a lot of people in the local community, and they use their connections to find out what happens. When someone comes in and asks about a rumor or piece of gossip, Elias said, the women start working to try and figure out what happened: "You know, everybody has different friends. I'll say, 'Vicky, text your friend.' She'll text her friend, and say, 'No, Di, she's saying this.' Then I'll text my friend, and I'll say, 'Well, she's saying this.' And this is how we're figuring it out. We're getting to be good investigators."

The diner sleuthing system works a lot of the time. But it's not foolproof. Elias learned the hard way about what happens when the system breaks down. She and her waitresses had heard that a local businessman named Ray had passed away. It seemed like everyone knew that he had died and was talking about it. Then, one day, Ray walked into the diner. "Did you hear it too?" he asked as he walked up to the counter. Flushed with embarrassment, Elias rushed over to apologize. "I'm sorry, Ray," she said. The man just smiled and shook his head. People all over town had been surprised that day to see him turn up after hearing that he had died. "Don't worry," he said. "I was already told at the butcher shop."

News about people dying tends to be one of the hardest pieces of information for residents to track down after a local newspaper closes. With a daily record of everyone who dies, the printed obituary in a local newspaper serves as a community resource to let others know who has passed and to record each deceased person's life story, often in the words of the people who knew them best. When that goes away, not only do false rumors spread about people dying when they have not, but after someone really does die, their friends might not find out for weeks, long after they are buried. A woman, thirty-seven, described how her mother and her mother's friends struggle to keep up with local deaths now that the *Daily News* no longer prints an obituary: "They don't necessarily have the social media contacts. If they don't have a younger person in their life, they don't really know. Like my mom's friend died, and nobody knew, because there's no obituary and older people don't really get on the internet."

The system of sharing information by word of mouth, like at Di's Kornerstone Diner, might not be reliable or efficient, but many people said they find out about what's happening exactly that way. They simply talk with other people in the community to see what everyone seems to be talking about at the Giant Eagle grocery store, at church on Sunday morning, or at the barber shop, the butcher shop, the library, and sporting events. Every person in their lives, from family members to neighbors next door, becomes a potential source of information, whether those people know what they're talking about or not. "Right now, I work a lot, and so on the way home, my mom will call me to tell me who is dead," a forty-five-year-old marketing director said. "'You know Mary?' Yeah, that kind of thing." Another person, a retired parole officer, talked about relying on his network: "You call people or you go to church, and then some people will say,

'Hey, whoa, did you hear about so-and-so dying' or whatever. . . . You get your information in church."

Individual citizens and community leaders said they turn to informal networks for information, even though they realize these sources might not always be that accurate or aware of everything that happens. Multiple people talked about how each person's level of awareness depends on who they know, the reliability of the people in their network, and whether they happen to see those people. A former police officer, fifty-seven, shared a concern about not knowing the full story unless he happens to learn about something through his limited number of contacts: "It breaks down the fabric of our social network, I guess you can say, with one another. We don't know about other people, with their family members or what have you, unless we run into people on the street or in a store, wherever we may be; then they fill us in with information that may interest us or what have you." A retired former newspaper reporter in another focus group said he worries about not finding out about everything that happens in the community, but instead only the bits that the people in his networks know about: "When I talk about people talking with people, I mean, that's how I find out a lot of things about McKeesport, but I'm sure that I'm missing a lot of areas, and a lot of other people and a lot of communities within the community that are just not part of my conversation. The conversations are going on for sure, but there's just no method for sharing them." Citizens do share information through their informal networks, but those networks are only as broad or as deep as the people in them, and they reflect the interests and ideas of those people. It makes sense that many other pieces of information get left out or ignored, or are just completely unknown to people outside of those circles. People in the traditional news situation had to rely on the subjective decisions of a professional gatekeeper to inform them about the world, but that seems far more reliable than having to depend on the whims of others who might not have any capacity to know whether the information they share has truth or value.

While informal news sources such as the church, the grocery store, and the hair salon do provide information, few in those places take the steps that professional journalists would to consider multiple, conflicting sources to understand the complete story, to verify information for accuracy, or to sort through all the gossip to determine what pieces are actually newsworthy. Elias and her waitresses do their best to make sense of the information they hear by attempting to verify rumors and cross-reference stories, but they have limited resources and few ways of detecting when a false rumor simply has been passed around enough that it seems true. As a result, people find out what happens by word of mouth, but they understand that they cannot rely on those sources for accuracy, fairness, or relevance.

Elias, for her part, said that ever since the supposedly deceased Ray walked into her restaurant that day, she has stopped repeating rumors unless she has verified the information from someone who would know. "If I really know the person, and I'm that close," she said as she reached across the counter, "and, I know, like, you know how you know your friends. If you're here, and if you tell me, 'Yes,' it's yes." Short of that personal confirmation from a trusted source, Elias said she no longer believes everything she hears—and she certainly does not repeat it.

Social Media

The woman with a six-foot-long Asian water monitor was happy to find out about the bag of pork patties sitting on top of the free food box on Locust Street (the lizard loves pork), but she was worried because they had been sitting outside for who knows how long.

Another woman who had been in a car accident wanted to know if anyone had seen what happened and whether the traffic cameras at the intersection actually worked. The police, meanwhile, wanted help with another accident in which one of the drivers left: "One vehicle fled the scene prior to any emergency services getting on scene. If anyone has any information about this accident please contact . . ."

It was "Wing Wednesday" at the American Legion's Canteen Kitchen ($1.25 each), while the Rotary Club was holding a lottery for a collection of Yeti insulated mugs and a gift certificate to a local Italian restaurant (two hundred chances at five dollars each). A bake shop started taking orders for Valentine's Day, while a resale shop opened despite road work taking place outside.

A local author planned to give an online talk about the "lost trolley parks of Western Pennsylvania" in an event sponsored by the McKeesport Regional History and Heritage Center, and the school board would be streaming its meeting online.

A woman wrote to thank first responders for finding her adult brother who had gotten lost, while another woman asked for help finding her black cat. A third woman posted a GIF with the words "God bless you" and wished everyone a "blessed Tuesday."

On this one January day, sixteen people posted separate messages to the McKeesport News & Events Facebook page, and more than one hundred users responded with comments or emojis. The posting about the food box and its pork patties elicited the most responses, with some people saying thanks, others wanting to drop off more food, and still others speculating about whether the pork patties were still safe for the Asian lizard to eat:

> **Person 1:** "it's 30 degree outside which is colder than most refrigerator temperature"
>
> **Person 2:** "true but I'm more worried about how long it's been there and if anything has gotten into it lol"
>
> **Person 3:** "that is true a rabid racoon could have got into the thing"

All of these exchanges took place over one twenty-four-hour period in just one Facebook group. Residents of McKeesport and the surrounding Mon Valley communities have created more than seventy-five local Facebook groups where people can post and discover a wide range of community information that includes gossip, emergency calls, political comments, jokes and complaints, updates on social and ethnic groups, and more. Users fill one page with nothing more than political jokes about liberals, while the largest one—with more than nineteen thousand followers—allows users to post messages about items they want to sell or give away.

Each group has at least one administrator, the person who runs the group and monitors the messages. Several of the administrators specifically say in the "about" section of their site that they seek to share local news and information; one administrator even calls her site McKeesport Daily News, and it has nearly six thousand members. Another large group, McKeesport and Neighboring Communities News Watch and Community Group, had more than 19,600 members until the administrator shut it down and archived the information. In that group's "about" section, the administrator posted a simple explanation for what she hoped to accomplish: "Since we no longer have the Daily News to keep us informed, this page can be used to post anything happening in the area. Anyone is welcome to post any local news or events." Local businesses were limited to posting twice a week, except restaurants, which could post their specials daily. Members of the group posted information about missing animals and charity events such as food drives, press releases from public officials and from local government agencies such as the school district, and information on local emergency calls. The administrator said she decided to shut down the group after being in the hospital and unable to keep it up to date; other users posted comments that the administrator had been upset that people had said rude things about her. (Although nothing obvious appeared on the thread, she might have removed them.) "I post as much as I can every day," she wrote when asked about why she turned off the posts. "I did slack off last week, but I was hoping people would be a little bit understanding since I almost died." Before shutting down the first group, she started another one that grew to include more than 4,400 members within a few months. The administrator said on the new site that she would not tolerate bullying and that she would remove people who she felt were behaving badly.

These Facebook groups have played a major role in informing the public, for better and worse, since the *Daily News* died. Community leaders and residents said they rely on Facebook pages and groups to find out information about the community and to share in local conversations. Even Mayor Cherepko said he turns to online sources to keep up. "Social media, obviously," he said. "A lot of people turn to that." Many leaders said in just a word or two during interviews that they look at Facebook as their primary social media platform to discover information, adding almost immediately that they do not find the content there reliable for many reasons. State Representative Austin Davis said, "[Facebook] certainly contributes in a way to people being informed. I don't know whether it contributes in a positive or negative way. It creates an outlet for people to voice their opinions, one way or another, whether they're right or wrong, but they have an outlet to voice their opinions. That's certainly a source where people get a lot of their news from in the local communities."

In addition to Facebook, community leaders and residents said they turn to other forms of technology for information about the community; these include Twitter, Instagram, Snapchat, and group text chats. Similar to word-of-mouth interactions, text chats allow individuals to share information directly with each other, but participants can share information more rapidly, among more people, and over wider geographic distances. Two women who participated in a library program for mothers said they rely primarily on group text chats to find out information. One said her family text chat group includes her two parents, her two sisters, and their two husbands, while her friend groups might have as few as two or three people. The other mother said she has one group text chat with nine-teen people drawn from family and friends, including several who used to live in McKeesport and who still want to stay in touch. The women said they share items they hear from news outlets, information they learn by word of mouth, and personal messages. One said that she has a group made up of friends who grew up together in McKeesport and who stay in touch with information about people who have died and items of local news. She said that some people in her group text chats live in other cities, and they had been taking the *Daily News* by mail just to keep up with their hometown; now they rely on other people to tell them what goes on in the community. "Some of my cousins are in other cities," she said. "My cousin in Philadelphia had a subscription to the *Daily News*. My cousin in California had a subscription to the *Daily News*."

Just as people turn to each other through personal interactions to learn about the community, they also turn to technological connections such as social media platforms and text chats to discover information. Again, like physical gathering places, however, it's rare that anyone fills the role of a journalist to verify information and sort through it for relevance.

In many ways, social media and other electronic means of conversation can act like word of mouth, except that they disseminate the information faster and more broadly. People who previously spent time looking at the local newspaper said that they now devote time on a regular basis to looking at Facebook for information about local events, for breaking news on crime and fire and medical incidents, and for community conversations. The newspaper used to provide a shared narrative for residents of the Mon Valley, and in its absence, people seek that community dialogue through online sources. These platforms work well for quickly and widely sharing information, and that provides a positive service when the information has been verified for accuracy and made free of bias. When the original news gets twisted each time it gets repeated, like in the children's game of telephone, this mangled information distorts and spreads more quickly online as well.

Official Sources

State Senator Jim Brewster, seventy-two, started out in newspapers, delivering the *Daily News* as a boy and then going to work as a newsroom assistant for the *Pittsburgh Post-Gazette* after college. He spent four and a half years going into the newsroom, helping reporters with research, and running errands. With the newsroom closed on Saturday mornings, he would go alone into the newspaper's quiet downtown offices, and he would make sure the Associated Press wire copy machines had paper. Before he left the newspaper to start a career in banking,

Brewster even wrote a few stories for the business desk, getting enough bylines that he ended up joining the newspaper guild. When celebrities and politicians, such as the presidential candidates who turn up every four years, visited the newsroom for editorial board meetings, Brewster would watch with a little bit of awe at the reverence that the newspaper and its journalists commanded. "It was a life-learning lesson," Brewster recalled years later. "I'm thinking, 'This newspaper is like the heartbeat of Pittsburgh.'"

Now, after living his entire life in McKeesport, working as vice president of operations for a major bank, and having served as the city's mayor and then representing the region in the state Senate, Brewster finds himself back where he started—letting people know what goes on in their community. When his cousin, a local businessman, saw work being done to clear out a property across the street that used to house a foundry, he called Brewster to find out what he knew. "Hey, this is right across the street from me," the cousin said. "What's going on?" Brewster did not know, so he called the mayor and found out that someone had bought the property and they were clearing it for a new bus depot. "I call my cousin back," Brewster said, "and he goes, 'That's good for me, JB, because they're gonna have to come out right past my business.'"

Before, when the *Daily News* existed, Brewster's cousin probably would have seen something in the newspaper about what was going on near his business. The *Daily News* would have recorded the property transfer, it would have reported when the new owner sought permission to tear down the old building, and it likely would have presented the plans for a new bus depot. Almost every step in the process could have prompted a reporter to write a story, or at least a brief, about the new development. "That's where the small newspapers filled that void," Brewster acknowledged.

Without the newspaper, Brewster's cousin had to do his own reporting to figure out what was going on after he saw work taking place at the former foundry. As he went about the process, the cousin had a major advantage because he could call Brewster's cell phone, realizing the politician would either know about the development or be able to find out. Community leaders enjoy more direct access to sources of information such as other government officials, incident reports, and financial data. As other citizens seek to learn about the community, they turn to these people to find out what they understand; citizens who have intimate connections to the leaders enjoy better access to information than those who are not able to call a government official's phone number and expect a call back in return. As a result of their special access, community leaders in a news desert often can control the amount and types of information they share with citizens who are desperate to find out what goes on.

When asked about how they learn about the community, many public officials in McKeesport shrugged or almost seemed baffled by the question because they already surround themselves with so many primary sources of information. They know what goes on in the city because they often have a role to play in the activity or they have direct access to the people who are working on the issue, whether it's responding to a fire or accident, approving changes to the city's code or taxes, or helping a developer start a new project. Brewster and Mayor Cherepko said they talk all the time.

"I really keep close tabs with the mayor," Brewster said. "We talk daily, and sometimes he'll know; sometimes he doesn't. Sometimes he'll know something, and I don't."

The fire chief, Jeffrey Tomovcsik, listens to the emergency call scanner, stays in direct contact with his firefighters about the incidents to which they respond, and often goes out on calls himself. If he wants to find out about any kind of emergency that involves the police department, he can simply call up his counterpart there and get the details.

Jennifer Vertullo, the mayor's assistant who used to work as a reporter at the *Daily News,* enjoys the sort of access in her new job that any city hall reporter would covet. She sits just outside the mayor's door, seeing every person who enters and overhearing many of their conversations. Half the time, she ends up answering questions from the public and other officials because she has direct knowledge about what happens in the community.

Even without the *Daily News,* McKeesport's community leaders remain steeped in the details of local life and government at all times, and they have many tools for figuring out what happens when they do not have direct knowledge. By contrast, many ordinary citizens do not share this same level of access and they often do not know. For those who have publicly challenged the mayor or spoken out against local government, it can be much harder to uncover what really goes on when they need to know.

Many community leaders said they have a hard time keeping up with the public's need to know since the *Daily News* died. It can be difficult to answer all the constant questions. Vertullo said people who knows she works for the mayor will seek her out with all sorts of questions, some important but many trivial. "There could be an incident at a house on our street, and if my neighbor wants to spy, she will immediately text me," Vertullo said. "Usually, it's like the neighborly stuff."

Few of these incidents rise to the level of actual community news, the kind of things that a local newspaper actually would cover if it were around. "If we were still relying on the *Daily News* for that kind of information," she said, "nobody would ever hear about the police being called to 123 ABC street at 10:59 on Thursday, because it was only because Bob was drunk, and then everybody went home."

As a main source of local news about the city, Mayor Cherepko maintains an open-door policy, meaning that residents may just stop by city hall and walk right into his office to ask a question. Many people take him up on the offer, showing up at his office with complaints and questions or hitting him up on social media. This results in the mayor and his staff spending a good portion of their day, both at work and at home, responding to citizens and trying to provide answers. "I make myself accessible as many different ways as possible," Cherepko said. He takes questions in person, via his cell phone, and through Facebook, and he tries to answer them at any hour. When the *Daily News* was operating, he said, people mostly wanted to share their opinion about what they had read; since the newspaper closed, more citizens have been seeking out the mayor for confirmation about something they heard by word of mouth or on social media:

> You definitely get more of your general, "Well I heard this is going on, I heard that." . . . Definitely, without question, I'd say now that the *Daily News* is gone, I get a lot more questions when I'm going places, about different things going on, than I did when the *Daily News* was here. People read back then. It would have been more, "Hey, I saw this is going on. That's wonderful. It's great to hear." So now that it's gone, it has gone from people really commenting on things that they already knew what was going on to now, "Hey, I heard this; is it true?"

The mayor and other public officials said they feel an obligation to fill some of the gaps that the *Daily News* left behind because people ask them so many questions. "They want more details because they didn't read it through the paper, the stories that would be covered through the *Daily News*," Cherepko said. "Right now, it's just like, 'Hey, I heard this; I heard that.' And then I confirm it."

People who do not have direct access to elected officials said they still seek them out for information, either informally or through the mechanisms of their office. One of the women in a discussion group said that she regularly looks up information on the city's website because she ran into the mayor and he told her to look there. A seventy-two-year-old retiree said that he often sees Senator Brewster holding informal conversations at a local chain restaurant: "I walk into

Eat'n Park and maybe once every couple weeks or so, he has a discussion booth for senior citizens in the middle of Eat'n Park. That's in McKeesport. They have about twenty senior citizens there." Other residents who want to stay informed said they show up at government meetings, where they can hear leaders discuss and vote on official business.

As much as they rely on public officials to find out what goes on, however, citizens also said they are aware that the information they receive from public officials often presents a jaundiced picture of the news that favors the perspective of the storyteller. Journalists at the *Daily News* might have had opinions about the news that influenced their coverage, but at least they had an outsider's perspective and attempted to provide a neutral look at the community. Public officials have no incentive but to share information that makes them look like they know what goes on, that they have things under control, and that they are being honest and transparent, whether they really are providing all of the information or not. A sixty-seven-year-old retired advertising executive who has lived in McKeesport all his life talked about getting a newsletter from Brewster's office and noting that while the information seemed factually correct, every story in it benefitted the senator. Of course the senator's own mailer presents him in the best possible way, making it seem like he did most, if not all, of the work to get grants and make positive developments happen. "It's factual," the retiree said. "What he's really good at is getting the federal and the state government to pump money into the Valley. And it'll have the dollar figures on the grants, and you'll have the numbers now. You have to question how much is his responsibility for getting those things." Even as he appreciates finding out about projects taking place in the community, the man said he has to feel skeptical about the information in the newsletter: "I mean, it's like every politician who ever lived takes, you know, claim for everything good that happens."

Community leaders enjoy outsize access to local news and information as compared to ordinary residents because they live in a world surrounded by primary sources, local activities, and official decisions. Residents seeking information may turn to these officials if they can access them, but the resulting information rarely tells the full story.

Traditional News

Nineteen miles south of McKeesport along the Monongahela River, the city of Monessen experienced a similar story of industrial strength and decline, followed by the collapse of its local newspaper after 113 years. The city's main employer, the Wheeling-Pittsburgh steel mill, closed in 1986, and the newspaper hung on for another thirty years. Publisher Richard Scaife had purchased the newspaper, like the *Daily News*, and added it to his Trib Total Media chain of local newspapers. When Scaife died and the Trib started looking for ways to stop losing money, it first tried to sell the *Valley Independent*; when it could not find a buyer, it decided to close it along with the *Daily News*.

The story in Monessen took a turn, however: four local businessmen decided in 2015 that they could run a profitable newspaper instead.[1] They acquired the subscriber and advertising lists from the old company and started their own newspaper called the *Mon Valley Independent*. The newspaper published its first edition in 2016, suffered through an initial period of financial losses, and had one of its founding investors end up in federal prison. A lawyer, he was convicted of defrauding an elderly client with dementia to steal money that he used, in part, toward his investment in the newspaper.[2]

Within four years, the publishers started breaking even by keeping their overhead costs low and tapping into a market underserved for both news coverage and local advertising. In February 2019, the *Mon Valley Independent* opened a newsroom bureau in McKeesport, inside the former home of the *Daily News*. Trib Total Media essentially donated the building to the city of McKeesport, which reopened the space as an office complex called the Tube City Center. The *Mon Valley Independent* maintains one full-time reporter in McKeesport, along with freelance contributors. Naz Victoria, one of the four founders of the *Mon Valley Independent*, explained his motivations: "The entire social system depends on somebody holding the public officials accountable. If not, then there is really no need for the newspaper. I believe that that's what the original meaning, the original purpose for the newspaper was, to hold our politicians accountable." Victoria said he gets upset anytime someone refers to McKeesport as a "news desert" because the city has the *Mon Valley Independent* now. "It is no longer a news desert," he said. "We have McKeesport, and the surrounding area is right up there with our largest subscription base that we have."

Since the *Daily News* died, residents of McKeesport have turned to other traditional media that serve their community. This includes two regional newspapers, the *Pittsburgh Post-Gazette*, and the Pittsburgh TV and radio stations. In that sense, McKeesport might not be considered a news desert. In reality, none of the regional news outlets provides the quantity or quality of local news that the *Daily News* once offered, and so, in many ways, the community does qualify as a news desert, particularly in the context of the Chicago columnist Laura Washington's original definition.

Many residents and community leaders said they look to these larger regional outlets for news, but they see differences in the numbers of stories about their community and the types of coverage. "You can still get your news nowadays," Tomovcsik, the fire chief, said. "You can put on KDKA or WTAE [the Pittsburgh TV affiliates] but you don't have the personal touch." Because these regional news outlets cover such a broad geographic area, they tend to focus on major negative stories such as shootings, murders, and fires. "When they want to come here and report something, then it . . . typically isn't something good," Tomovcsik added.

Fawn Walker-Montgomery, the community activist who used to serve on the McKeesport City Council, talked about dealing with a local issue when she ran for mayor. The regional news outlets—the *Post-Gazette*, the *Tribune-Review*, a local newspaper focused on Black issues called the *New Pittsburgh Courier*, and Pittsburgh's NPR affiliate, 90.5 WESA—all covered the conflict, but that hardly mattered to her campaign because so few local residents saw or heard these stories. Walker-Montgomery's daughter and some of her friends wanted to start a Black student union at their high school in McKeesport, and that caused tension with the school district, growing into a larger issue that received lots of regional media attention (and even some national news). A lot of that information never reached a lot of the people in McKeesport, she said, and the narrative would have been different if there had been a newspaper just for McKeesport telling the story. "It would have been, I think, a lot different because I would have been able to at least talk to them and get my side out more," Walker-Montgomery said. "Like the kids did an interview, but they did it with WESA. Not a lot of people around here know what WESA is."

Even before the *Daily News* closed, Jason Togyer, a McKeesport resident and former newspaper reporter, started a website called Tube City Online, which includes an internet news site called the Tube City Almanac and an internet radio station. The Almanac's news site lists obituaries, the local weather, and local news stories. Many of the community leaders said they turn to the website for information, and several said they have interacted with Togyer directly. "Jason Togyer filled that gap for the obituaries with the online thing, which reached most everybody," said Vertullo, the mayor's assistant. "I think that the older population now knows enough how to get online and do their thing." Mayor Cherepko agreed: "He's done a tremendous job. Once again, that's all online, so for me, I have no problem looking for information on there as mayor."

Again, however, the mayor and other community leaders questioned how many people in the city can access news and information on the internet, particularly among older and poorer residents. "You still have a high senior citizen population that's just unlikely to go online and read the Tube City Online," Cherepko said. When the fire department wanted to share information about giving away free smoke alarms, Chief Tomovcsik said he talked with Togyer about creating a commercial for his internet radio station but wondered if it would reach enough of the right people. "Jason does a great job pushing out his electronic stuff, but, you know, we just have that older generation now who just never had that internet," he said. Mark Holtzman Jr., the superintendent for the McKeesport Area School District, said he appreciates that the Tube City Almanac provides coverage of the community but questioned its reach. "They come around and spend some time with us, too, and they've been pretty fair as well," he said.

No one other than the publisher of the *Mon Valley Independent* has questioned whether McKeesport exists as a news desert since the *Daily News* closed. Community leaders said they appreciate reporting by the regional news outlets and the local online startup, but that even all that coverage combined does not equal what was lost when the *Daily News* went away. Some residents of McKeesport said that with the *Daily News*, they felt like they had their own newspaper with many reporters telling stories about their city and the surrounding communities. Now, McKeesport has to "share" the news coverage with other areas, Walker-Montgomery said. "Obviously they're trying to fill a gap the *Daily News* left, but it was a big gap," Tomovcsik said, "and the *Mon Valley Independent* is spread out over a lot of communities." Holtzman said the people at the *Mon Valley Independent* "make a really strong effort," but it's not the same. "I don't think it's quite like the *Daily News*," he said. "It's a little different than that. I think they . . . write in a little broader way. They incorporate some other communities and different things that maybe the *Daily News* was focused more around the McKeesport area."

A freelance reporter for the *Mon Valley Independent* participated in one of the focus group sessions, and he said people throughout the region tell him about how the newspaper only covers other communities: "When I interview people here [in McKeesport], or when I tell people, you know, that I do that, they say, 'That paper is all Charleroi and Monessen; it's all that.' Now, there was a person who was out of the office, I handled some work up in the Monessen, Donora area. And their complaint to me was that, 'It's all McKeesport coverage.' It's illustrative of the fact that everybody wants hyperlocal coverage."

Almost every leader interviewed mentioned the *Mon Valley Independent*'s McKeesport reporter, Jeff Stitt, by name. He shows up to city and school board meetings, he calls Tomovcsik whenever a fire emergency happens, he turns up at Di's Kornerstone Diner for meals, and he helps the library share news about upcoming events. Stitt tells the stories about anything bad that happens in the community, and he writes feature stories about the positive developments. While former reporters of the *Daily News* recalled the newspaper having as many as twenty reporters four decades ago, and at least ten reporters at the turn of the twenty-first century, Stitt and a small group of freelance reporters try to cover pretty much everything now. "You get one story a day because there's one guy, and it's not that I'm saying anything about the reporter, because he's doing his job," Vertullo, the former reporter, said. "He's a human and not a workhorse."

A community's relationship with its local newspaper goes both ways, and many residents and community leaders said McKeesport has not really given the *Mon Valley Independent* the same opportunity to become the newspaper of record. Many people said they know about the newspaper and see it for sale in stores, but they do not read it. As one woman, thirty-seven, said, "I see it, but I don't even, I can't even tell you what it contains." Mayor Cherepko said he cannot understand why residents refuse to consider the *Mon Valley Independent*, even as they complain of missing the *Daily News*. It might be that at first the newspaper had more news about areas further south in the Mon Valley, but since opening a bureau in McKeesport, the *Mon Valley Independent* often has one local story on the front page every day. Despite that, Cherepko said, many citizens will not give the new newspaper a chance to win them over: "The people, they couldn't even make the switch. Your older seniors, I mean, they'll go, 'Ever since the *Daily News* has gone, no one knows what's going on.' I'll say, well, the *Mon Valley Independent*, they're doing a good job with a printed paper, trying to get stories out. 'Well, it's not the *Daily News*; it's not the *Daily News*.' So a lot of people, as much as they miss the *Daily News*, it seems like many are reluctant to try the *Mon Valley Independent*." Holtzman compared starting a community newspaper with building up a low credit score: the *Daily News* had more than a century to build up its standing in the community, and it will just take the *Mon Valley Independent* time to earn trust among residents, even as they hunger for a local newspaper.

Victoria, the publisher and co-owner of the *Mon Valley Independent*, said he understands the community's frustration about not connecting with his newspaper. It costs money to market the publication, and the owners have invested limited resources into creating original content. "I just wish I could figure out how to get the word out to more people that we are there, and that we do service them and all of their neighbors," he said.

The newspaper's owners have made a deliberate move to tell stories about McKeesport, and they make sure their reporters emphasize positive issues that contribute to residents' sense of belonging, he said. Victoria also said the newspaper not only has to tell the stories of the community but also reinforce good things happening in the community: "Why is it important for me to do positive stories? Because the Mon Valley is so downtrodden that if you're from outside of the Mon Valley, you come in and you grab a newspaper at the store or whatever. If I have all over the front page of this paper, 'two murdered in McKeesport,' 'four arrested for drug dealing in Monessen,' 'Donora shuts down street because of a riot,' where am I going to? Do I want to stay here? Do I want to be here?" The newspaper has instituted a policy that stories about crime and drugs no longer appear on the front page unless they involve a public official or the issue presents a threat to public safety. Instead, the publishers would prefer to present stories about companies investing in the Mon Valley, business openings, infrastructure, development, and general "feel-good" topics. "We're also the face of the Mon Valley, and by being the face of the Mon Valley, we need to not only emphasize the ugly, but we need to really promote the beautiful," Victoria said.

Since the *Daily News* closed, residents of McKeesport have turned more to replacement news outlets for coverage of the community. None of these newsrooms—whether the regional TV stations or newspapers, the Tube City Almanac, or the *Mon Valley Independent*—has as many resources to cover the city with the volume of stories and attention to detail that the *Daily News* had at its peak. Regional outlets often tell only the negative stories of the community, while the news organizations with a presence in the city do not have the deep resources to tell the complete story in the ways that the *Daily News* previously did. Instead, residents and community leaders ultimately feel frustrated because they look for the news in places that purport to tell local stories and come away not seeing themselves represented in the ways they expected.

6

Sharing

The people of McKeesport who want to be informed, they keep
themselves informed. We've got a stable group. They come to every
council meeting. Those are the people who are out there, sharing
information. They want to be involved.

Traditional news gatekeepers do not have to think much about the
gates they use to share information because they exist as a natural part
of the job. For instance, when Mr. Gates was making decisions in the
1950s about what news stories to put into the local newspaper, he did not have
to consider how he would share the information; obviously, whatever he passed
through would go out to the public in that day's newspaper. Similarly, news gatekeepers today might consider the decisions they make about what to pass along
to the public, but they rarely have to dwell on how to share the information:
modern newsrooms have many methods for publishing information in print,
over broadcast airwaves, on the internet, and via social media platforms. A news
gatekeeper might have to decide what platforms make the most sense for sharing
a specific story or piece of information, but they do not have to go out and look
for the mechanisms to do so. They are all around.

As citizens start to take on the role of gatekeeping for local news and information, however, they also must identify the gates they will use to tell others about
what they have discovered. They might not consciously think about these gates
as they make decisions about what to share by word of mouth or what to post on
Facebook or Twitter, but they are actively choosing where and how to introduce
what they know into their community. In the absence of the local newspaper,

these citizens end up gathering in person and online to share information, and they look for creative ways to reach large numbers of people. Public officials, who enjoy greater access to taxpayer-funded methods for informing constituents, get into this game, too, by using their unique resources to inform thousands of people at once.

Informal Gates

Just as patrons turn to Di's Kornerstone Diner to find out what happens in their community, they also go to places like that to share what they have discovered. The exchange of information does not just work one way, and many of the customers who come to Diane Elias to find out what she knows are just as excited, perhaps even more so, to tell her what they know—or at least think they know. Places such as restaurants, beauty and barber shops, churches, and retail shops serve as informal gates where people with information gather to disseminate local news and information. Similarly, individuals turn to social media platforms, text chats, and other forms of technology to provide information to others. Through these informal exchanges—by word of mouth and with technology such as social media—individual citizens act as gatekeepers for the information they acquire as they decide what to repeat to others.

Elias has so much information only because she learns about the local news and gossip by listening to the people who come to her with stories. If someone calls to find out about a fire call, for instance, she will tell them to wait until the firefighters have come in for lunch, when she will find out what happened. "We sip a lot of tea around here," she said, employing a euphemism for listening to gossip. "We hear a lot of stuff." She compared working at the diner to serving as a bartender and listening to everyone's problems: "It's like when you work. When I was a bartender years ago, you know how you get stuck behind the bar and you listen to everything? I thought, Oh, I don't want to bartend anymore, but it's at any kind of our public job, I believe. You hear a lot."

In addition to in-person gathering places, community leaders and average citizens in McKeesport use social media and other technologies to post and share information, just as they use those same sites to learn about the community. The many Facebook groups related to McKeesport contain information that ordinary citizens post about moments in their daily lives, and some of it has more value than others. In one typical exchange, one citizen posted a photo and wrote that he could see police, fire, and ambulance vehicles with their lights on

Jay Dzub
April 2 at 10:53 PM · 😕 ···

Why is there dozens of police, fire and ambulance up over the hill from Harrison Village ?

Figures 3 and 4. A citizen posted this image (*above*) to Facebook and asked whether anyone knew about the emergency vehicles he could see in the distance. Other citizens replied (*right*) with information they had discovered about the incident, including an image from closer to the scene.

Chrissy Ross-Kuzel ···
Fire on Jenny lind
Like · Reply · 3d 1

Sue Ulm ···
Fire on Jennylind St
Like · Reply · 3d 1

Bill Chapman 🖐️ ···

Like · Reply · 3d 1

in the distance from his house. Within a few minutes, other residents replied to the original posting with information they knew about the incident. The first person wrote the name of the street where the action took place, and within a few minutes a second person confirmed the location while also correcting the spelling of the street name. A third person then posted another, closer photo, confirming that the emergency services crews had responded to a house fire; the image does not show exactly what was going on, but it does provide the context that the incident happened in a neighborhood with single-family homes.

By using social media, individual citizens are looking around at their community, acquiring as much information as they can find on their own, and then sharing it with other people to inform them—and to perhaps learn something more in return. Communicating via technology allows each individual to reach more people than trying to share and learn information through one-to-one and word-of-mouth interactions.

At another moment, during the COVID-19 pandemic in 2020, residents used technology to share information about community events and responses to the crisis: one person posted that police officers would be driving around the Easter Bunny so children could see him waving from a patrol car; another posted that high school seniors needed to check in with their English teacher for end-of-year assignments; a third told about where Christians could pick up palm leaves for Palm Sunday services; yet another offered information about the face masks she made and offered to others.

Without the ability to share information through a traditional news source such as a newspaper or radio station, residents told each other what they knew during the crisis by using social media. In return, other citizens were able to find out new information, share it with people in their networks, and add their own knowledge.

Every community leader except for one, the newspaper publisher, said they use Facebook to put out information for the community such as notices about upcoming events, highlights of people doing positive work, and images of politicians handing out government money. Even though the newspaper publisher does not personally use social media platforms, his newsroom editors and reporters certainly share information via Facebook and Twitter. Austin Davis, the state representative for McKeesport and surrounding areas, said he uses social media because it works to reach his constituents: "I tend to put a lot out. I hear a lot [of people] that say, 'I saw you posted this on Facebook,' even from people who I wouldn't expect, but they're like eighty-year-old people who say, 'I follow

Tammy Hoyman Moreno shared a **post**.
6 hrs ·

•••

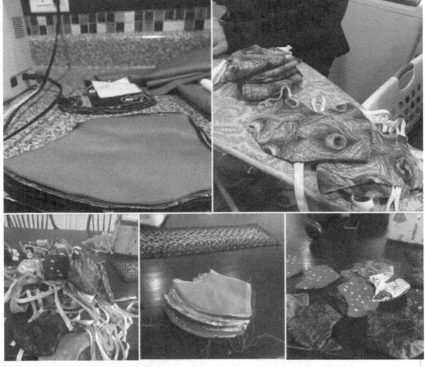

Tammy Hoyman Moreno
6 hrs ·

Mask making in the works.. does anyone need any?

FIGURE 5. During the COVID-19 pandemic, a resident of McKeesport turned to Facebook to tell others that she made masks and to offer them to anyone needing them.

you on Facebook.' They don't comment, they don't 'like' anything, they just kind of see it." Davis said he actually maintains three Facebook accounts—a governmental one, a political one, and a personal one—two Twitter accounts, and an Instagram account. When he was hosting a clinic on how citizens could apply to the state to expunge a criminal record, he shared the information on one of his Facebook pages, and within two hours, it had 87 shares and 250 likes. He said, "I usually share all the same content throughout all three of them, because some people are in different lists. The only thing I don't share on all of them is if it's a blatantly political thing; that doesn't go on my official page."

Elias said she started using Facebook to promote her restaurant after the *Daily News* closed and she no longer had a way to purchase affordable advertisements in a newspaper that would reach her target audience. She could buy an ad in one of the regional newspapers, but that would cost her a lot of money and the notice would end up going to a lot of people who live far away and never would visit her diner. With social media, she could post free messages on the Facebook pages that local residents use, and she could purchase targeted advertising based on the local geography, her customers' interests, and the actual number of people who saw her post. Elias at first felt uncomfortable posting about the diner, but now, she said, she and her customers have come to rely on it: "I was lost. That's when I started taking my own pictures and put them on Facebook. That's how I joined Facebook. Because I wasn't a Facebook person at all. Then the girls said, 'Hey, Di, take a picture and post your specials.' Now I just do three posts every day. People call me now and say, 'Di, you didn't post your specials.'"

Like Elias, Senator Jim Brewster said he did not really use social media until other people told him he needed to communicate better with his constituents: "Some of my colleagues are better at it than I am. I even said that to the mayor. He says—this is like a couple years ago—'You got to start using Facebook.' So, I asked him like nine months ago, I said, 'Hey mayor, what do you think of my work on Facebook?' He says, 'You're off the charts. In fact, it's to the point where it's nauseating.' I said, 'You asked for it.'" Brewster's office maintains two Facebook accounts, a governmental one and a political campaign one, and an Instagram account, and he gets help from his staff with sharing information. Typically, Brewster will share posts to promote something positive he has done in the community. For example, Brewster's staff shared on Facebook when he appeared before the borough council in nearby Port Vue to give a proclamation to someone who had served in local government for eighteen years. They posted again later that same night when Brewster went to the McKeesport Area School District's board meeting to receive an honor himself. "They're also going to recognize me because I've helped them get a significant amount of money for their recreational needs," he said. "So that will go on my business Facebook and also on my political Facebook."

The fire department not only shares information on social media about smoke detectors but also offers news items that might provoke a community conversation. The firefighters are trying to build an audience with popular, viral information so that people are paying attention when they want to raise awareness with a fire prevention message. When the Women's Basketball Hall of Fame announced that it would induct a McKeesport native named Swin Cash, the fire department shared that news with a congratulatory note for the popular hometown athlete. "It's good stuff like that that picks up and takes off," Fire Chief Jeffrey Tomovcsik said. "It's a feel-good story. People want to see the good stuff. So once that takes off, people share it and it gets shared, and they see it's been shared from our page, and we usually get some 'likes' out of it."

Citizens, whether they know it or not, serve as gatekeepers when they share news and information with the people they run into on the street and when they post to social media. People share information informally wherever they go, and they move these behaviors onto the internet as well, reaching broader audiences more quickly. Community leaders also use these networks to share information, but they often do so more formally, or with a definite sense of purpose.

Replacement Gates

When a former professional football player named Sam Davis went missing at age seventy-nine in McKeesport, his family looked for ways to get out the information quickly and to a large group of people. At one time, that might have meant calling up a reporter at the *Daily News*, but since the newspaper closed, people have had to get creative about sharing information to large groups.

Davis had lived in a senior assisted care facility, and someone there had seen him walk out of the building before 7:00 a.m.[1] Desperate to find his uncle, Davis's nephew found a photo of the two of them together, and he wrote a paragraph to describe his uncle's condition—"He suffers from dementia so he may be lost, confused or hurt and has trouble walking and seeing"—and tell people what to do if they found him. Without a local news outlet to notify, the nephew instead went to the Carnegie Free Library of McKeesport, about a ten-minute walk from his uncle's nursing facility. He walked up to the circulation desk, which sits in the middle of a large room filled with books, under a high ceiling. The nephew asked whether he could post the image and short paragraph to the building's glass doors. "We [knew Davis] because he lived up the road, so we shared that information with people because it was news," Colleen Denne, the librarian, recalled later.

By the time the McKeesport reporter for the regional *Mon Valley Independent* newspaper heard about the missing man later that afternoon, the journalist

Please share: My Uncle Sam Davis on the left has gone missing. All we know is he was last seen in McKeesport on Versailles Ave. Around 630am. He suffers from dementia so he may be lost, confused or hurt and has trouble walking and seeing. Thank you.

FIGURE 6. The nephew of Sam Davis, a former Steelers player, posted this photograph and message on the door of the Carnegie Free Library of McKeesport when Davis went missing in 2019. Photo by the author.

already had covered a local government meeting and did not have time to file another story. Normally in a football-crazed community, a story about a former Steeler who had won four Super Bowl championships would be major news, and it eventually was. But in the first moments, when the story was still just breaking, no local reporters were available to tell the story, and the people trying to get out the news went looking for their own outlet anyway. Davis turned up dead inside the nursing facility before the next day, and after that, regional television stations and newspapers were interested and providing their own versions of the story.

Although not as high-profile, moments like this happen all the time in McKeesport. Unable to tell their stories through a traditional media outlet, community leaders and residents said they look for other means of sharing information.

Few of these resources would qualify as journalism outlets, but they ultimately serve as alternative gates for citizens who want to quickly share news with large groups of people. Sharing information on a public message board or hanging posters about a lost cat on telephone poles does not require much innovation, but people become more reliant on these basic methods when they no longer have access to a traditional news outlet.

For many residents, the library serves as a key outlet for quickly sharing news with others. The castle-like stone structure has sat on a hill overlooking the Monongahela River for more than a century, since the steel industry baron Andrew Carnegie donated $50,000 for its construction at the end of the 1800s.[2] During a typical weekday, people come to the library to use computers, buy secondhand jewelry from a small table, and pick up forms for filing their federal income taxes; mothers and grandmothers gather in the basement children's area for reading time and crafts. Librarians stand at the oval-shaped information desk on the main floor, while downstairs one librarian reads to the children and another works at a second reference desk. "We are counted on for pretty much any kind of information that a person has, whether it be recreational or educational or life," Denne, the librarian, said. "They know that if 'I have this need; I need to file my unemployment,' they're coming here," she said.

The library maintains a message board by the main entrance, where it hangs up information when community leaders, local police, and ordinary residents bring messages for sharing. "We post it on our board for people who come in," Denne said. "We have a community board. We actually need it to be bigger, because there are a lot of people who do share things with us." The board includes information about upcoming community events, services available to people in need, job openings and volunteer opportunities, and missing people. "When people share it with us, we do, we will share," Denne said. Several residents confirmed that they turn to the library when they want to learn about what goes on in the community. A retired journalist, seventy, referred to the library as a "really a good resource," and a twenty-six-year-old woman who works at a Pittsburgh museum said she turns to the library for information.

Similar to hanging a flyer at the library, Mark Holtzman Jr., the superintendent, said the school district looks for ways to place simple messages in front of large groups of people where they pass regularly or gather. The district posts messages to an electronic sign board in front of the school complex along a busy road, and it hangs banners over the street for special events such as homecoming. "A lot of people really, believe it or not, catch things on [the message board]

FIGURE 7. A message board inside the main doors of the McKeesport Library holds messages about community events, information on social services, and flyers showing missing people. Photo by the author.

because it's on a main boulevard," Holtzman said. "We oftentimes will celebrate things there and get information out that way." Sporting events in McKeesport also represent a major way for reaching large numbers of people at one time, he said; when groups come to the school district looking for ways to share their messages, he often suggests they hang a sign or make an announcement at a football or basketball game, or other sporting event. "Sports is very important to this community," Holtzman said. "I often say sometimes we struggle to get parental involvement and things, but we can sure as heck get a couple thousand people for a high school football game. That's a tradition here that obviously is important to the community. We always tell people, if you want to get good information out, you want to share an idea, do it at an athletic event."

Other community leaders said they seek out alternative methods to reach people directly with information they want to share. Fawn Walker-Montgomery, the community activist who served on city council and ran for mayor, cofounded a group called Take Action Mon Valley, which opposes all forms of violence and has chapters in towns throughout the region. Walker-Montgomery said she works with volunteers to fan out across targeted neighborhoods to knock on doors and hand out flyers: "We just go out and knock. It depends on the area: McKeesport, we have eight of us in our chapter, Duquesne has three, and East Pittsburgh, we just started that one so we only have three. So we just go out and we door-knock. We'll see if we can leave a flyer on people's doors, like a restaurant: 'Can we leave one flyer here?'"

Tomovcsik, the fire chief, said he looks to groups that he can partner with to share local information. "Really, you gotta lean on groups in the community, not online, like churches, senior citizen groups, Boy Scouts," he said. "People like that. You got to rely on them to get information out in public."

Citizen gatekeepers look for creative, nontraditional ways of sharing information, on sites that would not qualify as traditional sources of journalism. Places where people gather—such as the library, high-traffic areas, and sporting events—allow citizens to reach large numbers of people quickly. People always have shared community information about missing pets, employment opportunities, bake sales, and more in public places, on message boards, and stapled to telephone poles. Without a local newspaper, however, the need to share information in these serendipitous ways takes on new urgency as individuals seek to reach large numbers of their fellow citizens.

Official Gates

The city of McKeesport changed garbage haulers in early 2020, and what should have been a routine transfer of contracts instead turned into a community crisis. People complained on social media about the new collectors missing their house or doing a poor job. At the same time, citizens started calling the mayor's office to ask about when to put out their recycling, even though that schedule had not changed. The city had released messages about recycling days on its website, and it had paid for a story to appear in a community magazine that goes to every home. Residents still said they didn't know. The mayor's assistant, Jennifer Vertullo, grew frustrated at answering the same question over and over when citizens called looking for answers. She said, "Now everybody's up in arms because they don't know when to recycle. People still don't seem to understand that, yes, your recycling pickup is going to follow the same weeks as it always did. And it's going to be on the same day as your new pickup day. Seems like really basic but people were still really crazy." If the *Daily News* were still in circulation, the newspaper would have carried multiple stories about the city council considering the new garbage collectors, the impact of the new contract, and the new days for garbage collection but not recycling. Many people who missed the messages on the city's website and in the printed magazine would have seen a story or stories in the newspaper about the change and how it impacted residents. Public officials would have issued press releases and talked with reporters about why they were changing services, and they could have used the newspaper as a free vehicle to inform people. Instead, without the newspaper and its journalists, the public officials had to find their own methods to share the information they wanted their constituents to know. They spend taxpayer money to share information on printed mailers, in newsletters and magazines, by phone, and through massive group texts and emails. As a result, community leaders may use these unique resources to present their ideas to large numbers of people, giving them greater control over what information to share and how to present it. Because they are providing these services on their own, however, these public officials have a mixed track record on whether their messages—such as the information about garbage pickup and recycling days—actually reach their targeted audiences.

Community leaders in McKeesport said they have tried to replace the *Daily News* through a variety of methods, such as email newsletters, print mailers, telephone calls that go to thousands of registered voters, websites, and social media. Plastic holders filled with government brochures sit on one wall of the lobby of Representative Davis's office, and people come in regularly to ask for help with government problems. Davis often uses the robocall system to reach thousands of people at once, although he feared that people would find the mass automated phone calls annoying. Instead, he said, many constituents seem to rely on them: "I get more people who come in who say, 'Hey, we appreciate your phone, your robocalls, because they're engaging. You're letting us know what's going on. You're keeping us informed.'" The city and the school district pay for a magazine insert that goes to every household, with eight pages dedicated to information that the elected officials want to share. The mayor makes good use of Vertullo's experience as a former journalist by asking her to write stories about his projects and programs that can be shared online and inserted into the community magazine. The school district has its own additional ways of reaching parents via letters sent to students' homes, an automated phone system, social media, and an app that the superintendent may use for emergency alerts. People who really want to know what goes on in the community have many ways of finding information via these government-sponsored sources, Tomovcsik said. "The people of McKeesport who want to be informed, they keep themselves informed," he said. "We've got a stable group. They come to every council meeting. Those are the people who are out there, sharing information. They want to be involved."

While using these methods to provide their own messaging and perspective, public officials have felt an additional responsibility to share news about McKeesport since the *Daily News* closed. "It puts a big burden on us," Brewster, the state senator, said. Because the community no longer has professional journalists, these community leaders attempt to fill the local knowledge gaps, but they do so from their own biased point of view, sharing only the information they want people to know. "I feel like we, as elected officials, try to fill in in some ways," Davis said. "We've tried to pick up some of that slack, to say there are positive things going on, making sure that we're pushing those things out. But we're not media organizations that are doing it every day, like the *Daily News* used to do."

Because they have access to taxpayer support, public officials have more resources, or gates, for disseminating information widely to large numbers of people via printed materials, phone calls, texts, the internet, and other means. These community leaders say they need these systems and rely on them more, since the *Daily News* closed, to inform people in the absence of a local newspaper that would share information for them. But it quickly becomes clear that these people—especially the elected politicians—have their own motivations for sharing their own biased point of view and giving out only the information they want people to know. They might be sharing their version of the news, but that does not make them journalists.

7

Discovering

I can tell you something. Then by the time it gets to, you know, your cousin's brother's janitor's whatever, it's completely different than what I said.

With great power comes great responsibility, as the comic book news photographer and Spiderman's alter ego Peter Parker might say. The democratization of information puts more power in the hands of ordinary citizens to determine what information their community knows—or thinks it knows. Once these people identify the gates they use for sharing information, they immediately and unconsciously start making decisions about what they will pass through those gates to the people around them. Unlike David Manning White's Mr. Gates, who likely had some formal training and who adhered to the norms of his profession, citizen gatekeepers lack training or expertise in how to use media frames to identify the positive and negative forces that exist in the information around their gates. These people must, instead, choose what to share on their own. As a result, they pass through all sorts of local news and information—some of it accurate and relevant, but much of it unverified, unsubstantiated, irrelevant, and skewed. They make uninformed decisions about sharing information that might be unverified or even inaccurate, that might seem extremely important to them even though it has little meaning to others, and that reveals their own unique bias or perspective rather than the full story.

Individual citizens often make these moves unwittingly, without realizing that they are poisoning the community conversation with bad information. Public officials, meanwhile, might make unconscious missteps, too, but they also quickly discover that with greater access to gates for reaching large numbers of people, they have the ability to shape what the public finds out—and what remains hidden.

Unverified and Irrelevant

When they talk with each other, people make unconscious decisions about what information to share, reaching into their well of knowledge to shape and expand the conversation. When several residents of McKeesport gathered for a focus group to talk about how they discover information, for example, they inadvertently started sharing what they knew about local news without even thinking about it.

One man, a seventy-eight-year-old retired shopkeeper, mentioned that he sometimes helps out at a local dealership by driving service customers while the shop works on their vehicles. While working the day before, he had run into someone he knew, a McKeesport native whose father used to own a gas station in the city. "Did you hear about the shooting last night in McKeesport?" the driver said, adding that he had heard about the fatal attack the night before. The other man answered, "This is the murder capital of Pennsylvania." Already, without taking time to think, these two men had made decisions about what information to share with each other based on what they deemed to be relevant. The retired shopkeeper had heard about a fatal shooting in the city, and he wanted to make sure the other man also knew about it. In reply, the man who grew up in the city added his own context to the story by sharing what he had heard, that McKeesport has more murders per capita than any other city in the state.

The exchange does not end there. As the driver later recounted his exchange, another woman in the focus group picked up on what she just heard. "I think it was 2018," she said. "McKeesport was put number one in crime in the whole everywhere." As it turns out, she had remembered pretty much correctly that in 2019 the National Council for Home Safety and Security looked at FBI crime statistics from the previous year and determined that McKeesport had the most violent crimes per capita of any Pennsylvania city and ranked it the fourth most dangerous city in the United States.[1]

In just a couple of exchanges, these people showed how news travels through a community. One person decided to share information about a fatal shooting, a second person provided context about the level of crime in the city, and then when the first person decided later to again talk about that conversation, a third person added another layer of context, affirming the narrative. None of these citizens consciously decided what information to share about the community; they just did it.

But what happens when the information people share turns out to be inaccurate?

Fire Chief Jeffrey Tomovcsik recalled an incident from social media in which a citizen posted a story to Facebook claiming that a police officer had been shot, with specific details about the situation, down to the street where it happened—except that the incident never actually happened. The original person perhaps misheard the information from someone else or misconstrued an actual incident that had gone differently. Either way, when they then shared the information about the supposed shooting on Facebook, the story started growing.

Within a few minutes, a second person posted online that they had "confirmed" the shooting by driving past the local hospital and seeing police cars everywhere outside the emergency room. A journalist would know that simply seeing police cars does not confirm anything, but to this citizen, it seemed to mean everything.

After another few minutes, a McKeesport police officer noticed the exchange and attempted to clear up the misinformation. "There was a McKeesport cop on there who was like, 'This is not true,'" Tomovcsik recalled. "And someone's like, 'Yes, it is; it's confirmed.' He's like, 'Look, I'm telling you, it's not true.'"

Even when faced with information from a primary source—a police officer who would know if one of his colleagues had been shot and hospitalized—these citizens refused to change their minds. Because they had seen the information on the internet, these people equated the exchange of information among uninformed citizens with the same quality of news one might get from a professional journalist who has been trained to identify news, verify it through reliable sources, and only then share it with the public. Instead, in this case, one person shared a detailed rumor, a second person added their own bad information to the rumor, and the story seemed to take on validity even though none of it had happened.

Challenging inaccurate or unverified information also requires convincing individuals to change their minds, to accept that what they thought was true had been misinterpreted or was simply wrong. Once someone has accepted a piece of information as reality, it can be nearly impossible to get them to admit they had made a mistake.

Ultimately in this case, Tomovcsik knew the Facebook administrator and reached out to her for help: "I said, 'Can you please delete this? This is going to get out of hand.'" The Facebook administrator deleted the thread at that point.

This social media exchange illustrates how one person can misconstrue something and share unverified initial information, and then how other citizens can compound the misinformation by sharing their own erroneous details. The first person thought they saw something, and they deemed it worthy enough to pass through their local information gates by posting it on social media; then, based on that first person's decision, others made subsequent choices to pass along other false details through their gates to continue the conversation on social media. It seems like no one acted maliciously in this exchange, but they had shared pieces of information without taking the time to verify that what they believed happened actually did. Because of the reach and speed of social media, other people saw the rumor and added their own unverified observations, giving the original information the appearance of veracity.

Informal networks, both in-person and online, ultimately can lead to misinformation as the news gets repeated. Tomovcsik said he routinely hears information at a local deli, the barber shop, and other places, but he often has to correct what he hears. "That's how the information gets around," he said. "But the danger you run into there is, I can tell you something. Then by the time it gets to, you know, your cousin's brother's janitor's whatever, it's completely different than what I said." Jennifer Vertullo, the mayor's assistant who used to work at the *Daily News*, agreed that informal networks of sharing information can be unreliable: "Word of mouth is a thing, but word of mouth is tricky . . . because it's a telephone game, and everything is wrong by the time it gets to the sixth person."

The Facebook administrator, meanwhile, could have served in the role of a traditional news editor by preventing irrelevant and unverified information from passing through an information gate to the public, but she apparently did not have the skills or enough information to make a decision about the false news and prevent it from being shared and snowballing. "People are posting stuff on there [Facebook]," Tomovcsik said, "and the average person who's an admin of a McKeesport group, they don't know if it's true or not."

Fawn Walker-Montgomery, the community activist who had served on city council, said the consequences of individuals sharing unverified information can be devastating for communities that gain an unfair reputation as a bad place because of so many inaccurate exchanges. "There's so much misinformation and people make up stuff," she said. "Like they say somebody was shot on the street, and it don't even be happening. Or they will hear stuff on police scanners and just kind of run with it." When this happens repeatedly, it starts to create an inaccurate, negative narrative about the community by making it seem like more

shootings and terrible crimes happen than actually do. Every small incident involving first responders gets elevated on social media by people sharing images of
flashing lights and speculating about what might have happened, rather than doing the work of journalism—asking questions about what actually occurred and
ignoring the minor events that happen in a community every day. A professional
news gatekeeper will examine a trivial incident and realize that it does not rise to
the level of community news that people will need to know or that will interest
them. But an untrained citizen gatekeeper might see something happening and
want to share what they have seen because it seems important to them.

People in McKeesport with knowledge of journalistic practices said they get
frustrated by the decisions citizens make about what seems worth sharing. Naz
Victoria, the publisher of the *Mon Valley Independent* in nearby Monessen, said
he tries to stay away from social media because of the misinformation that gets
shared: "What I don't like about it the most is probably how you can pretty much
say anything or send anything, and it gets repeated and there's no veracity to it
whatsoever. There's no fact checkers on social media."

Vertullo said she sees people sharing every little thing on social media—and
other people valuing that information because it came from the internet. "People
tend to think because of Facebook that every [emergency] call is significant," she
said. "People on Facebook turn that into, Oh, police were called out again in McK-
eesport, police are this, or police are that, and, it's like, no, they're doing their job
like they would anywhere." As a former newspaper employee, she noted that these
citizens do not have the professional skills to determine what qualifies as actual
news versus what may be just a routine police call. "They're just going with it," she
said. "I mean, they're making a mountain out of a mole hill." By sharing on social
media, citizen gatekeepers further amplify the insignificant or misinformation by
quickly reaching many people over a broad geographic area. "It just seems inappro-
priate, and it seems panic-inducing, and it seems like hysteria almost," Vertullo said.

For citizen gatekeepers who are making decisions about what to share, the
inconveniences that happen directly to them might seem to rise to the level of
information everyone should know, when they do not. For example, one person
posted on one of the McKeesport Facebook pages that they had gone to a fast
food restaurant only to find out that the workers had locked the doors and forced
everyone to go through the drive-through to place an order. If employees had
locked the doors because every restaurant had to shut down during the pandemic
or the health department had found multiple violations, the incident might interest many others. But if, as apparently in this case, the workers had acted because

they did not have enough employees to operate the restaurant or because they did not want to clean the dining room, that will interest only those people who really wanted to eat there. "John Q. Public does not have to notify the entire McKeesport region that the doors are closed, right?" Vertullo said. "Like, was I mad when that happened to Dunkin Donuts, and I really didn't want to sit through the drive-through, and I wanted to go in and get something? Yes. Did I tell anybody? No."

In gatekeeping theory, positive and negative forces exist around each gate, allowing keepers to decide which items to pass through and which to reject. Journalists use their training to notice the positive forces that make something newsworthy enough to pass through their gates to the public. When untrained citizen gatekeepers attempt to act like journalists, however, they often misconstrue these signals and see positive forces even when a piece of information will not matter to many. They lack the professional skills to understand what broad swaths of the community also will find newsworthy.

Community leaders, who enjoy the most access to primary sources of information, seemed the most upset about seeing and hearing people in the community sharing inaccurate and false details. "Word of mouth is, unfortunately, what gets twisted, what gets turned around," Mayor Michael Cherepko said. While maintaining an open door for people to ask questions wherever they find him, Cherepko said he tries to avoid reading Facebook posts because he sees so many people sharing information that he knows to be untrue: "It's just filled with absolute inaccuracies, lies. . . . If I read ten things on there that people claim to be facts, I promise you eight of them are false. Let's be conservative and say seven are absolutely without question false, and the other three, you might have two that might have some truth to them, and maybe one truth. That's like the best-case scenario." State Senator Jim Brewster, who worked early in his career as a news clerk at the *Post-Gazette*, said he has gained an appreciation as a public official for the choices that professional journalists make: "It was an art, and the people that I met at the *Post-Gazette*, the Trib, and at the *Daily News* were professional people."

With untrained citizen gatekeepers instead, the mix of stories they share creates a community narrative that seems confusing and unnecessarily negative.

Bias

The city of McKeesport pays for an insert in a monthly community magazine sent to every household, and the mayor's office controls the message. Cherepko used one of these opportunities to focus on his own initiative called "McKeesport

Rising." The main photograph shows a smiling mayor walking next to a city employee while a road crew works behind them to tear up a street for repaving or repairs. Text imposed on top of the image says, "We've all heard the hype about Mayor Michael Cherepko's McKeesport Rising Project, but do we truly know what the buzz is all about? Take time to read about the public safety, economic development, blight removal, budgeting, and programming that goes into McKeesport Rising." Subheads within the story refer to "safer neighborhoods" and "creating jobs," and the text includes bullet points listing recent public investments in economic development projects. The story does not list the number of violent crimes that take place in the community or McKeesport's distinction as a murder capital, and it does not list the businesses that have closed in the city. But why would it? A journalist might include that sort of perspective to show that while the city has scored some successes, it still has work left to do; the mayor, however, has little incentive to show the city's warts as he boasts about what he has accomplished. He sees this kind of messaging as his job: "That's one of the biggest obstacles I have as mayor is dealing with trying to market our city. I basically have to try to change the perception others have because of what the media puts in it."

While public officials said they have felt a burden to inform people since the *Daily News* died, and while they enjoy access to greater resources for telling the stories of the community through newsletters, emails, robocalls, and the like, they are not striving to serve as objective reporters. They have a particular point of view that jaundices the types of information they share and how they present it when they do; at the least, they want to show the community as a thriving, happy place, and at worst, they want to use the platforms they control to maintain their hold on political power.

Vertullo now writes much of the copy the mayor uses in the community magazine and in his other outreach efforts. She said she sees a clear difference in the type of material she writes for the administration versus the work she used to do as a reporter for the newspaper: The work now feels more like public relations than journalistic reporting. The stories she writes typically feature the mayor's initiatives, highlight companies making investments in the community, and talk about steps the city takes to fight blight, reduce crime, and provide public services. "It's another way for us to reach out to people who may not know where else to get that positive information that we want to use to help keep our community morale up, and keep people involved and keep people attending our events," she said.

It makes sense that public officials present subjective views of the best possible community because that reflects their role. While professional journalists seek objectivity in their reporting by presenting multiple, competing perspectives, and by identifying partisanship in their own work, citizen gatekeepers often lack the training or frames to see and remove the bias in their own messages—and many times they do not even want to remove the bias if they can see it. For those in power, the community leaders, it might mean presenting only the information that supports their hold on leadership and that portrays the community as a safe, healthy, and desirable place to live despite its challenges. Thinking back to Mr. Dooley, the fictional bartender who laid out the role of newspapers in his brogue in 1902, these public officials might seek to comfort the afflicted, but they rarely, if ever, afflict the comfortable by asking difficult questions of those in power or exposing their abuses.

Individual citizens make similarly self-centered choices when deciding what information to share with those around them. People rarely take the time to consider all sides of an argument in an effort to present an objective view of their community; instead, they look at the world from their own perspective and share information that supports their point of view. People, of course, do this with national issues by placing political signs in their yard, liking and retweeting social media posts that agree with their feelings (even when they have not actually fact-checked or even read them), and talking about issues that interest them in an effort to win over others. At the local level, these machinations can take on a more intimate feel as citizens speak for and against their elected representatives and argue with their neighbors over issues of taxes, street paving, garbage pickup, and all the pieces that make up community life. These attacks, when directed at the people of a neighborhood, can be even more biting and personal.

None of this should surprise anyone. Many people—both ordinary citizens and community leaders—said they often detect partisanship and personal bias when they look at social media sites related to local affairs. Social media users post commentaries for and against the local governmental administration, and they make claims with little or no verified evidence in support. Naz Victoria articulated a broad concern about seeing individual bias on social media platforms, and he talked about how people feel reluctant to entertain any perspective that disagrees with their own: "I want to use the word 'partisan.' I don't know if it's the right word to use, because what I mean by 'partisan' in my perspective is, like, things that they, that individual, believes in. . . . Too many people look for too many things and look at things from one point of view, and then they promote that point of view until the end. And if you come up with a different point of view, then you're 'an idiot' or, you know, you just don't know what you're talking about. I don't like social media."

Public officials voiced concerns about detecting bias, too, when they talked about people challenging their authority or their community view, often with what the officials see as misinformation. The same people who use their platforms to present a rosy image of the community blanch when others use competing information to challenge that view or question the steps leaders take to address problems. Mayor Cherepko said he avoids social media because of the people who post critical comments about him and his administration of the city, saying that the local Facebook groups are "absolutely worse than any tabloids you ever read." He added,

> I won't even get in there and start arguing because that's the other thing, I refuse to post anything on there because then you're just going to have your others that claim to know and claim you're lying or whatever. . . . Some of them, it's just so bizarre the things that they're saying either and claim are facts, and without question, I know these are the facts. Whether it's talking about me or whether it's talking about something else that I know has no truth in it, and they try to go, "Well, I know this for a fact because I worked here, I know this branch here," and they're outright lies. So to me, I stay away from them [the Facebook pages]. I don't even want to know what's on there.

Tomovcsik, the fire chief, cited an instance in which someone posted an allegation of corruption within the administration without citing any independent, verified evidence. A professional journalist would be required by code and because of civil laws to back up any claim with evidence and to give the subject of the claim an opportunity refute the evidence, but a citizen gatekeeper without any training or frames for determining what to post may go on social media sites, share almost anything, and claim it has validity. When the city sold its sewage plant, for instance, someone posted online a suggestion that the mayor's staff was stealing money even though the person did not provide any hard evidence and did not give the mayor a chance to defend himself or explain where the money went. "I just go into those [Facebook] pages, and I just, I cringe," Tomovcsik said. "Social media is—people just go on there and they post so much hearsay. They don't have an inkling of what they're talking about, but they're on there just spewing stuff."

At the same time, elected officials rarely hold each other to account or pro-duce investigative stories that reveal secret negotiations or inside information they do not want the public to hear. State Representative Davis said he under-stands that the news he shares with constituents will be very different from what a professional journalist might produce: "It's much more informational about something, either about my work in Harrisburg or about an event we're doing. Whereas I think a journalist would probably look at it from different angles, I'm very much probably looking at it from my one angle as a state representa-tive. Journalists might look at it from multiple angles." Davis said he would not produce an accountability report about another elected official with whom he must work politically. It would be suicidal for any politician's work and career to spend time undermining allies, even if they suspect or know that others have something to hide.

Politicians do feel motivated, at times, to conduct accountability reporting if it supports their position in the community. When environmental agencies cited an industrial polluter in Davis's district and citizens grew concerned about the health impacts, he used his platforms to call out the company, cite reports about the damage, and advocate for change. It looks politically good for the state representative to side with residents on a public health issue against a polluter that has been cited multiple times. "That probably doesn't make the community look the greatest," Davis said, "but it's, I think, an important story that we need to be talking about in terms of public health."

Public officials acknowledged that they see their work as different from a journalist's—and, significantly, they said they believe the public can tell the difference. Davis said he expects that people see that his messages have a pos-itive tone to them, as opposed to the more neutral, or even sometimes critical, voice the *Daily News* might have used. "They would look at it and just think that there's a slant," he said. "It's one thing when you read a newspaper: there's kind of the independence of it, of the news that you're getting. You're hoping you're getting balanced news." To his credit, Davis said he sees the need for independent sources to tell objective stories about the community and its leaders: "I think the [loss of] the *Daily News* is a result of a larger problem nationally, that we're seeing more publications going out of businesses and journalism and media are changing. To be honest, it's changing our society in a negative way. I'm an elected official, right? It's the public's job to hold me accountable for what I do as an elected official. They're not going to be able to do that if they don't know what I'm doing as an official."

The disappearance of objective reporting can have real impacts on residents. Walker-Montgomery, the former city council member who ran for mayor, said she sees the bias in public officials' messages, noting that the mayor controls the information that appears in the community magazine insert, and that he promotes only the community stories that he wants people to know about. "It's just who they like," she said. "When I was on council, my name was in it but that was about it. There's other people with my mindset who are getting treated the same way. And it's just, it's not fair." Walker-Montgomery had, for a time, been allies with the mayor and other political leaders, but when she started using her political platforms to question their actions, she became an outsider. In a system where elected officials control the message, people who question the official narrative can get shut out of the story that those in power want to tell. "If you go up against it, that's it, you're black-balled," Walker-Montgomery said. "It's a form of community violence because if you're given resources that are supposed to be used by the whole community, and you're only using it for certain things, that's violence." Public officials have a responsibility to tell the broader story with more perspectives because they are using taxpayer dollars from the entire community, Walker-Montgomery said.

When the newspaper existed, it did not do a perfect job of presenting an objective narrative about the community; just like Mr. Gates in the study on newspaper gatekeeping, the journalists had their own biases and might have favored people in power so they could maintain their own access to information. But the newspaper at least strived to be separate from the political process and called out corruption and bad behavior when it happened. The newspaper, at the least, provided another perspective on the work being done by public officials, rather than simply parroting one-sided messages.

Citizen gatekeepers lack the professional training to use frames that would allow them to identify and counteract their personal biases in order to present a full picture of what happens in the community, whether they agree with it or not. For many individuals, this means that they criticize public officials with little or no evidence, and other people build on this misinformation to form a biased public narrative. For community leaders, it also means that they tend to present information in a way that allows them to hold on to power by reinforcing the perception that they do a good job to create safe, livable spaces. Professional journalists would seek multiple perspectives by talking with many people to make sure they provide a full and varied picture, but citizen gatekeepers often lack the training, expertise, and occasionally even the motivations to present a balanced, objective view.

PART III
Obituary

8

When a
Newspaper Dies

We've had an information communication collapse in many communities. The term "news desert" is used, and it's a good term, but it understates the degree of the collapse.

The McKeesport experience clearly shows that few people realized the unique power of the local newspaper to communicate ideas—both complex and simple—widely through the community. It also reveals that none of the replacement strategies on its own offers a comparative ability for placing thoughts before a critical mass of people. After the *Daily News* died, residents felt a lost sense of knowledge, of course, but also lost opportunities for connecting with their neighbors, diminishing the opportunities for creating and maintaining value among their relationships, or social capital. Even when people choose not to be alone, they have a harder time discovering opportunities to interact with others.

This sense of depletion extends from individual citizens to community leaders, but they each find themselves encountering different types of loss. Individuals sense an acute diminished awareness about what goes on in their community, and they might start feeling frustrated by the lack of clear information and confused by stories that do not seem to accurately reflect their daily lives. Suddenly the emerging "news" sources to which they turn seem to be filled with endless examples of police calls, inconveniences like closed restaurants, and mixed-up stories about local government, while their daily experience does not seem to include any more mayhem than they experienced before. Community leaders, on the other hand, maintain an awareness of what happens because they have enough direct access to primary sources to know, but they feel a loss in how they communicate with the public, and a sense of diminished influence as a result. They might not have appreciated it before when the newspaper's reporters asked them difficult questions and challenged the decisions they made, but public officials certainly do not like it when no one at all pays attention to what they are doing. Overall, no matter how each feels about the death of the local newspaper, almost everyone in the community comes to mark its passing in one way or another.

Loss of Shared Narrative

People throughout McKeesport—from young adults to retirees, and from self-employed moms to the city's top elected officials—felt an unexpected and deep sense of loss from the closure of their newspaper, realizing only afterward that they saw themselves and their place in the community through the pages of the publication. For many people, the newspaper had been a part of their experience of growing up in the community, and it had been a part of their family story going back generations. This sense of nostalgia for the *Daily News* cut across all the community leaders and focus group participants with deep roots in McKeesport, and it underscored their sense of loss as they considered what the newspaper had meant to them. When the newspaper disintegrated over time and then abruptly disappeared, these citizens felt a loss of shared narrative that few expected. Even when publishers of a regional newspaper opened a bureau in the city, residents expressed a reluctance to embrace a different publication than the one that had told the stories of their lives previously. The *Daily News* had served as a source of information, but, unconsciously for many, it also served as an active connection to their presence as well as their shared past and collective sense of history.

Many people also lost their sense of awareness about their community when the newspaper died. Relatively inexpensive, and at the same time comprehensive, the publication had told detailed and nuanced stories on a daily basis; without it, people said they had fewer ways of discovering what happens in the community—from official government business, to local events and activities, to the small and often ordinary moments that make up life. The *Daily News* had told negative stories about crimes, incidents, and corruption, and it also reported on births, weddings and funerals, festivals, school activities, and local sporting events. Despite hollowing out over time with fewer reporters than it had at its peak, the newspaper chronicled a complicated narrative of life in the area. When the newspaper went away, citizens said they knew less about the operations of the local government, they found fewer opportunities for engagement with others, and they felt more disconnected.

Community leaders, meanwhile, still know about a lot of what happens in the community because they have access to many direct sources such as government documents, first-responders, and other people running the city. When the newspaper died, they lost their abilities to communicate with constituents through a neutral third party, and they experienced a shift to overwhelmingly negative stories in the community's shared narrative. The mayor talked about wanting to portray McKeesport in a positive way, as a place where people live and engage in the ordinary communal activities of daily life; the newspaper portrayed the community this way by telling many varied stories about the ordinary happenings that make people feel connected to each other. When the newspaper died, regional outlets continued to report on the major incidents in McKeesport, but these tend to be only the worst moments of civic life: TV news reporters show up more frequently to report on a murder, a house fire, or an incident of political corruption than to report on a community festival, a school activity, or an ordinary session of city council. Because traditional news gatekeepers at those regional news outlets operate at a distance from the community, local leaders have little influence over them and feel a loss of control over the shared narrative. Suddenly, every story seems negative.

Searching for Information

As people realize what they lost when the newspaper died, they also start the search for new ways of finding out what goes on in their community. They turn, as humans have done for all of time, to interpersonal relationships, first to each other through word-of-mouth interactions to learn what others have seen and heard and then, thanks to modern technology, to the internet, where people share this kind of anecdotal information more quickly and broadly. While few citizens think of themselves as journalists or actively work to aggregate and widely disseminate information, they do frequently rely upon their interpersonal networks to stay informed, media researchers found in a 2015 study released by Rutgers University and later republished in the journal *Digital Journalism.* "With limited and 'sporadic' local news coverage or for those lacking access to search for local news online, neighbors and interpersonal networks are turned to as a way to stay connected and informed," they wrote.[1] The dozens of Facebook groups that people have set up about McKeesport and the surrounding Monongahela River valley towns include all sorts of information, from snippets of news to the daily specials at local restaurants, to jokes about national politics and complaints about the local elected officials. People are using the social media platform to create and expand their interpersonal networks to discover more information, as flawed as it might be.

Realizing that community leaders still know what goes on, the people who can access these leaders turn to them for information, too, to learn about what happens and to confirm what they already have heard. People also search for news wherever they can find it, on startup online blogs and on larger, regional news outlets such as TV and radio broadcast stations. But compared to what they had been getting from the local newspaper, neither the small community sources nor the larger news outlets has enough resources to tell the complete story of their local community.

Media researchers have referred to communities that have lost their local news outlets as "news deserts" since at least 2011, when Chicago columnist Laura Washington first framed the term. Northwestern University's Penny Abernathy tracks where newspapers have died or retreated, and she counts the number of local independent digital news sites, ethnic media, and public broadcasting outlets as well. She defines a news desert as "a community, either rural or urban, with limited access to the sort of credible and comprehensive news and information that feeds democracy at the grassroots level."[2] Michelle Ferrier at Florida A&M University refers instead to "media deserts," or places where people lack access to basic technology as well. All these terminologies and definitions can feel misleading because, as participants at Newsgeist, the annual Google-sponsored media technology conference, asserted in 2019, news still happens in these places—even if the traditional media outlets are not present. Babies are born, people die, governments take actions that affect residents, and crises and corruption continue to occur. The problem for ordinary citizens who live in a news desert is not that the news has dried up but that without access to a local newspaper or other news source, they struggle to make sense of the overwhelming amounts of information around them—the incidents, events, and moments of community life—and they lack the resources that community leaders have for finding out.

As they start to become citizen gatekeepers, individuals must, on their own, look across all the bits of information in daily life—including the irrelevant, the rumored, the inaccurate, and the biased—to make sense of their shared narrative and to determine what has value. The McKeesport experience, however, shows that people face challenges in separating newsworthy information from gossip and deliberate misinformation. As they go out and attempt to make sense of their community, they absorb many different pieces and struggle to separate the accurate bits they need to know from the distracting background noise. Citizens might be aware of this need to be self-reliant in order to find and decipher news in the absence of traditional media, but that does not necessarily mean they are good at it. The researchers behind the Rutgers study found that citizens were "unaware of useful sources of news and information available to them or were not thorough in their use of sources."[3] Just because everyone has easy access to the tools of journalism does not mean they want to use them to gather and share information or that they know how to use them effectively.

Even with other resources for local news available since the *Daily News* closed, residents expressed a strong loss of awareness compared with what existed before. Similarly, residents' appreciation for their local newspaper runs deeper than just the news and information it provides: the *Daily News* built up a relationship with readers and the community over decades; a startup newspaper such as the *Mon Valley Independent* (and especially one that was previously identified with another, rival community) can begin to tell the stories of a community, but residents need time to understand how it tells *their* narrative. The publisher of the startup news outlet might argue that McKeesport no longer exists as a news desert because his reporter covers government meetings and positive developments. Based on the comments of community leaders and residents, however, any new local media outlet needs time to develop a relationship with readers, and it requires greater resources to tell the many nuanced stories that comprise the community narrative. No one else questioned whether McKeesport exists as a news desert.

Identifying Gates for Sharing

As ordinary people take on the role of citizen gatekeepers to local news and information, they look, often unconsciously, for methods—or gates—to share what they have discovered. Just as they turn to each other to find out what happens, people use one-to-one interactions to tell each other what goes on. They go to the places where people gather to let others know what they have found out, and to confirm their information while learning what others have heard. Many also turn to technology to share their discoveries more broadly and quickly over social media platforms, through group text chats, and by posting to websites. These citizens also look for alternative methods of disseminating information to large numbers of people where they gather or pass frequently, posting notes to public message boards and making announcements at sporting events, churches, schools, and group activities. These types of interactions are not new, but they take on greater importance after the local newspaper dies and people are looking for fast ways to inform and influence large groups. These interactions among citizens also have the potential to contribute to the creation of social capital because people are sharing what they know, how they feel, and what they understand about their community. In the process, they form new connections, both in person and online. The value of these linkages depends on the quality of information being shared; if people disseminate biased, inaccurate, irrelevant, and unverified information, that undermines the positive potential of the new social capital being created.

As people search for these gates of information sharing, public officials discover that they already control many taxpayer-supported means for reaching large groups of people, and that these means have greater worth now that the objective, third-party newspaper has gone away. Public officials might choose to send out printed mailers such as newsletters or magazine inserts that go to every home, make computer-assisted phone calls that ring at the home of every registered voter, use social media and other online technologies to share information widely, host public events, and directly interact with many people as part of their daily activities. With fewer means of finding out about the community, people come to rely on these political and government-controlled sources of information; at the same time, they might realize that the community leaders have inherent biases to share only the good news that helps them hold on to power.

Deciding What to Share

As citizen gatekeepers complete their evolution from being passive receivers of news to actively engaging with information, they must take the final step to make decisions, conscious and unconscious, about what to pass through their gates to others within their spheres of influence. Traditional newsroom gatekeepers use frames shaped by practice, tradition, and codes of conduct to look for positive and negative forces in the available information, and to let through only the pieces that they deem accurate and relevant, or newsworthy, for their audiences.

As much as journalists try to be objective, they still make subjective decisions about what seems important to them or what they think their audiences will want or need to know. But at least traditional gatekeepers have some broad guidelines that shape their decisions: most journalists look to disseminate stories that are based in fact and that have been verified, that present conflicting points of view when they exist, and that remain free of obvious bias even if they reflect the subtle decision-making that goes into any product.

Most citizens, however, lack any kind of serious training in sorting through vast amounts of information and quickly making choices about what to share with others based on its accuracy, verifiability, or attempted objectivity. Citizens often do share accurate, reliable, and neutral information, but it often appears alongside gossip, unverified claims, irrelevant details, and a mishmash of stories that might or might not have much meaning for most of the people in their community. Ultimately, citizen gatekeepers end up passing through a lot of inaccurate, unverified, and biased information as well. These messages can contribute to creating a negative, disorienting, and often false community narrative in which it seems crimes happen everywhere, local leaders engage in endless corruption, and no one really knows what actually happens. It also creates community conversations in which individuals feel uncertain about what seems like actual news versus what might just be opinion, misunderstanding, or deliberate attack.

Community leaders, meanwhile, enjoy easy access to information and have many ways of sharing what they know, but they have incentives to share only the bits of news that help them hold on to power. This makes sense: they want to portray the community as a safe, livable place with a highly functioning local government and little in the way of crime, and at the same time, they have little desire to point out their own mistakes, let alone their own corruption or that of others. They promote stories that show the pieces that work well, and they leave out evidence of malfunctions, back-office dealings, and the things they simply do not want the public to know. These decisions about what information to share do not necessarily make politicians bad people; it's just that they are not professional journalists, and they have a different community role to play. As a result, these community officials may share biased perspectives.

Faced with new realities for sharing information after a local newspaper dies, ordinary citizens and the people they elect to serve them must take greater responsibility for ensuring the free flow of reliable, objective news to preserve community cohesion. Leaders might feel the temptation to fill an information vacuum with their own self-serving perspectives, but for the broader good of the people they serve, they need to see beyond their own immediate motivations to understand the value that comes from supporting an objective third-party storyteller—even when they might not like every story that gets told. The Brazilian educator and philosopher Paulo Freire challenges people in power to see the widespread value in speaking honest, true words, and to engage with the public in a sincere dialogue that takes into consideration the community's challenges and differing perspectives. "It is not our role to speak to the people about our own view of the world, nor to attempt to impose that view on them, but rather to dialogue with the people about their view and ours," Freire wrote in *Pedagogy of the Oppressed* (1968).[4] In the case of a news desert, where community leaders enjoy an imbalance in power over the shared narrative, leaders must not abuse their advantages but instead work with the people on a narrative that matches everyone's understanding of their shared reality. Constituents see through the sham of one-sided interpretations of the news, and public officials can endear themselves to the people they serve by presenting a true picture even when it hurts them to do so.

Citizens, too, have key roles to play in ensuring that local information has reliable value in the absence of professional journalists. In a so-called news desert, the people must ensure that they not only dialogue with those in power but exact more control over the information they share too. They must ask the difficult questions that demand accountability from people in power, they must act fairly to present perspectives beyond their own narrow view, and they must work to ensure the information they share with others adds value rather than obfuscation. Peter Block, an author who writes about community building, argues that ordinary citizens have the ability, and perhaps the responsibility, to take control of the conversations that happen all around them: "Citizens have the capacity to change the community story, to reclaim the power to name what is worth talking about."[5] But in order to have that sort of impact, citizens must take an active role to ensure that the information they share has value: that it has been verified for accuracy, has relevance for wide swaths of their neighbors, and presents a fair view. Making that shift moves the citizen from a passive position as a consumer to one who is actively engaged with local news and information. It asks citizens to be, in Block's words, "accountable rather than entitled" to media coverage.[6] You can no longer blame the media if you *are* the media. "It moves us from having faith in professionals and those in positions of authority to having faith in our neighbors," Block writes.[7]

Every citizen gatekeeper who scours their community for relevant information and then shares it with others carries this weight of ensuring that it contributes in a positive way. In his book *On Tyranny*, the Yale University historian Timothy Snyder calls on individuals to take responsibility for information at the risk that inaction will allow others to control the narrative for their own personal benefit and political motivations: "Since in the age of the internet we are all publishers, each of us bears some private responsibility for the public's sense of truth. If we are serious about seeking the facts, we can each make a small revolution in the way the internet works. If you are verifying information for yourself, you will not send on fake news to others."[8] Snyder is talking mainly about how citizens should make good decisions about the journalists they follow and the news stories they tweet about, to ensure they are sharing actual facts rather than deliberately or carelessly fake news. Citizens might not see themselves as journalists or the work they do as reporting, but in a news desert, where professional journalists do not exist, ordinary people bear even more responsibility to ensure that they help weave a meaningful and relevant shared narrative by verifying statements, digging for the truth, and sharing only what has actual importance for the people around them. They might not want to do this work, but in many ways they already are; the situation of a news desert asks them to pay closer attention for their own benefit and that of their community.

Without a doubt, the internet has disrupted the old models and created an era in which people control the information, for better and worse. Initially, individuals giddily embraced this newfound power by creating new ways of sharing information without taking the time to see how they could misuse and abuse it. The dozens of Facebook groups that have sprung up in and around McKeesport reveal the public's enthusiasm for embracing technology to share their humor, their opinions, the news as they see it, and their peculiar hobbies. In the absence of a singular news source that attempts to present an objective view of the community, individuals have to realize they can use technologies to control their shared story and ensure that it contributes in positive ways. More people must begin to act like the diner owner who learned the hard way that sharing what one hears without verification can lead to the spreading of rumors—to telling others that a patron has died, and then to have him walk into the restaurant the next day. In response to this embarrassing blunder, the owner said she has learned to not say anything at all unless she has confirmed the information from someone in a position to know. In a news desert, the people—the citizen gatekeepers—can carry out a small revolution each moment by asserting power over their shared narrative to share only information that they have verified, that has meaning to their fellow neighbors, and that reflects a broader perspective than their own.

Impacts of Mortality

This story about McKeesport, Pennsylvania, repeats across the United States as traditional local newspapers shrink in size, reduce their delivery areas, cover fewer stories, and, in many cases, finally blink out of existence. From the perspective of a satellite map view, this looks like a growing wasteland emerging in small pockets and then spreading like a slow-moving virus that consumes small towns, urban neighborhoods, and ever-larger cities. Quantitative data exist to trace the path of this decline, especially since the mid-2000s with the Great Recession, the invention of the smartphone, and the expansion of broadband connectivity. Even where newspapers remain, many resemble a "ghost" of what they had been with fewer reporters and fewer news stories.[9] The subsequent economic recession caused by the COVID-19 pandemic, starting in early 2020, further eroded local news media by spurring new rounds of layoffs and cutbacks that consumed another sixteen thousand newsroom jobs.[10] "It's hard to imagine an industry being more poorly prepared for the arrival of a global pandemic than the media business," the *Columbia Journalism Review* reported in April 2020.[11]

At the local level, the impacts of dying newspapers appear even more devastating by undermining the ways people not only communicate with each other but also connect to build community: news continues to occur, and citizens must now figure out on their own what happens, how to communicate that, and where to meet their neighbors for both social events and solving common problems. Newspapers contribute to social capital in the communities they serve, and when they close, citizens feel less engaged and involved in civic life. In newly formed news deserts, residents talk anecdotally about no longer seeing themselves reflected in a local news outlet and about having less access to news about the functions of government and other institutions.[12] When a newspaper dies, the consequences add up for the places it used to serve. Joshua Benton, the founder of Harvard University's Nieman Journalism Lab, pointed out in 2019 all the things that newspapers do:

> What do strong local newspapers do? Well, past research has shown they increase voter turnout, reduce government corruption, make cities financially healthier, make citizens more knowledgeable about politics and more likely to engage with local government, force local TV to raise its game, encourage split-ticket (and thus

less uniformly partisan voting), make elected officials more responsive and efficient, and bake the most delicious apple pies. Okay, not that last one.

Local newspapers are basically little machines that spit out healthier democracies. And the best part is that you get to reap the benefits of all those positive outcomes *even if you don't read them yourself.* (On behalf of newspaper readers everywhere: You're welcome.)[13]

The death of a newspaper takes away those benefits, too, regardless of whether one maintained a paid subscription or not. And, obviously, many people did not: fewer Americans maintain subscriptions for printed local newspapers, and news outlets have struggled with convincing people to purchase digital subscriptions.[14]

The McKeesport experience reveals what happens as residents come to the realization of what they lost when their newspaper died, and how they have struggled since then to not only replace it but make sense of what happens around them. People who thought little about the newspaper when it existed, who grumbled about what a terrible job it did then, or who, like some of the elected officials, celebrated when it closed, suddenly saw that the demise of the *Daily News* also ate away at the way they saw themselves and how they fit into their community's larger narrative. Then, as they struggled to first find out about the community on their own and then make decisions about what pieces of information to share with their neighbors, it became clear that the job of discovering news, verifying it, and presenting a fair picture requires more work than it seemed from the outside.

The obituary for dying newspapers, however, does not have to be all bad. The McKeesport experience also uncovers many community assets that can be nurtured and developed to restore stronger journalistic storytelling at the local level. Individual citizens, whether they realize it or not, have taken up the mantle of shaping the narrative of where they live, creating countless Facebook groups, blogging on the internet, showing up in public gathering places to share information, and simply talking with the people around them. These people must first realize that the work they have been doing, often mindlessly, has real value and consequence: they are not just ephemerally tweeting but creating the dialogue that shapes their daily lives. Then, once they acknowledge the power they possess, they must develop the muscles to discern the truth, to identify harmful gossip, and to eliminate unintentional blunders along with the malicious lies that sprout up everywhere. As they embrace their newly discovered role and learn how to pursue it competently, these citizen gate-keepers can both inform others and rebuild the connections that make any community vibrant.

Accessing Critical Information

To measure what McKeesport has lost and gained since the death of the *Daily News*, it helps to consider how residents meet their critical information needs in the newspaper's absence. Media researchers at several American universities worked on a landmark study for the Federal Communications Commission in 2012 that considered the available data to determine the state of Americans' ability to meet their critical information needs and that offered recommendations for further study and possible solutions.[15] The researchers at the time believed their work might induce policy makers to take steps that would open some sociopolitical space for experimentation. "I actually saw in the writing of it a kind of proto-community information bill of rights or statement of community information needs," said researcher Lewis Friedland, who worked on the report and who founded the Center for Communication and Democracy at the University of Wisconsin-Madison.[16] Friedland's wishes for the report to catalyze a large national discussion came true, but not in the ways he expected: conservative social commentators such as Rush Limbaugh and Sean Hannity hijacked the conversation by focusing on what they claimed was government overreach. That redirection—away from threats to the free press—effectively killed any chance for further research, Friedland recalled years later.

In hindsight, the academics behind the report had sounded a clear alarm about the collapse of local journalism: yes, the internet has broken down many barriers to information sources that once were difficult for ordinary people to reach (such as information in medical journals); at the same time, disruptions to local news sources such as newspapers and broadcast television and radio stations have undercut people's ability to learn about their local community and respond (such as how to find a local doctor or to know about threats to local air quality). The loss of information at the local level, they wrote, represents a major threat to the United States' federal democracy: "Whether South Los Angeles or rural South Carolina, our needs for information are shaped by the places that we live in, our blocks and neighborhoods, cities or suburbs, and the people we live with."[17] Writing nearly a decade before the January 6, 2021, insurrection at the US Capitol Building—when the idea of Americans using metal poles, fire extinguishers, and other heavy objects to break into the seat of Congress in an attempt to stop the peaceful transfer of presidential power still seemed unthinkable—these researchers identified local journalism as a fundamental building block of American government: "In a federal democracy, the challenge of communication participation begins in local communities, and must stay rooted in local communities. Despite the vast amount of information, entertainment, and basic human connection that the internet provides, it cannot by itself substitute for meeting the local information needs of American communities."[18] The report seems predictive, then, that a violent attempt to overthrow American democracy might follow a long period in which local journalism has been decimated and destroyed.

Abraham Maslow in the 1940s developed a hierarchy of human needs, starting at the bottom with the basics such as shelter, food, and warmth and rising through safety, belonging and love, self-esteem, and self-actualization. Similarly, the researchers behind the FCC report identified eight basic information needs—ranging from specific, concrete ideas to broader, more general ones—that citizens require to "live safe and healthy lives; have full access to educational, employment, and business opportunities; and to fully participate in the civic and democratic lives of their communities should they choose."[19] Although they are not set in a hierarchical pyramid, these eight core areas can be seen as an informal rubric for measuring the effectiveness of local information sources in a place such as McKeesport after the *Daily News* died.[20] The researchers identified the following areas:

Emergencies and Public Safety

People need easy access to information about weather threats, environmental contaminations, biohazardous outbreaks, and similar challenges to public order. As a community within a larger media ecosystem, McKeesport's residents have access to regional online news outlets, broadcast stations, and print newspapers that cover major public safety concerns such as storms, domestic terrorism incidents, and mass shootings. If a line of threatening storms heads toward McKeesport, residents there have as much chance to be aware of the danger as anyone else living across the Pittsburgh metropolitan area who might learn of the weather from television, radio, and the internet.

Health

Residents need to know about the quality and cost of local health care options, about the spread of disease and vaccinations, and about health campaigns and interventions. McKeesport benefits from having a regional hospital that belongs to a larger university-based system, and residents therefore enjoy greater access to medical information than those of other communities that lack significant health facilities. Also, as part of a regional news ecosystem, McKeesport benefits from regional coverage of threats such as the COVID-19 pandemic and opioid addiction. Within the community, however, residents have few resources for learning about the effectiveness of individual doctors or medical facilities. Tube City Online, the local news website, posts information about vaccine clinics and opportunities for citizens to access public health resources. While government sources distributed information about the pandemic, residents have few robust, independent sources for discovering in depth how the crisis affected their neighbors and local businesses.

Education

Citizens, parents especially, need to know about the quality of local education sources, the decision-making within their school district, and the allocation of resources. This could include notices about the public and private K–12 options as well as information about adult education, job training, and higher education. In the absence of robust local news, the McKeesport Area School District has emerged as a leading source of information about itself: the district purchases pages in a community magazine for the superintendent to update residents on the district's activities, and it pushes out information to residents via email and mail. That kind of sourcing, however, takes place without the critical oversight of objective journalists to ask difficult questions and reveal the results of test scores and budget decisions. The *Mon Valley Independent* and Tube City Online have somewhat filled this role by reporting on the McKeesport school board's meetings and decisions, but the news outlets rarely have the resources to dig in depth or to cover all the surrounding school districts; Allegheny County, alone, has forty-three public school districts of varying sizes, with some having fewer than one thousand students.

Transportation Systems

People in a community need to know not only about how and when to move around efficiently but also about deeper issues such as decisions being made about the quality of infrastructure and mass transit. Regional broadcast news outlets in Pittsburgh provide overviews about daily bottlenecks and breakdowns, and the metro daily newspapers routinely go in depth about spending by the Pennsylvania Department of Transportation and the regional public transportation authority. Few resources exist for residents, however, to learn about changes to local bus lines or to understand how decisions made at the federal, state, and regional levels affect their access to transportation or the quality of roads and bridges.

Environment and Planning

Information about the local environment—including instructions for accessing clean air and water, alerts about acute hazards, reports on chronic threats, analyses about watersheds and habitats, and advertisements about recreational opportunities—shape the quality of everyone's daily life. The government generates primary source documents on the quality of the local environment as well as long-standing threats to air, water, and habitats, but people typically need access to technology to reach most of this information. Many McKeesport residents still lack easy access to computers and the internet, and even if they do have it, they also must know where to look for raw data and how to make sense of it. Government officials also may choose to highlight certain threats, such as the work State Representative Austin Davis has done to focus on air emissions from U.S. Steel's Clairton Coke Works, four miles south of McKeesport. When Davis wrote a public editorial about the situation in 2019, he submitted it to the *Pittsburgh Post-Gazette* for publication,[21] and the *Mon Valley Independent* provided coverage of a town hall event on the topic that Davis organized.[22] The *Allegheny Front*, a public radio news outlet devoted to environmental topics, and *Environmental Health News,* an online news outlet sponsored by the nonprofit Environmental Health Sciences, provide regional coverage that frequently focuses on the Monongahela River valley because of its persistent environmental challenges.

Economic Development

Information about employment opportunities, job training, starting a small business, and major business initiatives can help residents improve and maintain their quality of life. Like environmental topics, government resources exist for individuals to discover, but people need technology and an understanding of where to look. Regional news outlets provide reporting on major economic projects: for instance, the *Allegheny Front* has reported substantially on an ethane cracker plant being built in Beaver County, west of the Mon Valley.[23] The *Mon Valley Independent* and regional newspapers such as the *Tribune-Review* provide frequent coverage on topics such as local businesses, economic development projects, and regional issues such as fracking for natural gas. Government officials, such as the mayor, also provide information about economic development initiatives, but they typically highlight the successes and ignore the failures. The *Mon Valley Independent* makes a point to report on economic projects but also has some pressure, according to its publisher, to present the community as a business-friendly place.

Civic Information

Community life revolves around local institutions, membership groups, non-profits, religious organizations, and places offering recreational opportunities. Several sources provide this information throughout McKeesport, ranging from the information board in the local library to articles and notices in the *Mon Valley Independent* and Tube City Online, postings on social media sites, and notices from governmental agencies. The city's official website features a searchable calendar with information about free public concerts, local fireworks displays, and neighborhood celebrations. People use social media sites such as Facebook to share information about upcoming events.

Political Life

American-style democracy requires that citizens have information about elected officials and government agencies at all levels, from local municipalities up to the federal government. The *Mon Valley Independent* and Tube City Online cover some municipal and school board meetings and provide accountability reporting of public officials in their main coverage areas. When the *Mon Valley*

Independent's reporters believed that the mayor and city council in Monessen violated Pennsylvania's public records law known as Right to Know in 2020, it filed a lawsuit. A common pleas court judge ruled that the officials had violated the act, ordering them to undergo training and change their practices. Managing Editor Stacy Wolford said at the time, "As the Mon Valley's local newspaper, it is our job as journalists to be a watchdog over local government. We believe government should be open and transparent, and we filed this lawsuit for the public's right to know and to ensure that the Sunshine Act is upheld."[24] In other ways and across many other small communities throughout the McKeesport area, however, local officials have escaped the scrutiny they previously faced, and at the same time they have assumed a larger role in informing the public. As Davis pointed out, the ways he reports information about his activities often differ greatly from the way an independent journalist would, favoring positive information and ignoring or downplaying the negative.

McKeesport has fared better than other communities that have lost access to traditional news sources because it sits within a regional news environment; it retains significant infrastructure, such as active government officials, public agencies, and a hospital; and its residents still have a desire to engage with each other in person and online. Yet even here, with the death of the *Daily News*, the term "news desert" might not describe accurately enough what has happened. "We've had an information communication collapse in many communities," Friedland, the researcher of the FCC report, said.[25] "The term 'news desert' is used, and it's a good term, but it understates the degree of the collapse." With the gradual decline and then death of the newspaper, many people in McKeesport lost a lodestar for discovering information about their community and their place within it. In the absence, however, they also have started to discover new and unexpected ways of finding out about where they live and about each other.

9

A Prayer
for the Living

The hard truth is that development must start from within the community, and in most of our urban neighborhoods, there is no other choice.

Barely more than four years after the last edition of the *Daily News* rolled off the presses, more than a hundred people crowded into the former newspaper building's art deco lobby; ceramic tiles covered the walls and its neon map of the United States was lit up on the back wall. For most of the time in between, the building had sat empty with plyboard sheets covering its first-floor, plate-glass windows. After the newspaper died, many of its reporters simply had walked away—either to unemployment or to other news outlets—leaving their workspaces largely intact. The detritus of such an old newspaper seemed almost like a living time capsule of McKeesport's local history that included high school sports programs from decades earlier, old phone directories, and newsprint editions of historic events and anniversaries. A metal filing cabinet in the building's subbasement held the newspaper's handwritten financial ledgers from the 1950s. Painted portraits of the Mansfield family members who had served as publisher sat in their frames on the cement floor of a loading dock. Once a privileged space, the publisher's office sat open to anyone.

In the months after the newspaper closed, State Senator Jim Brewster and Mayor Michael Cherepko had started plotting ways to reopen the building. They convinced its owner, Trib Total Media, to sell the property to the city for only one dollar. The company previously had shored up the building by investing in a new roof, but president and CEO Jennifer Bertetto had been so pleased with the city's proposal that she also threw in a truckload of old furniture as well. Standing on the street outside the boarded-up building, Brewster tried to convince others of his vision for its new life, with multiple businesses inside, teaching space for retraining citizens in new skills, and a billboard on the roof signaling the rebirth of the space as Tube City Center, a nod to the area's industrial past.

That full vision had not come to fruition by February 2019 (after all, who could afford to erect a billboard), but enough of it had happened that the city prepared to reopen the building. City workers had removed the plyboard from the windows, secured any of the items that had historical value, and then spent weeks filling garbage bins with the remaining debris and washing every surface with rags and buckets of soapy water. Now as people crammed into the building's lobby, they looked up at a wooden stage erected near the back of the space, where Brewster, Cherepko, and several other officials sat on metal folding chairs waiting for their turn to speak. There would be a short ceremony and then the city would feed everyone light snacks and cake and hand out souvenir mugs printed with a likeness of the building with its new name.

Inside the newly minted Tube City Center, the county's district attorney runs a warrant office and a local company sells fire equipment from a second-floor office. Journalism happens in the building again too. Jason Togyer, the journalist who started Tube City Online, hosts an internet radio show and chronicles the stories of the community for local audiences and even, occasionally, national ones. Throughout 2020, Togyer wrote a series of columns for the *Columbia Journalism Review*, focusing on different ways the pandemic and the presidential election affected the Mon Valley. In one article, Togyer wrote about the precarious nature of depressed industrial towns besieged by violence, saying how insufficient it feels to report on someone's life through a few words about how they died—but how it would be worse to say nothing at all.[1] He also described the concern about attempting to cover many public school systems: "Our freelance writers do their best, but how many good news stories in these school districts go unreported simply because we don't have the time or resources to dig for them? How much of what residents know of their local schools is only in the context of official sources telling us about lower test scores and higher property-tax rates?"[2] Despite its limitations, Tube City Online celebrates the Mon Valley's rich history, marks the community's obituaries, and tells nuanced stories about its complicated present.

In another nearby space, more than a dozen people come out every other week to meet in the old newsroom to talk about writing and learn new skills. Part of the newly formed McKeesport Community Newsroom, these people range in ages from sixteen to seventy-five, and they represent the racial and cultural diversity of the community.[3] They work with a local freelance news photographer named Martha Rial, who won a Pulitzer Prize in 1998 for documenting the plight of Rwandan and Burundian refugees, and who now passes her knowledge on to almost anyone with a serious interest in making images and telling stories. The Pittsburgh Foundation has provided a series of grants to support Rial's work in the community with the goal of helping citizens develop the skills to chronicle their own lives and those of their neighbors. The community newsroom has hosted live storytelling events inside the former newspaper's lobby and on the sloping lawn of the city's library. The participants told stories about growing up in McKeesport, today and in the past, and they talked about their lived moments in the community. Besides the writers' group, a photography collective gets together regularly to learn about making images and to document community events such as the annual Fourth of July celebration and unseen places such as the long-abandoned upper floors of an underused downtown building. Young people in an afterschool program known as YouthCAST have gone around to playgrounds through McKeesport to record neighborhood residents talking about their lives and to interview community leaders such as police officers and the fire chief.

Even after the COVID-19 pandemic prevented people from gathering in person, citizens continued to meet through the community newsroom online with some technology support where needed. The writers' group started a blog about the pandemic, and one of the participants, Jim Busch, wrote a new post every day for a year about friends who had gotten sick, about his feelings of isolation and hope, and about his wife's cancer diagnosis while he had to wait outside for her in their car because of pandemic exposure protocols. The writers also produced a published anthology of their stories, in which two Black high school students wrote about African American history and how they rarely learn about it at school, and a third student wrote about racial discrimination and the death of George Floyd in Minneapolis. People wrote about growing older and litter by the side of the road. A woman who has autism wrote a first-person piece about her artwork, and another woman wrote about the struggle to give up gluten.

Another older man, Ed Boyko, wrote about growing up with the *Daily News*. He recalled how his dad would pick up a copy of the newspaper at Johnny Klucka's market as he walked up the hill home from work at National Tube Works. Boyko's mother would check the store ads for deals on steaks at Kudlik's butchery, groceries at Balsamo's market, and clothing at the city's three department stores. His dad would scan the obituaries for names he recognized, and then he would sit with his son and go over the box scores for teams in the local baseball league that carried the newspaper's name. In fifth grade, Boyko took over his own newspaper route, making a nickel per delivery and sometimes a dollar or two in tips; later, when he attended Duquesne University in Pittsburgh, he struggled to read the newspaper while riding the bumpy 56C streetcar into the city. Boyko wrote with a strong sense of nostalgia because almost everything about those days—the steel mill, the department stores, the streetcars—has gone away. He concluded the article with, "The last straw that changed McKeesport forever was the closing of The Daily News."[4]

Without a doubt, the ways people interact with information in McKeesport and the Mon Valley have transformed since the *Daily News* died, but not all the changes have been bad. Instead, people are finding new ways to connect with local news, and each other, in often unforeseen and unexpected ways.

Rise of the Citizen Gatekeeper

The concept of citizen gatekeeping builds on existing theories about media ecology, the flow of information through gates at traditional news organizations, and the creation of social capital to explore qualitatively what happens in a news desert, when people are left on their own to identify and share local news and information. In his own obtuse and often unsettling ways, the social scientist Marshall McLuhan described how culture evolves as media change with the advent of new technologies that irrevocably disrupt existing ones, and researchers since then have shown quantitatively that internet technologies have broken up traditional news organizations, contributing to the emergence and growth of news deserts. The McKeesport experience, by contrast, shows qualitatively how the residents of a newly formed news desert react to the death of their local news organization with confusion and unexpected feelings of loss.

Looking around at the world and how individuals' decisions affect the flow of everything from food to retail goods to information, the psychologist Kurt Lewin first proposed gatekeeper theory in 1947 to show how news may get stopped or be allowed to flow through gates to reach audiences and shape their understanding of the world. Later researchers developed this concept to explain how journalists at traditional news outlets, such as Mr. Gates in David Manning White's study of a midwestern newsroom in 1950, use their training and professional standards to identify positive and negative forces to sort information quickly. In the internet age, citizens might even influence the decisions that traditional gatekeepers make about the flow of information through gates.[5] The research in McKeesport also reveals that without any formal training, citizen gatekeepers left on their own struggle to make sense of all the information around them as they attempt to identify what pieces to consume and share with others.

Finally, social scientists as far back as Alexis de Tocqueville in the 1830s have demonstrated that news outlets, specifically newspapers, help citizens develop social capital in the ways they interact with each other—and that civic engagement declines when those local news outlets die. In McKeesport, people feel disconnected and uninformed after the death of their newspaper, causing them to miss out on opportunities for building social capital and to feel more isolated.

Ultimately, the forces of disruption have led citizens to take on the role of information gatekeeping to make better sense of their community as they look for ways to reconnect with neighbors and the people around them. This rise of the citizen gatekeeper puts more power in the hands of the public, allowing them to use it for the better by telling their shared narrative with more diversity from people overlooked and ignored by the traditional press, and for worse by muddling the conversation with innuendo and deliberate falsehoods.

Media Ecology Evolves

McLuhan showed how media ecology changes all the time with the advent of new technologies, and although he focused primarily on how television altered the way people acquired information in the mid-twentieth century, his theories seem prophetic for today's advanced computer age: the ways in which people access media unquestionably shape their culture, often leading to unexpected and unintended consequences. When consumers could turn to the internet for information, they no longer were limited by the decisions of a single journalist at a traditional news outlet deciding what stories to place in their local newspaper. Instead, they could go online to see almost limitless amounts of information and perspectives, from traditional news sources, from startups of all sorts, and from their fellow citizens who, as New York University's Jay Rosen might say, are using the tools of journalism to create and share stories of their own.

The residents of McKeesport are very aware of how the media ecology of their community has shifted, even if they would not articulate it that way. Many people talk wistfully about what existed previously when the *Daily News* employed many reporters and editors to tell their stories of their community. They understand that as subscribers started looking online for information, fewer of them continued taking the daily newspaper—and many of them made that same choice for themselves. Now, they also speak with frustration about how much things have shifted since the newspaper died, noting that even though other outlets have started up in attempts to replace the *Daily News*, they often somehow fall short, at least in many residents' perception. The citizens of McKeesport experienced deep and unexpected feelings of loss, not only in the ways they learn about their community but also in how they see themselves, how they tell their own shared story, and how they interact with each other.

Gatekeeper Role Shifts

Lewin first used gatekeeper theory in 1947 to consider how food moves from the farm to the grocery store to the dinner table, and he suggested briefly that the flow of information may also pass through gates before reaching audiences.[6] In this discussion, Lewin saw individuals weighing the positive and negative forces that exist around each item as they decide what to pass through and what to reject. A few years later, White built on the idea in a news context to show how Mr. Gates, one wire editor at a small-city newspaper, repeatedly made subjective decisions about what stories to publish: this one gatekeeper to information in the pre-internet age determined what stories people in that city read, and to a large extent how they understood the world. Researchers since then have shown how journalists, through practice and community standards, develop a framework to quickly sort large amounts of information to determine what pieces they believe will have value for their audiences.

The internet, of course, has untipped this whole process. People may now turn to multiple news sites for information, balancing the choices of one traditional gatekeeper against another as they attempt to see a clearer picture of reality. Mr. Gates might have discarded some stories because he had prejudices against Catholicism, and his subscribers had to live with that whether they even realized he had excluded those other perspectives. Today, a consumer who questions whether their newspaper gives them a full view of their religion may turn to countless other sources of information and, in the case of the Catholic religion, go directly to the Vatican News website to hear the Pope's unfiltered perspective.[7] The ways that citizens interact with the news also shape the actions of traditional gatekeepers by letting them see what stories get the most clicks or shares and then enticing them to share more similar content.[8]

None of these concepts on its own goes far enough to consider how citizens play a gatekeeping role around information when a traditional news outlet dies, taking its professional journalists with it. The experiences of people in McKeesport show that when the news gatekeepers disappear, the news does not stop happening; instead, individuals and community leaders attempt to fill the void by effectively taking up gatekeeping. Without any sort of training, however, they, too, frequently put little value in the significant role they play. They pass through their gates some information that has been confirmed but also other information that might be nothing more than a rumor or something that someone made up. They share items that seem significant to them, such as a police car showing up at a neighbor's house down the street, but that might have little actual significance and mean almost nothing to people who live on other streets in other parts of town. While the news shared by professional journalists might reflect their subjective decisions about what seems important, the information shared by citizen journalists often not only reflects their personal biases but also might lack accuracy or share only one part of what really happens. The combined results of these actions by citizen gatekeepers can lead to a shared narrative that seems depressing and uncertain, leaving citizens feeling frustrated because the stories told about where they live do not match the reality of their daily lives.

Finding Oases in a Desert

This study of McKeesport started out with a deficit narrative tied to the death of a community newspaper, but it uncovered many local assets that could be developed to provide stronger local storytelling. As researchers at Northwestern University's Institute for Policy Research, John P. Kretzmann and John L. McKnight looked in the early 1990s at how communities evolve, and they started seeing two divergent paths: one way focuses on the needs or deficits that might lead to residents' reliance on outside resources, and the other searches for assets that have the potential to empower residents to start solving their own problems.[9] Many people start down the path based on what the community needs, only to discover that the other way, with clues about what the community has to offer, presents more potential. If people want to improve their surroundings, they almost always have to do that work on their own with what they have on hand, Kretzmann and McKnight wrote in their book *Building Communities from the Inside Out* (1993):

"The hard truth is that development must start from within the community, and in most of our urban neighborhoods, there is no other choice."[10] This sentiment matches the reality of so-called news deserts, in which professional news outlets and journalists have withdrawn or disappeared, and residents, alone, are left to tackle the problem of sharing accurate, relevant information. People must take up the responsibility for telling their own stories, or no one else will.

Much of the national discussion about news deserts has focused on needs, with journalists and media academics pointing out how the traditional news industry has contracted and left behind communities without a dedicated media source or professional journalists. On heat maps, these look like places devoid of information sources, but that high-altitude view rarely tells the full story. In McKeesport since the *Daily News* closed, other assets for information-sharing have come about: a regional newspaper has opened a bureau in McKeesport, while an existing online news outlet continues to tell local stories; individual citizens have taken to social media sites such as Facebook and created dozens of places for local conversation; institutions such as the library and the school district have come up with creative ways of informing the public; even public officials have stepped into the void to provide more information about local government. All these resources can be seen as community assets despite their limitations, and with the right encouragement, residents could be inspired to feel that they can start to tackle their communications challenges on their own. The process of empowering residents starts with helping them see the positive developments happening around them so they can build on them with their available resources. In McKeesport, community members know they can share information on social media and through other means, but they rarely see the power embedded in what they do. Few people think of themselves as doing journalism or about how their social media postings contribute to a shared community narrative in a meaningful way.

With training and positive encouragement, people who are administering Facebook groups and who are sharing information at places such as the diner and library could come to see themselves as playing a more vital role in fostering the community conversation. When they start to see value in the work they already are doing, these people might also begin to take information gathering and dissemination more seriously, investing time to research issues for accuracy and to see them from the perspectives of others. Groups working to help citizens in news deserts should seek moments of awakening when citizens take responsibility for and ownership of local information.

Government can play a significant role in helping the public go through this process of self-actualization. McKeesport's public officials were among the first to realize that the death of the *Daily News* created a void, and they helped fill it with more of their own messaging. They have taken on this task, however, from the myopic perspective of sharing content that will help them maintain control of power, such as stories about the good deeds they have done, the economic developments they have supported, and the like. At the same time, even they realize that this jaundiced outlook does not really help the community see itself in the ways that it did when an independent newspaper told local stories. One-sided storytelling informs, but it cannot sustain the local community. Instead, by adopting an asset-based strategy, community leaders could help citizens see the good work people already are doing to tell and share local stories, and they could provide resources to help the public do a better job of this storytelling. McKeesport's public officials—in particular, Sen. Brewster and Mayor Cherepko—have taken steps to support local journalism by reopening the old Daily News Building and providing physical space at a reasonable cost. They came to see the value in supporting third-party news outlets. That type of strategy means that public officials risk having their constituents produce critical or disparaging content, but it also restores sincerity to the processes of gathering and sharing information. If citizens are going to become agents of change—as they already are doing on their own, with very little direction and mixed results—local governments and nonprofits could at least help them do a better job of it. Over the long term, everyone benefits.

Restoring Social Capital

The same technology that disrupted the traditional news model also has the potential to help citizens build social capital with each other, on their own terms. Realizing that potential requires them to take this new power seriously and to use it for their collective well-being. In his book about Chicago, *Great American City* (2012), Robert J. Sampson argues that communities matter because people appreciate the places where they live. They do so because of the connections, or social capital, that exist there as "a resource embodied in the social ties among persons—networks, norms, and trust."[11] When people of a community come to know and rely on each other, they create something of worth that can be invested or expended in ways that benefit their collective group.

Newspapers help weave together these networks among residents. Positing that "newspaper reading and good citizenship go together," Robert Putnam found that people who read newspapers are more likely to involve themselves in organizations, social clubs, community projects, and conversations with their friends and neighbors.[12] He divided this social trust into two forms: thick, such as that embedded in developed relationships, and thin, like that with new acquaintances or those that exist only through a single social media exchange. The more involved people get in their social and community networks, the more likely they are to feel a thick sense of trust, and that, in turn, helps citizens build and maintain social capital: "Other things being equal, people who trust their fellow citizens volunteer more often, contribute more to charity, participate more often in politics and community organizations, serve more readily on juries, give blood more frequently, comply more fully with their tax obligations, are more tolerant of minority views, and display many other forms of civic virtue."[13] By informing people about what goes on in their community and about how they can get more involved, newspapers help citizens develop that thick social trust that will bind them together when they need to tackle a crisis or address their community's weaknesses. Put another way, Alexis de Tocqueville realized that newspapers uniquely inform people about their shared values in ways that encourage them to engage with their community: "When no firm and lasting ties any longer unite men, it is impossible to obtain the cooperation of any great number of them unless you can persuade every man whose help is required that he serves his private interests by voluntarily uniting his efforts to those of all the others. That cannot be done habitually and conveniently without the help of a newspaper."[14] Conversely, the death of a newspaper can lead to lower levels of civic engagement measured by voting patterns, awareness of local issues, and involvement in community activities.[15] "When people's environments are rich in storytelling of their residential areas, they breathe it in, being more likely to participate directly with their neighbors in the process of imagining and constructing community," the media researchers Sandra J. Ball-Rokeach, Yong-Chan Kim, and Sorin Matei wrote in 2001.[16]

When the *Daily News* died, residents of McKeesport said they lost the piece of themselves that made them feel a part of a community, a sense of who they are in relation to the people around them. The connections fostered by the newspaper ran back for generations, so that reading the local newspaper served as a means by which members of the community identified with each other and with a shared sense of history, growing out of the practice of doing something that their parents and grandparents had done before them. The newspaper, owned at times by people with various forms of privilege—white, wealthy, and politically connected—presented a particular perspective of the community but one that many others still could recognize. The *Daily News* not only told about the community but reflected what it means to be part of a community, with detailed stories from births to deaths and everything in between. The newspaper's owners promoted the publication as a "community institution," and residents came to see it as serving a central role in civic life, physically at the center of the region and symbolically as the chronicler of daily existence. These notions have resonance with the quote from the book *Observations by Mr. Dooley* (1902), in which the fictional, satirical bartender describes the newspaper doing everything for readers. Because the community had one shared story, even people who had just moved into the area, and those who had moved far away, still could gain access relatively easily and affordably to share in the city's experiences. The newspaper created a foundation for other activities, such as attending community events and church, knowing about births and funerals, celebrating successes, and better understanding failures. The newspaper had become such a part of residents' shared sense of self that they had taken it for granted, and they could not anticipate the wide-ranging impacts its disappearance would cause. The ripples of that loss continue to wash over the community more than five years later.

Paradoxically, by taking an asset-based approach to solving their communication problems now that the newspaper has closed, citizens have the power to harness the disruptive technologies that killed the *Daily News* and use them to build social capital in ways that could be more meaningful than before, when only a few gatekeepers to news and information decided the narrative. People now experience the internet daily and must realize, like Tocqueville in his time, that it has infinitely more power than the printed page to place a single idea before masses of people. Today, citizen gatekeepers can determine what they value on their own and tell those stories, and they can set the parameters for how well information-sharing happens. Putnam saw that internet technologies would have the power to shape social capital, but also that it would be up to individual citizens to determine what form that value takes:

> No sector of American society will have more influence on the future state of our social capital than the electronic mass media and especially the internet. If we are to reverse the adverse trends of the last three decades in any fundamental way, the electronic entertainment and telecommunications industry must become a big part of the solution instead of a big part of the problem. . . . The recent flurry of interest in "civic journalism" could be one strand to this strategy, if it is interpreted not as a

substitute for genuine grassroots participation, but as a goad and soapbox for such participation.[17]

Yes, citizens can speak out about their communities via the internet, but they must take responsibility for the words they share so that other people can trust in this content enough for it to catalyze civic action. Only in that way, by forging a meaningful, trustworthy shared narrative, can citizen gatekeepers hope to create the conditions that might lead once again to creating meaningful opportunities for restoring social capital.

Hope for the Future

As the local news industry has collapsed, foundations and individuals have started stepping in to replace what has been lost by supporting experiments such as nonprofit newsrooms, university-based programs, and professional development for journalists. Estimates vary, but foundations have put billions of dollars into journalism programs this century in attempts to replace what has been lost as newspapers have closed. An entire organization, the Philadelphia-based Media Impact Funders, has existed as a nonprofit since 2008 to assist funders who want to apply their resources to helping solve the problems of local journalism. All of that might seem like a lot of money and support, but the spending must be seen in the context of the vast need and in the ways that donors distribute resources. An analysis by the Shorenstein Center and Northeastern University in 2018 looked at $1.8 billion that foundations had given to journalism projects between 2010 and 2015, and it discovered that 44 percent went to public media, 20.5 percent to university programs and museums, 12 percent to national nonprofit news outlets, 7 percent to professional development, 5 percent to magazines, 4.5 percent to local nonprofit news outlets, 4 percent to research, and 2 percent to university-backed journalism.[18] By comparison, foundations in the study gave just $13 million directly to citizen journalism programs, with nearly all of it going to two organizations: Witness Inc., an international nonprofit that uses technology to protect human rights, and the Global Press Institute, which provides journalism training to people in underreported countries. Compared with the collapse of local journalism taking place across the United States, the response has so far failed to meet the challenge.

Solutions to solving the problems of places that have lost traditional journalism start with harnessing the energy of the information-sharing that already occurs, albeit in serendipitous and often perplexing ways. More support should go toward helping citizens play a bigger role in local storytelling, both in areas where fewer journalists remain and where they no longer exist at all. The McKeesport experiment reveals that when a newspaper dies, people start trying to discover and tell news on their own—but they need help. They struggle to identify accurate, relevant news amid overwhelming amounts of information, much of it unverified or, worse, made up. They rarely see themselves playing a vital journalistic role in their community either.[19] Yes, they create Facebook groups and share what they know with others, but they do not often see this as journalism or the kind of fact-based reporting that any community needs to thrive. Because they devalue what they have to contribute, they rarely take it seriously or take the time to do it well. When citizens tweet something, they are not just sharing a fleeting thought that will disappear but contributing to their community's conversation and knowledge base, for its benefit or detriment.

We need to help people, first, appreciate the significant role they already play in shaping local conversations; then, we need to help them do a better job of it.

None of the information failures that occur after a newspaper dies should suggest that a meaningful, citizen-driven narrative cannot exist in a news desert. Instead, the power to control information inexorably gives people the ability to control their conversation. They just need help.

Professional journalists have long worked to separate the work they do from the typical activities of everyday people, correctly pointing out that professionals go to great lengths to find stories, research them, and present them in coherent ways. This type of thinking led to the creation of the Society of Professional Journalists and its professional code of ethics, which separated working journalists from amateur citizens. To reimagine the news industry, however, these walls need to come down so that journalists recognize the work that citizens already are doing in their communities by going to meetings, searching for information, and telling others about it. In places where journalists have left and are not coming back, citizens play an even bigger role. Everyone needs to celebrate this work—even with all its flaws—so that people start to see the value in what they are doing, often without even thinking about it. Just as journalists had to fight for their work to be seen as a profession, everyone must now lift up citizens when they perform acts of journalism.

Once people start seeing that they have the power to shape their community's conversations, they need training to do a better job of it. The media researchers Kathleen McCollough, Jessica K. Crowell, and Philip M. Napoli talked with citizens in six focus groups across three communities for a 2015 report to gauge people's interest and ability to conduct journalism on their own.[20] They found skepticism among the public about the real value of what they were doing because it did not seem like journalism, and few people formally involved themselves in aggregating and sharing information. The researchers also discovered a need to help citizens develop more skills: "If communities are going to rely, to some extent, on citizen journalism filling important gaps in local journalism, then our findings suggest that more may need to be done to encourage, support, train, and motivate community members to engage with their communities in this way."[21] More also needs to be done, they argue, to bring marginalized groups into these community newsrooms so that people who have been left at the edges of the conversation in many traditional models now have the ability to communicate their perspectives and values widely as well. A community-engaged newsroom brings many different voices into the conversation rather than simply turning to the local leaders with the loudest megaphones.

In places where even a few professional, trained journalists remain, these chroniclers must come to see their job differently so that they no longer keep citizens at a distance while seeking to tell the stories of the people they cover. Instead, they must begin to work with citizens, and even coach them to do a better job of identifying relevant information, verifying its accuracy, and setting aside their personal feelings. Rather than using the Society of Professional Journalists' guidelines to exclude amateurs, the rules of journalism can be used as guardrails for bringing more people into the practice of telling community stories.

For newsrooms that already struggle to report the news with fewer hands, it can seem like an extra or unnecessary burden to work with citizens because it takes more time and increases the risks. As foundations look for ways to support local journalism, they can help fill these gaps by giving newsrooms resources to train citizens in basic skills and by defraying the costs of paying ordinary people to contribute to news coverage, at least until they develop those abilities to contribute in reliable ways that also generate revenue for news outlets. It takes time to convince people they have a role to play, to educate them on meaningful ways to tell stories, and to have them contribute to the success of a news organization. Foundations can provide a runway for these activities.

The payoffs for professional journalists can be significant when they invest time to work collaboratively with the public to tell stories. The traditional journalists who engage citizens in storytelling will, first, develop richer narratives that include more perspectives and, over time, expand their ability to tell more stories. A few journalists can only be in so many places, but a few journalists working with motivated and trained citizens can cover a lot more local meetings and tell many more stories about community life.

Reaching the goal of restoring robust local storytelling in places where traditional news outlets are dead or dying also demands more of the public. When journalists control the news product and its content, they tell citizens what seems important; when citizens run their own local news networks, they make these decisions for themselves. The new opportunities created by democratizing technologies also carry additional responsibilities. Everyone who has access to the now-familiar technologies of smartphones, tablets, and laptop computers has the power to publish and broadcast information to others. At the same time, they also now share the burdens of getting their story right, asking fair but difficult questions of people in power, and speaking up for the less fortunate around them. The universal practice of sharing information must be seen as a deliberate act with actual consequences. Just as a professional journalist would not consciously share lies, rumors, or unverified information, citizens must realize the responsibility of making sure the information they share is based in truth and has broad relevance. Without a traditional news gatekeeper setting the agenda, the situation in news deserts has the potential to "leave the consumer vulnerable to the vagaries of the mob, unable to distinguish good information from garbage," as the media researcher Tom Fiedler warned in 2009.[22] Worse, Melissa Wall, a professor at California State University Northridge, points out that a lack of training and sophistication can leave people susceptible to being used: "This manipulation is exactly what critics of citizen news have long warned about: The lack of professional routines among bloggers and other citizens trying to collect information could make them more likely to commit ethical gaffes and more likely to be preyed upon by sophisticated entities seeking to take advantage of their lack of savvy or simply their lack of resources."[23] If citizens do not take more responsibility for how they consume and share information, community leaders who have greater access to primary sources and to mechanisms for sharing their perspective will come to dominate. That not only has the potential to skew the shared narrative in unnatural directions but also will leave out broad groups of people who do not enjoy the favor of those in power.

Citizens also shape the news they receive by the choices they make about what they consume. In places where professional journalists still exist, those journalists pay close attention to the stories people are reading, watching, and hearing. With online analytics, newsroom managers can tell when the public gravitates to certain types of bite-size breaking news stories, to sports articles, and to clickbait about sensational local controversies. In the many newsrooms that now measure their successes in internet clicks, these news producers will respond to the public's appetite by creating more stories that generate views even if they do not necessarily contribute to knowledge in substantive ways. The kinds of information that journalists create and that people consume matter: newsrooms cannot give people only vegetables to eat, but neither can the public subsist on candy alone.[24] The public decides what kind of information they receive from traditional news outlets, and they vote every time they turn to an online news story, whether they go directly to a news source or happen to get there through a social media platform. People must choose wisely about the stories they want to read and share.

Citizens who truly care about local news must go a step further by putting their resources into the places generating the information they value. At least ten million Americans who paid for a printed news subscription a decade ago no longer do.[25] Presumably many of these former subscribers figure they do not need to pay for information if they can instead turn for free to online news sites and social media platforms. They figure that if something significant happens, they will learn about it eventually because a computer algorithm will place it before them or someone in their interpersonal networks will make them aware. This passive approach to the news, however, ignores the fact that someone in the community must find this information in the first place and make the gatekeeping decisions about whether it has enough value and relevance to share with others. If people want access to reliable local news and information, they must support the journalists—professionals and citizens—who gather and disseminate valuable stories about their communities. No one should have to work for free, and no one should expect them to do a great job if they do.

The answers to solving the problems of disrupted local newsrooms start in realizing that many ordinary citizens continue to have a deep interest in knowing about their community. They want to find out what their neighbors are talking about, and they want to know about the things that shape their lives—decisions elected officials make about spending tax dollars, companies moving in or out, crimes that take place, and the many moments, good and bad, that weave together the texture of daily life. They might click more often on breaking news and sports stories, but many of them also want to know that the elected officials running their community are making good, thoughtful decisions that protect their homes, educate their children, and pave their streets. Citizens want to know

that someone is asking challenging questions of public officials and community leaders to hold them accountable and keep them honest—the work that
journalists at their best always have done. In a horizontal world where everyone
has access to information, citizens have to not only support local journalists
but also take up the responsibility of asking meaningful questions about their
community, digging for answers, and letting others know the objective truth.

No one has to convince citizens to go out, gather information, and share
what they know with others. People on their own are setting up Facebook groups
and blogging online, they are putting up flyers when they need to inform large
groups, and they are gathering in the places where people talk in person and
online. They might not think of what they do as journalism, but millions of
ordinary people collect information and make gatekeeping decisions about what
to share every day. Professional journalists, news organizations, social media
platforms, and foundations can help individiuals recognize and celebrate the
work they already do, then give them the training to improve. People like to share
their opinions, but few of them deliberately want to get facts wrong: they just
need the resources—education, guidelines, and practice—to start separating
verified and relevant news from gossip, lies, and bias. Citizens, meanwhile, must
collectively choose through their behavior whether they will carry out the little,
daily revolutions advocated by the historian Timothy Snyder to demand more
accountability from themselves for what they consume and share.[26] Collectively,
if enough people embrace the work of citizen gatekeeping and pay attention to
what they share with those around them, they can bring sense and direction to
an otherwise confusing, and overwhelmingly negative, community story.

Epilogue

As if the death of the *Daily News* had been a whodunit, the conclusion of this story brings with it an unexpected twist: just when things seemed bleakest for local journalism in McKeesport, the community got back a newspaper—or at least a newsroom.

In the summer of 2021, the owners of the *Mon Valley Independent* daily newspaper, based in Monessen, nineteen miles south along the Monongahela River, lost their building location there. After looking around for a new office space—and with help from Sen. Jim Brewster and Mayor Michael Cherepko—they decided to move a half dozen reporters and editors to McKeesport, into the *Daily News* building, which had been abandoned by its newspaper more than a half decade before. While the COVID-19 pandemic has delayed the workers' return to the office, they plan to come back, and the building's first-floor space once again will have journalists sitting at desks, working on deadlines, and churning out original local copy.

All along, the *Mon Valley Independent*'s copublisher Naz Victoria had fought against the idea that McKeesport could be a news desert. It remains true that his newspaper has far fewer resources than the *Daily News* enjoyed at its peak, and Jeff Stitt, the reporter assigned to McKeesport, must attempt to capture both the actions of local government and the nuances of daily life. The *Mon Valley*

Independent also seeks to cover a broad area of the Mon Valley, the many communities between the two newspapers that died—the *Daily News* in McKeesport and the *Valley Independent* in Monessen.

Perhaps no one solution, not even a new printed newspaper, will completely quench the thirst for information in a community that lost a traditional newspaper that existed for more than a century. But in the attempt to find out and chronicle what goes on—through a restored newsroom, in print and online news outlets, on the library's message board and lawn, and in Facebook community groups—citizens can and do continue to tell their own story.

CHARACTER PROFILES

Interview Subjects

Jim Brewster, state senator. A Democrat, Brewster was elected to the state Senate in 2010, representing the Forty-Fifth District in both Allegheny and Westmoreland counties. He previously served as mayor of McKeesport, from 2004 to 2010, and as a member of city council for seven years before that. He previously worked as vice president of operations for Mellon Bank. See https://www.senatorbrewster.com.

Michael Cherepko, mayor of McKeesport. A Democrat, Cherepko was first elected to office in 2011. Before that, he served on city council and worked as a fifth-grade teacher in the McKeesport Area School District. See https://www.mckeesport-pa.gov/171/Mayors-Office.

Austin Davis, state representative. A Democrat, Davis was elected in 2018 to serve the Thirty-Fifth District, which includes McKeesport. He became the first African American to represent the district. In high school, Davis founded and then served as chairman of the Mayor's Youth Advisory Council, under Mayor Jim Brewster. See https://www.davisforpa.com.

Colleen Denne, library director (former). With a master's degree in library science, Denne became director of the Carnegie Library of McKeesport in 2018. She stepped down in 2020.

Diane Elias, owner of Di's Kornerstone Diner and vice president of the McKeesport Area School District's board of directors.

Mark P. Holtzman Jr., superintendent of McKeesport Area School District. A graduate of McKeesport's high school in 1997, Holtzman became district superintendent in 2017. He previously served as the district's high school principal and director of secondary education. See https://www.mckasd.net.

Jeffrey Tomovcsik, chief of the City of McKeesport's Bureau of Fire. Tomovcsik took over as chief in 2015 after serving as a firefighter in the city for ten years.

Jennifer Vertullo, McKeesport mayor's assistant. Before joining the administration of Mayor Cherepko, Vertullo worked as a journalist for the *Daily News* in McKeesport. When she started in 2000, the newspaper had ten news reporters and two interns; she was one of four news reporters when she left in 2014.

Naz Victoria, copublisher of the *Mon Valley Independent*. When Trib Total Media closed the *Valley Independent* newspaper in Monessen in 2015, Victoria joined with three other investors to start up a new print newspaper the following year. See https://monvalleyindependent.com.

Fawn Walker-Montgomery, cofounder of Take Action Mon Valley. A former member of McKeesport's city council and a candidate for mayor in 2019, she started TAMV in 2014 as a way to highlight and combat incidents of violence in the Monongahela River valley. See https://www.tamv.org.

METHODOLOGY

I conducted ten interviews with community leaders, two focus groups with citizens, and one combined interview with two citizens. I also collected artifacts from the research site. The work took place over ten weeks, from January 6 to March 10, 2020, concluding just days before Pennsylvania governor Tom Wolf issued a stay-at-home order for all residents because of the COVID-19 pandemic. I digitally recorded each conversation, transcribed the information using Otter.ai software, and analyzed the data with NVivo software.

For the interviews, each of the subjects agreed to be identified by name, title, and demographic information. They included six men and four women, eight white people and two Black people. I met with each person in a location of their choosing, including seven offices and three restaurants. After I provided a transcript to each subject for review, one person requested to redact a portion of what they said, and I removed that information.

I also conducted two focus groups and a joint interview with citizens who were de-identified to allow them to speak freely about their experiences. The thirteen people ranged in age from twenty-six to eighty-five, and they included nine people who had lived in McKeesport longer than ten years (including five life-long residents), two people who recently had moved into the city, and two people who live in nearby communities. The groups included seven women and six men, nine white people and four Black people. The author asked each person in the focus groups and discussion to draw an image that shows how they find out about what goes on in McKeesport, and those drawings helped inform the research.

TABLE 1. Focus Groups and Joint Interview

Focus Group 1	2/13/20			
Age	**Gender**	**Race**	**Occupation**	**Hobbies**
26	Female	White	Bakery sales clerk, movie extra	Blogging, singing, crafting, dancing, writing
41	Female	Black	Coach	Sports, reading
41	Female	White	Professor	Writing, weight lifting
45	Female	White	Marketing director	Yoga, hiking, RVing
67	Male	White	Retired advertising executive	Art, writing, metalwork, woodwork
70	Male	White	Retired journalist	Golfing, reading, eating
75	Male	White	Retired	Sports
Focus Group 2	**3/10/20**			
Age	**Gender**	**Race**	**Occupation**	**Hobbies**
57	Male	White	Professor / Retired policeman	Gaming, music
67	Male	Black	Retired	Working with youth
78	Male	White	Retired shopkeeper	N/A
85	Female	Black	Retired	Reading
Joint interview	**2/20/20**			
Age	**Gender**	**Race**	**Occupation**	**Hobbies**
37	Female	Black	Personal caregiver	Crafting, event planning, treat making
37	Female	White	Business analyst	Biking, kickboxing

TABLE 2. Interview Subjects

Order	Title	First	Last	Race	Gender
1	State senator	Jim	Brewster	White	Male
2	Mayor's assistant	Jennifer	Vertullo	White	Female
3	Mayor	Michael	Cherepko	White	Male
4	State representative	Austin	Davis	Black	Male
5	Librarian (former)	Colleen	Denne	White	Female
6	Newspaper publisher	Naz	Victoria	White	Male
7	School superintendent	Mark	Holtzman Jr.	White	Male
8	Fire chief	Jeffrey	Tomovcsik	White	Male
9	School board director	Diane	Elias	White	Female
10	Former councilwoman	Fawn	Walker-Montgomery	Black	Female

AUTHOR'S NOTE

I thought I had coined the phrase "news deserts" around 2016 when I started hearing from residents of southwestern Pennsylvania who no longer had professional journalists covering their communities. That summer, as I worked to set up the Center for Media Innovation at Point Park University as a laboratory for local journalism, I started getting phone calls from people near Pittsburgh asking me where the journalists had gone. At first, I did not know what they meant, but after a little research I realized that the region's two dominant newspapers had withdrawn their coverage areas, leaving behind pocket communities that no longer had local reporting. This seemed to me something similar to food deserts, where people lack easy access to fresh, locally sourced fruits, vegetables, and more.

Of course, in the internet age, it seems very hard to be the first at anything. I quickly discovered that researchers had started collecting quantitative data to track the growth of news deserts across the United States. A Chicago columnist had started formulating this idea of deserts in 2011 when she pointed out that some places even within metro coverage areas receive very little local reporting.

The concept still resonated with me: if we allow places to exist without independent news coverage, it threatens the core of our democracy. Our system of government depends on individuals having enough accurate, objective information to ask honest questions of elected officials and to know what goes on in their community. In one of the local places I heard from that first summer, a resident told me she thought her township manager had been stealing from the taxpayers, and she wondered who would investigate if no reporters were coming around. Ultimately, I reached out to a reporter who had been covering the community before the cutbacks, and he looked into the claim.

Local journalism forms the bedrock of our American way of life, even if people took it for granted until it started disappearing. After graduating from Columbia University's School of Journalism when many of my classmates were going off to cover foreign wars, national politics, and business stories, I headed out to cover local municipal meetings in a small but rapidly growing Florida city, Port St. Lucie. One of my first big stories was about whether residents would be required to pay for installing public water and sewage. The topic sounds boring, but it means a lot to local residents: on one hand, each property owner would have to pay thousands of dollars to be hooked into the utility system; on the other, so many homes were being built that residents were drinking well water from the same shallow aquifer where they and their neighbors were emptying their septic tanks. Fixing the problem would cost a lot, particularly for retirees on fixed incomes, but ignoring it could lead to a major health crisis. Residents relied on the newspaper to present these options, to ask hard questions of elected officials, and, when the resolution ultimately passed, to make sure that the utilities were installed with minimal wasteful spending.

Throughout my career, I have seen local journalists fulfill this role of independent watchdog, holding powerful people to account for their actions and speaking up for those who felt like they could not be heard on their own. There was the retired World War II veteran who nearly lost his home because he could not afford to pay both his wife's medical bills and his local taxes. After I knocked on his door and then reported what was happening to him and many others like him, the city changed its policies to work with seniors on payment options rather than just foreclosing.

Another time, in Cincinnati, we chronicled repeated incidents of police officers killing unarmed black suspects in the late 1990s and pointed out the patterns of what happened until the people got fed up and angrily demonstrated—and then rioted in the streets. Journalists told the stories of each police killing, they asked difficult questions of both the police officers and the public, they followed the riots, and then they explored possible solutions. Ultimately, the city ended up identifying a history of racial bias in policing decades before Minneapolis officers killed George Floyd and set off a national conversation about these same issues.

Yet again, in Pennsylvania, when state lawmakers voted in the early morning of July 4, 2005, to give themselves hefty pay raises, figuring the public would not be paying attention on the holiday, local reporters told the story—and pointed out the secrecy and hypocrisy over the following weeks and months. Ultimately, the legislators felt so much pressure from the public that they gave back the money. If they legitimately felt the need for more pay, they should have raised the issue in the light of day, held hearings, and made their case to the public.

Much of this work by local journalists goes on with people paying little attention until it abruptly disappears. In that moment, when people start looking around and asking where the journalists went, they start to realize all that their local newspaper had been doing for them. Not only does the local newspaper ask questions and report the answers, but it provides a forum for people to discuss the issues they care about and to let others know about the moments when they can come together—both around issues of significance, but more routinely around the points of civic life that mean so much, like Friday night high school football games, school recitals, church events, and community festivals. Many people can remember a first moment their name or photo appeared in the local newspaper—often as the result of sports or a school activity—adding their small contribution to their community's local story and giving their parents and grandparents a clipping to hang on the refrigerator or bulletin board. Those moments matter when they happen, and their importance lingers when they no longer exist.

Even public officials start to see what happens when their local newspaper suddenly goes away. They might celebrate at first, thinking that no journalists will be at their meetings to ask challenging questions about how they award contracts, choose what streets to repair first, or decide how much they pay themselves. Then, after the journalists stop coming around, they start to realize that for every negative story in the newspaper, the reporters also were telling many positive stories about their plans for the community, about every check they handed out for local developments, about the constituent work they do to win reelection.

While data researchers track the spread of news deserts across the United States, now consuming more than half of all counties that have only one newspaper (often a weekly) or none at all, this book tells the story of what happens in one of those places when the local newspaper suddenly disappears. I have been working in this community over the five years since the newspaper died, helping citizens come to terms with their unexpected loss and then giving them the tools to start telling their own stories. They have a long way to go toward replacing the work that professional journalists were doing—but at the same time, they have come a great distance toward developing new community conversations.

This story repeats itself all across the United States every time a newspaper closes, pulls back its coverage area to leave behind communities that no longer have reporters, or cuts its resources and stops reporting in detail on the many local neighborhoods that make up larger cities. This book, then, serves as part autopsy and part obituary, as a guide to grieving, and as a map to the path forward. Through its telling, I hope that people in places that have lost local news coverage will find lessons for what they can adopt or hope to avoid—and that everyone else who still enjoys local reporting will see its value before it potentially goes away.

ACKNOWLEDGMENTS

I tried to not tell my wife, Tania, about one of my deadlines for this book, but she figured out something was up anyway. She does this all the time. She said I had changed my demeanor, my eyes looked different, the tone in my voice seemed sharper. She's like that, paying attention to all the little details to read what's up with the people she cares about. Everyone should be so lucky to have someone in their lives who cares so deeply about them. I am blessed. My children, Noah and Claudia, are charting their own unique academic paths. No two of us are the same, and I am proud of them for working to find what drives them—and then to pursue that direction without caution. I am grateful that they indulged me in the pursuit of my own research, even though it often took me away from spending time with them.

My family has been there all the way, encouraging me, pushing me to be my best, and offering insights and wisdom. Special thanks to my parents, Olive and George; my in-laws, Pam and Al Miller; Donna Searles; Elizabeth and Iwan Fuchs, Johann, André, Cameron, and Nikolai; and Al and Jessica Miller and Claire.

To my community engagement professors at Point Park University, thank you for expanding my vision of the world, for helping me work to be a better and more engaged person, and for allowing me to straddle the role of student, colleague, and friend. Special thanks to my dissertation committee: Heather Starr Fiedler, Sera Mathew, and Britney Brinkman. Thank you also to Mitch Nickols.

I'm grateful to Keino Fitzpatrick for putting my ideas to work with Youth-CAST and for introducing me to Aaron Johnson. I'm particularly thankful for Harold Allen, who has helped me so many times in my work in McKeesport, who does so much to lift up the young people around him, and who bailed me out at a critical moment in my research.

I owe special thanks to Martha Rial, who runs the McKeesport Community Newsroom. I also feel a special debt of appreciation to the people who work with me at the Center for Media Innovation every day and to those who have worked with me in the past: Tara Maziarz Myers, Lisa Knapp, Chris Hays,

Jennifer Szweda Jordan, Casey Hoolahan, Stacey Federoff, Ashley Murray, Amy Philips-Haller, Olivia Valyo, Wayne Gaines, Tanner Knapp, Eddie Robas, Jacob Balistreri, Nick Ruffolo, Tyler Polk, Colten Oakes, Nick Tommarello, Chris Sichi, and too many others to name. I'm grateful to my Point Park University community: Presidents Don Green and Paul Hennigan; Provosts Michael Soto, John Pearson, and Jonas Prida; Dean Bernie Ankney; and my colleagues, especially Thom Baggerman.

My friends make everything possible: Mark Houser; the Dandy Gents—Todd Anderson, Vince Benincasa, Ken Dornback, Scott Goldman, Mark O'Matz, and Steve Posti; and too many others to name here.

Special thanks to Gail Waite, operations assistant at the McKeesport Regional History and Heritage Center, for helping me locate original news clippings from the day in 1947 when two first-term lawmakers, Richard M. Nixon and John F. Kennedy, came to town to debate labor legislation. The center provides a meaningful resource for the people of McKeesport, for the Mon Valley, and for those of us who celebrate the region's industrial and ethnic history.

Above all, I owe a debt of gratitude to so many residents of McKeesport and the Mon Valley who graciously share their insights with me, invite me into their lives, accept me, and challenge me to always be better. Some of these people are named in the report through the interviews I conducted, and many more of them remain anonymous. I hope each of you knows how much I value the time you spend with me and how much I admire your undying love for your community.

NOTES

Chapter 1: Place of Death

1. "Nixon, Kennedy Debated Labor Bill Here in '47," *Daily News* (McKeesport, PA), July 21, 1960, 1.

2. "Congressmen Debate Merits of House-Passed Labor Bill; Nixon Sees Rights Protected, Kennedy Fears Civil Strife," *Daily News*, April 22, 1947.

3. E. F. Goldman, "The 1947 Kennedy-Nixon 'Tube City' Debate: A Little-Remembered Duel Between the Two Fledgling Congressmen at McKeesport, Pa.," *Saturday Review*, October 16, 1976.

4. "Nixon, Kennedy Debated Labor Bill Here in '47," *Daily News*, July 21, 1960, 1.

5. Jason Togyer, "National Tube Company: A Timeline," Tube City Almanac, 2017, http://www.tubecityonline.com/steel/nat_works_timeline.html.

6. Carol Waterloo Frazier and Jeffrey Sisk, "Daily News Thanks Mon Valley, Publishes Final Edition after 131 Years," *Pittsburgh Tribune-Review*, December 31, 2015.

7. Jonathan D. Silver, "Main Street McKeesport: A Painful Decline," *Pittsburgh Post-Gazette*, June 15, 1999, http://old.post-gazette.com/regionstate/19990615mmckeesport3.asp.

8. John F. Kennedy, "Remarks at City Hall, McKeesport, Pennsylvania," John F. Kennedy Presidential Library and Museum, October 13, 1962, https://www.jfklibrary.org/asset-viewer/archives/JFKPOF/041/JFKPOF-041-001.

9. Jason Togyer, "Looking Back: McKeesport's Kennedy Connection," Tube City Almanac, November 22, 2013, http://www.tubecityonline.com/almanac/entry_2393.php.

10. Jason Togyer, "JFK-Nixon Debate to Be Marked April 21," Tube City Almanac, March 13, 2012, http://www.tubecityonline.com/almanac/entry_1873.php.

11. Frazier and Sisk, "Daily News Thanks."

12. Frazier and Sisk, "Daily News Thanks."

Chapter 2: Time of Death

1. Maria Sciullo, "It's the End of an Era for the McKeesport Daily News," *Pittsburgh Post-Gazette*, December 31, 2015.

2. When using the term "citizen," the author intends the broader meaning of the word to include all people residing in an area regardless of their citizenship status.

3. Many quotes throughout this book come from personal interviews and focus groups with McKeesport residents. See the methodology chapter for more information about the author's approach to these interviews. Colleen Denne stepped down as library director in 2020.

4. Penelope Muse Abernathy, *The Expanding News Desert* (Chapel Hill: Center for Innovation and Sustainability in Local Media, University of North Carolina at Chapel Hill, 2018), https://www.usnewsdeserts.com/reports/expanding-news-desert/.

5. "State of the News Media (Project)," News Media Trends, Pew Research Center, August 25, 2021, http://www.pewresearch.org/topics/state-of-the-news-media/.

6. Brian McNair, "Trust, Truth and Objectivity: Sustaining Quality Journalism in the Era of the Content-Generating User," in *Rethinking Journalism: Trust and Participation in a Transformed News Landscape*, ed. Chris Peters and Marcel Broersma (New York: Routledge, 2013), 75–88.

7. Christopher Ali and Damien Radcliffe, *New Research: Small-Market Newspapers in the Digital Age* (New York: Tow Center for Digital Journalism, 2017), https://www.cjr.org/tow_center_reports/local-small-market-newspapers-study.php.

8. "State of the News Media."

9. "State of the News Media."

10. Marcel Broersma and Chris Peters, "Rethinking Journalism: The Structural Transformation of a Public Good," in Peters and Broersma, 1–12.

11. David Shedden, "Today in Media History: Mr. Dooley: 'The Job of the Newspaper Is to Comfort the Afflicted and Afflict the Comfortable,'" Poynter, October 7, 2014, https://www.poynter.org/news/today-media-history-mr-dooley-job-newspaper-comfort-afflicted-and-afflict-comfortable.

12. Robert G. Picard, "Twilight or New Dawn of Journalism?" *Journalism Studies* 15, no. 5 (2014): 500, https://doi.org/10.1080/1461670X.2014.895530.

13. Tom Fiedler, "Crisis Alert: Barack Obama Meets a Citizen Journalist," in *Citizen Journalism: Global Perspectives*, ed. Stuart Allan and Einar Thorsen (New York: Peter Lang, 2009), 209–20.

14. "State of the News Media."

15. "State of the News Media."

16. Abernathy, *Expanding News Desert*.

17. Abernathy, *Expanding News Desert*.

18. Doug Muder, "Expand Your Vocabulary: News Desert," *The Weekly Sift* (blog), December 5, 2011, https://weeklysift.com/2011/12/05/expand-your-vocabulary-news-desert/.

19. Tom Stites, "Layoffs and Cutbacks Lead to a New World of News Deserts," NiemanLab, December 8, 2011, http://www.niemanlab.org/2011/12/tom-stites-layoffs-and-cutbacks-lead-to-a-new-world-of-news-deserts/.

20. Steve Franklin, "The News Desert We Live In. Please Come and Visit," Chicago Is the World, April 14, 2011, http://chicagoistheworld.org/2011/04/the-news-desert-we-live-in-please-come-and-visit/.

21. Franklin, "News Desert."

22. Franklin, "News Desert."

23. Stites, "Layoffs and Cutbacks."

24. Michelle Ferrier, *The Media Deserts Project: Monitoring Community News and Information Needs Using Geographic Information System Technologies* (Scripps College of Communication, February 2014), introduction, para. 2, Academia, https://www.academia.edu/11469030/The_Media_Deserts_Project_Monitoring_Community_News_and_Information_Needs_Using_Geographic_Information_System_Technologies.

25. Ferrier, *Media Deserts Project*. See also Michelle Ferrier, Guarav Sinha, and Michael Outrich, "Media Deserts: Monitoring the Changing Media Ecosystem," in *The Communication Crisis in America, and How to Fix It*, ed. Mark Lloyd and Lewis A. Friedland (New York: Palgrave, 2016), 215–32, https://doi.org/10.1057/978-1-349-94925-0.

26. Ferrier, Sinha, and Outrich, "Media Deserts."

27. C. W. Anderson, Emily J. Bell, and Clay Shirky, *Post-industrial Journalism: Adapting to the Present* (New York: Columbia University Tow Center for Digital Journalism, 2014), https://academiccommons.columbia.edu/doi/10.7916/D8N01JS7.

28. Anderson, Bell, and Shirky, *Post-industrial Journalism*, 1.

29. Jay Rosen, "A Most Useful Definition of Citizen Journalism," *PressThink* (blog), July 14, 2008, http://archive.pressthink.org/2008/07/14/a_most_useful_d.html.

30. "Generation C," February 2004, *Trendwatching* (blog), http://trendwatching.com/trends/GENERATION_C.htm.

31. Lydia Polgreen, "Introducing HuffPost Opinion and HuffPost Personal," HuffPost, January 18, 2018, https://www.huffpost.com/entry/huffpost-opinion-huffpost-personal_n_5a5f6a29e4b096ecfca98edb.

32. Polgreen, "Introducing HuffPost Opinion," para. 8.

33. Polgreen, "Introducing HuffPost Opinion," para. 9.

34. See Kelly Kaufhold, Sebastian Valenzuela, and Homero Gil De Zúñiga, "Citizen Journalism and Democracy: How User-Generated News Use Relates to Political Knowledge and Participation," *Journalism & Mass Communication Quarterly* 87, no. 3–4 (2010): 515–29, https://doi.org/10.1177/107769901008700305; McNair, "Trust, Truth and Objectivity"; and Jane B. Singer and Ian Ashman, "User-Generated Content and Journalistic Values," in *Citizen Journalism: Global Perspectives*, ed. Stuart Allan and Einar Thorsen (New York: Peter Lang Publishing, 2009), 233–42.

35. McNair, "Trust, Truth and Objectivity," 81.

36. Singer and Ashman, "User-Generated Content," 242.

37. Ryan Chittum, "Advance Publications Scraps AnnArbor.com," *Columbia Journalism Review*, September 9, 2013, https://archives.cjr.org/the_audit/advance_publications_scraps_an.php.

38. Stefanie Murray, "AnnArbor.com's Offices Will Be in Heart of Downtown Ann Arbor," *Ann Arbor News*, June 3, 2009, accessed via the Internet Archive WayBack Machine, http://web.archive.org/web/20090606090454/http://annarbor.com/2009/06/annarborcoms-offices-will-be-in-heart-of-downtown-ann-arbor.html.

39. Amy Maestas, "Ann Arbor: Citizenship and the Local Newspaper," in *Thwarting the Emergence of News Deserts* (Chapel Hill: Center for Innovation and Sustainability in Local Media, University of North Carolina at Chapel Hill, 2017), 38–42, http://newspaperownership.com/wp-content/uploads/2017/03/Symposium-Leave-Behind-Web-Final.pdf; E. White, "'Ann Arbor News' Prints Last Edition after 174 years," *Editor & Publisher*, July 23, 2009.

40. Maestas, "Ann Arbor."

41. Maestas, "Ann Arbor," 42.

42. "AnnArbor.com Moving to MLive.com on Sept. 12," *Ann Arbor News*, September 4, 2013, http://www.annarbor.com/news/annarborcom-moving-to-mlivecom-on-sept-12/.

43. J. D. Lasica, "Blogs and Journalism Need Each Other," *Nieman Reports* 57, no. 3 (Fall 2003), https://niemanreports.org/articles/blogs-and-journalism-need-each-other/.

44. Lasica, "Blogs and Journalism," 70.

45. Picard, "Twilight or New Dawn," 505.

46. Andrew Keen, *The Cult of the Amateur* (New York: Doubleday/Currency, 2007).

47. Seth C. Lewis, Kelly Kaufhold, and Dominic L. Lasorsa, "Thinking about Citizen Journalism," *Journalism Practice* 4, no. 2 (2010): 163–79, https://doi.org/10.1080/14616700903156919.

48. Lewis, Kaufhold, and Lasorsa, "Thinking about Citizen Journalism," 160.

49. Henrik Örnebring, "Anything You Can Do, I Can Do Better? Professional Journalists on Citizen Journalism in Six European Countries," *International Communication Gazette* 75, no. 1 (February 2013): 35–53, https://doi.org/10.1177/1748048512461761.

50. Örnebring, "Anything You Can Do," 43.

51. Axel Bruns, "News Produsage in a Pro-Am Mediasphere: Why Citizen Journalism Matters,"

in *News Online: Transformations and Continuities,* ed. Graham Meikle and Guy Redden (London: Palgrave Macmillan, 2011).

52. Lewis, Kaufhold, and Lasorsa, "Thinking about Citizen Journalism," 170.

53. "Citizen Journalism Publishing Standards, HuffPost, April 14, 2009, https://www.huffing-tonpost.com/2009/04/14/citizen-journalism-publis_n_186963.html.

54. "SPJ Code of Ethics," Society of Professional Journalists, September 6, 2014, https://www.spj.org/ethicscode.asp.

55. Gallup, *Indicators of News Media Trust: A Gallup/Knight Foundation Survey* (Knight Foundation, 2018), https://kf-site-production.s3.amazonaws.com/media_elements/files/000/000/216/original/KnightFoundation_Panel4_Trust_Indicators_FINAL.pdf.

56. De Tocqueville, *Democracy in America,* chap. 6, para. 4.

57. L. J. Hanifan, "The Rural School Community Center," *Annals of the American Academy of Political and Social Science,* no. 67 (September 1916): 130–38.

58. Hanifan, "Rural School Community Center."

59. Pierre Bourdieu, "The Forms of Capital," in *Handbook of Theory and Research for the Sociology of Education,* ed. J. Richardson (New York: Greenwood, 2009), 9.

60. Robert D. Putnam, *Bowling Alone* (New York: Simon & Schuster, 2000), 218.

61. Penelope Muse Abernathy, *The Rise of a New Media Baron and the Emerging Threat of News Deserts* (Chapel Hill: Center for Innovation and Sustainability in Local Media, University of North Carolina at Chapel Hill, 2016), 6, https://www.usnewsdeserts.com/reports/rise-new-media-baron/new-media-barons/.

62. Michael Barthel et al., *Civic Engagement Strongly Tied to Local News Habits: Local Voters and Those Who Feel Attached to Their Communities Stand Out* (Washington, DC: Pew Research Center, 2016), http://www.journalism.org/2016/11/03/civic-engagement-strongly-tied-to-local-news-habits/.

63. Abernathy, *Expanding News Desert.*

64. "Food Access Research Atlas: Documentation," US Department of Agriculture, Economic Research Service, December 5, 2017, https://www.ers.usda.gov/data-products/food-access-research-atlas/documentation/.

65. Paolo Freire, *Pedagogy of the Oppressed,* 30th anniversary ed. (New York: Continuum, 2010), 30.

66. De Tocqueville, *Democracy in America,* chap. 6, para 2.

Chapter 3: Cause of Death

1. David Manning White, "The 'Gatekeeper': A Case Study in the Selection of News," *Journalism Quarterly,* no. 27 (Fall 1950): 383–90.

2. White, "Gatekeeper," 386.

3. White, "Gatekeeper," 387.

4. White, "Gatekeeper," 390.

5. White, "Gatekeeper," 390.

6. White, "Gatekeeper," 384.

7. Kurt Lewin, "Frontiers in Group Dynamics II: Channels of Group Life; Social Planning and Action Research," *Human Relations* 1, no. 1 (1947): 143–53, https://journals.sagepub.com/doi/pdf/10.1177/001872674700100201.

8. Lewin, "Frontiers in Group Dynamics," 145.

9. Lewin, "Frontiers in Group Dynamics," 145.

10. Upton Sinclair, *The Brass Check: A Study of American Journalism* (1919; repr., Urbana: University of Illinois Press, 2003), 153. Citations refer to the reprint edition.

11. Robert W. McChesney and Ben Scott, introduction to *Brass Check,* by Sinclair, ix–xxxiii.

12. Walter Lippman, *Public Opinion* (New York: MacMillan, 1961), 354.

13. Pamela Shoemaker and Timothy Vos, *Gatekeeping Theory* (New York: Routledge, 2009).

14. Eric Norden, "Playboy Interview: Marshall McLuhan," *Playboy,* March 1969.

15. Richard Metzger, "When John Lennon & Yoko Ono Met Marshall McLuhan, December 1969," *McLuhan Galaxy* (blog), September 25, 2017, https://mcluhangalaxy.wordpress.com/2017/09/25/when-john-lennon-yoko-ono-met-marshall-mcluhan-1969/.

16. Norden, "Playboy Interview."

17. Norden, "Playboy Interview."

18. Norden, "Playboy Interview."

19. Norden, "Playboy Interview."

20. "About AT&T," AT&T, https://about.att.com/pages/corporate_profile. "AT&T's WarnerMedia and Discovery, Inc. Creating Standalone Company by Combining Operations to Form New Global Leader in Entertainment," AT&T, May 17, 2021, https://about.att.com/story/2021/warnermedia_discovery.html.

21. Marshall McLuhan and Quentin Fiore, *The Medium Is the Message: An Inventory of Effects* (Corte Madera, CA: Gingko Press, 1967), 63.

22. Neil Postman, *Technopoly: The Surrender of Culture to Technology* (New York: Alfred A. Knopf, 1992), 20.

23. Chris Peters and Marcel Broersma, eds., *Rethinking Journalism: Trust and Participation in a Transformed News Landscape* (New York: Routledge, 2013), 5.

24. McLuhan and Fiore, *Medium Is the Message,* 81.

25. Todd Gitlin, *The Whole World Is Watching: Media in the Making and Unmaking of the New Left* (Berkeley: University of California Press, 1980).

26. Ken Doctor, *Newsonomics: Twelve New Trends That Will Shape the News You Get* (New York: St. Martin's Press, 2010), 10.

27. Doctor, *Newsonomics,* 15.

28. "Facebook Journalism Project," Facebook, accessed August 10, 2021, https://www.facebook.com/journalismproject.

29. Brandy Zadrozny, "In a Pennsylvania Town, a Facebook Group Fills the Local News Void," NBC News, April 5, 2021, https://www.nbcnews.com/tech/social-media/pennsylvania-town-facebook-group-fills-local-news-void-rcna577.

30. "We're Launching New Engagement Features, Ways to Discover Groups and More Tools for Admins," Facebook, October 1, 2020, https://www.facebook.com/community/whats-new/facebook-communities-summit-keynote-recap/.

31. Andrew Conte, "On Media: Local Journalism Must Be of the People, and Not Just for the People," NEXTpittsburgh, March 16, 2021, https://nextpittsburgh.com/features/on-media-local-journalism-must-be-of-the-people-and-not-just-for-the-people/.

32. Todd Graham, "Talking Back, but Is Anyone Listening? Journalism and Comment Fields," in Peters and Broersma, 115.

33. Shoemaker and Vos, *Gatekeeping Theory.*

34. Shoemaker and Vos, *Gatekeeping Theory,* 124.

35. Robert D. Putnam, *Bowling Alone* (New York: Simon & Schuster, 2000), 288–89.

Chapter 4: Losing

1. Robert G. Kaiser and Ira Chinoy, "Scaife: Founding Father of the Right," *Washington Post,* May 2, 1999, A1.

2. David Conti, "Trib Circulation Pulls Away from Post-Gazette's," TribLive, *Pittsburgh Tribune-Review,* May 17, 2014, https://archive.triblive.com/local/pittsburgh-allegheny trib-circulation -pulls-away-from-post-gazettes/.

3. Walter S. Abbott and William E. Harrison, *The First One Hundred Years of McKeesport* (McKeesport, PA: Press of McKeesport Times, 1894).

4. Jason Togyer, "George Washington Slept Here—No, Really," Tube City Almanac, last updated 2010, http://www.tubecityonline.com/history/.

5. Togyer, "George Washington."

6. "National Tube Works Historical Marker," Explore PA History, last updated 2019, https://explorepahistory.com/hmarker.php?markerId=1-A-252.

7. Western Pennsylvania Brownfields Center, "McKeesport (US Steel National Tube Works)," case study, Summer 2007, https://www.cmu.edu/steinbrenner/brownfields/Case%20Studies/pdf/mckeesport.pdf.

8. Jonathan Silver, "Main Street McKeesport: A Painful Decline," *Pittsburgh Post-Gazette,* June 15, 1999, http://old.post-gazette.com/regionstate/19990615mmckeesport3.asp; Jason Togyer, "City Coming to Grips with Blight, Vacancies in Downtown Area," Tube City Almanac, October 1, 2019, http://almanac.tubecityonline.com/almanac/?e=1597.

9. Togyer, "City Coming to Grips."

10. Steven R. Lease, *McKeesport and Glassport: The Changes through the Years—an Ethnographic Research Project for the Steel Industry Heritage Corporation* (Homestead, PA: Steel Industry Heritage Corporation, n.d.), 13, https://riversofsteel.com/_uploads/files/mckeesport-and-glassport-final-report.pdf.

11. Togyer, "City Coming to Grips."

12. US Census Bureau, 2017, https://data.census.gov.

13. "Primary and General Election Results," Allegheny County Election Resources, last updated 2021, https://www.alleghenycounty.us/elections/election-results.aspx.

14. "Trib Total Media Journalists Nab 15 Golden Quills," TribLive, *Pittsburgh Tribune-Review,* May 23, 2014, https://archive.triblive.com/local/pittsburgh-allegheny/trib-total-media-journalists-nab-15-golden-quills/.

15. "Trib Takes High Honors in Keystone Awards," TribLive, *Pittsburgh Tribune-Review,* March 29, 2014. https://archive.triblive.com/local/pittsburgh-allegheny/trib-takes-high-honors-in-keystone-awards/.

16. Karen Carlin, Press Club of Western Pennsylvania board member, email message to author, June 26, 2021.

17. The author conducted interviews and focus groups in 2020. For a detailed discussion of this process, please see the methodology section.

Chapter 5: Searching

1. Jim Iovino, "Rising from the Ashes in the Mon Valley," NewStart, West Virginia University, last updated November 11, 2019, https://newstart.wvu.edu/testimonials/mon-valley-independent.

2. Torsten Ove, "Former Charleroi Attorney Sentenced for Stealing More than $500K from Elderly Woman," *Pittsburgh Post-Gazette,* March 14, 2018, https://www.post-gazette.com/local/south/2018/03/14/attorney-Keith-Bassi-sentenced-stealing-elderly-woman-Nancy-Lutz/stories/201803140121.

Chapter 6: Sharing

1. "Former Steeler Sam Davis Found Dead after Reported Missing from McKeesport Nursing Home," *Pittsburgh Post-Gazette*, September 10, 2019, https://www.post-gazette.com/local/east/2019/09/10/Former-Steelers-lineman-Sam-Davis-missing-from-McKeesport-nursing-home/stories/201909100152.

2. "Carnegie Library of McKeesport's History," Carnegie Library of McKeesport, 2000, https://mckeesportlibrary.org/about-us/.

Chapter 7: Discovering

1. "Top 100 Most Dangerous Cities in America," Alarms.org, last updated January 14, 2020, https://www.alarms.org/top-100-most-dangerous-cities-in-america/.

Chapter 8: When a Newspaper Dies

1. Kathleen McCollough, Jessica K. Crowell, and Philip M. Napoli, "Portrait of the Online Local News Audience," *Digital Journalism* 5, no. 1 (March 11, 2016): 111.

2. Penelope Muse Abernathy, *The Expanding News Desert* (Chapel Hill: Center for Innovation and Sustainability in Local Media, University of North Carolina at Chapel Hill, 2018), https://www.usnewsdeserts.com/reports/expanding-news-desert/.

3. McCollough, Crowell, and Napoli, "Portrait of the Online," 113.

4. Paulo Freire, *Pedagogy of the Oppressed*, 30th anniversary ed. (New York: Continuum, 2010), 96.

5. Peter Block, *Community* (Oakland, CA: Berrett-Koehler, 2009), 46.

6. Block, *Community*, 48.

7. Block, *Community*, 54.

8. Timothy Snyder, *On Tyranny: Twenty Lessons from the Twentieth Century* (New York: Tim Duggan Books, 2017), 79.

9. Abernathy, *Expanding News Desert*; "The layoff tracker," *Columbia Journalism Review*, December 17, 2019, https://www.cjr.org/analysis/journalism-layoff-tracker.php; Jonathan O'Connell, "Ghost Papers and News Deserts: Will America Ever Get Its Local News Back?," *Washington Post*, December 26, 2019, https://www.washingtonpost.com/business/economy/ghost-papers-and-news-deserts-will-america-ever-get-its-local-news-back/2019/12/25/2f57c7d4-1ddd-11ea-9ddd-3e0321c180e7_story.html; Sara Fischer, "More than Half of Media Jobs Lost This Year Are in News," Axios, December 8, 2020, https://www.axios.com/media-unemployment-job-loss-44acca2d-a339-463f-924d-c7963f5d5601.html.

10. Fischer, "More than Half"; Elizabeth Grieco (Pew Research Center), "U.S. Newspapers Have Shed Half of Their Newsroom Employees since 2008," *Editor & Publisher*, April 20, 2020, https://www.editorandpublisher.com/stories/us-newspapers-have-shed-half-of-their-newsroom-employees-since-2008,960?; Matthew Ingram, "Coronavirus Continues to Take Its Toll on the Media Industry," *Columbia Journalism Review*, April 20, 2020, https://www.cjr.org/the_media_today/coronavirus-toll-media.php.

11. Ingram, "Coronavirus Continues to Take," para. 1.

12. Lara Takenaga, "More than 1 in 5 U.S. Papers Has Closed. This Is the Result," *New York Times*, December 21, 2019, https://www.nytimes.com/2019/12/21/reader-center/local-news-deserts.html.

13. Joshua Benton, "When Local Newspapers Shrink, Fewer People Bother to Run for Mayor," NiemanLab, April 9, 2019, https://www.niemanlab.org/2019/04/when-local-newspapers-shrink-fewer-people-bother-to-run-for-mayor/.

14. Clara Hendrickson, "Local Journalism in Crisis: Why America Must Revive Its Local Newsrooms," Brookings, November 12, 2019, https://www.brookings.edu/research/local-journalism-in-crisis-why-america-must-revive-its-local-newsrooms/.

15. Lewis Friedland et al., *Review of the Literature Regarding Critical Information Needs of the American Public* (Washington, D.C.: Federal Communications Commission, July 16, 2012), ii.

16. Lewis A. Friedland, in discussion with the author, July 19, 2021.

17. Friedland et al., *Review of the Literature*, ii.

18. Friedland et al., *Review of the Literature*, 90.

19. Friedland et al., *Review of the Literature*, iii.

20. Friedland et al., *Review of the Literature*, 6–40.

21. Austin Davis, "Austin Davis: A Plan to Protect Pennsylvania's Air and Its Communities," *Pittsburgh Post-Gazette*, August 20, 2019, https://www.post-gazette.com/opinion/Op-Ed/2019/08/20/Austin-Davis-Pennsylvania-air-quality-clean-Clairton-Coke-Works-fire-public-health-safety/stories/201908200020.

22. Jeff Stitt, "Lawmakers' Air Quality Hearing Draws Huge Crowd," *Mon Valley Independent*, February 8, 2019, https://monvalleyindependent.com/2019/02/lawmakers-air-quality-hearing-draws-huge-crowd/.

23. "The Coming Chemical Boom," *Allegheny Front*, August 6, 2021, https://www.allegheny-front.org/chemicalboom/.

24. Kristie Linden, "Judge: Sunshine Act Was Violated," *Mon Valley Independent*, December 17, 2020, https://monvalleyindependent.com/2020/12/judge-sunshine-act-was-violated/.

25. Lewis A. Friedland, in discussion with the author, July 19, 2021.

Chapter 9: A Prayer for the Living

1. Jason Togyer, "Year of Fear, Chapter 15: In Towns like McKeesport, the Future Was Already Precarious. Then Came Coronavirus," *Columbia Journalism Review*, May 22, 2020, https://www.cjr.org/special_report/year-of-fear-mckeesport-crime-covid-19.php.

2. Togyer, "Year of Fear," para. 14.

3. The McKeesport Community Newsroom exists as a program of the Center for Media Innovation at Point Park University, which the author directs.

4. Ed Boyko, "Growing Old with the McKeesport Daily News," in *Tube City Tales*, ed. Martha Rial (McKeesport, PA: McKeesport Community Newsroom, 2020), 12–13. See also https://www.mckeesportcommunitynewsroom.com/blog.

5. Pamela Shoemaker and Timothy Vos, *Gatekeeping Theory* (New York: Routledge, 2009).

6. Kurt Lewin, "Frontiers in Group Dynamics II: Channels of Group Life; Social Planning and Action Research," *Human Relations* 1, no. 1 (1947): 143–53, https://journals.sagepub.com/doi/pdf/10.1177/001872674700100201.

7. Vatican News, "About Us," accessed December 1, 2021, https://www.vaticannews.va/en/about-us.html.

8. Shoemaker and Vos, *Gatekeeping Theory*.

9. John P. Kretzmann and John L. McKnight, *Building Communities from the Inside Out: A Path toward Finding and Mobilizing a Community's Assets* (Chicago, IL: ACTA Publications, 1993).

10. Kretzmann and McKnight, *Building Communities*, 4.

11. Robert J. Sampson, *Great American City: Chicago and the Enduring Neighborhood Effect* (Chicago: University of Chicago Press, 2012), 38.

12. Robert D. Putnam, *Bowling Alone* (New York: Simon & Schuster, 2000), 218.

13. Putnam, *Bowling Alone*, 136–37.

14. Alexis de Tocqueville, *Democracy in America: In Two Volumes*, trans. Henry Reeve (1835/1840; repr., Chapel Hill, NC: Project Gutenberg, 2006), chap. 6, para. 1.

15. Barthel et al., *Civic Engagement Strongly Tied to Local News Habits: Local Voters and Those Who Feel Attached to Their Communities Stand Out* (Washington, DC: Pew Research Center, 2016), http://www.journalism.org/2016/11/03/civic-engagement-strongly-tied-to-local-news-habits/.

16. Sandra J. Ball-Rokeach, Yong-Chan Kim, and Sorin Matei, "Storytelling Neighborhood: Paths to Belonging in Diverse Urban Environments," *Communication Research* 28, no. 4 (2001): 392–428.

17. Putnam, *Bowling Alone*, 410.

18. Matthew Nisbet et al., "Funding the News: Foundations and Nonprofit Media," Shorenstein Center on Media, Politics and Public Policy, June 18, 2018, https://shorensteincenter.org/funding-the-news-foundations-and-nonprofit-media/.

19. Kathleen McCollough, Jessica K. Crowell, and Philip M. Napoli, "Portrait of the Online Local News Audience," *Digital Journalism* 5, no. 1 (March 11, 2016): 100–18.

20. McCollough, Crowell, and Napoli, "Portrait of the Online News Audience."

21. McCollough, Crowell, and Napoli, "Portrait of the Online News Audience," 113.

22. Tom Fiedler, "Crisis Alert: Barack Obama Meets a Citizen Journalist," in *Citizen Journalism: Global Perspectives*, ed. Stuart Allan and Einar Thorsen (New York: Peter Lang, 2009), 215.

23. Melissa Wall, "The Taming of the Warblogs: Citizen Journalism and the War in Iraq," in Allan and Thorsen, 37.

24. Hat tip here to the author's friend and colleague Luis Fabregas, the executive editor of Trib Total Media.

25. "Newspapers Fact Sheet," Pew Research Center, June 29, 2021, https://www.pewresearch.org/journalism/fact-sheet/newspapers/.

26. Timothy Snyder, *On Tyranny: Twenty Lessons from the Twentieth Century* (New York: Tim Duggan Books, 2017).

BIBLIOGRAPHY

Abbott, Walter S., and William E. Harrison. *The First One Hundred Years of McKeesport.* McKeesport, PA: Press of McKeesport Times, 1894.

Abernathy, Penelope Muse. *The Expanding News Desert.* Chapel Hill: Center for Innovation and Sustainability in Local Media, University of North Carolina at Chapel Hill, 2018. https://www.usnewsdeserts.com/reports/expanding-news-desert/.

Abernathy, Penelope Muse. *News Deserts and Ghost Newspapers: Will Local News Survive?* Chapel Hill: Center for Innovation and Sustainability in Local Media, University of North Carolina at Chapel Hill, 2020. https://www.usnewsdeserts.com/reports/news-deserts-and-ghost-newspapers-will-local-news-survive/.

Abernathy, Penelope Muse. *The Rise of a New Media Baron and the Emerging Threat of News Deserts.* Chapel Hill: Center for Innovation and Sustainability in Local Media, University of North Carolina at Chapel Hill, 2016. https://www.usnewsdeserts.com/reports/rise-new-media-baron/new-media-baron.

Alarms.org. "Top 100 Most Dangerous Cities in America," January 14, 2020. https://www.alarms.org/top-100-most-dangerous-cities-in-america/.

Ali, Christopher, and Damian Radcliffe. "New Research: Small-Market Newspapers in the Digital Age." *Columbia Journalism Review,* November 15, 2017. https://www.cjr.org/tow_center_reports/local-small-market-newspapers-study.php.

Allan, S. "Histories of Citizen Journalism." In *Citizen Journalism: Global Perspectives,* edited by Stuart Allan and Einar Thorsen, 17–32. New York: Peter Lang, 2009.

Allan, Stuart, and Einar Thorsen, eds. *Citizen Journalism: Global Perspectives.* New York: Peter Lang, 2009.

Allegheny Front, The. "The Coming Chemical Boom." August 6, 2021. https://www.alleghenyfront.org/chemicalboom/.

Altschull, J. Herbert. "A Crisis of Conscience: Is Community Journalism the Answer?" *Journal of Mass Media Ethics* 11, no. 3 (1996): 166–72.

Anderson, C. W., Emily J. Bell, and Clay Shirky. *Post-industrial Journalism: Adapting to the Present.* New York: Columbia University Tow Center for Digital Journalism, 2014. https://academic-commons.columbia.edu/doi/10.7916/D8N01JS7.

Anderson, Rob, Robert Dardenne, and George Killenberg. *The Conversation of Journalism: Communication, Community, and News.* Westport, CT: Praeger, 1994.

Ann Arbor News, The. "AnnArbor.com Moving to MLive.com on Sept. 12." September 4, 2013. http://www.annarbor.com/news/annarborcom-moving-to-mlivecom-on-sept-12/.

Atton, Chris. (2013). "Separate, Supplementary or Seamless?: Alternative News and Professional Journalism." In *Rethinking Journalism: Trust and Participation in a Transformed News Landscape,* edited by Chris Peters and Marcel Broersma, 131–43. New York: Routledge, 2013.

Aupperlee, Aaron. "Tribune-Review Adapts to Changing Newspaper Industry." TribLive, *Pitts-*

burgh Tribune-Review, November 29, 2016. http://triblive.com/local/allegheny/11475091–74/
digital-bertetto-trib.

Backlund, Harry. "Is Your Journalism a Luxury or a Necessity?" City Bureau, July 18, 2019. https://
www.citybureau.org/notebook/2019/7/17/journalism-is-a-luxury-information-is-a-necessity.

Ball-Rokeach, Sandra J., Yong-Chan Kim, and Sorin Matei. "Storytelling Neighborhood: Paths to
Belonging in Diverse Urban Environments." *Communication Research* 28, no. 4 (2001): 392–428.

Barnhurst, Kevin G. "'Trust Me, I'm an Innovative Journalist,' and Other Fictions." In *Rethinking
Journalism: Trust and Participation in a Transformed News Landscape,* edited by Chris Peters
and Marcel Broersma, 210–20. New York: Routledge, 2013.

Barthel, Michael, Jesse Holcomb, Jessica Mahone, and Amy Mitchell. *Civic Engagement Strongly
Tied to Local News Habits: Local Voters and Those Who Feel Attached to Their Communities
Stand Out.* Washington, DC: Pew Research Center, 2016. http://www.journalism.
org/2016/11/03/civic-engagement-strongly-tied-to-local-news-habits/.

Barzilai-Nahon, Karine. "Toward a Theory of Network Gatekeeping: A Framework For Exploring
Information Control." *Journal of the American Society for Information Science and Technology*
59, no. 9 (May 13, 2008): 1493–1512. http://citeseerx.ist.psu.edu/viewdoc/download;jsessionid
=FDCEA5742CC12B8CF95158105446EFFA?doi=10.1.1.476.8484&rep=rep1&type=pdf.

Bauder, David. "Loss of Newspapers Contributes to Political Polarization." AP News, January 30,
2019. https://apnews.com/ecf440606c824f9d9671f2fb22a2ffce.

Benton, Joshua. "When Local Newspapers Shrink, Fewer People Bother to Run
for Mayor." NiemanLab, April 9, 2019. https://www.niemanlab.org/2019/04/
when-local-newspapers-shrink-fewer-people-bother-to-run-for-mayor/.

Block, Peter. *Community.* Oakland, CA: Berrett-Koehler, 2009.

Bourdieu, Pierre. "The Forms of Capital." In *Handbook of Theory and Research for the Sociology of
Education,* edited by J. Richardson, 241–58. New York: Greenwood, 2009.

Boyko, Ed. "Growing Old with the McKeesport Daily News." In *Tube City Tales,* edited by Martha
Rial, 12–13. McKeesport, PA: McKeesport Community Newsroom, 2020.

Brants, Kees. "Trust, Cynicism, and Responsiveness: The Uneasy Situation of Journalism in Democracy." In *Rethinking Journalism: Trust and Participation in a Transformed News Landscape,*
edited by Chris Peters and Marcel Broersma, 15–27. New York: Routledge, 2013.

Broersma, Marcel, and Chris Peters. "Rethinking Journalism: The Structural Transformation
of a Public Good." In *Rethinking Journalism: Trust and Participation in a Transformed News
Landscape,* edited by Peters and Broersma, 1–12. New York: Routledge, 2013.

Brown, Juanita, and David Isaacs. *The World Café: Shaping Our Futures through Conversations That
Matter.* San Francisco: Berrett-Koehler, 2005.

Bruns, Axel. "News Produsage in a Pro-Am Mediasphere: Why Citizen Journalism Matters." In
News Online: Transformations and Continuities, edited by Graham Meikle and Guy Redden,
132–47. London: Palgrave Macmillan, 2011.

Bruns, Axel, and Timothy Highfield. "Blogs, Twitter, and Breaking News: The Produsage of
Citizen Journalism." In *Produsing Theory in a Digital World: The Intersection of Audiences and
Production in Contemporary Theory,* edited by R. A. Lind, 15–32. New York: Peter Lang, 2012.

Bucay, Yemile, Vittoria Elliott, Jennie Kamin, and Andrea Park. "America's Growing News Deserts." *Columbia Journalism Review,* Spring 2017. https://www.cjr.org/local_news/
american-news-deserts-donuts-local.php.

Buni, Andrew. *Robert L. Vann of the* Pittsburgh Courier: *Politics and Black Journalism.* Pittsburgh,
PA: University of Pittsburgh Press, 1974.

Center for Innovation and Sustainability in Local Media. *Thwarting the Emergence of News Deserts*. Chapel Hill: Center for Innovation and Sustainability in Local Media, University of North Carolina at Chapel Hill, March 2017. http://newspaperownership.com/wp-content/uploads/2017/03/Symposium-Leave-Behind-Web-Final.pdf.

Chittum, Ryan. "Advance Publications Scraps *AnnArbor.com*." *Columbia Journalism Review*, September 9, 2013. https://archives.cjr.org/the_audit/advance_publications_scraps_an.php.

CNN Wire. "The Growing Problem of 'News Deserts' In Local Communities." Fox4, November 4, 2018.https://fox4kc.com/2018/11/04/the-growing-problem-of-news-deserts-in-local-communities/.

Coleman, James S. "Social Capital in the Creation of Human Capital." *American Journal of Sociology* 94 (1988): 95–120.

Columbia Journalism Review. "The Layoff Tracker." December 17, 2019. https://www.cjr.org/analysis/journalism-layoff-tracker.php.

Conte, Andrew. *The Color of Sundays*. Indianapolis: Blue River Press, 2015.

Conte, Andrew. "On Media: Local Journalism Must Be of the People, and Not Just for the People." NEXTpittsburgh, March 16, 2021. https://nextpittsburgh.com/features/on-media-local-journalism-must-be-of-the-people-and-not-just-for-the-people/.

Conti, David. "Trib Circulation Pulls Away from Post-Gazette's." TribLive, *Pittsburgh Tribune-Review*, May 17, 2014. https://archive.triblive.com/local/pittsburgh-allegheny/trib-circulation-pulls-away-from-post-gazettes/.

Creech, B., and A. L. Mendelson. "Imagining the Journalist of the Future: Technological Visions of Journalism Education and Newswork." *Communication Review* 18, no. 2 (2015): 142–65. https://doi.org/10.1080/10714421.2015.1031998.

Daily News, The (McKeesport, PA). "Congressmen Debate Merits of House-Passed Labor Bill; Nixon Sees Rights Protected, Kennedy Fears Civil Strife." April 22, 1947.

Daily News, The (McKeesport, PA). "Nixon, Kennedy Debated Labor Bill Here in '47." July 21, 1960.

Davis, Austin. "Austin Davis: A Plan to Protect Pennsylvania's Air and Its Communities." *Pittsburgh Post-Gazette*, August 20, 2019. https://www.post-gazette.com/opinion/Op-Ed/2019/08/20/Austin-Davis-Pennsylvania-air-quality-clean-Clairton-Coke-Works-fire-public-health-safety/stories/201908200020.

Deuze, Mark, and Tamara Witschge. "Beyond Journalism: Theorizing the Transformation of Journalism." *Journalism* 19, no. 2 (2018): 165–81. https://doi.org/10.1177/1464884916688550.

Doctor, Ken. *Newsonomics: Twelve New Trends That Will Shape the News You Get*. New York: St. Martin's Press, 2010.

Dulac, Donald T. "40 Years Ago: Nixon, Kennedy Debated in City." *Daily News* (McKeesport, PA), April 17, 1987.

Facebook. "We're Launching New Engagement Features, Ways to Discover Groups and More Tools for Admins." October 1, 2020. https://www.facebook.com/community/whats-new/facebook-communities-summit-keynote-recap/.

Ferrier, Michelle. *The Media Deserts Project: Monitoring Community News and Information Needs Using Geographic Information System Technologies*. Scripps College, February 2014. Academia, https://www.academia.edu/11469030/The_Media_Deserts_Project_Monitoring_Community_News_and_Information_Needs_Using_Geographic_Information_System_Technologies.

Ferrier, Michelle, Guarav Sinha, and Michael Outrich. "Media Deserts: Monitoring the Changing Media Ecosystem." In *The Communication Crisis in America, and How to Fix It*, edited by Mark Lloyd and Lewis A. Friedland, 215–32. New York: Palgrave, 2016. https://doi.org/10.1057/978-1-349-94925-0.

Fiedler, Tom. "Crisis Alert: Barack Obama Meets a Citizen Journalist." In *Citizen Journalism:*

Global Perspectives, edited by Stuart Allan and Einar Thorsen, 209–20. New York: Peter Lang, 2009.

Fischer, Sara. "More than Half of Media Jobs Lost This Year Are in News." Axios, December 8, 2020. https://www.axios.com/media-unemployment-job-loss-44acca2d-a339-463f-924d-c79 63f5d5601.html.

"Former Steeler Sam Davis Found Dead after Reported Missing from McKeesport Nursing Home." *Pittsburgh Post-Gazette*, September 10, 2019. https://www.post-gazette.com/local/east/2019/09/10/ Former-Steelers-lineman-Sam-Davis-missing-from-McKeesport-nursing-home/stories/201909100152.

Franklin, Steve. "The News Desert We Live In. Please Come and Visit." Chicago Is the World, April 14, 2011. http://chicagoistheworld.org/2011/04/ the-news-desert-we-live-in-please-come-and-visit/.

Frazier, Carol Waterloo, and Jeffrey Sisk. "Daily News Thanks Mon Valley, Publishes Final Edition after 131 years." *Pittsburgh Tribune-Review*, December 31, 2015.

Freire, Paulo. *Pedagogy of the Oppressed*. 30th anniversary ed. New York: Continuum, 2010.

Friedland, Lewis, Philip Napoli, Katherine Ognyanova, Carola Weil, and Ernest J. Wilson III. *Review of the Literature Regarding Critical Information Needs of the American Public*. Washington, DC: Federal Communications Commission, July 16, 2012. https://transition.fcc.gov/ bureaus/ocbo/Final_Literature_Review.pdf.

Friedman, Thomas L. *Thank You for Being Late: An Optimist's Guide to Thriving in the Age of Accelerations*. New York: Picador, 2016.

Gahran, Amy. "HuffPost Publishes Citizen Journalism Standards." Poynter, April 9, 2009. https:// www.poynter.org/news/huffpost-publishes-citizen-journalism-standards.

Gallup. *Indicators of News Media Trust: A Gallup/Knight Foundation Survey*. Knight Foundation, 2018. https://kf-site-production.s3.amazonaws.com/media_elements/files/000/000/216/ original/KnightFoundation_Panel4_Trust_Indicators_FINAL.pdf.

Gaventa, John. *Power and Powerlessness: Quiescence and Rebellion in an Appalachian Valley*. Urbana: University of Illinois Press, 1980.

Gitlin, Todd. *The Whole World Is Watching: Media in the Making and Unmaking of the New Left*. Berkeley: University of California Press, 1980.

Goldman, E. F. "The 1947 Kennedy-Nixon 'Tube City' Debate: A Little-Remembered Duel between the Two Fledgling Congressmen at McKeesport, PA." *Saturday Review*, October 16, 1976, 12–13.

Gordon, Rich, and Zachary Johnson. "Linking Audiences to News: A Network Analysis of Chicago Websites." Chicago Community Trust, April 1, 2011. https://www.issuelab.org/resource/ linking-audiences-to-news-a-network-analysis-of-chicago-websites.html.

Graham, Todd. "Talking Back, but Is Anyone Listening? Journalism and Comment Fields." In *Rethinking Journalism: Trust and Participation in a Transformed News Landscape*, edited by Chris Peters and Marcel Broersma, 114–27. New York: Routledge, 2013.

Green, Gary Paul, and Anna Haines. *Asset Building & Community Development*. Thousand Oaks, CA: Sage, 2012.

Grieco, Elizabeth. "U.S. Newspapers Have Shed Half of Their Newsroom Employees since 2008." *Editor & Publisher*, April 20, 2020. https://www.editorandpublisher.com/stories/ us-newspapers-have-shed-half-of-their-newsroom-employees-since-2008,960?.

Griffin, Emory A. *A First Look at Communication Theory*. 7th ed. Boston: McGraw-Hill, 2008.

Grubisich, Tom. "Despite Many New Local News Sites, 'Media Deserts' Are a Stubborn Reality." StreetFight, June 26, 2014. http://streetfightmag.com/2014/06/26/ despite-many-local-news-sites-media-deserts-are-a-stubborn-reality/.

Hanifan, L. J. "The Rural School Community Center." *Annals of the American Academy of Political and Social Science* 67 (September 1916): 130–38.

Hanitzsch, Thomas. "Journalism, Participative Media and Trust in a Comparative Context." In *Rethinking Journalism: Trust and Participation in a Transformed News Landscape*, edited by Chris Peters and Marcel Broersma, 200–209. New York: Routledge, 2013.

Harris, C., photographer. "President Kennedy Campaigns for Pennsylvania Democrats in McKeesport, October 13, 1962." Pittsburgh, PA: Carnegie Museum of Art, October 13, 1962.

Hassan, Zaid. *The Social Labs Revolution: A New Approach to Solving Our Most Complex Challenges.* San Francisco: Berrett-Koehler, 2014.

Hendrickson, Clara. "Local Journalism in Crisis: Why America Must Revive Its Local Newsrooms." Brookings, November 12, 2019. https://www.brookings.edu/research/local-journalism-in-crisis -why-america-must-revive-its-local-newsrooms/.

Hoerr, John. *And the Wolf Finally Came: The Decline and Fall of the American Steel Industry.* Pittsburgh, PA: University of Pittsburgh Press, 2014.

Hoskins, Andrew, and Ben O'Loughlin. "Remediating Jihad for Western News Audiences: The Renewal of Gatekeeping?" Open University, 2010. http://www.open.ac.uk/researchprojects/ diasporas/sites/www.open.ac.uk.researchprojects.diasporas/files/diasporas_working-paper-21.pdf.

HuffPost. "Citizen Journalism Publishing Standards." Last updated May 25, 2011. https://www .huffingtonpost.com/2009/04/14/citizen-journalism-publis_n_186963.html.

Ingram, Matthew. "Coronavirus Continues to Take Its Toll on the Media Industry." *Columbia Journalism Review*, April 20, 2020. https://www.cjr.org/the_media_today/coronavirus-toll -media.php.

Innis, Harold. *The Bias of Communication.* 1951. Reprint, Toronto, Canada: University of Toronto Press, 1982.

Iovino, Jim. "Rising from the Ashes in the Mon Valley." Mon Valley Independent, NewStart, West Virginia University. Last updated November 11, 2019. https://newstart.wvu.edu/testimonials/ mon-valley-independent.

Johnson, J. B. "City's 'Great Debate': Nixon-Kennedy in '47." *Daily News* (McKeesport, PA), April 21, 1977, 1.

Kaiser, Robert G., and Ira Chinoy. "Scaife: Founding Father of the Right." *Washington Post*, May 2, 1999.

Kaufhold, Kelly, Sebastian Valenzuela, and Homero Gil De Zúñiga. "Citizen Journalism and Democracy: How User-Generated News Use Relates to Political Knowledge and Participation." *Journalism & Mass Communication Quarterly* 87, no. 3–4 (2010): 515–29. https://doi. org/10.1177/107769901008700305.

Keen, Andrew. *The Cult of the Amateur.* New York: Doubleday/Currency, 2007.

Kellerhals, Blair. "Breaking Down the Gates with Participatory Journalism: Leveraging User-Generated Content for Today's Journalistic Practices." Master's thesis, Colorado State University, 2018. ProQuest, https://search.proquest.com/docview/2116576491.

Kennedy, John F. "Remarks at City Hall, McKeesport, Pennsylvania." John F. Kennedy Presidential Library and Museum, October 13, 1962. https://www.jfklibrary.org/asset-viewer/archives/ JFKPOF/041/JFKPOF-041-001.

Kretzmann, John P., and John L. McKnight. *Building Communities from the Inside Out: A Path toward Finding and Mobilizing a Community's Assets.* Chicago, IL: ACTA Publications, 1993.

Lasica, J. D. "Blogs and Journalism Need Each Other." *Nieman Reports* 57, no. 3 (Fall 2003), https:// niemanreports.org/articles/blogs-and-journalism-need-each-other/.

Lauterer, Jock. *Community Journalism: The Personal Approach*. Ames: Iowa State University Press, 1995.

Lease, Steven R. *McKeesport and Glassport: The Changes through the Years—an Ethnographic Research Project for the Steel Industry Heritage Corporation*. Homestead, PA: Steel Industry Heritage Corporation, n.d. https://riversofsteel.com/_uploads/files/mckeesport-and-glassport-final-report.pdf.

Lewin, Kurt. "Frontiers in Group Dynamics II: Channels of Group Life; Social Planning and Action Research," *Human Relations* 1, no. 1 (1947): 143–53. https://journals.sagepub.com/doi/pdf/10.1177/001872674700100201.

Lewis, Seth C., Kelly Kaufhold, and Dominic L. Lasorsa. "Thinking about Citizen Journalism." *Journalism Practice* 4, no. 2 (2010): 163–79. https://doi.org/10.1080/14616700903156919.

Linden, Kristie. "Judge: Sunshine Act Was Violated." *Mon Valley Independent*, December 17, 2020. https://monvalleyindependent.com/2020/12/judge-sunshine-act-was-violated/.

Lippman, Walter. *Public Opinion*. 17th printing. New York: MacMillan, 1961.

Luengo, Maria. "Constructing the Crisis of Journalism." *Journalism Studies* 15, no. 5 (2014): 576–85. https://doi.org/10.1080/1461670X.2014.891858.

Maestas, Amy. "Ann Arbor: Citizenship and the Local Newspaper." In *Thwarting the Emergence of News Deserts*, 38–42. Chapel Hill: Center for Innovation and Sustainability in Local Media, University of North Carolina at Chapel Hill, 2017. http://newspaperownership.com/wp-content/uploads/2017/03/Symposium-Leave-Behind-Web-Final.pdf.

Maslow, Abraham H. "A Theory of Human Motivation." *Psychological Review* 50, no. 4 (1943): 370–96. https://doi.org/10.1037/h0054346.

Mathie, Alison, Jenny Cameron, and Katherine Gibson. "Asset-Based and Citizen-Led Development: Using a Diffracted Power Lens to Analyze the Possibilities and Challenges." *Progress in Development Studies* 17, no. 1 (2017): 54–66.

McChesney, Robert W., and Ben Scott. Introduction to *The Brass Check: A Study of American Journalism*, by Upton Sinclair, ix–xxxiii. Reprint, Urbana: University of Illinois Press, 2003.

McCollough, Kathleen, Jessica K. Crowell, and Philip M. Napoli. "Portrait of the Online Local News Audience." *Digital Journalism* 5, no. 1 (March 11, 2016): 100–18.

McLuhan, Marshall. *Understanding Media: The Extensions of Man*. 1964. Reprint, Cambridge, MA: MIT Press, 1996.

McLuhan, Marshall, and Quentin Fiore. *The Medium Is the Message: An Inventory of Effects*. Corte Madera, CA: Gingko Press, 1967.

McNair, Brian. "Trust, Truth and Objectivity: Sustaining Quality Journalism in the Era of the Content-Generating User." In *Rethinking Journalism: Trust and Participation in a Transformed News Landscape*, edited by Chris Peters and Marcel Broersma, 75–88. New York: Routledge, 2013.

Metzger, Richard. "When John Lennon & Yoko Ono Met Marshall McLuhan, December 1969." *McLuhan Galaxy* (blog), September 25, 2017. https://mcluhangalaxy.wordpress.com/2017/09/25/when-john-lennon-yoko-ono-met-marshall-mcluhan-1969/.

Moellinger, Terry. "To Think Different: The Unexpected Consequences of Personal Computer and Internet Use." PhD diss., University of Oklahoma, 2010. ProQuest.

Muder, Doug. "Expand Your Vocabulary: News Desert." *The Weekly Sift* (blog), December 5, 2011. https://weeklysift.com/2011/12/05/expand-your-vocabulary-news-desert/.

Mumford, Lewis. *Technics and Civilization*. New York: Harcourt Brace & Company, 1934.

Murray, Stefanie. "AnnArbor.com's Offices Will Be in Heart of Downtown Ann Arbor." *Ann Arbor News*, June 3, 2009. Accessed via the Internet Archive WayBack Machine, http://web.archive.org/web/20090606090454/http://annarbor.com/2009/06/annarborcoms-offices-will-be-in-heart-of-downtown-ann-arbor.html.

Nicolas, Alexandra. "How Journalists Can Use Location-Based Apps as a Reporting Tool." Poynter, March 21, 2013. https://www.poynter.org/news/how-journalists-can-use-location-based-apps-reporting-tool.

Nisbet, Matthew, John Wihbey, Silje Kristiansen, and Aleszu Bajak. "Funding the News: Foundations and Nonprofit Media." Shorenstein Center on Media, Politics and Public Policy, June 18, 2018. https://shorensteincenter.org/funding-the-news-foundations-and-nonprofit-media/.

Norden, Eric. "Playboy Interview: Marshall McLuhan." *Playboy Magazine*, March 1969.

O'Connell, Jonathan. "Ghost Papers and News Deserts: Will America Ever Get Its Local News Back?" *Washington Post*, December 26, 2019. https://www.washingtonpost.com/business/economy/ghost-papers-and-news-deserts-will-america-ever-get-its-local-news-back/2019/12/25/2f57c7d4-1ddd-11ea-9ddd-3e0321c180e7_story.html.

Örnebring, Henrik. "Anything You Can Do, I Can Do Better? Professional Journalists on Citizen Journalism in Six European Countries." *International Communication Gazette* 75, no. 1 (February 2013): 35–53. https://doi.org/10.1177/1748048512461761.

Ove, Torsten. "Former Charleroi Attorney Sentenced for Stealing More than $500K from Elderly Woman." *Pittsburgh Post-Gazette*, March 14, 2018. https://www.post-gazette.com/local/south/2018/03/14/attorney-Keith-Bassi-sentenced-stealing-elderly-woman-Nancy-Lutz/stories/201803140121.

Paglia, Ron. "After 113 Years, the Valley Independent Prints Final Edition." TribLive, *Pittsburgh Tribune-Review*, December 31, 2015. https://archive.triblive.com/news/after-113-years-the-valley-independent-prints-final-edition/.

Parkinson, Hannah Jane. "Click and Elect: How Fake News Helped Donald Trump Win a Real Election." *Guardian*, November 14, 2016. https://www.theguardian.com/commentisfree/2016/nov/14/fake-news-donald-trump-election-alt-right-social-media-tech-companies.

Pew Research Center. "Newspapers Fact Sheet." Research Topics. June 29, 2021. https://www.pewresearch.org/journalism/fact-sheet/newspapers/.

Pew Research Center. "State of the News Media (Project)." News Media Trends. August 25, 2021. http://www.pewresearch.org/topics/state-of-the-news-media/.

Picard, Robert G. "Twilight or New Dawn of Journalism?" *Journalism Studies* 15, no. 5 (2014): 500–510. https://doi.org/10.1080/1461670X.2014.895530.

Polgreen, Lydia. "Introducing HuffPost Opinion and HuffPost Personal." HuffPost, January 18, 2018. https://www.huffpost.com/entry/huffpost-opinion-huffpost-personal_n_5a5f6a29e4b096ecfca98edb.

Postman, Neil. *Technopoly: The Surrender of Culture to Technology*. New York: Alfred A. Knopf, 1992.

Putnam, Robert D. *Bowling Alone*. New York: Simon & Schuster, 2000.

Rafsky, Sara. "Does the Media Capital of the World Have News Deserts?" *Columbia Journalism Review*, January 7, 2020. https://www.cjr.org/tow_center/new-york-city-local-news.php?ct=t.

Reisdorf, Bianca C., Laleah Fernandez, Keith N. Hampton, Inyoung Shin, and William H. Dutton. "Mobile Phones Will Not Eliminate Digital and Social Divides: How Variation in Internet Activities Mediates the Relationship between Type of Internet Access and Local Social Capital in Detroit." *Social Science Computer Review*, March 16, 2020. https://doi.org/10.1177/0894439320909446.

Roberts, Chris. "Gatekeeping Theory: An Evolution." Paper presented at the Association for Education in Journalism and Mass Communication, San Antonio, Texas, August 2005. http://www.chrisrob.com/about/gatekeeping.pdf.

Rosen, Jay. "A Most Useful Definition of Citizen Journalism." PressThink, July 14, 2008. http://
     archive.pressthink.org/2008/07/14/a_most_useful_d.html.

Rubado, Meghan E., and Jay T. Jennings. "Political Consequences of the Endangered Local Watch-
     dog: Newspaper Decline and Mayoral Elections in the United States." *Urban Affairs Review* 56,
     no. 5 (April 2019): 1327–56. https://doi.org/10.1177/1078087419838058.

Sampson, Robert J. *Great American City: Chicago and the Enduring Neighborhood Effect.* Chicago:
     University of Chicago Press, 2012.

Schieffer, Alexander, David Isaacs, and Bo Gyllenpalm. "The World Café: Part One." *World Busi-
     ness Academy* 18, no. 8 (July 2004): 1–9.

Sciullo, Maria. "It's the End of an Era for the McKeesport Daily News." *Pittsburgh
     Post-Gazette,* December 31, 2015. http://www.post-gazette.com/business/2015/12/31/
     It-s-the-end-of-an-era-for-the-McKeesport-Daily-News/stories/201512310188.

Serrin, William. *Homestead: The Glory and Tragedy of an American Steel Town.* New York: Crown, 1992.

Shaker, Lee. "Dead Newspapers and Citizens' Civic Engagement." *Political Communication* 31, no. 1
     (January 2014): 131–48. https://doi.org/10.1080/10584609.2012.762817.

Shedden, David. "Today in Media History: Mr. Dooley: 'The Job of the
     Newspaper Is to Comfort the Afflicted and Afflict the Comfort-
     able.'" Poynter, October 7, 2014. https://www.poynter.org/news/
     today-media-history-mr-dooley-job-newspaper-comfort-afflicted-and-afflict-comfortable.

Shoemaker, Pamela. *Gatekeeping.* Newbury Park, CA: Sage, 1991.

Shoemaker, Pamela, and Timothy Vos. *Gatekeeping Theory.* New York: Routledge, 2009.

Silver, Jonathan. "Main Street McKeesport: A Painful Decline," *Pittsburgh Post-Gazette,* June 15,
     1999. http://old.post-gazette.com/regionstate/19990615mmckeesport3.asp.

Sinclair, Upton. *The Brass Check: A Study of American Journalism.* 1919. Reprint, Urbana: University
     of Illinois Press, 2003.

Singer, Jane B., and Ian Ashman. "User-Generated Content and Journalistic Values." In *Citizen
     Journalism: Global Perspectives,* edited by Stuart Allan and Einar Thorsen, 233–42. New York:
     Peter Lang, 2009.

Snyder, Timothy. *On Tyranny: Twenty Lessons from the Twentieth Century.* New York: Tim Duggan
     Books, 2017.

Society of Professional Journalists. "SPJ Code of Ethics." September 6, 2014. https://www.spj.org/
     ethicscode.asp.

Stites, Tom. "Layoffs and Cutbacks Lead to a New World of News Deserts." NiemanLab,
     December 8, 2011. http://www.niemanlab.org/2011/12/tom-stites-layoffs-and-cutbacks
     -lead-to-a-new-world-of-news-deserts/.

Stitt, Jeff. "Lawmakers' Air Quality Hearing Draws Huge Crowd." *Mon Valley Independent,*
     February 8, 2019. https://monvalleyindependent.com/2019/02/lawmakers-air-quality
     -hearing-draws-huge-crowd/.

Terry, Thomas C. "Community Journalism Provides Model for Future." *Newspaper Research
     Journal* 32, no. 1 (2011): 71–83. https://doi.org/10.1177/073953291103200107.

Tocqueville, Alexis de. *Democracy in America: In Two Volumes.* Translated by Henry Reeve.
     1835/1840. Reprint, Chapel Hill, NC: Project Gutenberg, 2006.

Togyer, Jason. "Year of Fear, Chapter 15: In Towns Like Mckeesport, the Future Was Already
     Precarious. Then Came Coronavirus." *Columbia Journalism Review,* May 22, 2020. https://
     www.cjr.org/special_report/year-of-fear-mckeesport-crime-covid-19.php.

Togyer, Jason. "Year of Fear, Chapter Three: Red Streets v. Blue Streets in McKeesport." *Columbia*

Journalism Review, February 27, 2020. https://www.cjr.org/special_report/year-of-fear-mck-eesport-pennsylvania.php.

Tribune-Review (Pittsburgh, PA). "Trib Takes High Honors in Keystone Awards." TribLive, March 29, 2014. https://archive.triblive.com/local/pittsburgh-allegheny/trib-takes-high-honors-in-keystone-awards/.

Tribune-Review (Pittsburgh, PA). "Trib Total Media Journalists Nab 15 Golden Quills." TribLive, May 23, 2014. https://archive.triblive.com/local/pittsburgh-allegheny/trib-total-media-journalists-nab-15-golden-quills/.

Tucker, Patrick. "Fighting the Cult of the Amateur." *Futurist* 42, no. 1 (2008): 33–34.

US Census Bureau. "QuickFacts: McKeesport City, Pennsylvania." Accessed November 29, 2021. https://www.census.gov/quickfacts/fact/table/mckeesportcitypennsylvania/COM100217.

US Census Bureau. "QuickFacts: United States." Accessed November 29, 2021. https://www.census.gov/quickfacts/fact/table/US/PST045219.

US Department of Agriculture, Economic Research Service. "Food Access Research Atlas." December 5, 2017. https://www.ers.usda.gov/data-products/food-access-research-atlas/documentation/.

Vitak, Jessica, Paul Zube, Andrew Smock, Caleb T. Carr, Nicole Ellison, and Cliff Lampe. "It's Complicated: Facebook Users' Political Participation in the 2008 Election." *Cyberpsychology, Behavior, and Social Networking* 14 (2011): 107–14.

Volkmer, Ingrid, and Amira Firdaus. "Between Networks and 'Hierarchies of Credibility': Navigating Journalistic Practice in a Sea of User-Generated Content." In *Rethinking Journalism: Trust and Participation in a Transformed News Landscape*, edited by Chris Peters and Marcel Broersma, 101–13. New York: Routledge, 2013.

Wall, Melissa. "The Taming of the Warblogs: Citizen Journalism and the War in Iraq." In *Citizen Journalism: Global Perspectives*, edited by Stuart Allan and Einar Thorsen, 33–42. New York: Peter Lang, 2009.

Warner, Dave. "Billionaire's Support for Pittsburgh Paper Is at Issue in Court Case." *Columbia Journalism Review*, December 17, 2014. https://archives.cjr.org/united_states_project/richard_mellon_scaife_tribune_review_trust.php.

Washington, Laura S. "The Paradox of Our Media Age—and What to Do About It." *In These Times*, April 5, 2011. http://inthesetimes.com/article/7151/the_paradox_of_our_media_ageand_what_to_do_about_it/.

Western Pennsylvania Brownfields Center. *McKeesport (U.S. Steel National Tube Works)*. Western Pennsylvania Brownfields Center, 2007. https://www.cmu.edu/steinbrenner/brownfields/Case%20Studies/pdf/mckeesport.pdf.

White, David Manning. "The 'Gatekeeper': A Case Study in the Selection of News." *Journalism Quarterly*, no. 27 (Fall 1950): 383–90.

White, E. "'Ann Arbor News' Prints Last Edition after 174 years." *Editor & Publisher*, July 23, 2009.

Witschge, Tamara. "Transforming Journalistic Practice: A Profession Caught between Change and Tradition." In *Rethinking Journalism: Trust and Participation in a Transformed News Landscape*, edited by Chris Peters and Marcel Broersma, 160–72. New York: Routledge, 2013.

Zadrozny, Brandy. "In a Pennsylvania Town, a Facebook Group Fills the Local News Void." NBC News, April 5, 2021. https://www.nbcnews.com/tech/social-media/pennsylvania-town-facebook-group-fills-local-news-void-rcna577.

INDEX

Praise for *The Joy of Strategy* and Allison Rimm

"Sixteen years of experience improving Massachusetts General Hospital convinced strategic planning and management coach Rimm that achieving personal happiness is not as difficult as it appears. We can give ourselves a kick-start on the path to personal and career satisfaction by designing a business plan for our lives—a process that includes setting core values, identifying goals, and coming up with a strategy for achieving those goals. In her first book, Rimm helps the reader break free from inertia by choosing a mission that encompasses his or her interests and talents, envisioning what success is going to look like, getting past roadblocks, analyzing strengths and weaknesses, and making the most of our most precious commodity: time. Suggestions are supported with accessible and inspiring exercises to help readers figure out what's truly important. While the subject matter is not new, the book makes change seem truly achievable. Readers who feel stuck in their lives will find Rimm's optimism infectious: 'Life is a wild, wondrous adventure and you never know what awaits you around the next bend...Stick to your plans as long as they continue to guide you toward the results you desire....Have a great trip and keep in touch.'" —*Publishers Weekly*

"This is a fantastic guide to living: well-conceived, beautifully written, filled with wonderful, real-life examples and inspiring messages. Rimm infuses the book with the credo for her own life—to laugh loudly, love deeply, and nourish all with food for thought. *The Joy of Strategy* is truly balm for the soul."
—Suzanne Bates, CEO of Bates Communications, Inc., best-selling author of *Speak Like a CEO: Secrets for Commanding Attention and Getting Results*

"One of academia's greatest challenges is mastering the essential art of mentoring. *The Joy of Strategy* not only provides the insight and tools to nurture the extraordinary talents of our young professionals; it demonstrates for mentors how best to mentor. This book should be required reading for organizations that want to reach their full potential."

—Gary Gottlieb, MD, MBA,
president and CEO, Partners HealthCare

"I've had the privilege of seeing Allison Rimm in action. She conveys the *why* for personal strategy development and then the *how* in a very understandable and effective manner. This book is a must-read for anyone who would like to help improve their individual effectiveness in both work and personal aspects of their life."

—James I. Cash, James E. Robison Professor of Business
Administration, Emeritus, Harvard Business School

"This is a wonderful and practical book based on the simple premise that work is only part of our life and that work and life should—make that must—be joyful. You'll find the book loaded with strategies on how to achieve this joy."

—Lawrence Fish, chairman of
Houghton Mifflin Harcourt Corporation

"Having a background in strategic planning, I approached the book with much skepticism, but I became engaged within the first few pages and ultimately became convinced of the importance of having a personal strategic plan. The author's stories and subtle humor bring to life her approach to strategy and make the book a joy to read. Her ideas are enlightening and well-grounded in practice. Her promise of being able 'to focus on what matters most and to spend your time and talent where it can make a meaningful difference' is a compelling reason to undertake a personal strategy development process. In fact, I began to put into practice some of the ideas as soon as I put the book down."

—Raymond V. Gilmartin, former chairman, president, and CEO
of Merck and adjunct professor at Harvard Business School

"Blending a delicious mixture of classic strategic planning techniques, time management tools, and unique life planning exercises, Allison Rimm's *The Joy of Strategy* offers a fresh and compelling method to help people facing a life transition, looking to achieve an ambitious goal, or just stuck in their careers. The special added ingredient comes from an emphasis on seizing joy and happiness along the way. Allison brings her ideas to life with compelling vignettes from her extensive practice, making *The Joy of Strategy* a very authentic and practical guide for a diverse audience. This book will change people's lives!"

—Celia R. Brown, EVP, group human
resources director, Willis Group, LTD

"Inspirational leaders know that their primary role is to create and sustain a healthy work environment. This timely book shows readers how to employ the business tools and life lessons Rimm provides to be the leaders of their own balanced and fulfilling lives. She has generously shared her experience, knowledge, and skill, including rich examples of the results people have achieved by putting her techniques into practice. Her work exemplifies leadership at its best. This helpful book provides a wealth of strategies that will help everyone from emerging leaders to seasoned veterans be more effective managing themselves and others."

—Jeanette Ives Erickson, DNP, RN, FAAN, SVP for Patient
Care and Chief Nurse at Massachusetts General Hospital
and co-author of *Fostering Nurse-Led Care: Professional
Practice for the Bedside Leader*

The
Joy
of
Strategy

The Joy of Strategy

of

A Business Plan for Life

Allison Rimm

bibliomotion
books + media

First published by Bibliomotion, Inc.
33 Manchester Road
Brookline, MA 02446
Tel: 617-934-2427
www.bibliomotion.com

Printed in the United States of America

Library of Congress Cataloging-in-Publication Data

Rimm, Allison.
    The joy of strategy : a business plan for life / Allison Rimm. — First Edition.
        pages cm
    Includes index.
    ISBN 978-1-937134-55-6 (hardcover : alk. paper) —
ISBN 978-1-937134-56-3 (ebook) — ISBN 978-1-937134-57-0 (enhanced ebook)
    1. Strategic planning.   2. Goal setting in personnel management.   3. Job satisfaction.   I. Title.
    HD30.28.R556 2013
    650.1—dc23
    2013016000

To my grandmother, Frances Hirshon, who taught me what unconditional love really means. And to my mother, Jocelyn Caplan, who personifies grace in adversity and proves that true wisdom doesn't come from a textbook, but from knowing what truly matters and giving it your all.

Contents

Foreword

By Nancy J. Tarbell, M.D.

I first met Allison Rimm when I arrived at Massachusetts General Hospital in 1997 as the new division chief of Pediatric Radiation Oncology and the founding director of the Office for Women's Careers. For many years, she had led hospital-wide strategic planning efforts, rallying hundreds of professionals in the bargain. Allison was also in charge of the Office of the President and served on the committee that created the new department I was hired to lead with the goal of promoting the careers of female faculty at the MGH. From the start, I relied on her expert advice, steadfast advocacy, and ability to get things done in that highly complex organization.

By the time I participated in Allison's groundbreaking course, *The Business of Life: Bringing Organization to Souls* in 2008, I was already a full professor at Harvard Medical School and the founding director of the newly created Office for Faculty Development. I had found my calling and was enjoying a hugely satisfying career treating kids with cancer, leading my division, and helping to develop the careers of the next generation of doctors and scientists.

But I was lucky. I'd never thought of being a doctor until my college friend saw something in me and encouraged me to pursue a career in medicine. It was a moment in a friendship that led me to join the long and hopeful battle to cure children with cancer.

Not everyone is so fortunate to have such an insightful—and forceful—friend. All around me, family, friends, and acquaintances, seemed to be juggling so many commitments that they were utterly exhausted, yet many of them expressed that they didn't feel like much of that activity really mattered much in the long run.

At work, several of my peers and much of the junior faculty were struggling with all manner of professional challenges while also trying to have a family and maintain some sense of sanity in the process. This was especially true for the women faculty who, despite the tentative progress we'd made in gender equality, were still primarily responsible for childcare and household administration in addition to their responsibilities at work. It was in my heart, and my job description, to help them reach their professional goals and find some semblance of work/life balance.

Allison's course not only offered us all a strategic framework to approach managing our careers and our lives, it gave us the time, space, and guidance to consider what was truly important to us and the tips, tools, and techniques necessary to make progress on the most essential initiatives. But she didn't stop there. She blended her skills as a strategist with soulful wisdom and gave us permission to think about what made us joyful at work and at home. Now, that was a first in the highly traditional world of academic medicine! But if you stop to really think about it, doctors—or anyone for that matter—who are happy at work and thriving in their careers will bring that sense of joy into the examining room when they see patients. They will bring it to their laboratories, administrative roles, and any other endeavors they pursue. And that positive attitude fuels their ability to be effective in their many roles.

But that doesn't just happen. Finding fulfillment and satisfaction requires that we have the tools and know-how needed to set priorities, manage our time, and cope with our own habits that stand in the way of us achieving our goals and enjoying the process. Over the years, Allison has shared the tricks of the trade that helped her rise to her senior leadership position in one of the world's most highly esteemed institutions with hundreds of faculty and staff at the MGH through her Business of Life courses. With her warm, candid, and compassionate approach to teaching solid self-management and project management skills, Allison created an environment where the people felt safe to express their deepest professional concerns and their career ambitions. And then they helped each other address their challenges by sharing their own stories with one another.

Perhaps the most profound shift in the classroom took place when these faculty-turned-students gave themselves the credit they deserved for achieving what they had accomplished already and cultivated some patience with themselves as they faced their next challenge. It was wonderful to witness the optimism—and relief—they experienced when they learned about the concrete steps they could take to achieve the results they desired. While I wish I had thought about some of these things earlier in my own career, I was glad to have had the opportunity to offer this experience to our faculty *and* be a participant.

In the *The Joy of Strategy*, Allison has recreated that space where her readers can learn her novel approach to thinking about their lives and careers strategically. This book is readable, entertaining, and provides practical, doable step-by-step guidance to make a business plan for your life. These principles come alive with the stories of people who have used these techniques to solve problems and make their dreams come true. All the while, Allison maintains a focus on finding some daily pleasures while working toward longer-term goals.

Anyone who cares about using their talents to do something meaningful with their lives should grab a notebook, read this book, and complete the exercises in it. Then they should create a plan and make it happen. Reading the *The Joy of Strategy* is a great first step.

Dr. Nancy J. Tarbell is the Dean for Academic and Clinical Affairs and the C.C. Wang Professor of Radiation Oncology at Harvard Medical School. She is a longstanding advocate for faculty development initiatives including mentoring programs for junior faculty and numerous efforts on behalf of women and minorities.

Acknowledgments

For a pursuit as solitary as writing, it's remarkable how many people have contributed to bringing this work into being. During the writing phase, my thoughts vacillated between moments of panic and "pinch me!" wonder at how lucky I am to have so many people in my corner.

First, my deepest gratitude goes to my all my friends and family for your love, patience, and encouragement. I must mention just a few: Jeri Weiss is my amazing alter ego and Matt Goldman our treasured co-conspirator. Alma Berson offered endless shots of courage. Meir and Claire Stampfer hosted countless dinners and made sure my family never starved for company or sustenance.

I am thankful to my coaching and consulting clients and the thousands of people who have attended my lectures and participated in my workshops, seminars, and courses. You have taught me so much and your accomplishments motivated me to write this book. I'm honored to have played a small part in your journey. I am particularly grateful to those of you whose stories appear on these pages. Thank you for serving as role models and inspiring others.

Finding my voice as a writer was a high hurdle and I couldn't have cleared it without Louisa Kasden and Donna Frazier Glynn. Jennifer Caplan and Willow Clark were among the first to read early chapters and gave me the courage to show them to others and Ellen Alfaro gave me the gift of her company on a writing retreat.

Andy O'Connell, my friend, and Harvard Business Review editor patiently challenged me to refine my message, always keeping the readers' needs in mind. His insights have been invaluable.

A gigantic thank you to everyone who read each chapter and provided priceless comments: Jennifer Caplan, Ellen Alfaro, Eric Rimm, Hannah Rimm, Sara Rimm-Kaufman, Trudy Craig, Alma Berson, and Bob Malster. Carey Goldberg must be singled out here for providing the most expert, insightful, and compassionate editorial advice anyone could hope for. I'd be more emphatic about her contributions, but she allows no exclamation points.

Of course, writing the book wasn't enough. Finding the right publisher was essential and it took a village. Thanks to Karla Todd who introduced me to Stacy DeBroff who introduced me to Lisa Butler who introduced me to Kate Sweetman who led me to Madelyn Sierra who introduced me to Carolyn Monaco who persistently pushed me to contact the extraordinary Erika Heilman. I can't imagine a better group than the gang at Bibliomotion: Erika, her co-founder and president, Jill Friedlander, Jill Schoenhaut, Susan Lauzau, Susanna Kellogg, Emily Hanson, and Shevaun Betzler. It's a joy to be a part of your spectacular community.

Dr. Jim Cash has been an important, generous mentor. Countless others have kindly shared their experiences and expertise. I could never list them all, but trust they know how much they mean to me. Thanks to my associates past and present, especially Peggy Meehan, Manny Correia, Lee Ann Ross, Bonnie Michelman, and Mary Finlay.

Finally, no one endured more "stuff" than those who lived with me while I wrote (and wrote and wrote). Hannah and Isaac's notes of encouragement grace the walls of my tiny office. Their many "mini-visits" just to say hi or plant a kiss were precious. Eric Rimm, my cherished husband and partner in life, patiently reassured me over and over, and was constantly available to serve as a sounding board. If that isn't enough, he makes me laugh every day. His support and friendship blow me away. I can't imagine traveling this road without him.

Introduction

What Is a Strategic Plan and
Why Do You Need One?

The joy of a life well lived—our work well done, our cherished ones well loved, our potential realized. Isn't that what we're all after? You don't need to leave your dreams to chance. However, achieving this most fundamental and often elusive goal doesn't just happen. It requires a strategy. To create a meaningful plan, you need a structured approach that guides you, step by step, through the process of defining what is most important to you and what you must do to get it. The world's most successful businesses do this as a matter of course, and there is no more essential business than the business of your life.

Here's my story. In 1995, I was recruited to lead Massachusetts General Hospital, the nation's top-ranked hospital,[1] through a strategic planning process and bring order to the chaos that was the chief executive's office. Chaos at MGH? Doesn't everyone know that stands for Man's Greatest Hospital? From the outside, everything looked great for this world-renowned institution and, for the most part, it was. But as the health care industry rapidly changed around it, the formula that brought this prestigious medical center legendary success for nearly two centuries would send them into a slow death spiral if they didn't develop a strategy to thrive in the evolving landscape.

While the hospital worked to position itself for continued success in the new millennium, the CEO was seriously overcommitted. His calendar was consistently over-booked and he needed a system to ensure he spent his time on matters that required his personal attention.

More than that, in this time of unprecedented change, he needed to improve communications with the hundreds of clinical and administrative leaders who had to carry out this new agenda *and* reduce the time they spent in meetings so they could get this extra work done while providing the exceptional patient care for which they were so well known. Like the hospital he was tasked to run, he needed a strategic plan of his own.

While we didn't call it that at the time, that CEO was my first coaching client. He urgently needed to set priorities and make his actions reflect them. He had to stop allowing his assistant to overbook his calendar and I told him so during my job interview. So when the request came in for him to attend a vendor selection meeting for their computer system during our interview, he turned to me and asked if he should accept. I told him if he didn't have people he could count on to attend that meeting and give him a recommendation he could trust, he was in bigger trouble than he thought. He offered me the job that very day. Thus began my sixteen-year stint running the executive office for him and the two presidents who followed.

Your Joy in Jeopardy

Chances are you are a lot like this CEO, highly accomplished in your own way and with so many demands coming at you that it's hard to get through the day in one piece, let alone feeling fulfilled and joyful. As a person with your own unique gifts to offer, it is your responsibility to use your talents wisely and it is your right to enjoy yourself while doing so. Happiness is so fundamental, in fact, that its pursuit is even stated as a right in the United States' Declaration of Independence. Yet despite achieving phenomenal career successes, countless professionals are experiencing feelings ranging from vague dissatisfaction to utter misery.

As a senior executive and management consultant, I'm astonished that more leaders don't pay close attention to how their employees *feel* about their work, or at least they don't do this formally. To put it in economic terms, I've come to appreciate over the years that happiness on the job is a leading indicator of an individual's ability to sustain high levels of passion, performance, and productivity over the long run. Because any organization's greatest asset is the people who work there, supporting joy on the job seems an obvious way to protect that investment.

This just makes intuitive sense to me—so much so that I even invented a metric and an instrument to measure it. Productivity indicators for individual performance are common, as are profitability measures for organizations. I also track people's joy quotient, which is simply a measure of the joy-to-hassle ratio of a given situation. And I measure it on my joy meter, which I keep in my office. When I worked in the executive suite of Mass General Hospital, countless people would come into my office, close the door, and point the dial on my meter toward hassle or joy, depending on what had happened recently. You'd be surprised by the number of very senior, world-famous physicians who have had a go at it.

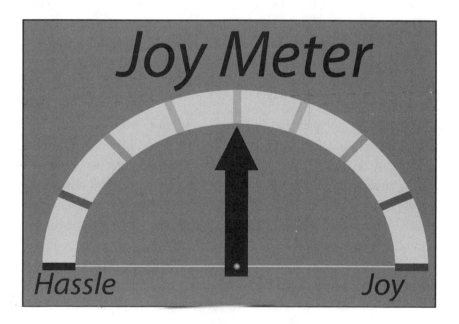

With so many experts exhorting us to work smarter, not harder, why are so many smart people working so hard? Even smart people need help. Like the overcommitted CEO, they need a solid framework to guide decisions large and small. In this book, I will be your coach as you create a business plan for your life so you can enjoy success on your own terms. This eight-step process mirrors the strategic planning steps that may be quite familiar to you, but here we will mix in some tools that may surprise you to bring you joy *and* success. I will teach you some hard skills to accomplish this and will offer firm but gentle guidance to support you when the work itself is tough.

Self-Management and More

The great news about learning how to create a business plan for your life is that you can apply this newfound knowledge so you can be more effective in everything you do. Beyond managing yourself, you will be better equipped to lead teams and projects at work, rally the troops for a community service initiative, manage your family life—you name it. The investment you are about to make in yourself will pay huge dividends for the rest of your life and in ways that may surprise you.

The Time for Your Passions Is Now

Helping such a complex and historic institution as MGH determine its future was an intriguing intellectual challenge. And gaining the support of the hospital's leaders to implement the resulting plan, with its inevitable winners and losers, called on all of my diplomatic skills and powers of persuasion. My accomplishments were rewarded with more: more responsibility, more people to lead, and larger budgets to manage until I had hundreds of people and tens of millions of dollars under my direction. More of what many professionals regard as indicators of success.

And then came the year that changed everything. After enduring a string of heart-wrenching personal losses, I was thrilled when I became pregnant with the baby we'd worked so hard to conceive. But elation turned quickly to fear when we learned his heart didn't appear to be developing properly and it was not clear if he would survive. We had to make some impossibly difficult decisions. If that wasn't enough, in the midst of that pregnancy, my husband was diagnosed with a potentially life-threatening condition that required a risky surgery to repair. Facing the very real possibility that I could lose the husband and child I cherished so deeply, I realized our time was short and I needed to make the most of it—*now*.

That meant leading with my heart and emotional intelligence after years of putting my intellectual gifts first. I'd spent my life thinking that if I worked hard enough I could fulfill my potential: put myself through college; earn a graduate degree from Harvard; effectively manage huge projects and successful teams; and win big contracts, awards, and promotions; and I did all that. Yet, at the pinnacle of my career, I knew that snuggling up with big budgets wasn't enough and that my real satisfaction came from connecting deeply with other people and making a positive difference. After a great deal of introspection, I realized that my unique ability to combine the techniques I'd employed so effectively in business with some hard-won life lessons to help others to find soul-satisfying success was a great way to do that. So while mixing soul with strategy isn't exactly the most intuitive combination, it is a lot more spiritual than leaving your dreams to chance or, worse, letting them go because you don't know how to pursue them. I've met a lot of souls that need organizing. More than that, many organizations need soul. After conducting dozens of workshops for people ranging from physicians to firefighters, I could see that using my strategic planning and executive skills was the perfect way to put my passion into practice.

What Is a Strategic Plan and Why Do You Need One?

"Good plans shape good decisions. That's why good planning helps make elusive business dreams come true."[2]

—Lester Robert Bittel, industrial engineer and management guru

In its simplest form, strategic planning is the process of identifying your purpose and core values, setting goals, and developing the approach that is most likely to achieve them. A strategic plan serves as a road map that defines your destination and shows how you can use your talents to take you there. Several routes are possible, and this map lays out which way is most likely to get you there quickly and reliably.

Are you thinking this just isn't for you and that you might put down this book? Not so fast! I've seen time and again that the people who resist this process are the very people who need it most. If the term strategic planning makes you think "I'd rather have a colonoscopy," rest assured I will walk you through a focused, streamlined process aimed at giving you practical news you can use and not a bunch of jargon-filled fluff. Drawing a map that takes you someplace you actually want to go requires some careful thought and quiet reflection. Working with this book, you will create the space that makes that possible.

> *"I went to the woods because I wished to live deliberately, to front only the essential facts of life, and to see if I could not learn what it had to teach, and not, when I came to die, discover that I had not lived."*[3]
> —Henry David Thoreau, *Walden*, 1854

No business could attract investors without clearly stating what its purpose is and what it hopes to achieve. Further, backers would not be satisfied by a fledgling business "hoping" to fulfill its mission: they require a detailed business plan showing the specific actions the business will take to accomplish what it sets out to do. In the business world, no one is going to take an uncalculated risk. Savvy investors know how to pick a winner, and winners have a clear sense of where they are going and how they are going to get there. Furthermore, their plans are doable and have a high degree of probability that they will yield the results needed for a successful return on investment.

Asset Management

Once you have gotten clear about what you want to achieve, you can be a responsible steward of your limited resources—time, money, talents—and utilize your assets in ways that are most likely to get you the results you desire.

Your Life Is Serious Business...

Just like that business, *you* need a clear picture of what you want to accomplish and what success means for you in order to focus your efforts and achieve your goals. Don't leave fulfilling your dreams to chance. If you don't take the time to decide where you want to go, it is impossible to draw a map that will help you reach your destination. Lacking direction, you could spend endless days simply responding to what others want from you. Years of this condition can leave you feeling unfulfilled and asking "Is this all there is?"

So You Need a Business Plan for Life

Most people don't live deliberately and they skip the critical step of deciding what is most important before they act, a state Thoreau sought to avoid for himself with his reflective sojourn in Walden Woods. Without a clearly defined purpose, many people find they are not living their lives. Their lives are living *them*. Your own strategic plan is the result of a structured, systematic process and provides you with the basis from which you can make good decisions, both personal and professional.

Step off the Treadmill and Break Free from Inertia

Let me tell you about Danielle. In the first several years we knew each other, I rarely saw her fully dressed and never saw her completely happy. Our lockers were located close together at our health club and we chatted every morning as we dressed to go off to work. We would discuss what was ahead of us that day and quip about funny things that we'd seen at the gym.

While I'd usually be excited about a talk I was giving or an interesting client I'd be meeting, Danielle was not so enthusiastic. She worked in the fashion industry and would often regale me with outrageous tales of her company's dysfunction. While her stories were devilishly funny, they revealed how truly miserable she was. Her job was eating away at her spirit and each day she dreaded going to work. The problems only compounded when her company was bought out and a new management team took over.

One morning, Danielle came into the gym more excited than I'd seen her in months. She and her colleagues were going to be laid off at the end of the summer and if she stayed with the company until the agreed-upon date, she would get a sizable bonus. The end was in sight.

She was counting the days until she could leave when she showed up at the gym one day deflated. Her new manager told her she was needed to help with the transition. While she was desperate to leave the company, she needed the bonus to give her time to pursue new career options. Over the ensuing months, as this demand was repeated and she was promised ever-growing bonuses, she stayed even longer. During this period, she was contacted about a senior position in a competing company and was actually considering pursuing another job in the industry she couldn't wait to leave.

It was clear to me that Danielle was allowing herself to be swept away by the inertia brought about by circumstances rather than taking the lead role in her life and writing her own script. I suggested she participate in the Business of Life workshop I was giving later that month and she gratefully accepted. This day would allow her to sit back and think about what was really important to her. With that in mind, she could consider how this decision would impact her life and whether it was a wise move. She had never stepped off the treadmill long enough to see how the decisions she was making impacted her health, relationships, and general sense of joy and purpose. In order to do that she needed a plan, and this workshop was just the opportunity she needed to take charge of her own well-being. We will meet up with Danielle later in this book to see the changes she made.

Get Clarity and Get Going

There's nothing mysterious or overly complicated about this kind of planning and strategizing. But for many people, it's the missing piece, the step-by-step breakdown that shows them very concretely what they need to do to put their own dreams first every day and how to find effective strategies to deal with what's derailed them in the past.

Those who achieve *soul-satisfying* success don't rely on intellect alone. These people know that to be truly happy, they need to focus on what's most important. They have more than a high IQ. They have a plan. A strategic plan. I know because I've taught them how to create one. They are smart enough to know what they don't know and they're not afraid to ask directions. They have attended my workshops and courses or have hired me as their coach. And you are about to learn what they have discovered.

This book guides you through that process, which begins by connecting you with your deepest life purpose and then walks you through bringing that ideal into reality. It's not just about visualizing. It's also about looking carefully at what you have, what you need, and how to get it. A strategic plan, unlike other things you may have tried (vision boards, simple lists, resolutions), helps you create strategies for moving steadily toward your target—based on who you really are, strengths, weaknesses, and all.

If you're worried that this work will take some of that precious time you just don't have, rest assured that once you sharpen your tools, your future efforts will be far more precise and efficient. As Melissa, an operations manager and early graduate of this program, said, "The best thing about your class is how timeless everything was. It was such a great investment of time because I still use your techniques [five years later] for goal setting all the time and I know I always will. It's just the way I think now." You will see how Melissa employed these techniques at work and at home with relative ease and achieved her two most important goals—getting promoted and finding a husband—in short order.

Zen Garden in the Shark Tank

Predictably, as I rose through the ranks at MGH, ultimately becoming a senior vice president, more and more people sought me out for coaching and mentoring. It's very satisfying to help earnest, able professionals advance their careers and enjoy life outside of work and I was glad to do it. MGH is blessed with countless bright and dedicated professionals contributing to its worthy mission. Yet even in such a rich environment, the uncompromising drive for excellence can be daunting and stressful, taking its toll over time. My office became known as an oasis of serenity in the hospital's relentlessly fast-paced environment as I guided people to make choices that brought them professional *and* personal satisfaction.

If the notion of monitoring people's joy on the job sounds frivolous to you, I have some outcomes of my own that validate the utility of paying close attention to your employees' happiness and engagement in their work. In my sixteen years at MGH, not a single one of my department heads left the institution. In fact, up until a few months before I left, there was zero turnover among my direct reports. That one change occurred when the hospital CIO was promoted to lead the IT enterprise for our entire system, a move I heartily endorsed. That loyalty and longevity doesn't just happen.

If these empirical data aren't enough to convince you, a recent study by Dr. Michal Biron of the University of Haifa's Graduate School of Management showed that employees are less likely to take time off for stress-related illnesses when they receive "emotional and instrumental support" from their supervisors. Absenteeism due to stress-related illnesses cost U.S. businesses an estimated $225.8 billion annually.[4] If you need a reason to support your workers, there are a quarter trillion good ones right there.

When the demand for individual mentoring sessions rose beyond what my calendar allowed, I created a course to teach groups of leaders the skills they needed to manage their careers and their lives. The course, called The Business of Life, was instantly oversubscribed and the classes have been full ever since. As word spread, I developed courses for the doctors and research faculty at the hospital and created programs for my coaching and consulting clients in financial services, broadcasting, marketing, higher education, government, and a wide variety of other industries.

Recently, I met with a group of physicians and surgeons who had taken my course six weeks earlier to check in on how they were putting their new knowledge into action. In spite of being brilliant and virtuous doctors, or maybe because of that, they had been feeling pretty dissatisfied. After just one day of learning about the Business of Life, they were able to make small changes in their habits that made a huge impact on their outlook and experience. They felt more in control. More like they were running the show rather than the show running them. Here are just a few examples of what they had to say about their experience:

- "It was life changing."
- "I let go of trying to do everything. Your challenging me to ask myself, 'what would happen if this doesn't get done' was so eye-opening. Often, the answer was 'not much,' and sometimes even 'I can do something that is much more important.' So basic. Why hadn't I figured that out long ago?"
- "This experience completely changed the lens I look through when evaluating work requests. I allowed myself to feel anger for the first time when a colleague tried to dump his work on me instead of worrying about how I was going to please him. And for the first time, I simply said no. I was shocked when all he said was 'OK, I'll try someone else.' Sh*t, that's liberation!"

It is so fulfilling to hear how people have used what they've learned in my classes over the years not only to transform their own lives, but also to do amazing things that help countless others in myriad ways. I knew I needed to broaden my reach so even more people can do the same. That defines my mission. I've written this book to coach you through the process of creating a business plan for your life so you can fulfill your potential and make your own special contribution.

Who Will Benefit from This Book?

The beauty of this process is that it meets you where you are and takes you where you want to go. Whether you are looking to find direction and transform your life, fine-tune an otherwise pretty good life, or just figure out how to manage your time so you can get home for dinner by six every night, you will find help reaching your goal. If you are looking for a new job or more satisfaction from the one you already have, you will find tools and suggestions on these pages.

You will take from this process what you need. That was made very clear to me the first time I taught the Business of Life workshop in a large company. At the end of the course, several people came up to the podium to thank me for such an enriching experience. First in line was the manager of the company's parking garage. He said, "That was the best time management class I've ever had." The very next person in line declared that "this was a life-altering experience," and the tools he'd learned helped him and his wife make some major life decisions after they had already achieved their career goals. You will see the results Bruce accomplished later in this book.

As a strategic planner, of course I believe everyone should have a life plan, one that balances career, relationships, mind/body/spirit, and community service priorities. My programs have been enormously popular with professionals across a wide range of disciplines and industries. Business leaders often find that sharing my methods with their staff helps with team bonding and makes them more effective at assigning people to the roles that play to their strengths and ignite their passion at work. People from all walks of life have benefitted from my workshops, often at times of transition such as career shifts, nests emptying, and retirement, to name a few. I frequently hear from course participants that they've shared their materials with a spouse or a friend. Who wouldn't benefit from taking a careful look at her life so she can make conscious, well-considered choices?

Left and Right Brains Unite

One thing that is so appealing about the strategic planning process is that it works for just about everyone. Some people love the conceptual work and find that creating a vision comes naturally, but the practical steps to bring it to life often elude them. Others, who are more left-brain and analytically oriented, are quite comfortable making lists and getting things done. For them, the challenge is focusing on the big questions like their life's purpose so they can be sure all those completed tasks contribute to their most meaningful goals. If life planning has fallen short for you in the past, it is probably because you neglected half the story.

After decades of working with people all along that spectrum, I can warn you right now, parts of this process may well put you a bit outside of your comfort zone and you may find yourself resisting certain activities. Do them anyway. The parts that are hardest for you are likely the ones that will have the biggest payoff—much like exercising when you're out of shape. It's not easy, but you know this investment will make you stronger. And after some practice, it becomes much more natural.

Some Artists Take the First Step

Peggy and Gail are artists with a burning desire to inspire "peace, spirit, and healing" in a supportive environment for children and teens touched by cancer. As breast cancer survivors, they were struck by how isolating it is to be so sick and also by the way the medical system cured their disease but left them on their own to heal their souls.

As artists, they had no trouble visualizing how they could help these kids, but they had no idea how to start the practical tasks of making it come about. I taught them the fundamentals of developing a strategic plan and coached them to start with one small action that very first day. I sent them off with the simple assignment of buying some beautiful folders and a colorful rack that appealed to their aesthetic so they could file away all their papers. Now they had an office set up. It was starting to look real. They were surprised by how quickly small, concrete actions added up to tangible results. You will watch their Our Space, Inc. story unfold throughout this book.

Ticked off Tasks Don't Add Up

Stan is a coaching client whose work life defined the term "rat race." He started working right out of business school, where he'd gone for that most practical reason: he wanted to make money. That he has done. And like a lot of people, once he set out on his path, way back in his early twenties, he never changed course or even gave much thought to what he really wanted to do with his life. There was no time for that. He spent nonstop days reacting to the fast-paced drama of the stock-trading floor. The problem was, after the first few years, none of that activity ever added up to anything he cared about.

Like Danielle, Stan got the shock and opportunity of a lifetime when he was downsized right out of his rut. At first, losing his job seemed like a crisis. But then, he used that "crisatunity" to refocus— or maybe to focus on the big questions for the first time.

How This Book Is Organized

Over the years, I have streamlined the strategic planning process to address the most essential elements you need to consider to achieve your goals efficiently. I keep it simple because the work it guides is not easy. We start with simple exercises so you can ease in and gain confidence as the complexity of the tasks grows. You will see stories every step of the way that illustrate how real people have used this program to address all kinds of goals and challenges. The names and/or details in some of these examples have been altered to maintain anonymity or to illustrate a specific point. In a few cases, the characters presented are composites of more than one individual.

I will be your guide as you work through my 8-Step Strategic Planning Program. In each section, you will complete exercises to accomplish all the necessary steps. You will find tools you can gather to address your particular needs and assemble your own custom toolbox. We start with an assessment of who you are, what you care about, where you want to go, and how well you're positioned to get there. You will do some organized, strategic soul-searching.

Step 1—Mission: Find Your Purpose

Step 2—Vision: Imagine the Sweet Smell (Sound, Look, and Feel) of Success

Step 3—Name Your Critical Success Factors: What You Need to Succeed

Step 4—Find Your Sweet SWOT

From here, we move from who you *are* to what you're going to *do* to express your essential self, employing your talents and putting your passions into play.

Step 5—Set Goals: What You Need to Do to Get the Results You Desire

Next, we do some diagnosis: how well are your activities aligned with your goals? Where are you off track and why?

Step 6—Perform a Time and Emotion Study

Finally, you will find treatments for whatever is standing between you and your goals—practical advice and tools to help you choose the strategies that are most likely to get you the results you want. You will learn new ways to excavate time from your calendar to invest in your most worthy pursuits. You will find tips and tools to help you get back on track if you find you've strayed off the path. The process ends with you devising an action plan that will break down your next steps into bite-sized, doable pieces that banish procrastination and set you in motion toward your vibrant future. Today.

Step 7—Select Successful Strategies
Step 8—Get Going! Your Simplementation Plan
Step Back—Tips and Tools to Get Back on Track and Stay the Course

How You Will Work with This Book

You are about to get very organized. You will also eliminate the anxiety that comes from trying to keep myriad details in your head by putting everything on paper. For this, you will need a notebook to record your thoughts and complete the exercises. Then, you will organize the most critical pieces into a one-page designer document that will make it easy for you to track your progress regularly and make timely course corrections.

Your Custom Closet

Ask anyone in the know what the greatest pitfall of strategic planning is and she will likely say it's when a company spends tons of time and money creating a huge, impenetrable document that gets put aside and collects dust.

Well, this isn't another plan to put on the shelf—it *is* the shelf.

I will confess to being an organization junkie to the point that cleaning out my closets gives me a sense of order when life feels like it's getting out of control. So it seems an apt metaphor to use a custom closet to organize the essential elements of our life plan. You can use this to clear out the clutter of your life, eliminate anything that no longer fits or that blocks your view of the clothes you'd rather wear each day, and make space for new ideas and priorities. With your essentials

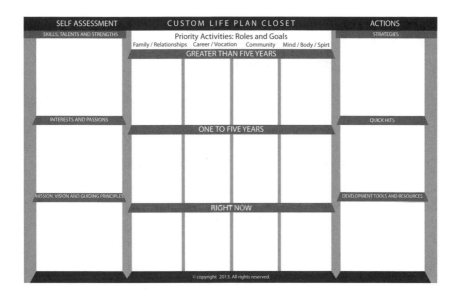

easily visible, you can try mixing and matching them in new, intriguing combinations.

Okay, I can almost hear you snickering at my obsessive devotion to getting organized, but this isn't just about indulging my infatuation with the velvet-lined jewelry drawers you can build into those high-end closets. According to Merriam-Webster's online dictionary,[5] the word *organize* means "to form into a coherent unity or functioning whole." Isn't that what we're after? Aren't we all seeking the integrity that comes when what we do is in harmony with what we believe so that we feel balanced and whole? Organizing ourselves is critical to making that happen.

I just Googled the term "work–life balance" and it returned 208 *million* results. That's a serious problem. I believe the reason that work–life balance is so elusive is that our definition of balance is fundamentally flawed. If you, like so many, are looking to allocate the "right" number of hours to work versus life activities, you've set up a false dichotomy and an equation that can't be solved. My friends, life *is* work. Keeping your house clean, staying fit, and maintaining healthy relations all require work. But work doesn't necessarily suggest drudgery. Your work—at the office or on behalf of your community, health, or home life—can be rewarding, joyful even, when it is contributing to your individual vision of success. That kind of balance you can achieve.

Your closet captures your mission, vision, goals, and strategies, balanced by your own priorities, and it will serve as an easy way to track your progress and course correct for years to come. And it's a custom closet because you can use the shell I've created (you can download one from joyofstrategy.com) or modify it in any way that serves your purposes. Laid out in the way that works best for you, everything you need is right there in one place. Can't get to one of your priorities right now? Put it on a shelf so you will remember to get to it when you're ready. Now that it's written down, you can stop worrying that you'll forget about it when the time comes.

Your Toolbox

This book is full of news you can use. Sprinkled throughout are Toolboxes that you can use to address challenges you may be facing at any point throughout the process. You will also find many tips and techniques to help you get and stay on a fruitful path toward achieving your goals. Whenever any of these speaks to you, you can record them in your notebook or put them on a shelf in your closet so they are available for ready access whenever you need them.

Reservoirs of Joy Create Resilience

I thought I was organized until Lauren, a Wall Street analyst and consulting client, showed up to our first meeting with a file full of color-coded folders, one for each topic we were to cover and another summarizing all of the research she'd conducted to back up every point we'd address in her organization's strategic plan. You can imagine that two methodical planners hit it off and we became great friends once she'd launched her successful strategy.

Over lunch about a year later, she confessed that she had been skeptical about "the joy thing." While she had nodded politely when I described that part of my approach, she was secretly thinking, "*I* don't need that," and dug into the project in earnest when we got to the "real" work. So it was a true gift when she told me that some part of her had absorbed the message. She was concerned that her tween-aged son was too serious and worked too hard. As they planned his summer activities, she remembered about those reservoirs of joy I'd mentioned and she shipped him off to spend the summer with relatives in Europe with nothing but good times with good people on the agenda. She was thrilled when he returned from his visit with his crazy cousins with an easy laugh and quick wit he'd rarely demonstrated before his trip. These qualities eased his transition to high school, where he easily made new friends. And he was a lot more fun at the dinner table, a bonus Lauren truly treasured.

Lauren realized that her son's time in Europe had created joyful memories that he could draw on when he returned to the pressure of his schoolwork. And when he needed a break, he could relieve some stress with a good chortle. She was sold.

These reservoirs of joy make us more resilient dealing with the daily stresses we all face. Have you ever noticed that you can put up with tedious tasks when you are surrounded by colleagues you respect and enjoy? Or that your annoying coworkers don't bother you so much when your work is enormously fulfilling? That's your joy quotient in action: the joy you feel offsets the inevitable hassles you have to face. And having a deep reservoir to call on will help take you through the joy drought brought about by a particularly difficult situation. That's another way you can capture that sense of balance that eludes so many.

Don't Die with Your Song Still Inside You

When I was in the third grade, my music teacher, Mr. Series, directed me to stand in the back row of the chorus and silently mouth the words to the song we were rehearsing for the winter concert. With that one dismissive act, he extinguished the enthusiasm of an exuberant (if not tonally superior) student who had, moments before, been singing with gusto and glee.

Decades later, just after my fortieth birthday, I was sitting in the audience of a concert at a national convention where my daughter's musical ensemble had been invited to sing with the choir. As several musical luminaries joined one another to jam onstage and make beautiful music, I thought wistfully how tragic it was that I loved to sing so much and couldn't carry a tune. Then a lightbulb went on over my forty-year-old head as I realized that I hadn't yet done everything possible to develop my singing ability and that the real tragedy would be to have had the raw talent all along without ever knowing it or developing it. So, I resolved that day to give it my best shot before giving up on something that would bring me so much joy.

That week, I registered for a weekend-long workshop that promised to "have you singing the way you've always wanted to" and that "not an ounce of talent" was required. It took every bit of courage I could summon to mount the stage and sing in front of a group of strangers, but I was determined not to die with my song still inside me, quite literally.

The leader of my singing workshop saw the reticent little third grade girl Mr. Series had silenced so many years ago now standing onstage, choking on my fears and croaking out a feeble tune. He saw that I had to get out of my own way and told me to try again, this time pretending to be a New York City truck driver. I dropped my register and belted out like a tough guy used to shouting at other drivers at the top of his lungs. The crowd laughed and sang along and then jumped to their feet cheering when I triumphantly finished my song.

Shame on Mr. Series for not doing his job: teaching that eager third grader how to sing on key. But as an adult, I am responsible for my own experience. What's holding you back from pursuing your dreams? If it's that you don't know how to start, or are stuck, your excuses are gone. I challenge you to defy any limiting beliefs and to take decisive action toward making those dreams come true. Don't die with your song still inside you.

Step ❶

Mission: Find Your Purpose

"Hide not your talents, they for use were made: What's a sun-dial in the shade?"[1]

—Benjamin Franklin

Every great strategic plan starts with a declaration of an entity's purpose that expresses why it exists, what its members value, and what these people intend to accomplish. Your mission is nothing short of your purpose here on earth, and you'll start your personal plan by spelling it out. I know that sounds lofty, as though we're trying to find the meaning of life. But the answer to the question "What am I here to do?" isn't as remote as you might think. What do you love to do? What are you good at? You'll find your mission right there—it's as accessible and profound as that. I love author Matthew Kelly's definition of what we're after: "Mission is where our talents and passions collide with the needs of others and the world."[2]

Wouldn't it be reassuring, when you are making decisions, to have a filter that separates what is important from what is not? That's what a good mission statement can do for you, and creating one is the first step in engaging your heart and mind in making a plan to fulfill your most deeply held desires.

As with any organization, if you don't have clear intentions, you will have great difficulty focusing your efforts to achieve a *deliberate* result. Something will happen, all right, but you may not like it. Lack of clear direction is the reason so many of us career from task to task, collapsing in an exhausted heap at the end of the day feeling like we haven't really accomplished anything of value. So how can you get ahead of the daily deluge of incoming demands and opportunities and focus on what's truly important? You need to start with knowing your own purpose, what matters most to you.

Mission Critical

While you may find it tempting to dismiss talking about abstractions such as defining your purpose as, well, abstract, discussing your intentions actually leads to very practical actions. Defining your mission is critical to allocating your resources, time, and abilities wisely.

This was evident when I was assigned the task of solving a problem that had plagued Massachusetts General Hospital's Board of Trustees for years. The trustees wanted to feel more closely connected to this esteemed institution and to make better use of their legendary expertise. The board is a treasure trove of talent that includes captains of industry, bank presidents, a National Football League team owner and a Major League Baseball team owner, leading academics, philanthropists, and community leaders. But when they came together for board meetings, the management team spent so much time presenting vast amounts of information that the trustees reported it was like trying to drink from a fire hose. Furthermore, there was little, if any, time left for discussion, so the trustees didn't feel like they were making much of a contribution. And they had so much to offer.

It was my job to find innovative ways to make better use of that invaluable asset and the scant twenty hours of meeting time we had each year. That required educating the trustees so they could advise the hospital leadership on matters of strategy, quality of care, and financial performance. It also meant inspiring them with stories of heroic care delivery and innovation so the trustees could be passionate advocates of the hospital's work. How did I accomplish that goal? It all started with a focus on the hospital's mission. I optimized their precious time together by planning board meeting agendas a year at a time to make sure they addressed all four key components of the mission: patient care, research, education, and community health improvement. We also began the tradition of holding an annual retreat for trustees so they could more thoroughly examine different aspects of the health-care system and the hospital's mission to deepen the trustees' understanding and commitment. And we created subcommittees that gave board members opportunities to contribute their special expertise where it could have the greatest impact.

Isn't that what you want for yourself? To focus on what matters most and to spend your time and talent where it can make a meaningful difference? So, just like MGH and all great organizations, you need a clear statement of your purpose. If you are paralyzed by the idea of starting this process because of the enormity of this first step, take a deep breath. We will ease into it with surprisingly simple, even fun, exercises. Help is here for you at every turn.

What Is Your Personal Mission?

You may have noticed that I asked you what *your* mission is. It is important to start by thinking about what's most important to *you*. I am asking you to listen to your own voice. Not your parents' or your boss's or the neighbors', or the voice of the ever-popular "they" who always seem to have a lot to say about just about everything. Your plan will not be successful unless it reflects your most authentic passions and employs your own brand of genius.

When I first set out to write my own mission statement, I was surprised by how many voices I recalled telling me what I should do. My mother thought my talents for healing would lead me to a career in medicine. A former teacher thought my skill with puzzles and problem solving would make me a great engineer. It took a while to sort through all that input and think about what I loved doing and where I could make a unique contribution. Since physics was among my least favorite subjects in school, engineering was clearly *not* it. So, do take some time to consider the advice of others, and decide how well it fits. Your mission must be an authentic reflection of you or it will not serve its intended purpose.

Joy Notes

Feeling like we've spent our time well is essential to our happiness. We have opportunities every day to add to our reservoir of joy when we perform good acts or just connect meaningfully with others. When we are able to use our unique gifts to help someone or make something better, we feel like we're making a meaningful contribution and our lives matter. American psychologist Abraham Maslow showed in his famous hierarchy of needs that self-actualization is the highest driver of human motivation. According to his well-regarded theory, people who fulfill their potential experience moments of profound happiness and harmony. Furthermore, people must do what they are individually suited to do in order to be at peace with themselves.[3]

So, what talents and passions do you have that we can set on a (very friendly) collision course with the needs of others? When we were kids, we had no trouble tooting our horns or saying what we loved. We declared with glee what we wanted to be or do when we grew up and we never questioned whether we could do whatever we wanted. Have you ever heard a toddler say, "I want to be a fireman when I grow up, but I'm afraid I won't be good enough?" If your ability to declare your talents has been socialized out of you, you'll need to flex that muscle. And if you can't say off the top of your head what you love doing, you will have to work on that too. Let's start with a warm-up exercise that's fun and easy and can help you get back in touch with what makes your heart sing.

EXERCISE

Part One: Proud Accomplishment

Start by thinking of an accomplishment you're proud of, something that succeeded because of the unique blend of talents you provided. This could be anything. Maybe you pulled off a marketing coup, made a stellar presentation, or defused a volatile family situation. Perhaps you realized that some of the kids at your child's school didn't have coats and you organized a clothing drive. Or, it could be that you threw a killer salsa dance party that people still talk about years later.

Grab your notebook and start writing. What was it you did that makes you smile just to remember the experience? It should be comforting to know that there are no wrong answers here. One of the most valuable lessons I learned happened when I was helping our local National Public Radio affiliate with its strategic plan. At that time, John Davidow was the news director at WBUR and he said something that has stuck with me for years. He talked about how talented his reporters were and yet so different from one another. "If I gave the same story idea to five reporters, they would come back with five very different stories, all excellent. There are many good ways to tell a story." So, just get started writing and don't worry about getting it "right." Just tell your story. You can always come back to this exercise and add and edit as you see fit.

Part Two: What Made You So Successful?

There, that wasn't such heavy lifting, was it? Now that your muscles are warmed up, it's time to complete the second part of this exercise. Jot down in your notebook what it was about you that made you so successful. What combination of skills and abilities made you uniquely suited to pull it off?

Whatever the specifics of the accomplishment you chose, you're looking for a feeling of success and ease, the sense that you were the right person for the task because it called on your passions and talents so that you were naturally drawn to do it. These are the hallmarks of your calling.

Look a Little Deeper

Now that you're warmed up, it's time for some more self-reflection. Who *are* you? When is the last time you really looked at yourself: your skills, passions, and desires? What drives you? If you've been around any teenagers lately, chances are you've seen them hanging around in front of a mirror, playing with their hair, making funny faces, or trying out different voices. They spend a lot of time considering who they are and how they want to present themselves to others. But at some point, that self-examination stops and we get caught up in the busyness that keeps us from looking inside ourselves with any regularity.

This process of self-reflection often makes me think of my annual hiking trips through the national parks. Most of these parks have some pretty gorgeous scenery you can see from the car as you drive through them. And it's wonderful that so much beauty is accessible to anyone who makes the trip. It's always striking to me, however, that there's so much more splendor and adventure waiting for those who are willing to take the time and make the effort to explore what's beyond the surface. Sometimes it's scary to confront the power of nature and to find the energy for a big climb. But if you're willing to go inside and work a little harder than the average bear, you are usually rewarded with some spectacular views and peak experiences.

And so it is with our selves. It takes some effort to look at our innermost thoughts and desires. It can require some real courage if we're afraid of what we might see. Honest self-examination can indeed open up some new frontiers or require us to face some facts about ourselves that we'd just as soon ignore. Yet we turn a deaf ear to our inner voice at our peril. Failing to pay attention to what our hearts are trying to tell us can mean missing out on discovering what's really going to fulfill us.

What Is Holding You Back?

Fear is often at the root of what is holding us back from pursuing our deepest desires and getting what we really want. We're afraid that if we try, we might fail. Even though we know, on some level, that failure is guaranteed if we *don't* try, it somehow feels less risky not to put ourselves out there. It is often quite liberating when we face our fears head on. I've seen coaching clients and workshop participants address fears they'd been carrying with them for years and get past them in a matter of minutes once they were able to name the problem and make a plan.

Examine Your Self-Doubt

When I was a hospital senior vice president, Brenda came to interview for a job opening in one of my departments. She was a program coordinator who administered the complex logistics of a training program that was integrated with Harvard Medical School. It was clear from our discussion that she was able to manage lots of details, cope with some challenging personalities, and meet countless deadlines. So I asked her why she was interested in this administrative assistant position that was clearly less involved than what she was already doing and several pay grades below her current position. She said that what she really wanted was a management career and that "sometimes you need to take a step back in order to take a step forward." When I pointed out that this move would be a step *away* from reaching her goal, her face fell and her shoulders drooped. But something sparkled in Brenda and I was impressed by her talent and earnest desire to make a bigger contribution to the hospital. Something was holding her back and I wanted to help her figure out what that was and how to drive past that roadblock so she could get what she really wanted. I offered to mentor her through the steps necessary to become a manager. She gratefully accepted.

Brenda came to our first meeting eager to get on the path to becoming a manager. We started by reviewing her résumé with an eye toward identifying where she was relative to where she needed to be to land a job in management. The most glaring hole was readily apparent—she didn't have a college education. When I asked her why she never pursued the bachelor's degree that was essential for her to achieve her goal of becoming a manager, she told me that she was no good at math and there was no way she could make it through college. I asked her where she got that idea. She told me about her middle school math teacher who had humiliated her in front of her class and told her publicly that she had no aptitude for math. Hello? Within minutes, we had reached the source of the dilemma that had plagued her for decades. Shame on her math teacher who, thirty years earlier, had robbed a young girl of her confidence. But now we knew what we were dealing with and what was really holding her back.

Question Your Limiting Beliefs

I pointed out to Brenda that in order to be successful in her current job, she did math every day, some of it very sophisticated. So, when she turned to making her list of strengths, she could include math among them. Suddenly, all kinds of possibilities opened up for her. You will see her story unfold as you move through the rest of the steps in this book.

The Foundation of YOUR Mission

Let's go on with creating the building blocks for your mission statement. In this section, you will continue to look at your passions and talents. You will also look at your core values and the principles that will guide your way. Taken together, these elements will illuminate your purpose so that your mission statement can reflect who you are, what you intend to do, and why it is important. This statement should inspire you and ignite your commitment to fulfilling it.

It is now time to round out a description of your talents. If you find it hard to wax on about what you're really good at doing, it might help to think about how others see you. Who knows you best? What would they say are your greatest strengths?

EXERCISE

Talent Inventory

Here are some more questions to ask yourself to help you get started. Then, take it as far as you can go and record your findings in your notebook.

- What are my unique skills, talents, and strengths?
- What's my first instinct when approaching a new challenge?
- What Is the first thing I do when I enter a room?[4]
- What do I spontaneously contribute to the activity of a group?
- What do I feel compelled to do for others?
- What are others seeking when they come to me for help?

To illustrate how this all works, let's look at Raymond, a fictional coaching client (who draws on aspects of a few real-life clients) with an innovative ear for music and a passion for blending harmonies. When he thought about his musical gifts in relation to these questions, Raymond realized that he had an unusual set of skills. He was one of those rare artists who had lots of left-brained analytic and organizational abilities to complement his considerable creative talents. He had a unique ability to interpret great works and to imagine how to blend the many orchestral instruments to create arrangements that had a visceral impact on the audience. His colleagues always looked to him to find the flourish that would add the necessary flair to elevate a piece from well executed to exceptionally moving.

Raymond's father, an aspiring concert pianist who never fulfilled his own ambitions, saw the creative genius his son possessed and was thrilled at the notion that someone in his family could rise to the heights he'd once imagined for himself. Raymond took his father's enthusiasm to heart and always assumed he'd become a pianist wowing crowds across the globe with his brilliant interpretations of classical compositions. He was excited to have so many talents on which to build an amazing musical career. He crafted a mission statement that really lit him up: "To beautify the world with musical harmonies that soothe the soul and ignite the spirit."

Often, what you are good at is highly correlated with what you enjoy doing. One of the reasons I'm so passionate about creating a personal strategic plan is that I want to make sure my life is full of the things that I love most. To do that, you need to know what those things are. As sad as it might sound, a lot of us just haven't given much thought to what lights us up from the inside. Here in your virtual Walden Woods, you have the perfect opportunity to pay close attention to what you enjoy most.

EXERCISE

Name Your Passions

What are you most passionate about? You can free-associate and write down anything that comes to mind. If you're stuck, here are a few provocative questions to get you going.

- What are some peak experiences I've enjoyed in my life?
- What activities am I naturally drawn to?
- What is my favorite kind of vacation?
- How do I spend my spare time?
- What are my hobbies?
- What do I do when I'm procrastinating?

It's about this time in the Business of Life workshops that a lot of light bulbs start going off. Remember Danielle, the disgruntled fashion buyer who was stuck by inertia in a job she hated? As she worked on these questions in the hushed room of the workshop she attended, she blurted out that she'd been working for more than twenty years and hadn't done a single thing she loved doing. At that moment, she resolved to make a major change. While inertia had her in a holding pattern with fear of letting go of the familiar, she saw that it was actually riskier to stay in a soul-sapping situation than to cut her losses and try something new. The cost of staying put and hating her life was too high. Especially now that she saw, on paper, that her love of cooking and the arts found no expression in her current life. While she couldn't yet see how it would, she knew that it must.

Doing What Comes Natur'lly

A wonderful benefit of creating a mission built on the foundation of your talents and passions is that you're likely to craft one that plays to your strengths and comes naturally to you. When that is the case, success comes with relative ease. Has anyone ever complimented you for doing something that comes so easily to you that you didn't even recognize it was a special talent? Did you respond by saying, "Oh, that was nothing, anyone can do that"? Well, not everyone can compose a symphony or twirl a baton while reciting poetry. If someone has indeed complimented you on one of your particular aptitudes, what is it that you can do that you thought anyone could do? Go back and put that on your list of talents.

I asked a client I'll call Thelma if I could interview her about how she applies what she learned in the Business of Life management course offered her by her employer a couple of years earlier. She had mentioned she used many of the tools in both her work and personal life since taking the class. I told her I was interested in her experience because she's one of the most strategic thinkers I know and she works so well with the planning framework in the workplace. As if to make my point for me, she said she was glad I saw those traits in her because they happen so instinctively, she wasn't even aware of them.

Have you ever seen a job description that seemed to be written for you, almost as though the person writing it knew you and wanted you to have the job? It's an amazing feeling to see the details of what you love listed as qualifications you miraculously possess. That is like the time a family friend won a college scholarship designated for a student of high academic achievement who played piano and excelled on the high school tennis team. Now there's a niche not many people could fill, but it played right into his quirky mix of gifts.

Core Values

The final building block of your mission embraces your core values. These are the principles you hold most dear that will guide your path toward fulfilling your mission. My daughter calls these her "words to live by."

What matters most to you? You need to think about that because what you value will illuminate your way, guide how you conduct yourself, and determine what you leave behind. Guiding principles serve as an excellent filter when setting priorities. For example, after all my struggles to have my second child, being fully present for my kids and showering them with love was my highest priority, along with keeping up with my many responsibilities in the executive suite at work. Achieving both objectives took laser-like focus, and using my guiding principles helped me make decisions that would keep my energies focused on what was truly most important to me.

What Are Core Values?

Core values reflect the underlying philosophy that determines how you want to conduct your business and life. Organizations frequently use their statement of core values to describe how they expect their employees to treat their colleagues and customers as they work to carry out their mission.

While I was the senior vice president for strategic planning at Massachusetts General Hospital, we updated the institution's mission statement to reflect the hospital's passionate commitment to patient-centered care as well as to improving the health of people in the surrounding communities. In this example, you can see how the hospital's dedication to excellence and quality combines with its core values of compassion, collaboration, and innovation to infuse the MGH's purpose of providing patient care, research, and education with passion and commitment.

MASSACHUSETTS GENERAL HOSPITAL'S REVISED MISSION STATEMENT

Guided by the needs of our patients and their families, we aim to deliver the very best health care in a safe, compassionate environment; to advance that care through innovative research and education; and to improve the health and well-being of the diverse communities we serve.

This revision replaced a far more utilitarian version:

To provide the highest quality care to individuals and to the local and distant communities we serve, to advance care through excellence in biomedical research, and to educate future academic and practice leaders of the health-care professions.

Can you feel the difference between these two statements? The earlier version espouses some important values such as quality and excellence. The revision built on that foundation, but made explicit the desire to place patients and families at the center of the mission and to bring safety and compassion into the mix. In this way, both the people who work at the hospital and those who use its services can see how vital they are to the hospital's purpose. We shared a draft of the revision with hundreds of employees, staff, and patients to get their responses. Hospital leadership settled on this version only after ensuring that it reflected their values and made them proud to be affiliated with this august institution.

Some Common Core Values

I have worked over the years with many organizations to articulate their core values. Here is a sample of some frequently cited guiding principles:

Accountability	Dedication	Honesty	Passion
Collaboration	Efficiency	Innovation	Quality
Commitment	Excellence	Integrity	Relationships
Compassion	Fun	Loyalty	Spirituality

It's hard to argue with any of these, but you will likely value some more than others, relatively speaking. And, of course, there are many other possibilities that may speak more directly to you. You will create your own list and it should reflect what matters most to *you*. It seems like mom and apple pie, but some people do lose sight of what truly matters and stray from their right path from time to time.

Live Your Values

Miranda looked for success in all the wrong places. Trying to impress others and please her parents, she set out to shatter the glass ceiling and to do whatever it took to make it to the corner office. And she did. The only problem is that she didn't really *want* to be there. She got so caught up in winning the game she had been playing for so long, she'd forgotten why she'd started playing it in the first place. Driven to win the approval of others, Miranda compromised her personal values so many times to climb the corporate ladder that she lost many friends and her sense of spirit along the way.

Looking back on it all in her late fifties, she realized in a rare moment of self-reflection that she'd sacrificed her soul to acquire all the outer trappings of success. She'd become the CEO of her large corporation, served on the boards of international companies, and sported a diamond the size of a skating rink. Yet despite the rewards and recognition, she was spiritually bankrupt. She hated just about everything to do with her job and looked at her cutthroat colleagues with suspicion and disdain. Sadly, she saw pretty much the same thing when she looked in the mirror. As Miranda imagined herself rocking on the porch swing in her twilight years, she saw herself surrounded by people whom she paid to take care of her. She saw herself feeling empty, alone, insecure, and unfulfilled. And despite her undeniable professional achievements, she still had the urgent sense that she wasn't good enough and never would be. She had lost herself in her quest to impress others. Worse, those people she had impressed didn't like her much and certainly wouldn't choose to spend their free time with her.

During her coaching sessions, Miranda discovered that she had been chasing external validation of her worth and had failed to look deep inside her own self to discover what truly mattered most to her. She finally understood that she would have to take responsibility for her actions by defining her personal values and adopting principles that would guide her future choices. She realized that she wanted to help new generations of women avoid the mistakes she had made that had taken such a toll on her and everyone who had been on the receiving end of her legendary bursts of anger. Later in this book, you will read more about Miranda's quest to put her considerable talents to use in a way that would empower young women to find career success. She learned to create meaningful, authentic relationships, both personal and professional, and experienced true joy for the first time that she could remember.

EXERCISE

Words to Live By

What ideology guides your actions? Think about the values and underlying philosophy that determine how you intend to live your life. These are your guiding principles. Record them in your notebook.

Putting It All Together

You've identified where your talents make you shine, where you feel most satisfied sharing them, and the issues, causes, people, and arenas that capture your passion. You've also zeroed in on the guiding principles you'll use as a compass. Hopefully, as you look at these elements together, you see your mission coming into focus and are ready to capture that clarity in a mission statement. As you prepare to write your statement, I offer some final questions to help you integrate what you've listed in the previous exercises into a statement of your purpose.

EXERCISE

Part One: Answer these Guiding Questions

- What would you want people to say about you at your funeral? Or maybe you'll find it less morbid to imagine people holding a "lifetime achievement" dinner in your honor. What are they saying about you? Your accomplishments? How you lived out your purpose? What are they saying was your unique contribution to the world? What would you say if you could write your own obituary (way, way in the future, of course)?
- If you didn't have to earn a living, how would you spend your time?
- If you had a million dollars to donate, what cause would you support?
- What would you do if you knew you couldn't fail?

Record your answers in your notebook.

Part Two: Write Your Mission Statement

This is a declaration of your life's purpose—why you are here. Craft your mission statement as if you couldn't fail. Think big and be aspirational. Don't worry that your mission seems too big or grandiose. Just write down what feels right. You are taking this one step at a time. Following this exercise are some frequently asked questions and sample mission statements for you to review now or after you take a first stab at your mission statement.

Frequently Asked Questions

At this point in the process, many people have questions about how to produce an effective mission statement. Here are some of the most common queries I've received.

- *What is a good mission statement and how is it written?* An effective mission statement describes your primary purpose in a way that inspires you to take values-based action to fulfill it. It serves as a filter to help you focus your actions in accordance with your intention. Use language that motivates you and is clear and memorable.

- *How long should my mission statement be?* I'm often asked about the "right" length for a mission statement. Some say it needs to pass the coffee mug test, meaning it should be short enough for you to look at as you sip your daily cup of joe. In truth, the length needs to be what's right for you, and you are the only one who can determine that. If it motivates and inspires you, it's right. It's often helpful to keep it short enough so you can remember and recite it easily. A passing glance at a framed version should energize and inspire you.

- *Will you share some sample mission statements?* I used to share my own personal mission statement in my workshops as an example of what one looks like, but stopped doing that because people would sometimes make a Mad Libs version of mine and call it their own. I will share examples from previous workshop participants to show you some effective statements. You will see mine later on, but please do create yours before you read it.

Sample Mission Statements

Use the following examples as models for crafting your mission statement, but please avoid the temptation to make a few edits to someone else's statement and call it a day.

Personal Mission Statements

With thanks to the talented managers who took my leadership development course at MGH and gave me permission to share their personal missions, here are several examples of well-crafted mission statements.

- "To achieve personal and professional success by utilizing my knowledge and skill set when and wherever possible. I will also strive to help others and give back to the community in every way that I know how."
- "To operate from a balanced mental, physical, and spiritual center while sharing my creative talents in both my professional and personal life."
- "Through my compassion and generosity, I will set the best practice for my philanthropic endeavors and will inspire others to do the same. I will fulfill the need for humane education: teaching others the principles of kindness, compassion, and respect for all life."
- "My personal mission is to be a great mom, a true and faithful partner to my husband, a good citizen, a caring daughter, daughter-in-law, and family member as well as a good friend. With my husband, we will raise smart, happy, good and independent children who will grow up to be productive and successful adults. I will have fun at the same time as accomplishing these goals. I also want to be faithful to God and want to help others in their time of need by donating time, talents, and money whenever possible."

- "To strive to achieve consistent growth and education in my professional career, in conjunction with a harmonious family life."
- "My personal mission is to value myself first, so that I can give more to others with a clear mind and open heart. I will rely on my humor and empathy to help others when they need it and give to those who need it most."
- "To provide compassionate care for less fortunate and needy throughout the local community and the entire world."
- "I am an adoring mother driven by passion for my children, husband, and family. I strive to support, motivate, and bring joy to those I encounter throughout my life. My life is enriched and rounded out with family, friends, career, volunteer service, spirituality, and my adorable dog, who always makes me smile."

Organizational Mission Statement

Remember Peggy and Gail, the cancer survivors who wanted to start a program for kids? Here's their organization's mission statement.

OUR SPACE, INC. MISSION

The mission of Our Space is to embrace children and teens who have faced or are confronting cancer. Our Space will inspire peace, spirit, and healing within a supportive community, through play, learning, and creative exploration.

My Own Mission Statements

I had occasion to use my own personal mission statement to help me make an important decision very recently. While writing this book, I was confronted with a choice. My son was preparing for his bar mitzvah, an important rite of passage for Jewish boys on their thirteenth birthday. As part of this ceremony, which marks a young man's entry into manhood, he needed to lead a large portion of the service as well as write and deliver a commentary. This required work of epic proportions and not a small amount of his mother's attention to teach him the skills he'd need to excel. As the date neared, it became clear to me that I could not keep up with my consulting obligations, help my son prepare fully, and devote the intense focus necessary to write my book all at the same time. Something had to give, and the book was the only thing that had any give in the short term. Facing the prospect of falling three weeks behind on my writing schedule (remember, you're dealing with a planner here; procrastination is painful for me), I needed centering to make a clear decision and allow myself to fully commit to whatever I chose to do. So, I turned to my personal mission statement:

> Devoted to delighting my family, friends, clients, colleagues, and community, I strive to laugh loudly, love deeply, and nourish all with food for thought and balm for the soul. To use my unique talents fully to inspire others to connect with their passions and fulfill their potential so together we shine our light, spread joy, and leave the world a better place for having lived here—with purpose.

In an instant, I knew that putting my book aside for those three weeks was what I needed to do. Concentrating my efforts to help my son fill his potential at this critical juncture was central to my personal mission. I picked up the phone and told my husband what I'd discovered and prepared him for the fact that I'd be "going underground" after the bar mitzvah to spend some intensive time writing to get the book back on schedule. With Plan B firmly in place, I was able to put my attention where it was needed. And when my son delivered the performance of a lifetime and basked in the pride of knowing he'd done his very best, there was no doubt I had made the right decision.

Following my personal mission in no way meant compromising my professional ideals, but I want to emphasize that while critically important to me, my career is only one aspect of my life's mission. My work and business has its own mission:

To guide individuals and organizations in identifying their unique talents, passions, and purpose and to provide the tools necessary to harness this power to ensure the joyful fulfillment of their individual and collective missions and, in so doing, improve the world.

You will notice that the two statements complement one another and work in harmony. But a balanced life is about much more than work alone, so that is reflected by the fact that I have more than one statement. My associates and I are all well aware of the company's mission statement and it guides all of our decision making relative to business matters. Likewise, many families have a family mission statement that helps members of that important operating unit get on the same page and operate in solidarity.

Take one last look at your mission statement (of course, you can go back and revise it whenever you like) and put some final flourishes on it if you are so moved. Record your mission statement, guiding principles, and the most essential insights from your self-assessment on the left side of your Custom Life Closet for easy reference. You may even wish to make an attractive printout of your mission and hang it where you can see it every day to be reminded of what matters most to you. You may also want to consider writing another mission statement for any aspect of your life that seems to call out for its own. Most essentially, use your mission statement(s) to remind yourself of what brings you joy and matters most.

Toolbox

Breath

Accessible to anyone at any time, focused breathing is a tool you can use to center yourself and get clarity as you contemplate your mission or at any point in the planning process. Whether you call focusing on your breath for a few moments meditation or just taking a breather, take regular moments to jump off the treadmill to reclaim your focus. Taking time to just be quiet and listen to what your inner voice has to say to you is a critical step in finding your metaphorical song so you bring your beautiful music to life.

Step ❷

Vision: Imagine the Sweet Smell (Sound, Look, and Feel) of Success

"If you don't know where you are going, any road will get you there."[1]
—Lewis Carroll

Congratulations. You have named your life's mission and you *are* going to put your talents to work to meet a need in the world. So how do you begin to do that? By stepping into the future and imagining that it's already done.

Creating a vision statement is step two of building your strategic plan. You will paint a vivid verbal picture of what life looks like when you are using your gifts fully, doing what you love most, and accomplishing what you set out to do. Your vision statement describes the point on the map you want to reach. While it won't tell you how you'll get there, it serves as your inspiration and the foundation for your business planning. You can't figure out what stands between where you are and where you want to be and how you'll travel the distance until you can clearly see your destination. It's your personal definition of success.

But in the Business of Life, your vision is more than just the X that marks the spot labeled "I've arrived." It's also a description of the journey—the life you'll savor along the way. Think of yourself as a skier standing at the trail map on the mountain. Your task is to choose the path that matches your ability, passions, and resources. Maybe you have a natural gift for skiing, love the exhilaration of flying down the mountain, and have a great pair of high-performance skis.

You might choose the double black diamond slope, with its bumps and adrenaline-pumping jumps. Or perhaps you're more laid back and would prefer a contemplative cross-country meander through the valley to the waterfall.

Your vision statement will capture all of this: the endpoint—where you're enjoying the fruits of doing what you set out to do—as well as the path and cadence that bring you pleasure as you head in that direction. In this chapter, you will complete a series of exercises that will define the elements of your vision. By the end of this phase, you will put them all together in a comprehensive picture so you can create the steps that will take you toward this satisfying future.

Visioning may sound a bit ethereal if you're a left-brain analytic person, but it's absolutely pragmatic. These compelling images will motivate you and keep you energized and moving forward productively. Whether you are creating a plan for a project at work, making more space for your family and hobbies, or taking on your whole life's mission, your vision statement puts a picture of what you are trying to achieve in your mind's eye and gives you a target to shoot for. It also reminds you very clearly of why hitting that target is worth it.

Bill is an architect who has run his own successful firm for decades. As the president of a million-dollar-plus nonprofit organization, he asked me to guide the board of trustees through a strategic planning process. After working on the mission statement, he was eager to jump right to setting strategies for achieving it. That's step five and, like a lot of people, he wanted to cut out the "softer" preliminaries and just get right to it. So it was gratifying to see the light bulb go on over his head as I explained the importance of creating a vision statement. He exclaimed, "Oh, I see now. If we can say more clearly what we want, we can figure out which strategies are most likely to get us there." As simple as this sounds, it was a revelation to him.

Interestingly, as an architect, Bill used visioning quite naturally with his clients by asking them how they wanted to use the space they had engaged him to design and what they wanted to accomplish there. Furthermore, he recognized that the other trustees who worked in a variety of industries needed a common understanding of the organi-zation's aspirations and that taking time at the outset to sharpen that vision would avoid time-stealing disagreements later in the process.

If you are leading a group at work, think about your people rowing toward a goal. Imagine what would happen if one person was headed in another direction. At best, he would slow the team's progress and at worst he would get your boat spinning in circles, making everyone seasick in the process.

And so it is for you. When a vision statement does its job, it's so vivid that you can easily see yourself in the new reality you would like to create. And it will get all parts of you working in harmony; your heart *and* head will be rowing in the same direction so you don't spin from inner conflict. If you're clear on where you're headed, it's much easier to see what it will take to accomplish your goals. And because it requires thinking about all the things you need to enjoy your life, creating your vision statement is actually fun and inspiring.

Having a Wonderful Time, Wish You Were Here

Think of your vision statement as a postcard from the future. You imagine yourself at a point a year or five or ten years down the line where you are happy and fulfilled. As you put yourself firmly in this picture, you use all of your senses to fully experience this vision—what true success would be like for you. Are you running a new busi-ness? Serving a needy population with an entrepreneurial nonprofit organization? Are you sitting in a beautifully decorated office? Cut-ting the ribbon for a new school you've helped open? Are you thriving at your demanding job, but this time making room for all the other things that mean so much to you, such as running outside with the dog or going out for real romance with your spouse? What are you seeing, smelling, hearing, feeling? Who is with you? You're on vaca-tion? Are you trekking through the mountains in Nepal or lounging in a hammock with a good book? Take time to note all the elements that surround the future you, and imagine this delicious scene in all its glory, with you at the center.

Many Western definitions of success focus on achieving a goal such as reaching a career milestone and crossing it off the list, but a well-lived life includes so much more. The soul-satisfying activities that make you feel whole belong in your vision, too. Interestingly, as you'll see throughout this book, bringing more *you* to your life can increase your effectiveness at work exponentially.

Life is serious business, but who said the ride shouldn't be fun? It isn't just about achieving results; it's about creating warm relationships, giving of yourself, and feeling joy and pleasure. In fact, a happy and fulfilled you is one of the greatest gifts you can give to the world. So, let's get started creating the building blocks of your vision statement.

EXERCISE

Postcard from the Future

I invite you to have some fun fantasizing about what a perfect day looks like for you. Sit comfortably with your notebook or computer. Put your mission statement firmly in your mind. Close your eyes for a few moments and picture yourself at some point in the future, fully living your dream and fulfilling your purpose. Breathe deeply and engage all of your senses. Describe what you experience as you imagine moving through your day. As you write it all down, be sure to state everything in the present tense and keep it positive. You experience what you put your attention on, so focus on pleasant images and describe what you see as though it were happening right now.

- What are you doing?
- Where are you?
- What does the space look like? Are you indoors or outside? Is it sunny and warm or are you in a dark room filled with technol-

ogy? What colors do you see? Is every room filled with fresh flowers? Are there whiteboards on the walls?

- Who is with you? Are you working in blissful solitude or surrounded by an unruly bunch of creative types? How are you relating to one another?
- Are you working in peace and quiet or is there music playing in the background?
- What do you need to have to make every day a joyful pleasure? The chance to connect deeply with other people? A fix of chocolate? Lots of laughter?
- What must you avoid to be happy? Do you hate conflict? Barking dogs? Traffic?

Write down anything that comes to you in your notebook and just start a stream-of-consciousness brain download. Answer all the questions above and anything else that comes to you. You will add to your "postcard" as you work your way through the following sections and you'll refine your vision in the final exercise.

Mission + You = Vision

In case you are feeling any pressure about getting your vision statement "right," let me assure you this task is eminently doable and virtually impossible to get wrong. That's because it's all about *you*, and you're the owner/operator of that fine operation.

One of the most important factors that separates inspired leaders from the sea of competent managers is a clear vision. It's hard to persuade other people to contribute to your success if you can't tell them what you want. And now that you are running the business of your life, it's time you get clear on what *You, Inc.* is going to produce. No one knows you better than you, so there is no one more qualified to define success on your terms.

You used your talent inventory in the last chapter to help define your mission, and it may be quite similar to other people's statements.

A lot of people and organizations have missions that overlap, or even sound nearly identical. But the visions they have for fulfilling those missions can be quite different, because each is built on the visioner's guiding principles and unique skills, experiences, and passions.

How you choose to carry out a given mission is a reflection of who you are: your own skills, likes, values, and quirky sense of what's fun or fulfilling. You're looking for the path that's a perfect fit for your talents, something that excites you and feels easy because it lets you do what comes naturally to you.

Say you identified feeding the hungry as your life's mission. The task of nourishing the world is enormous, and there are endless possible visions for accomplishing it. A right-brain, creative type might take on this mission by creating delicious new recipes for food that is stable without refrigeration and can easily be shipped and stored in areas without electricity. An analytical left-brain thinker might be intrigued by the logistics of creating a distribution system that delivers her creative friend's innovative cuisine to hungry people in remote third world villages. Yet another person with the very same mission might enjoy solving the puzzle of how to get around corrupt governments and bandits who siphon off the aid being offered by relief groups to the souls whose survival depends it.

Each of these people is working toward a common purpose, and all make an essential contribution in their own way.

EXERCISE

Pack It with Passion

To infuse your vision with passion and fun, go back to the lists of your talents and interests that you made in step one. How many of your passions can you pack in as you carry out your mission? Love problem solving? How can you bring your sleuthing skills into the picture? Would people laugh with recognition to see you, a dog lover, as a detective in the canine unit? Put that possibility on the table. What else makes you smile? You'll want your vision to be sprinkled with those feel-good spices.

The Magic Word for
a Powerful Vision: AGLOW

"Neither do men light a candle, and put it under a bushel, but on a candlestick: and it gives its light unto all that are in the house."

—Jesus of Nazareth

Your vision statement isn't something you'll write and file away. You'll refer to it often, even daily, so it should be inspirational. Create an image that propels you forward, compelling you to pursue goals that will move you along your path. It should light you up from the inside with a glow that radiates to everyone around you. Just reading it should energize you.

You can ensure that your vision statement has the power to set you AGLOW by making it:

Authentic
Grand
Laudable
Optimistic
Wondrous

EXERCISE

Get Glowing

Grab your notebook and record your thoughts as we drill down into each of these elements. The insights, images, and desires that surface as you go along may become the pearls that you string together to create a complete vision.

1. Make it authentic: First and foremost, your vision must allow you to be true to who you really are, not someone else's vision of what they'd like you to be. What do you most value? What are the gifts that only you can share with the world? That must be expressed in your vision statement. You will not heed your calling if you are trying to be a pale imitation of someone else. You need to focus your energies on being the best YOU possible. As motivational speaker Mike Robbins says in his book of the same name, "Be yourself. Everyone else is already taken."[2]

I can't stress enough the importance of authenticity in writing your vision. Make it reflect your genuine dreams and desires. You've put a lot of effort into finding your personal genius and thinking about how to put that to work in service of the world. Stay focused there. Dig deep.

2. Make it grand: This is the time to think big, audacious thoughts. One of my students told me that his grandfather used to say, "Shoot for the sky and you might hit the top of the coconut tree. Shoot for the tree and you may hit the ground." Take his advice and aim high. Writing a vision statement is about defining your ideal, not what you think may be possible. This is *not* the time to limit your thinking and cut off your options because you believe your fantasy is too big, too bold, or too anything ever to come true. We will test those limiting beliefs later. You may be quite surprised to see what's feasible once you have a vivid vision of where you're headed and you're armed with the information and tools presented in the upcoming chapters. So, suspend disbelief for now and think big.

If you knew you couldn't fail, what would you include in your picture of your perfect future? Would you be hanging out with rock stars? Write it down. Selling your artwork in high-end art galleries? Record that. Your fantasies need a place to live. For now, that will be in your notebook. Later, who knows? One thing is for sure. If you cross your dreams off your list, they won't come true. At least give them a shot.

3. Make it laudable: Since your mission is about using your talents to meet a need in the world, your vision should describe how your little corner of the world will be better because of the work your mission has set in motion. This doesn't mean you have to be Mother Teresa. A personal shopper who helps people find flattering styles that make them feel attractive and confident is providing a helpful service. You can be helpful without being perfect. What does the world need that you have to offer? Which population do you want to serve? Animals? Do you want to be a veterinarian, a conservationist who saves endangered species in the jungles of Africa, or a dog walker? Do you want to raise happy children and send them into the world? Help the hungry and homeless? Heal the sick? Tell killer jokes and relieve the stress of overwrought executives? Write it down.

4. Make it optimistic: This is essential. To be effective, your vision statement should describe your life in positive, present-tense language as though you were already living your ideal. The whole point of creating a vision is to help you picture what you are trying to achieve so you can focus your efforts on filling in the colors in your paint-by-numbers future.

When you were a kid, what got you excited? Write that down. Your younger self may well have a lot to teach you. So put yourself in your size four Keds and try to remember: What did you want to be when you grew up? Think about how you would have answered that question at several points in your childhood. The answers may give you additional clues about your gifts and passions. You may no longer want to fight fires, but when you ask your younger self why he wanted to do that, he may tell you that he likes helping people and the excitement that comes with the urgency of a crisis. Not to mention, he'd get to drive really cool trucks and slide down a pole in the middle of the night.

Do those things still float your boat? You may want to look for activities that include them and make them part of your vision. How can you get that adrenaline rush while helping people? Or was it the shiny brass pole that caught your imagination? I hear pole-dancing classes are popping up in health clubs across the country.

5. Make it wondrous: Your vision should leave you in a state of "pinch me" wonder, where you are thrilled to look around at a life that includes everything you value and that rewards you for giving exactly what you're here to offer. The more you paint a picture with all the shades that inspire and energize you, the more committed you will be to breathing life into it. And commitment is what we want. Your mission depends on it.

Pull It Together

Take a moment to review this section and make sure you've recorded all of the elements that will make your future glow.

Igniting Your Glow May Feel Undoable, but Try It Anyway

Bruce and his wife, Mara, were thrilled that their careers were going so well, and they were proud of their two beautiful children. Yes, they'd hoped for three, but other than that, they couldn't quite figure out why their jobs and kids weren't enough to make them happy. With this vague sense of dissatisfaction, Bruce, a mid-level manager (ironically enough, a strategic planner) took one of my Business of Life courses. Besides learning some concrete business skills he could use on the job, Bruce was hoping to get to the bottom of his discontent and to develop a plan to bring more joy into his life to match the success he seemed to have on paper.

Bruce's personal mission was "to create a harmonious home life, raise happy, healthy, and productive children, and make a positive difference with my professional and volunteer work." That statement reflected who he was, but it gave him no clues about what was missing, so he was excited by the idea of imagining his perfect day and conjuring up the details of what he needed in his life for it to feel fun, fulfilling, and meaningful.

He nodded when I told his group to consider what would make them the happiest, rather than focusing on what wasn't working in their lives. As a strategist, he knew well that working toward a positive vision is much more productive than dwelling on shortcomings. It was pretty easy for him to come up with this vision statement:

BRUCE'S VISION STATEMENT

It is five years from now and our household is a crazy, mixed-up bastion of creative, controlled chaos. Our three little girls, ages three, six, and eight, are growing, giggling, and thriving at their preschool and public schools. They enjoy their friends and each other. Each girl has her own distinct personality, but they share our family's common values and there is always love and compassion present, even during their disagreements. I enjoy being their personal riding toy and delight in showering them with love, wisdom, and thousands of kisses.

My wife and I have reclaimed some of the time we had devoted to establishing our careers and made a commitment to a weekly date where we can focus on our love for each other and remember to laugh together. Every Saturday night, we get dressed up, go out for dinner, and do something that reminds us of why we fell in love so many years ago. Fun is a requirement. We remember to be silly with each other, not just with the kids. I remember, weekly, to look deeply into Mara's eyes and really see her. This fuels me and allows me to keep a sense of humor about all the times my kids' demands pull me away from my work. Because it reminds me that raising happy, productive children *is* my work, and this memory makes me smile and relax.

Just writing his vision down made Bruce smile and relax. He had a big *aha* moment when he put his finger on what had been making him dissatisfied in his otherwise pretty great life: he'd gotten into a groove so deep it was more like a rut. He and Mara had been having what could best be described as an "administrative relationship." Their brief time together each day was spent figuring out the family's complicated logistics and assigning chores. They'd stopped expressing their real love for each other, let alone having fun together. This became immediately apparent to Bruce as he envisioned his ideal life. And when he mentioned it to Mara, she nodded with recognition and pledged immediately to join him in making some changes.

Bruce's shiny vision ultimately transformed their lives, but committing it to paper was a struggle for him. He hesitated to write down what he longed for because there seemed to be no way he and Mara could have a third child and keep it all together—not with *their* schedules.

When I saw his brow furrow while he was writing his vision statement in class, I walked over and asked if he needed help. He said that his vision seemed impossible and he was trying to figure out a vision that was feasible, so I reminded him not to edit down his dreams. We're going for grand, optimistic, and wondrous, after all, and that means coming up with a picture of the ideal, not simply what's practical. A vision statement helps you figure out *what* you want. The work that follows in a strategic plan is about figuring out *how* to get it, even when it seems wildly impractical.

Bruce took a deep breath and went determinedly (if a bit skeptically) back to his writing. We'll meet up with him later in this book to see how he dealt with the nuts and bolts of living out his vision. For now, all I will say is that he figured out a lot of stuff—and lit his wife's light in the process. He even improved his work life. And it all started with stretching his imagination and expanding his notion of what was possible.

Toolbox

Suspend Disbelief

You are going to learn some skills and techniques later in this book that may well give you the tools to accomplish what now seems completely out of the question. So before you discount any dream or desire as unattainable, put your doubts aside and, for now, continue with the assumption that anything is possible.

Feel the Pull

Just as a magnet draws metal effortlessly toward it, an effective vision statement pulls you toward its fulfillment. There's something irresistible to your mind and heart about imagining yourself enjoying your life while you are using your native talents to do great things. Who wouldn't be lured by such a force? And, when you layer on those things that make your hours joyful, you look forward to the process of arriving at your vision.

As I wrote this book—a project with the simple, utilitarian mission: Complete Writing the Book—I was pulled along by a vision that had me sitting in my beautiful office with soothing, cheerful colors, a cup of tea, music playing, and my lush garden on view through the window. Because my vision had spelled out not only my larger goals for the book but also what would make my journey the most satisfying, I made sure that I had all the little touches in my office that made me glad to be there. The space was clean and peaceful. I enjoyed a lovely solitude when it was needed and made plans to be with cherished friends and family later, so I was alone, but not lonely. My kids knew they could pop in for a kiss or a question, but not linger. So, I was productive, but not isolated. In short, my office was someplace I wanted to be and, as a result, it wasn't a struggle to get my butt in the chair and get down to work on this enormous undertaking.

The hard work of writing was sweetened immeasurably by the grace notes I strung through my vision. And I read the comments of people whose lives had been changed for the better after taking my workshops. The image of readers lighting up as they figure out what they want and discovering a path to make it happen kept me going, knowing I was fulfilling an important mission.

Did my vision "attract" the experience it described? Well, what you think about, you bring about, as the saying goes. We also tend to act on impulses that arise from what we focus on. We visualize writing in a serene space, and soon comes the impulse to clear and paint the room, set up the desk, put down the first few sentences. And in that way, we move toward creating that new reality.

You will do things randomly if you haven't consciously chosen a direction, so crafting a vision statement means taking active control of your thoughts, focusing them on creating a deliberate reality that is fulfilling and provides lasting value.

Remember Raymond, the imaginary musician from the last chapter whose mission was to become a concert pianist? He had a remarkable gift for blending notes and melodies to interpret great works in astonishing ways that still respected the compositions' integrity. Further, he found that his gift compelled him to create new musical pieces that stretched the music-loving public's imagination.

Now, as he closes his eyes and imagines his happy future, he sees himself surrounded by other musicians. He is listening, enraptured, to a harmonic blend of orchestral instruments sending their sweet sounds through the air of a great theater, and he is thrilled to contribute to the symphony. While he is there, he feels the joy that comes with living this reality.

When he wakes from his reverie and finishes writing down his vision, he realizes that it's been a mighty long time since he's actually played the piano. He's so excited to get started, he immediately picks up the phone to call the maestro from his local symphony hall to find the name of a piano teacher who can help him hone his skills until he is an accomplished enough performer to flourish as a soloist. He's on his way to leading the life he's dreamed of.

Vision has an amazing way of giving birth to action.

EXERCISE

Joy Notes

Because you'll want to be sure that your vision is full of elements, large and small, that give you pleasure, spend some time taking note of just what those things are. I often suggest that my students carry a notebook for a day, even a week, and jot down the things they enjoy. Puzzles? A walk across the park on the way home? A bounding yellow lab puppy jumping on you as you walk in the door? If it makes you happy, write it down, and be sure there's room for it in your vision.

Finding Focus

I've seen many people make changes, large and small, based solely on the power of their mission and vision statements, together with their guiding principles.

Take Sandra, for example. She's the compassionate, ambitious professional we met in the last section whose mission statement described the way she wanted to "support, motivate, and bring joy to those I encounter throughout my life."

She'd been tested, strengthened, and ultimately inspired by a long struggle with infertility, and when she sat down to write her vision statement, she reached back to that experience and confirmed for herself that helping others with that issue would be an important part of her future. She'd been thinking about starting a nonprofit organization, and because that dream seemed grand and a bit daunting, she set her vision five years in the future:

SANDRA'S PERSONAL VISION STATEMENT

I have a loving husband and two happy children who are self-confident and aware of themselves. We laugh and love together every day.

I am instrumental in developing and leading the inpatient and outpatient Diabetes Wellness Center at my hospital. I grew this center from its nascent stages to the award-winning center it is today.

I am the cofounder of Fertility Within Reach, a successful nonprofit organization aimed at helping individuals who are impacted by the disease of infertility become their own best advocates for change. I personally advocate for insurance coverage of infertility services nationwide. As a result of these efforts, individuals gain the confidence they need to navigate the struggles of infertility, and thousands of babies are born to couples faced with the challenge of infertility.

I enjoy my vast network of friends, each of whom brings me something different. We laugh together, support each other, and help each other grow.

Sandra came to the Business of Life class because she had an ambitious agenda and needed a set of tools to manage everything she wanted to do at home, at work, and in her community. With so much fire in her belly, she ran the risk of burning herself out if she tried to do too much. And like a lot of capable people who can handle many things well, she faced the very real possibility that she'd expertly execute the wrong things—initiatives that didn't mean much to her. That could bring her external rewards, but not genuine success.

Her vision statement helped her keep her passions front and center, and laid the groundwork for setting some short- and long-term goals. Just one year later—not five, as she'd expected—she's gotten Fertility Within Reach off the ground. The project took off as she discovered the power of concentrating her abundant energy on her own passions. And the joy that infused her vision is now part of her everyday life.

Later, you'll see the shifts Sandra made, and the new habits that took shape, as she began setting priorities based on her vision.

Use Your Vision to Make Decisions

Perhaps you are considering making a big change. Your vision statement can give you some objectivity in moments of doubt. As I contemplated what it would mean for me to leave my senior position in one of the world's most prestigious institutions to work on my own without a safety net, I looked to the vision statement I'd written years earlier. To my great surprise, the words "Massachusetts General Hospital" did not even appear in the document. So, while I likened my departure from MGH after sixteen years of devoted service to bungee jumping, my vision statement confirmed that this leap was worth making.

MY PERSONAL VISION STATEMENT

Every day is productive and filled with joy and laughter. I feel happily connected to others and my life's purpose at all times. My time is spent with people I love, respect, and enjoy. I have enough time to myself, but never feel alone or lonely. I feel guided and protected, safe to explore all aspects of who I am and to express my being fully.

My family is thriving. Indeed, all of my relationships are harmonious, loving, and mutually beneficial. My children are healthy, happy, and fulfilled. They enjoy a strong sense of self and their place in the world. We remain deeply connected while they enjoy their independence. They are fine human beings with wonderful values and are contributing their special gifts to benefit the world. My husband and I continue to grow together while also pursuing our individual interests. We nurture and support one another and have a lot of fun. We are learning what we need to know about each other and we enjoy and appreciate being together. Our connection continues to deepen and grow.

My work is another way to fulfill my sense of purpose. I lead a team of talented people with great integrity, commitment, and good humor. Our work is devoted to helping, empowering, and healing others and reflects back on us daily. I have enough flexibility to balance work with family life and the pursuit of my other personal interests. I consistently feel deeply satisfied with my work and can see tangible benefits of my contributions.

I have ample time to enjoy nature. My life is structured to allow for lots of hikes and other ways to enjoy the outdoors with friends and family or in solitude. It is easy to "get away from it all" whenever the need arises. I am surrounded by beauty: in my home and work environments, on the faces of the people I see, radiating from my own heart.

My life has a profound positive impact on all it touches. I am rewarded enough financially to support myself and my family and to contribute significantly to worthy causes. My future is secure. I may retire comfortably whenever I am ready. My needs, both material and emotional, are modest and easily met. All of this joy and bounty flows easily to and through me. I enjoy good health and vitality, easily maintaining my fitness level and a healthy, comfortable weight. I have more than enough energy to accomplish anything I choose to do. I enjoy inner peace and have learned to accept myself with love, unconditionally.

I have found the balance of work and other pursuits that works for my family, friends, colleagues, clients, and community. I am fully present at all times and true to myself. The people in my life know, honor, respect, and support me and the choices that I've made. We all live together in joy, good health, and harmony.

This statement reflects my aspirations and serves as a daily reminder to make decisions that support living in the manner this vision describes. In many ways, my vision statement is a great affirmation that I'm already acting in accordance with my values and that much of what's written here is part of my reality. That's worth appreciating, and I most certainly do. It's also there to pull me back on track when I stray from some of my own principles. You may have noticed that I speak of ease in my statement because, as a driven achiever, it's good to be reminded that I could lighten up from time to time. That reminder truly does help me make more mindful decisions that continuously nudge me in the right direction.

Evaluate an Opportunity

Your vision statement can help with all kinds of decisions. A new opportunity presents itself. Should you take it? A quick look at your vision statement will help you decide whether doing so will contribute to your idea of success or whether it will take you in some random, aimless direction.

Say you're offered a job as a financial analyst. It sounds like an interesting challenge, and it's a promotion. You're momentarily intrigued. Then you look at your vision statement and realize your mission to become manager is going to require that you get some experience supervising people. The only thing you'll be supervising as an analyst is a bunch of spreadsheets. The new job would move you up all right, but in a direction that moves you away from your goal, not toward it. No, this isn't the best strategic move you can make. But it's a useful wake-up call. You are due for a promotion and resolve to make an appointment today to talk to your boss about giving you a project with a few people to manage.

Should I Say Yes or No?

Your vision can also be a useful filter for deciding what to add to your already overflowing plate. Does serving on that fundraising committee at your church contribute to your vision of the perfect day, month, or life? It's a good fit for a vision that says: "I am happily engaged with other people in all my pursuits; I am very active in my community." Serving on this committee will give you time to spend with people you like and respect while contributing to your church, which is very important to your life and the fabric of the community. So, it's a big YES; you're happy to serve.

Or your experience may be more like that of my coaching client Brandon, a busy executive juggling family and a career. His vision of a balanced life showed him thriving at work yet being available to attend his children's soccer games and concerts without drawing the disapproving glares of his colleagues.

When he was asked to join the board of directors of a prestigious company, he was flattered, and his first instinct was to say yes and enjoy hobnobbing with other high-powered businesspeople. However, when he asked for more details, he learned that there would be at least an additional fifteen to twenty hours of work per month involved, and that the board meetings were held in the evenings, making it difficult to free himself for those important events at his kids' school. So, with disappointment but not regret, he turned down the offer with the confidence that another opportunity would arise when his kids were older and his priorities shifted.

You can use your vision statement to make less momentous decisions, as well. For instance, is an intriguing invitation a distraction or a pleasant diversion? Imagine that a friend invites you to come for a weekend at her house by the seashore. You love the beach, and spending time by the water is part of your vision. But you're on deadline with a project and worry you can't fit it in. Your spirits sink at the idea of missing all the fun, so remembering your vision, you tell your friend about your dilemma, instead of automatically saying no. She surprises you by suggesting that you take the bedroom in the back of the house where you can work in peace. Now you can go to the beach for a couple of hours, go back and work with intense focus during peak sun hours, and join up with your pals for a nice dinner out. Sounds splendid, and it will actually help you be efficient and meet your deadline. You start packing.

Vision at Work: Tapping Into Passion

There's another benefit to having a juicy vision: that inspiring image is a great way to get others on board and supporting you in whatever you want to do.

I recently chaired the search committee for a rabbi of a good-sized synagogue. We had just completed a strategic plan for the congregation so we were clear about the kind of spiritual leader we wanted to recruit. We were told there was a shortage of rabbis nationally and that we'd be lucky to get a dozen candidates. Astonishingly, more than forty rabbis applied for the position. When we asked the candidates what attracted them to the job, they all cited the same thing: the vision statement described such an exciting future, they wanted to be a part of making it happen.

Whether you're leading a team in your workplace, on a football field, or even at home, the shinier and more inspiring the vision, the more vigor and commitment your players will bring. And the more that you can make your collective vision reflect elements of each team member's personal vision, the more passion they will bring to the project. They'll want to join you in making it succeed because it satisfies *them* too.

Tips for Making Your Vision Statements Glow

By now, I hope you see what a vision statement can do for you, and how richly you'll be rewarded for putting time and care into creating one. You started your visioning when you wrote your description of a perfect day and considered the elements that set it AGLOW. As we get ready to fold that work into your larger vision statement, I'll offer a few last guidelines.

• **Details matter:** A good vision statement draws you in and pumps you up with the enthusiasm you need to make it a reality. It doesn't need to be a piece of literary art, but it should include as many specifics as you can muster so that you can easily picture yourself doing the things you describe in an atmosphere that inspires you and brings you joy.

• **Positive language will give you more energy:** As I've said before, you are looking to feel empowered and excited, so pay close attention to how your chosen words make you feel. Try this experiment: state, in positive terms, how you are surrounded by people who get along with one another. The scene is serene and you are at ease. You are enjoying uncomplicated, effortless relationships with everyone in your life. It's an encouraging vision, right?

But how inspiring is this? "I am surrounded by troublemaking jerks, but they don't bother me much anymore. They aren't picking fights and making me quite as insane as usual. And, I can win the fights they do start." Do you find yourself holding your breath as you see these button-pushing words? See how much more encouraging the first version is than one that dwells on ridding yourself of negativity?

The words you use can have a profound impact on your emotions. This is the place to make them shiny and bright.

• **Give yourself time:** How far in the future should your vision be? That really depends on the distance between where you are and where you want to be. It could be a wide gap if you have a huge vision such as joining NASA and walking on the moon. You might want to pick a longer time line, too, if you're overcoming a setback, say recovering from a major surgery, and you've got some work to do just to prepare for your journey. Choose a time that seems reasonable for the size of your vision. Generally speaking, six months is a good lower boundary and five years is a reasonable upper limit.

You want to achieve this vision, of course, so you want the time frame to reflect steady, relentless progress toward your goal, but you don't want it to be so aggressive that you couldn't possibly meet the time frame and still have any joy in the journey. So give yourself some positive pressure, but don't go overboard and create one more source of unnecessary stress.

• **One page is a good goal:** My students often tell me that they've posted their mission and vision statements in a place where they can read them daily to stay focused and motivated. It's ideal if they are detailed and nuanced, but succinct enough so you can refer to them often for quick inspiration.

There's No One Right Answer

We all bring our own unique perspective to everything we do. We see things through our own lens, filtered through our own experiences. One view isn't right and another isn't wrong. The way we picture something is just a reflection of our perspective and worldview. Let me show you what I mean. Look at how the smallest shifts change your perception of the Koffka Ring[3] below. The gray ring is exactly the same in each of the three images even though it looks quite different as the background shifts and changes.

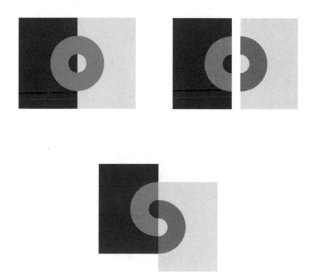

Is one perception right and another wrong? Not at all. The way you see something has everything to do with the way you look at it. The "right" vision is the one that's right for *you*.

EXERCISE

Your Personal Vision Statement: Weaving the Threads

Set aside some time when you will be free of phones, e-mail, and interruptions so you can quietly reflect. Read through the whole exercise and then review everything you wrote down as you worked through this chapter. It is time to weave all the threads of your vision into a tapestry that excites and inspires you.

You are defining your destination: Where are you headed on your map? Be very specific. What do you need for each day to be joyful as you move toward your destination? What does your life look like when you are using your special gifts in the way only you can?

Give yourself permission to shed your limiting beliefs and envision your ideal life. Close your eyes and take a few deep breaths. Place yourself at some point in the future. Your life is going just the way you want it. You wouldn't change a thing. What do you see, hear, smell, taste, feel? How do you look? Write down whatever comes to you in your notebook or on your computer. Do *not* censor yourself or constrain your thinking by practical limitations. Ask yourself one more time:

- What do I need to have in my life to feel joyful and fulfilled?
- When do I feel at my best?
- What are some of the peak experiences of my life? What was special about them that I want to have more of in my daily life?
- If I/my organization/my project is wildly successful, what is happening?
- If I didn't have to make money to live, how would I spend my time?
- Whose life do I envy? What do they have that I want in my life?
- Who are the people in my life who support my vision? How are they helping me? How am I interacting with them?

As you answer these questions, keep in mind that there is a difference between lasting joy and fleeting pleasure. Many people begin this exercise with a fantasy of chilling on the beach with a frozen umbrella drink, but soon come to the conclusion that doing that for a lifetime would be rather meaningless. Pleasure is great, and you should most certainly include a good dose of that in your vision. But to be fully gratified and successful achieving your mission, you will want to focus a fair bit of energy thinking about how you are employing your special gifts to serve a conscious, worthy purpose.

Reflect on your responses to these questions and everything else you've recorded. Write your personal vision statement incorporating all the elements that mean the most to you. Whatever you have written, this is the kind of exercise you may want to allow to marinate over a few days. Allow your vision to be present in your thoughts when you are going for a walk, taking a shower, shaving, or doing any repetitive, relaxing activity. You may want to keep your notebook close at hand so you can take down any inspiring thoughts that pop up when you're in a peaceful state and not forcing yourself to think about your vision. Inspiration can come at any time, so be alert to thoughts, feelings, and signals. When an image quickens your heartbeat and nudges the corners of your mouth into a smile, pay attention to what's causing that excitement. It may well be something that belongs in your vision.

Mini-Visions

I do a visioning exercise every day during my early-morning swim. After my workout, I get into the pool for my cool-down and meditation. Using the rhythm of my breath and strokes to get into a relaxed, focused state, I set an intention for each day. I think about what I want to accomplish and how I want to feel. Then I concentrate on that intention and what I need to do to make it happen. These are what I call my "mini-visions."

I've got an overall vision statement for my life and business that is filled with details of what that all looks like as well as a vision for my typical day. (I started to type average, but of course, my vision is *aglow*, so my envisioned days are anything but average.) Now, in order to fulfill my big mission and vision, I have many small and medium-sized projects that need to be done. Each of these can have its own vision statement. At some point in the future, you may want to consider doing the same. For now, writing a vision statement for your overall mission is a great place to start.

Themes May Be Clear but the Specifics Are Elusive

Creating a vision statement can be a very abstract exercise for people who would naturally prefer to do, do, do and skip the dreaming phase. So how can a task-focused doer cross the vision statement off the to-do list? Start with what you know.

Lee Ann lost her cherished mother to cancer a few years ago. It was a wrenching heartache. When her beloved aunt was struck with the same fatal disease a short time later, Lee Ann couldn't justify staying in her successful management job, particularly since the last few years at work had become increasingly unfulfilling. She retired from her position and devoted herself to providing care, comfort, and companionship to her aunt during her illness. When her aunt passed away, Lee Ann was ready to resume her career, but didn't know what she wanted to do. It needed to be more meaningful, that much was clear. And she wanted to help people coping with cancer. That kernel of an idea, along with her firm commitment and intention, didn't add up to a full-blown vision, but it wasn't a bad place to start.

As we sat across the table from each other in her first coaching session, I asked her what brought her joy and what renewed her energy as she cared for her dying aunt. I also asked her what talents she drew on that gave her a sense of mission. Having no children of her own, she loved doing craft projects with her nieces. One of her favorite things was making killer Halloween costumes for the girls every year and she'd recently taken up painting to renew her spirit. She also said she is very organized and has a real talent for figuring out a series of steps needed to achieve her goals. She had drawn on these skills throughout her highly successful management career.

Neither of us knew where this combination of talents and passions would take her, but now she knew where to start looking. You will see as her story unfolds later in this book that her ability to articulate even a bit of what she wanted to do, and whom she wanted to help, would enable her to enlist the help of others to find a precise vision that fit.

So, if you're stymied, start with what you've got and write down whatever you can. Is there a specific group you want to serve? What activities bring you joy and satisfaction? What refills your spiritual cup? Go back to your talents and interests. What are you good at? What do you have to work with? Jot it all down. Don't push too hard. Enjoy some time just imagining yourself in an environment that juices you up. Get as specific as you can without straining. Then you may want to consider talking to some like-minded souls or other people you admire and start sharing the elements of your vision that you *can* describe.

Solicit the ideas, guidance, and suggestions of other people who may be able to help you round out your vision. There is no dishonor in asking for help. Keep on thinking, feeling, and talking, and be patient if it takes a while. Spend some time in quiet introspection. Give it regular thought and keep revisiting it until the pieces of your vision crystallize. Write them down as they come to you. This process should feel joyful as it unfolds. It's okay if it takes time, as long as you commit to sticking with it until a compelling vision comes into focus.

Now You'll Know You're on Track

Put the key elements of your vision into your custom closet, where you can look at them often and continue moving forward in your own special style—whether you're schussing down the slopes with exhilarating speed or striding over for a view of that waterfall you hear roaring in the distance. It's not unusual for people who have taken the Business of Life course to tell me that they're still pulling out their closets years after their class for inspiration and confirmation that they're still on the right track.

With a clear vision firmly in your mind's eye, you are ready to move to the next steps in the planning cycle: naming what you need to have in place to succeed and sizing up your ability to secure all you need to bring your vision to life.

Toolbox

Focus

We create our own reality, and what we think about, we bring about. This is not as metaphysical as you might think. You experience what you think about, so why not choose your thoughts deliberately? Cultivate the discipline to focus your thoughts on those experiences you want more of in your life and less on those you don't. Focus will also bring clarity and guide you to spend your precious resources getting the results you want.

Step ❸

Name Your Critical Success Factors

"Success is where preparation and opportunity meet."[1]
—Bobby Unser, Three-Time Indianapolis 500 Winner

You have created an ambitious, glowing vision, but perhaps it seems far off and out of reach. So now what? How do you go from dreaming to doing? The key is to examine the elements that set your vision aglow and to list everything you need to bring it to life. By writing it all down, you are taking a tangible step toward making real progress. This is a very brief but essential step. By accomplishing this simple task, you build positive forward momentum that moves you in the right direction before the glow dims and you go back to doing things the way you've always done them.

What You Need to Succeed

You already know where you're headed. If you were sketching out a map, your destination would be the vision you've so carefully created. It is time to get specific about what you need so you can figure out how you will make it happen. So, first things first: you will make a list. This step seems so obvious that many people skip right over it. But pausing for a moment to make sure you've documented what you need improves the odds that you will put everything in place to get where you're going.

You can't make a suit without taking careful measurements, creating a pattern, and procuring fabric, notions, and a sewing machine.

Your list of success factors will also help you assess the distance between where you are and where you're headed. In turn, that will help you see how far you have to travel and how long it might take to arrive.

Let's look at Raymond, the would-be concert pianist we met in earlier chapters. What would he need to fulfill that vision? With his ambition to be a musician of worldwide renown, here's a decent list of what he might need:

- Access to a piano
- A concert-level piano teacher
- Space to practice
- Aptitude for the piano
- Money to pay for the piano, space, and lessons
- Membership with an ensemble to practice with other musicians
- Knowledge of music theory

When Your Vision Seems Impossible to Achieve

Diane is a primary care physician at a highly traditional academic medical center. She came for some coaching as she considered the options for advancing her career while reserving ample time to spend with her two young daughters. As always, we began her planning with her creating an inventory of her strengths, interests, and values, and then she wrote her mission and vision statements. Thinking about how she could fulfill her vision overwhelmed her because she didn't have any role models who had done what she hoped to pull off for herself. She simply couldn't picture how to make it happen. Her vision included her cooking with her kids several nights a week and enjoying family dinners that they'd created as a team. Her husband, a busy attorney who shared this desire, was willing to commit to being home for those meals and offered to take on cleanup duty. That part seemed doable.

But Diane wanted to establish herself as a national thought leader in medicine, which, following the traditional career path, would require her to set up a research group, secure grants, and publish scholarly articles in prestigious journals. The problem with that scenario is that it didn't fit well with her busy primary care practice, to which she was passionately committed, and her active home life. Securing research funding is highly competitive and requires long hours in order to excel. Her ambition to have a soaring career while being an involved parent seemed impossible when held up against the realities of her chosen field.

I reminded Diane that until she fully explored all of her options, it was too early to dismiss her ideal as impractical and settle for something less. She was game to move forward, if not terribly optimistic. So I asked her to continue suspending disbelief for a while longer and just list what she would need to have in place for her to achieve this seemingly unworkable balance. She thought it might be more feasible to pull off this feat if she were able to do some of her work at home, so she came up with this list:

- A home office setup, with computer
- A morning clinical schedule that allowed her to be home after school hours
- Deep expertise in an issue of importance to her medical peers
- A platform to communicate her ideas
- The support of her division chief
- Salary for her nonclinical hours

Just committing her list to paper made it seem less overwhelming. While she still couldn't see how she would make this happen, she could begin to imagine how she might set some goals to further refine her vision. We'll meet up with Diane in the next step.

When You Don't Know Where to Start

If your vision is multifaceted, you may want to break it down into separate sections and make an inventory of success factors for each one. Organize them in whatever way works for you. I find it helpful to use different color markers to highlight the various parts of my vision, such as relationships, work, community, and mind/body/spirit pursuits. However you choose to approach this, make sure to include the joy notes that will make working toward your vision a pleasant journey.

Because my own vision encompasses many disparate yet harmonious activities, I have broken it down into projects and made a list of success factors for each one. For example, writing this book is one aspect of fulfilling both my personal and professional visions. I needed some obvious things:

- A computer
- Time, time, and more time to review and organize mountains of materials
- Welcoming work space
  - Attractive office with soothing colors
  - Clean, orderly desk
  - Inspiring photos
  - Pots of tea
  - Music
- Scheduled breaks for exercise and human contact
- Interviews with clients and program participants

This was also an opportunity to get some good "twofers"—activities that serve you in more than one way. Reviewing my vision statement was a great way to see the potential. When I rethought my writing schedule so that I could help my son prepare for his bar mitzvah, I had planned to get back on track by "going underground" to spend some concentrated time writing free from the competing demands of family, consulting projects, and coaching clients. A review of my vision statement reminded me that spending time in nature is critical to nourishing my spirit. Connecting with cherished friends is also central to my well-being, and is a particular challenge given the solitary nature of writing. So, I added to my list of critical success factors:

- Getting "off the grid" for five days
- Time in nature
- Good company for breaks

Just to show you where this is all leading, I'll jump ahead a couple of steps and demonstrate how this list of success factors led me to a strategy that fulfilled my whole list. I knew from past experience that trying to write for sustained periods from my office was a setup that would lead to distractions and frustration. Blocking off a few hours a day is usually doable, but the time required to get back on schedule meant that wasn't feasible. So, I decided to rent a cottage on Cape Cod for a few days and invite my sister to join me. The cape is very quiet and beautiful in the autumn and I was able to find a perfect space at off-season rates.

It was a magical time. I had the concentrated periods of quiet time I needed to reimmerse myself in this massive project and I had scheduled breaks for exercise and time in nature when we walked the beaches in the cool breeze. We were delighted by the rare opportunity to spend so much time together and we had the special treat of watching seals playing in the surf. The invigorating walks renewed me for a few more hours of writing. Then we capped off the day with dinner out. We made a point of testing the cosmopolitans in each restaurant we tried, so we accomplished some important research as well. Most important, I made up for lost writing time and returned home with renewed focus, successfully reconnected with this intense project.

Hopefully, it is now clear how listing your success factors will form a basis for creating strategies that are likely to help you achieve your goals. And, as important, to enjoy the process as much as is possible. So remember to add some spice and make your main course as delicious as it can be. Consider these factors as the ingredient list for your recipe for success.

EXERCISE

Make Your List

Pull out your vision statement and take a look all the individual aspects that comprise your ideal future. Grab your notebook and simply make a list of those things that need to be in place for you to fully occupy the picture you've drawn for yourself. Be as thorough as possible. In the next step, you will take an inventory of those factors that you have in place and those that you will have to acquire. The more detail you can develop here, the better your chances of getting them in place.

Step ④

Find Your Sweet SWOT

"When I…use my strength in the service of my vision, it becomes less and less important whether I am afraid."[1]

—Audre Lorde

With your list of critical success factors in hand, it is natural to ask with some trepidation: Do I have what it takes to get there? A strategic plan doesn't leave you wondering. It gives you a clear, calm, and brilliantly easy way to find out. It's called a SWOT analysis. I don't have much use for business jargon, but I make an exception for SWOT, an acronym for strengths, weaknesses, opportunities, and threats. You can use your SWOT to size up what you have to work with—or work around—as you move into action on your project. With a clear picture of your assets and liabilities, you will be in a great position to figure out where to invest your efforts and resources so they will return the greatest dividends.

Size Up Your Position

Now comes a little reconnaissance. Is your vehicle the right one for the trip you want to take? Are there obstacles to steer around or particular routes that will send you flying toward where you want to go? A SWOT analysis will tell you, so you can plot out your next moves in a way that's custom designed to boost your chances for success.

The great thing about SWOT is its simplicity. It gives you a wealth of information by having you focus on just four key areas:

- Your strengths—the skills, talents, and resources you'll use to fulfill your vision.
- Your weaknesses—factors that could impede your progress. A weakness could be a skill or resource you need but don't have. It might also be a behavioral pattern that holds you back or a tendency to undermine yourself by doing things like thinking too small.
- Your opportunities—situations that could give you a chance to leverage your skills and talents.
- Your threats—outside factors that could get in your way.

You'll start by looking internally, at your own strengths and weaknesses. Next, you will scan your environment for potential opportunities and threats, the external factors that are out of your control but may have an impact on your success. Once you've recorded what you find, you'll be able to test how well your mission fits with your talents and circumstances, and evaluate the potential for challenges ahead. Armed with this information, you can set goals that will make the most of your assets and opportunities, fill in gaps, and mitigate potential threats.

Putting everything on a grid like the one below makes it easy to assess advantages and risks, and provides you with a checklist you can use when you set goals and create strategies to achieve them. Once again, by documenting key information, you reduce both the odds that you will forget something important and the anxiety that goes along with worrying that you'll drop a detail.

Internal factors	External factors
Strengths	Opportunities
Weaknesses	Threats

Will your trip toward your vision be easy or difficult? Your SWOT will reveal that at a glance so you can put yourself on track for success.

SWOT in a Nutshell

To see a SWOT in action, let's look at how Raymond's circumstances line up with his mission, vision, and critical success factors. Here's his list once again:

- Access to a piano
- A concert-level piano teacher
- Space to practice
- Aptitude for the piano
- Money to pay for the piano, space, and lessons
- Membership with an ensemble to practice with other musicians
- Knowledge of music theory

Strengths:	Opportunities:
• I live right down the street from the conservatory	• The conservatory has world-class instruments, practice space, and faculty
• My musical talent qualifies me for admission and a scholarship	• It has an ensemble orchestra for regular group practice and the camaraderie I need to enjoy the process

Weaknesses:	Threats:
• I lack the manual dexterity to play intricate pieces	• Federal funding for the arts may be cut, threatening my scholarship

Especially after working through his critical success factors, Raymond knew a lot about himself and the environment surrounding his vision. That intelligence is pulled together here.

When he looked at his SWOT, Raymond was reassured that he had the skills to be a great musician, and the fine conservatory recognized and rewarded his talent. But the SWOT forced him to consider a weakness he hadn't focused on much in the past; he didn't have the skill to play the piano at the level that would allow him to give full expression to his musical genius. As his fictional luck would have it, he learned he had arthritis and his fingers just couldn't fly over the keyboard at the speed needed to play Chopin concertos in allegro. Now what? Is his music career over? He felt surprisingly calm when he received the diagnosis.

This analysis drove Raymond to look at his options. He could try treating his condition and seek occupational therapy to shore up this weakness. Or he could go back and review his other strengths, and examine his mission and vision for alternatives. No wonder he was unruffled by his diagnosis. His mission "To beautify the world with musical harmonies that soothe the soul and ignite the spirit" did not require him to play the piano to fulfill it. Furthermore, when he looked at his vision statement, he was reminded that it is working with other musicians to create exquisite harmonies that really excites him. Finally, when he looked at his skills inventory, he recalled his unique ability to interpret great works and to imagine how to blend the many orchestral instruments to create arrangements that thrilled his audiences and fellow musicians. As he mused on his situation, he realized he'd been swept along by his father's expectation that his gifted son would have the piano career that had eluded him. That didn't fit with the authenticity that should define his own vision of his future. Here's what he realized when he revisited his vision statement to make sure it reflected his own definition of success:

I see myself surrounded by musicians and creating beautiful music with pianos, but, son of a gun, I don't need to be sitting at the piano to do that. As a conductor, I could blend magnificent harmonies and even a ham-fisted guy like me can wave a baton. My rhythm and timing are impeccable. What else do I need to succeed as a conductor and how do my strengths play into that? How would this shifted role play to my strengths? In addition to my great ear, it turns out I have a real knack for imagining how dozens of instruments can be layered on top of one another to create the most exquisitely nuanced version of a concerto the world has ever seen. Voilà! *That* is my true personal genius at work. My work will bring classical pieces alive and make fine music more accessible to the masses. The classical music industry, once in decline, has a shiny future, thanks to me. And to think, I once only wanted to play the piano.

Raymond's SWOT provided him with a reality check and an opportunity to make sure his ambitions really matched his passions and abilities. It offered him a chance for an early course correction that saved him from wasting precious time and effort pursuing an avenue that would never fulfill his vision of playing on the world music stage. In other words, he could choose a path that is likely to make the most of his strengths and give him some success to build on. He could also take advantage of the opportunities the conservatory offered and make contingency plans for alternative funding sources should his scholarship money dry up.

Notice that, as you move through the strategic planning process, you get steadily more concrete, attaching more detail and more analysis that's aimed at increasing the odds that the journey toward your vision will be full of wins and pleasure. The process is all about success.

EXERCISE

Swift SWOT

If you're a person who likes to skip the manual and get straight to assembling the furniture, feel free to do a preliminary SWOT of your project now, following the instructions in the exercise below. You can refine your SWOT as you move through the rest of this section. Draw a SWOT grid like the one above in your notebook or download a copy from joyofstrategy.com.

1. Take a look at your vision statement and your critical success factors. What strengths can you draw on that will position you for success? List them in the Strengths space.
2. What do you need to be successful that you don't have? List those missing ingredients in the Weaknesses box. Are you

      doing anything (or not doing something) that undermines your objective? Add that as well.

3. What's happening around you that could present a great opportunity? Mark that down.

4. Do you perceive hazards in the environment that have the potential to blow you off course? Make a note of those issues in the Threats space.

SWOT Step by Step

The SWOT analysis is the point in the strategic planning process where we finish looking at who we are and prepare to think about what we *do*. And this completed self-assessment is the basis for all the action steps that come next. So now let's move through it element by element.

Strengths: Using Your Greatest Talents

In peak form, Michael Jordan flew down the basketball court, a perfect match of talent and passion, with results that put him in the record books. All that innate athletic ability, honed by focus, ambition, and hours of practice, landed him in the basketball pantheon. Did he have the strengths to be a basketball great? It seems absurd to ask. His remarkable skills and talents propelled him toward his mission and made him a star.

Now think back to Michael Jordan, baseball rookie. Same man, same talents. But notably, he was a man whose talents and skills were not the same tight match with his new sport. During that forgettable byway of his career, Jordan struggled for one lusterless season in the minors. And then he returned to the Chicago Bulls, a champion once more. As that humbling life experiment proved, he had enough raw athletic prowess to get through the door of another sport, but not enough to excel there. On the diamond, he was a jewel forced into the wrong setting. His talent was still beautiful, but it just didn't fit.

Your talents can wax the slide for you, and they can send you on the ride of your life—as long as they're a good match for your mission. When the fit is right, they're strengths. When it's not, you might just feel like Michael Jordan in a batting helmet.

The strengths part of a SWOT is a place where you can see how much your talents are stacking the deck in favor of success with the direction you've chosen. The more specific skills you have that support your vision, the more your journey will be a smooth, swift arc toward your target. No forced effort, just a natural expression of who you are and what you do best.

The "Stuff" of Strengths

Obviously, success takes more than talent. You'll also need other things, like time, materials, money, and staff. The resources you have in hand are *also* strengths, and of course you'll need to take them into account. Your talents and skills, though, are what turn stuff into results.

The skills and resources you need for your vision are spelled out right there on your list of Critical Success Factors, so there's no need for guesswork. You can get a good picture of your strengths by going down the list item by item and answering the question: Do I have it? Every "Yes" is a specific strength related to reaching your vision.

Peggy and Gail were encouraged and energized when they saw how many strengths they had for opening Our Space, their arts center for kids with cancer. As they started their SWOT, they could see a kind of critical mass building. Every time they confirmed that they had one of their critical success factors, it felt like an affirmation. And it was. Their "yeses" are listed in the "Do we have it?" column:

Skill/Resource We Need	Do We Have It?
Ability to attract critical mass of parents and kids interested in our services	1. We have an inspiring mission and vision.
	2. We're strong advocates with a good message.
	3. Our research revealed a receptive group of kids and families facing cancer.

(Cont.)

Skill/Resource We Need	Do We Have It?
Service providers: teachers, therapists, yoga instructors, artists	Yes: we are teachers ourselves and our network of colleagues is full of people willing to volunteer their services
Art supplies	We own a lot of supplies and we know several others who are willing to donate even more to help sick kids

Looking at the list of strengths you bring to your project can give you a great sense of confidence. It can also give you information that could nudge you in a new direction. Or, like Michael Jordan on his baseball detour, you might discover that your proposed mission, wonderful as it is, isn't the best match for your unique talents. Pay attention if you don't have a solid "I'm on the right track" feeling when you finish listing your strengths. Those strengths are the fuel for your journey.

EXERCISE

Record It

Go through your Critical Success Factors and for each one, as Peggy and Gail did, answer yes or no to the question, "Do I have it?" The details you put under each "yes" answer are strengths. Put them in the Strengths section of your SWOT grid.

Weaknesses: Skills or Resources You Lack

As you went through the inventory above, looking at the skills and resources you need for your project and answering the question "Do I have it?" Your eye may have been drawn to the spots where the answer was no. The "nos" are weaknesses.

A weakness can be a skill or resource you need for your project that you don't have. It might also be an inner quality, such as fear or a bad habit, that's holding you back. Building a house but don't have lumber? That's a weakness. Lack of carpentry skills would be too, as would a fear of hammers.

The very word weakness makes many people uncomfortable, but keep in mind that a SWOT doesn't judge, it simply tells you what you need so you can decide how you'd like to get it. Do you feel bad about yourself if you don't happen to have fresh pineapple in your fridge, but need it for a recipe? Probably not—you just put pineapple on your shopping list. And that's how it works with weaknesses. You spot them and you address them.

One assumption I'd like you to take off the table is that you have to be a one-person show who can—or should—do everything yourself. Weaknesses are often areas that don't tap your personal genius, and that's invaluable information for you to have. Remember that a strategic plan is all about finding ways to use your resources wisely. You'll get the best results if you put your time, energy, and focus into areas that make the most of your talents. The rest you can hand off to someone who can do the job better.

As a person who really likes to be able to say, "I can handle that," I know that it can be tough to admit that you're not the perfect person for every job. But I can tell you that there is grace in letting go of the notion that you have to do everything yourself. It's a relief. Once you know what has to get done, and acknowledge what part of it lies outside your wealth of talents, you can find help. There's probably someone whose strengths are a perfect match for your weakness.

I could do a decent job on my accounting if I really wanted to file my taxes on my own. It would certainly save me money. But I'd have to invest a lot of time because I'm not experienced enough to do it efficiently. Not to mention that I'm anything but passionate about adding up columns of numbers. Knowing this about myself, I can figure out what's in shorter supply: time or money, and then decide the best use of my resources. I'm not flawed because tax codes leave me cold, I'm just wired differently from those remarkable souls who love to curl up with the latest tax-rule changes. Fortunately, some of those tax mavens see their mission as helping poor schlubs like me stay on the good side of the IRS. My weakness is their strength, and a happy partnership is born.

Your Strategic To-Do List Is Taking Shape

I've described how energized Peggy and Gail were when they looked at their array of strengths for their arts drop-in center. That was a good thing, too, because they began to panic a bit when they got to weaknesses. But they were doing a strategic plan in the first place because they felt stuck when it came to making their vision come alive. This exercise showed them why that was and gave them clues to what to do about it. The "nos" in the "Do we have it?" column below reflect Peggy and Gail's weaknesses:

Skill/Resource We Need	Do We Have It?
Space to create and connect	No, and space is expensive
A step-by-step start-up plan	1. We have no idea where to start, or what to do to get our center out of our heads and into the real world
	2. We don't know how to plan
	3. We lack experience starting a business
Start-up cash	1. We don't have any extra money for this
	2. We don't have fundraising experience
	BUT
	1. Gail is a stand-up comic with the gift of gab; she'd be great at fundraising if she tried
	2. We also have artwork of our own that we could auction off or sell to raise cash
	3. We know a lot of people who will help us with fundraising
Publicity/marketing	We need help with a website, graphics, and printing

The pair, usually so full of energy and laughter, almost physically deflated as they confronted this litany of "nos." "Arggh," Gail moaned, head in her hands. "I knew this was just pie in the sky. Look at us. We're artists. This really brings it home—we don't know the first thing about starting a business."

That was one truth, I told her, but there was another: now that they were clear about what they lacked, they could find ways to get it. They had actually begun doing that automatically when they listed their obstacles with start-up cash. Even as they were writing down their weaknesses on that front, they could see that they had strengths and opportunities there, too. Not cash—not yet—but ideas for raising it. When you see yourself wrestling with a particular item on the weakness list, it's a strong sign that the issue is so important to the overall success of the project that it's really an undertaking of its own.

The real stoppers on your weaknesses list, the ones that knock the air out of you, often deserve deeper attention. Peggy and Gail finished the SWOT for Our Space, then went back to do a separate SWOT for the financing piece, so they could look more closely at the opportunities they sensed there. And those "buts" they had noted on their list of weaknesses, they realized, were strengths.

EXERCISE

Record It

Go back to your Critical Success Factors "Do I have it?" list and transfer the details you put under each "no" answer to the Weaknesses section of your SWOT grid. Note any "big" weaknesses that might benefit from a SWOT of their own.

Your Weakness Is Someone Else's Strength

As so often happens, serendipity was afoot as Peggy and Gail faced their weaknesses. Talking with them about their lack of planning skills, I found myself thinking about my client Lee Ann. She's the manager we met earlier who was looking for a way to return to work in a meaningful way after leaving her high-level job to care for her aunt as she succumbed to cancer. Lee Ann, a gifted project manager, was extraordinary in her ability to translate a vision to reality, but after she lost her aunt, she couldn't see the path that would let her express her new mission: to use her skills to help cancer patients in a meaningful way.

One answer, though, was right in front of us. Peggy and Gail's puzzle was missing a piece shaped exactly like Lee Ann, and her puzzle was missing a piece shaped just like them. I arranged to bring the three of them together. As if to confirm that the universe was at work in making the connection, when Lee Ann pulled into the parking lot for her first meeting with Peggy and Gail, she saw a car—that turned out to be Peggy's—with a bumper sticker that read "Grace Happens." It was the very bumper sticker she kept in the glove compartment of her own car as a tribute to her mother, Grace. Tingling, and covered in goose bumps, Lee Ann went in to meet with the visioneers of Our Space.

She was dazzled by the artists' energy, craft, and vision, and also by their appreciation as she walked them through the first steps of finding support for their center and breaking down a huge, daunting project into manageable steps. With her guidance and coaching, they learned the basics of project management and gained the confidence to take action in unfamiliar areas to support their vision.

They also gave Lee Ann an important and unexpected gift: a new perspective on her talents. Often, we assume that the skills that come so easily to us are easy for everyone. But in meeting Peggy and Gail, who were astonished by her ability to handle their business planning, Lee Ann was able to see her talents as the distinctive gift they really are. That gave her the clarity and confidence to envision her own next steps.

You become part of a much larger circle when you match your weaknesses with someone else's strengths. For that to happen, though, you have to take a look at what you lack and what you need. Then ask for help.

Are You Getting in Your Own Way?

There's a group of weaknesses that can be a little trickier to see than a simple accounting of what you need and don't have. These are the fears and limiting beliefs that keep you from using your talents fully. Behavior patterns that often find their roots in fear can be so familiar to you that you may not even notice them. What you might perceive instead is that while you have all the strengths and opportunities you need to glide toward your vision, something keeps pulling you off track. That "something" is often fear.

Seven Fears That Can Block the Way

In my work as a senior executive, teacher, and coach, I've identified several patterns of self-defeating behavior people indulge at the expense of achieving their goals. Take a look at some of the most common fear-based behaviors below. Do you see yourself in one or more of these patterns or personality types? I ask this question with great compassion and empathy, as many of us struggle with one or more of these issues. Treat this exploration as another simple inventory. And if you recognize yourself, treat that knowledge as valuable information that will bring you closer to your vision.

1. People Pleasing

The inability to say no may well be the most common problem that diverts people from their own goals. People with the disease to please say yes a lot when they mean no because they fear disappointing someone. My client, Jim, was so worried about disappointing his parents that he went to law school even though he dreaded the very thought. Without some new strategies, he could easily have spent a lifetime in a career he hated, wondering why he felt so empty—and why he still hadn't won the approval of those for whom he'd sacrificed so much.

This problem is particularly prevalent among people in the healing professions. I've worked with countless doctors and nurses whose identity is so connected to helping others that they often put their own needs behind everyone else's. That would be okay if it didn't lead to burnout and resentment, which it frequently does.

2. Perfectionism

My client Miranda was a top executive, superb at execution, completing tasks, even identifying vision. But she was also extremely hard on herself and others, ferocious when she or anyone under her fell short of her unreachable expectations. She found money and prestige but very little satisfaction until she took some rare time for introspection and realized she'd spent her life driven by the need to win her parents' approval. She believed that they wouldn't love her unless she was perfect, and "perfect" was always just out of reach.

3. Inertia

Danielle, the unhappy fashionista we met earlier, managed to spend two decades in a career she hated. How could that happen? Fear of leaving her familiar gilded cage, with its high salary, honors, perks, and benefits, had prevented her from taking a hard look at the truth that she confronted every day even though she tried not to think about it: she was miserable. And because she'd been afraid to admit it, she had condemned herself to keep going mindlessly until a string of difficult days added up to an unhappy twenty years.

4. Ego Identification and Control Issues

Another client, Angie, quit her job as a bank vice president when her first child was born so she could spend time nurturing her beautiful baby and enjoying her growing family. Soon enough, though, she was channeling every bit of her business drive into her kids' schools and organizations, which she turned into a full-time job. All because she couldn't turn off the chatty ego voice inside that wanted her to look good, keep up appearances, impress. She was afraid of giving herself over to the "unglamorous" job of simply being Mommy and so, ironically, had little time left for her children. She was too busy volunteering.

5. Listening to Naysayers

Remember Brenda, the woman we met in step 1, the "Mission" chapter, who was told by a teacher way back in middle school that she was no good in math? It was an assessment she never challenged. She simply crossed off the list any path that required her to use numbers. But after years of denial and misguided career choices, she finally faced the fact that she couldn't have the career in management she'd always wanted without a college degree—and getting a degree required, *gasp,* taking some math courses.

6. Succumbing to the Yeah-But Habit

For Stella, a student in my Business of Life course, every big dream seemed to come with a whole army of reasons why it was impossible to pull off. The "yeah-buts" popped up all over, and the funny thing is, with her confirmed yeah-but habit, they seemed to be a sign of realism rather than pessimism or a block. But beneath it all was fear—fear of failure, embarrassment, wasted effort. Or fear that what she wanted most in life just "wasn't meant to be."

7. Procrastination

So much to do, so little time for what's important. That's the dilemma of the chronic procrastinator. Easily distracted by the Crackberry, e-mail, web surfing, other people's conversations—and any number of other wheel-spinning diversions—people like my client Jerry are, paradoxically, busy, busy, busy. They're the ones who careen from one task to another all day, yet go home without accomplishing a single thing of value to them. One of the characteristics of a workaholic is procrastination. Eastern philosophers call this paradox active laziness, a way many people avoid looking deep inside to see what's really important. Procrastination keeps them from focusing on tasks that could have an impact and use their real talents. Most of us procrastinate from time to time without serious repercussions. But the fear of many habitual procrastinators is that their vision is too big, too hard, or too impossible, and they just can't risk failing. Or even starting.

Toolbox

Mirror

Pause a moment for some honest self-reflection. Look in the mirror or quietly close your eyes and ask yourself if you have any fear-based habits that are standing in the way of fulfilling your dreams.

For our purposes, how any of us wound up with these patterns isn't important. That's in the past, and we are here, right now, in the present. The goal is to move from where you are to where you want to be, and recognizing these patterns is the first step toward breaking free of them. If you can keep your focus there, putting aside judgment or labeling, you liberate the energy these patterns can trap and channel it in a more productive direction.

If you notice one of these patterns is at work in your life, one helpful thing to do is to consider what it's costing you. Often, I frame the situation this way for a client: What's more important to you? That Patsy, whom you'll never see again, will like you better because you made brownies for the school bake sale or that you write your novel? Are you pouring your energies into something that will never satisfy you, just to tiptoe around a fear?

Use the weaknesses section of your SWOT to identify what might be going on in your inner world that could be hindering your progress. You can unearth causes later and figure out how to address any problems. For now, knowledge is the first step to change and to reclaiming your power. Put a checkmark next to any of the patterns that resonate with you, and we'll return to them. And if one of these patterns is causing you deep distress, keep in mind that one highly effective strategy might be to work on it with a therapist, even as you continue building your strategic plan.

EXERCISE

Record It

Do you find that you act in ways that are not working for you? Mark it on your weaknesses list. Just a brief note, such as "I procrastinate" or "people pleasing," will suffice.

Opportunities and Threats

If our visions existed in a vacuum, we could boil down SWOT to SW (though it might be a little tough to say). But the cherished projects we conjure up in our minds are meant to be carried into the world. And out there, many factors are beyond our control. A SWOT takes them into account with an external analysis that helps you identify the factors that could smooth your way and even put some wind in your sails, so you can take advantage of them. Or anticipate those things that could impede you, so you can steer around them or push them aside.

For a company that makes sports caps and equipment, the Olympics might be an incredible opportunity to offer new products or snag an endorsement contract. And for a wedding planner in an Olympic host city, the weeks surrounding the games might be a threat that makes it hard to book venues and get attention. Or perhaps they'd be a great chance to offer sports-themed ceremonies. These imaginary businesses have no control over the timing of the Olympics or the ripples it sends into the environment. But they can anticipate and adjust their planning. Scanning the environment and becoming aware of the outside forces that can affect them, they gain an advantage that will let them surf the big waves or get out of the water before the typhoon hits.

As Jimmy Dean once said, "I can't change the direction of the wind, but I can adjust my sails to always reach my destination."[2] So let's do that. We'll look at opportunities and threats together, because the difference between an opportunity and a threat often depends on your point of view.

Opportunities

When a vision takes hold in your mind, much of the excitement surrounding it comes from seeing a need in the world for what you do best. You feel the pull of your calling. When you keep your focus there, on the match between your talents and the world's needs, you'll naturally begin to see situations with your name written on them, problems with solutions *you* can provide.

Remember the definition: an opportunity is a situation that gives you a chance to leverage your skills and talents. That's what you'll be looking for all around you.

Stella's dream was to open a religious bookstore that would create community and spread the wisdom and comfort she found in her beliefs. With her "yeah-but" tendencies, she felt stymied. After all, she said, she needed to keep her day job, with its steady paycheck and health benefits, so fulfilling her dream was out of the question.

I asked her if she'd considered running the store part time herself and hiring someone to mind the store while she was at work. "Yeah," she replied, "but I can't afford the rent and the salary until the store starts turning a profit, and I really want to keep my prices low so anyone can have access to the message in these books."

I counseled Stella to keep her eyes open and hold her vision of the bookstore so firmly in her mind that she would be open to interpret anything she saw in her daily travels as an opportunity to make her dream come alive. She kept pulling her mind toward her vision, and that very weekend, when she went to church, she saw her first big opportunity, one that had been right under her nose for years. Her church was located on a busy corner in the downtown section of a city with lots of foot traffic. The front door to the sanctuary was on one street, and the church building had an empty storefront on the perpendicular street. Stella recalled that the minister had long been concerned that the vacant display windows would invite vandalism.

After services, Stella approached the minister and asked him what he would think of her opening a bookstore in that empty space, with hours on weekends and a few selected evenings. He was delighted with the idea that the space could be used to further the church's mission and would make the space look occupied and less vulnerable to vandals. He offered her the opportunity to use the space rent-free, and she offered to donate a portion of her profits to the church.

She was overjoyed. The power of holding her vision firmly in her mind's eye had proven itself immediately. That old saying, "What you focus on, you find," is quite true. If you put your attention on something, it's possible that you draw the "pulling power of the universe." What's certain is that you draw on the power of your own vision by keeping alert to the possibilities to make it happen.

Coincidence—like meeting someone who knows a person you need a connection to, or suddenly being offered a gift that provides just what you were seeking—feels like serendipity. But I think it's often focus finding opportunity. There are plenty of opportunities staring us in the face if we're focused enough to see them.

EXERCISE

Seize Opportunities

Think about the factors in the world around you that could support your vision: helpful people, events you've noticed, anything that might potentially give your project a boost. List these opportunities on your SWOT grid. Then spend a week keeping your vision in front of you (read it every morning, or set a reminder on a calendar that prompts you to think about it). As the week unfolds, be open to interpreting anything you see as an opportunity to bring your vision to life. As ideas occur, keep adding to your list of opportunities.

Threats

The best-laid plans can be derailed by factors large and small. Life happens. The price of gas triples just as you're getting ready to open your Humvee franchise. A stock market bubble bursts. A Starbucks announces that it's opening across from your mom and pop coffee house. You have no control over outside events like this, but by being aware of your environment and the forces that threaten to derail your journey toward your vision, you can tailor your responses, tweak your plans, even find a catalyst for inspired new possibilities.

So if the idea of actively looking for "threats" sounds too, well, threatening, think of it this way: you're living out the old Boy Scout motto that smartly advises "Be prepared." Putting your head in the sand won't make the threats go away. But as we'll see, examining them closely, or standing them on their heads, just might.

Businesses commonly scan the horizon for what the competition is up to, how their current and potential clients might be changing, and what's going on with new laws, regulations, and technology. For your SWOT, look around the wider world that surrounds your project and see what could have a negative impact. Your threats could include someone who doesn't support your vision for whatever reason, like a spouse who would rather see you stay home and clean house than pursue a dream. Or it could be something less intimate: the credit crisis that makes cash hard to come by or the rainy season coming to drown out your lemonade stand.

If you have "yeah-but" inclinations that tend to make the environment look especially threatening, use this opportunity to list every possible element that could take the spark out of your project. That will enable you to deal with each one in a methodical, practical way instead of staying paralyzed. Threats, by definition, are factors that are out of your control, but you are very much in control of how you interpret and respond to them. The first step is to look for them and name them. Then you can make plans to deal with them.

As Peggy and Gail looked around for threats, their list was short— one big, overarching threat and another one that helped them think about how they might want to use one of the opportunities they'd pinpointed.

Peggy and Gail's threats:

- The economy is still slumping, so all those foundations and individuals who used to have a lot of money to give have less. There's ~~a lot of competition when it~~ comes to fundraising, and we're

- 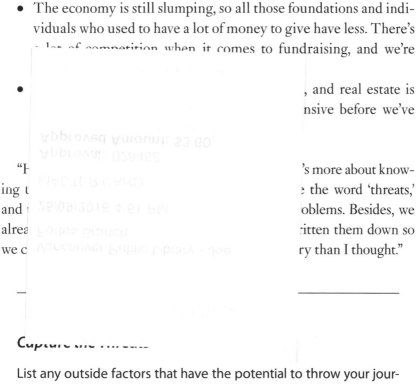, and real estate is nsive before we've

"H 's more about know-
ing t the word 'threats,'
and oblems. Besides, we
alrea :itten them down so
we c ry than I thought."

Capture the Threats

List any outside factors that have the potential to throw your journey toward your vision off track. Are there people, events, or situations that could have a negative impact? Put them in the threats section of your SWOT.

Is That Hazard Really a Threat?

I'm a threat skeptic. When people suggest that a situation is dire, that some turn of events has blasted a hole in their boat and their vision is going down, I'm sympathetic, but I'm also inclined to ask: Really? Are you sure? In fact, are you sure you even need a boat to get where you're going?

I've seen many times that one person's threat is another's opportunity. Does every cloud have a silver lining? Well, maybe not. But if you've ever talked to someone ramping up a cleanup business after a natural disaster or watched people take a difficult experience (say, going through chemotherapy for cancer) and transform it into an inspiring vision ("let's create a center to help kids getting chemo"), you know the power of perspective.

Toolbox

Reframing

Look at your *conclusions* about the situation you've labeled a threat and ask: "Are you absolutely sure this is a threat?" You will need to learn the difference between assessing a fact (the economy is tanking) and your conclusions (we're doomed). Once you do that, the fact is just a fact and you can consider it objectively and reframe your reaction.

The trick to reframing is to question all of your limiting beliefs and to not simply believe the naysayers, as Brenda did with her math phobia. How do you do that? It's as simple as recasting yourself as an observer. With a little objectivity, you can resist jumping to "obvious" conclusions and can ask several questions that allow you to find more creative answers. With Brenda, we reframed her certainty that she was not good at math by asking if that was really true. Yes, her middle school teacher made that assertion, but what did the evidence show? In fact, her job responsibilities required her to create elaborate spreadsheets and to track complex statistics. She did it so naturally that she didn't even realize her facility with figures was actually a *strength*. Her only weakness in this regard was her misperception that she didn't possess this talent. Her new awareness eliminated that weakness for the most part. It was with some trepidation that she recorded math in the strengths quadrant of her SWOT.

I found myself using reframing to good effect after the stock market crashed in 2008 and the economy tanked. A lot of coaches I know panicked, certain that no one would be able to afford the luxury of hiring a coach. That sounded logical on the surface. But as I centered myself

- The economy is still slumping, so all those foundations and individuals who used to have a lot of money to give have less. There's a lot of competition when it comes to fundraising, and we're going to need money to establish ourselves.
- We will eventually need a permanent space, and real estate is very expensive. It may get even more expensive before we've gotten our fundraising skills up to speed.

"Hmm, this doesn't seem so terrible," Gail said. "It's more about knowing the possibilities than anything else. I don't like the word 'threats,' and these things we turned up are just potential problems. Besides, we already knew they were there. All we've done is written them down so we can figure out how to deal with them. It's less scary than I thought."

EXERCISE

Capture the Threats

List any outside factors that have the potential to throw your journey toward your vision off track. Are there people, events, or situations that could have a negative impact? Put them in the threats section of your SWOT.

Is That Hazard Really a Threat?

I'm a threat skeptic. When people suggest that a situation is dire, that some turn of events has blasted a hole in their boat and their vision is going down, I'm sympathetic, but I'm also inclined to ask: Really? Are you sure? In fact, are you sure you even need a boat to get where you're going?

I've seen many times that one person's threat is another's opportunity. Does every cloud have a silver lining? Well, maybe not. But if you've ever talked to someone ramping up a cleanup business after a natural disaster or watched people take a difficult experience (say, going through chemotherapy for cancer) and transform it into an inspiring vision ("let's create a center to help kids getting chemo"), you know the power of perspective.

Reframing

Look at your *conclusions* about the situation you've labeled a threat and ask: "Are you absolutely sure this is a threat?" You will need to learn the difference between assessing a fact (the economy is tanking) and your conclusions (we're doomed). Once you do that, the fact is just a fact and you can consider it objectively and reframe your reaction.

The trick to reframing is to question all of your limiting beliefs and to not simply believe the naysayers, as Brenda did with her math phobia. How do you do that? It's as simple as recasting yourself as an observer. With a little objectivity, you can resist jumping to "obvious" conclusions and can ask several questions that allow you to find more creative answers. With Brenda, we reframed her certainty that she was not good at math by asking if that was really true. Yes, her middle school teacher made that assertion, but what did the evidence show? In fact, her job responsibilities required her to create elaborate spreadsheets and to track complex statistics. She did it so naturally that she didn't even realize her facility with figures was actually a *strength*. Her only weakness in this regard was her misperception that she didn't possess this talent. Her new awareness eliminated that weakness for the most part. It was with some trepidation that she recorded math in the strengths quadrant of her SWOT.

I found myself using reframing to good effect after the stock market crashed in 2008 and the economy tanked. A lot of coaches I know panicked, certain that no one would be able to afford the luxury of hiring a coach. That sounded logical on the surface. But as I centered myself and looked around, I asked the questions I coach my clients to use: Does this situation, bad as it looks, create a new opportunity? Does it create a need my talents can fill?

That's when I began to notice the glut of talented financial services professionals who'd been laid off, all of them now competing for the same handful of jobs in their shrinking field. How could they stand out? How could they use the opportunity of a career transition to assess what they wanted to do in the next stage of their careers? Those are the kinds of questions I specialize in helping people answer, and in the context of this new environment, I found lots of opportunities— speaking about "personal branding" to professional groups, coaching people through job transitions. I had as much business as I could possibly handle, even as many others threw up their hands, positive that they were no match for an economic meltdown.

Reframing takes practice, but it's worth the effort.

Roadblock or Vantage Point?

A boulder in the road is a big piece of rock. That's a fact. But is it a threat? That depends. If you're driving fast and don't see it soon enough, yes. It's a big, potentially fatal threat. But if you're walking, the same boulder might give you a chance to climb up, survey the landscape, and figure out the easiest way to proceed. Perspective is everything. So take a close look at every threat on your SWOT. Hidden there, waiting for you to see it, might be an amazing opportunity.

EXERCISE

Test Your Assumptions

For every threat on your list, ask yourself these questions:

- What is the *fact* of the perceived threat?
- What is my assumption/conclusion about that threat?

- Is that assumption correct?
- How do I know?
- Can I be sure?
- Is there something I can do to change the fact?
- What is another way to interpret the implications of the fact?
- How else could I look at this?

Did you find new possibilities that flip your threat into the opportunities column? If so, note the changes on your grid. You'll have a chance to practice much more with reframing in step 7 when you assemble your toolkit.

When the SWOT Delivers News You Didn't Expect

Now that you've got all the pieces of your SWOT, you have an intimate feel for the terrain you'll be traveling. And at this point, it occasionally happens that people realize that they're in for such a rough trip they're on the wrong journey. That is, they've chosen the wrong mission. You can fool yourself with a fantasy, but it's hard to fool a SWOT.

Mission Misfit

I like to give my students the following scenario so they can see the value in a SWOT that lets them know when the strengths they need for a mission just aren't there. Say I've always wanted to win the Miss America Pageant, and I've put that goal at the center of my mission. Tall, lithe blondes have an advantage in the competition, and I'm five two and brunette, so a quick SWOT might reveal that I have no real strengths except for being Miss Congeniality, and I've got a boatload of weaknesses: height, age, gravity...I can't think of many opportunities, and the threats abound—thousands of tall, thin, young blondes, for example.

This SWOT would probably send me scurrying to reconsider what my mission ought to be. And that's not a bad thing. It means the SWOT served its function, alerting me that perhaps beauty contests are not the place where my talents and passions intersect with the needs of the world. (The world does *not* need to see me in the bathing suit competition, I assure you.) This kind of SWOT might well be painful, but it could save me a lot of useless effort and expense trying to become something I'm not.

The truth is, you probably won't get to the point of doing a SWOT analysis only to discover that your mission is so far off base. Certainly, in doing an assessment of my skills, talents, and passions, I wouldn't have found the stuff of beauty queens. And when I set to work on my vision statement, I wouldn't have gotten past the A in "AGLOW." There is nothing authentic about my chasing after a pageant title. It's not at all true to who I am and what I value most. Chances are, if you complete your SWOT and find you need to change direction, you are looking at a more modest redirection rather than a total reboot.

Alternative Approach

Annette came to me for coaching when she couldn't get traction on her mission to work with medical practices to provide a more holistic approach to patient care. She was particularly interested in advocating for progressive health policies and insurance coverage for nonmedical interventions such as in-home support for people who need help buying groceries and filling prescriptions. When we reviewed Annette's strengths, she had passion for this issue, having seen how the medical community fell far short of meeting her husband's needs when he was terminally ill. Insult was heaped upon injury when he lost his rich health benefits once he was no longer able to work—just when he needed them most.

She was driven to make sure others didn't suffer the same fate. Her intimate knowledge of the problem she was trying to solve was another strength, as was the faith she'd leaned on to get through her ordeal.

However, when I asked her how these strengths would bring value to a medical practice such that they would want to hire her for this worthy purpose, she was hard-pressed to give a compelling answer. What she was offering appealed to some providers in principle, but that wasn't much of an opportunity. And the growing pressure for doctors to cut medical costs was a real threat. The pieces just didn't fit.

Annette already knew this on some level and the SWOT just confirmed it. But before she had time to get discouraged, I asked her to expound more on the faith she kept mentioning and her conviction that this was a calling that came from a higher authority. She became so animated that I had to stop her and ask her to reconsider whether she wanted her nonprofit to work in partnership with doctors' offices or whether running a religious organization was more in harmony with her mission to advocate for patients. Without hesitation, she said this was a faith-based pursuit.

Immediately, she had much more clarity about how she could move forward gathering support for this reframed endeavor. Her SWOT redirected her by showing how her initial approach wasn't a great fit for her strengths and circumstances. When she factored in all the pieces of her SWOT, Annette was able to find a better way to address her mission. As a result, her next steps became obvious and she was able to move forward after years of being stuck.

Harmonizing with Your Strength and Passion

You're looking for a mission, a vision—a life—that will let you be a star, a great fit with your talents and values. So if you find yourself getting a troubling message from your SWOT analysis, take a deep breath and have another look at your strengths and passions. You deserve a mission that makes the most of them, and it's worth investing the time to find it. Like Raymond, you just might find that your mission calls for you to play even bigger than you'd originally envisioned. He had to question an assumption about how he would express his musical gifts, namely that his father would fulfill his own musical dreams vicariously through his son. Pursuing that path would have meant falling short of his true potential. The apparent misfortune of arthritic joints saved him from pursuing the wrong path.

EXERCISE

Sum Up the SWOT

Be sure you have captured all of your SWOT information on your grid, where you can pull it out and refer to it as needed. As you complete your self-assessment and move toward goal setting, finish filling out the left-hand side of your custom closet. Make sure you put any core strengths or talents you've found in this chapter on the appropriate shelf for easy reference as you move to the next step in the process.

Peggy and Gail's final SWOT analysis looked like this, and as we saw above, new opportunities began presenting themselves almost as soon as the two artists began looking for them. Weaknesses were answered by new strengths.

Strengths	*Opportunities*
• Inspiring mission and vision	• Vision fills an important void
• Strong, creative, passionate advocates	• Growing awareness that children with cancer have special needs that are unmet by medical field or other providers; that should help with fundraising
• Big network, comedy skills, and art collection to support fundraising effort	
• Excellent staff and supplies	

Weaknesses	Threats
• We are disorganized and don't know what steps to take to incorporate	• Struggling economy may impede fundraising
• No business planning experience	• Real estate is very expensive even in a depressed market, and prices may rebound before we get a handle on fundraising; that would mean even more trouble finding affordable space
• Need help with website, graphics, printing	

By just putting the potential threats to their endeavor on paper, Peggy and Gail began to see ways to address the problems and find alternate ways to deliver services much faster than they'd originally envisioned. We will catch up with Peggy and Gail later to see what they were able to accomplish.

Postscript: Keep SWOT in the Lineup

Now that you know the basics of performing a SWOT analysis, you'll find that it's a versatile tool for getting an overview of a problem or project and figuring out what needs attention. If your undertaking is complex, like starting a new business or changing careers, you might want to break it down and perform multiple SWOTs of individual elements.

Here's how: take out your vision statement and list of critical success factors. Underline the key elements and assess your strengths, weaknesses, opportunities, and threats for each one. Don't get too hung up on getting it "perfect." As you've seen, perfectionism can be a weakness when it comes to getting things done.

No need to get swamped in SWOTs. Just keep the tool in your back pocket and pull it out whenever you need the perspective it can bring. The process is dynamic, and focusing on the information you've collected here will lead you directly to setting smart, effective goals and priorities, the task of the next step in the process.

Step ⑤

Set Goals: Your Steps to Success

"Vision without action is a daydream. Action without vision is a nightmare."

—Japanese proverb

Y ou have done a lot of important work, so take a moment to pause, reflect, and acknowledge what you've already accomplished. Don't worry that you're not "finished." As long as you're living and growing, you never will be. That's a good thing. You can go back to the foundational steps you have just completed and update them at any time as new information, experiences, circumstances, and feelings arise. This is a dynamic process that invites regular reviews and adjustments.

Up until now, your work has been to do some strategic soul-searching and analyze what you need to succeed in the business of your life. Your vision statement describes what success means to you and your critical success factors are a list of things you'll need to make it come to life. Your SWOT (strengths, weaknesses, opportunities, and threats) summed up your position and provided you with intelligence about what you have to work with and work around. So you now have a great foundation on which to build an action plan.

A vision is just a pretty picture until you actively breathe life into it. Your prioritized list of goals gives you a wonderfully effective way to think about how you'll want to spend your precious resources of time, energy, money, and attention that works in harmony with your core values, mission, and vision over time. The next step is to determine what you need to *do* to make real, steady progress toward living your envisioned ideal. That includes finding pleasure in each day while you work on getting "there." To do that, you will set some goals. Accomplishing them will give you an energy boost and keep you moving forward. Especially when some of those goals include spending more time with people you love or having a peanut butter and pickle sandwich every day if that's your thing.

Later in this chapter, we will look at how to make your goals as effective as possible. Taking the time in the goal-setting phase to ensure they are specific, measurable, and timely will make it possible to create successful strategies for accomplishing them and tracking your progress toward fulfilling your vision.

These early steps were just what Sandra needed to get motivated to work in a more holistic manner. Because of her left-brained, "let's get it done" tendencies, the conceptual work involved in creating a vision gave her focus and brought her pleasure as she contemplated a fulfilling future. For someone so task-oriented, it provided a well-rounded basis for setting goals and choosing carefully considered tasks likely to bring her great results as she crossed them off her list. Creating a vision did two other important things for her:

- She noticed that among the many aspects of her personal vision, she felt a particular urgency to launch Fertility Within Reach, her nonprofit organization that aims to empower infertile couples to advocate for themselves in order to build their families.

- She realized that, as a leader, she had been "pretty loose" about project management and, as a result, several initiatives languished. Involving her team in creating a collective vision for their department created a new sense of commitment to their work. Setting clear goals to make it happen was an important motivator and those goals were the basis for establishing the accountability needed to keep herself and her group on target. She no longer leaves it to chance.

Sandra's SWOT told her a lot about her considerable assets— strengths she needed to leverage and opportunities she could seize.

She also confronted a weakness she'd never really looked at as such until performing this analysis. Sandra, who is mindful in many ways and extraordinarily effective in completing projects, discovered that her way-too-long to-do list spread her attention too thin and threatened her ability to concentrate enough effort on her highest priorities. This was an important wake-up call and something she could readily address. Her vision statement snapped her right into focus and guided her next steps.

Move from Dreaming to Doing

Formulating goals is the step that creates the bridge between dreaming and doing. As you will see, the more specific you can be about what you will do to bring your vision to life, the more likely you are to do it. Your goals articulate *what* you want to accomplish. The strategies you will develop specify *how* you will accomplish it all. For now, your job is to get clear on what you want to do. Many people get so hung up on how they will get things done that they get stuck right here. If you're not clear on what you want, it will be hard to figure out how to get it. So, your task for this step is to stay focused on setting your goals. Once again, the key is to not cut off your options too soon by worrying about how you will achieve them. That is the work of the next step.

Bruce is the strategic planner whose vision included having a third child. He had a hard time committing his vision to paper because he couldn't see how he'd ever accomplish that when his life was already so busy. Now that he had it written down, he felt more committed than ever to doing whatever he could to make it happen. So he wrote down a specific goal—he wanted to have a third kid within the next two years. How he and his wife would find the time to devote to another child was not yet clear, but he wanted it enough that he would give his full attention to finding a way.

Remember, you were challenged to aim high and create a grand vision. In his book *Good to Great,* Jim Collins talks about the importance of setting "BHAGs"—big hairy audacious goals.[1] For a company, this is a high-reaching goal that reflects its peoples' passions, their ability to be the best, and something that will drive their economic engine. For you, audacious goals may also reflect your passions, tap your unique talents, and be something that will pay major dividends—such as bringing you joy, fulfillment, or financial rewards.

If you are like most people and organizations, you will have many more goals than you can tackle all at once. You will need a way to look at everything you'd like to accomplish so you can put first things first. It probably won't surprise you that, once again, the first step in that process is writing it all down so you can get a good visual of the *what* and *when*. Your custom closet holds the key—and your priorities.

Devise and Conquer

It's time to dig in and organize your thoughts. Here's how you will do it so you can get a well-rounded look at what matters most to you across some key areas. We've talked about the elusive balance that everyone seems to be seeking and not finding. The largest section of your custom closet is devoted to displaying your goals and priorities in a way that lets you visualize the balance you are emphasizing. Creating a clear picture will make it easier to see how to make it happen. There are two important dimensions to consider when setting and prioritizing your goals: *what* you want to do and *when* you want to do it.

WHAT You Want

One way to attack the challenge of deciding what your priorities should be is to set goals in each of four major areas:

- Family and relationships
- Career or vocation

- Community engagement/service
- Mind/body/spirit

Remember that this is a *custom* closet, so it is up to you how much emphasis you want to place on each of these areas. Balance is a function of *your* individual priorities.

WHEN You Want It

The second dimension you will consider is the time horizon. I happen to believe you can have it all—just not all at once. Nor would you want to, really. How can you be fully present to experience everything all at once? So, you will think about when you want to get to everything over time. Once again, you can customize your closet to reflect the time frames that make the most sense for you given the nature of your goals and their relationship to one another.

People often ask me about the "right" time frame for goal setting. The answer to that question always depends on the nature of your goals and your particular circumstances. The goal of curing cancer would obviously take a lot longer than finding retail space for your new bakery. Likewise, the goal of earning your MBA will take longer to achieve if you don't have your undergraduate degree than it would if you already have that credential.

As you consider your priorities, it's easiest to begin by thinking about what you want to accomplish right now. What do you need to do to fulfill the vision you've established for yourself? Do you have a good balance of activities across the many roles you play, given your current circumstances? Are you getting enough exercise? Sleep? What represents a good balance for you today may not be so relevant next year. If you're working full time and pursuing that MBA at night, your goal may just be to hold it all together until you earn your degree. A year from now, with classes behind you and a new credential, you may have very different goals. In fact, it's not unlikely that earning your degree is a short-term goal that you undertook in order to fulfill a longer-term ambition.

If you have small children at home, you may have some things you'd like to pursue once they go off to college. Or, if you're facing retirement, you may be looking forward to how that new phase of your life could be most satisfying. If your current circumstances won't last more than a few years, thinking in one- and five-year increments might make a lot of sense for you. This is particularly true if you need to do something in the short term to be ready to meet your long-term objectives.

On the other hand, you might have such consuming short-term goals that taking a long-range view is too overwhelming for you. Only you can determine the appropriate time frame for your own goal setting in this moment. You will have ample opportunities to review your goals and add to them as it makes sense for you to do so. Set long-term goals if they serve you. Just be sure to avoid being so rigidly attached to making them happen that you pursue them even if they no longer fit a few years down the road.

What Goal-Setting Looks Like

Let's take a look at Regina, a project manager in a large information technology operation, who took my Business of Life course offered through her employer. She had an eighteen-month-old baby girl, and just the mention of her name lit up Regina's face. Her career was thriving and, overall, things were going pretty well. Her major issue: she was overweight and exhausted. While she had a satisfying job and a family she adored, she experienced melancholy that sometimes bordered on despair. As she considered her priorities, she realized that, as is all too common with working mothers, she was ignoring her own health just to get through her epic daily to-do list. It was clear that she needed to put some emphasis on taking care of herself since her bouts of depression coincided with the ebbs in her energy level. Her goal-setting exercise made it very clear how she could accomplish this goal while meeting other key objectives at the same time.

REGINA'S PRIORITIES EXERCISE

	Family/ Relationships	Career/Vocation	Community	Mind/Body/ Spirit
Long Term (1-5 years)	Have a second child	Get promoted	Serve on a nonprofit board of directors	
Medium Term (within a year)		Take courses toward MBA offered by employer		
Short Term (now)	Date night with husband every other Saturday night Take baby for walk		Sing in church choir	Get to the gym 3x a week Take baby for walk other 4 days Sing in church choir

Regina was relieved to see her priorities seemed doable once they were laid out before her. She was happy to see that she could do things that brought her joy, met her family goals, and put her health in the mix. She vowed to get some physical activity daily and committed to getting to the gym three days a week. On her off days, she would take the baby for a walk. In that way, she could spend some time on her family priorities and get some exercise at the same time. Likewise, she loved to sing and decided to join her church choir That gave her some much-needed connection to her community and built in time to attend to her spirit. Just seeing these few shifts boosted her morale and gave her hope that her health—and moods—would improve.

You're In Charge

I'd like to underscore the importance of this exercise reflecting *your own* priorities. It's very easy to get so caught up with people pleasing and other tendencies that you end up spending inordinate amounts of time on activities that don't really mean that much to you. This can be an insidious problem because we're often fooled by the way the invitation or request is framed. Like the time my nine-year-old niece told my sister-in-law, "It's Mother's Day. You can use whatever kind of fabric softener you want." Generous offer indeed, but who said she wanted to spend her special day indulging her laundry habit in the first place? So beware, this is one way to get pulled into doing some-one else's bidding even if we're invited to do their thing our way.

The Goals of Goal Setting

A detailed list of goals acts as a ready reminder of your priorities and serves as a rudder that guides your investments to produce the best possible results given your current circumstances, while still taking the long view.

Decision-Making Filter

This tool worked so well for reordering my priorities when my son was born, after I'd spent my whole pregnancy wondering if he would survive birth. Thankfully, he did, but we weren't out of the woods. He had an unusual set of cardiac anomalies that required we keep close watch on him because sudden death was a lurking possibility for the first two years of his tender life. There was no question that family was my top, burning priority in those years. Community service, as important as it is to me, would have to wait until I saw my son through this critical time. Other people could support worthy causes, but only I could mother my son.

Once his condition no longer required such vigilance and I could do a limited amount of volunteer work, my priorities were clear. After facing the prospect of losing my precious child, I knew that as long as my children lived at home, family life was my absolute top priority and other decisions would be shaped by what was best for them. So as I added community service back into the mix, I had specific criteria for which projects I would accept. The organization requesting help would have to:

1. Benefit my children or family
2. Need a skill that I uniquely possessed
3. Require a time-limited commitment
4. Have a pleasant team capable of sustaining the value of our work

If those conditions were met, I would accept. If not, I would politely decline, saying I'd consider it once my kids moved on to college. Done. No guilt. No second-guessing myself.

Balance and Perspective

Many professionals I work with struggle with finding a good balance of work and personal life. Paul is no exception—except he had no awareness of his problem until he got to the goal-setting exercise in his Business of Life workshop. He'd signed up for the course because he had just relocated to Boston to take on a new position as finance manager in a large corporation. He felt that all he'd learned in his MBA program years earlier was a bit rusty, so he thought the class would be a good chance to brush up on his skills. He came expecting to focus on strategic planning and implementation techniques. But when he started filling in his priorities in his Custom Life Closet, he was slightly alarmed to see that he had put all of his attention on his career and he'd paid scant attention to any other aspects of his life. He was living in a new city where he didn't know anyone and had no connection to the community. What's more, he was so concerned about meeting the expectations of his new boss that he'd not focused much on his own health or recreation. This look in his closet was a big wake-up call.

Melissa is a manager who came to my Business of Life course hoping to find a way to be recognized by her vice president as the leader she was and to upgrade the status of her position to reflect that understanding. Achieving this goal would also affect her forty colleagues holding the same title. Almost as soon as her six-week course began, she realized that she had a number of additional areas to improve beyond work, and creating a business plan for her life was the key:

> The most important thing I learned from the class, what really turned things around for me, was setting long-term goals. I'd been a big fan of to-do lists and loved crossing completed tasks off my list. But I'd never really stepped back to think about what I wanted to accomplish over time. Changing the operations coordinators jobs to operations managers wouldn't have happened if we weren't able to take that longer-term view. Everything I'd done up until then was just responding to doing what needed to be done. Thinking about what I wanted to accomplish long term let me set goals and make strategies to accomplish them. That was big.

Taking the long view also allowed Melissa to see that just "going along to get along" was driving her to make decisions that were in conflict with her personal goals. She described it this way, "The closet also really helped me see I was putting all my effort into work and my personal life was suffering. So I used the same goal setting to accomplish personal goals as well. This made it possible for me to find balance between my office and home life."

Melissa's vision statement had her in her new position as an operations manager and working on mastering the art of managing other people. But her vision expanded well beyond work and included a vivid description of her joyful home life that included a husband and children. Until she started working on her priorities, she hadn't really thought much about how that was going to happen.

Many times we're doing something that keeps us from fulfilling our desires that is so obvious, but only once we stop to look at it in context. Yes, Melissa wanted to get married and build a family. But it wasn't until she looked at this goal with the intention of creating a plan to make it happen that she could see she was doing things that were not conducive to finding a husband. Not only was she focused almost entirely on her career, she had allowed her brother to move into her tiny apartment rent-free. With little free time and no privacy at home, it would be hard to find and nurture an intimate relationship with anyone else.

Within a year of developing her plan, she'd worked with the other operations coordinators to develop a forum where they could share challenges and best practices. I was delighted when she asked me to facilitate a retreat for this group and help them develop a strategy to get their positions upgraded, even at a time when her employer was facing layoffs and budget cuts. Melissa was fortunate that Jeanette, her senior vice president, had created an environment that encourages innovation from all the clinical and administrative staff and "supports their power to create positive change." Melissa's director, George, attended the retreat she organized. While the leadership needed to eliminate some positions, Melissa and her colleagues agreed to cover more units if their positions were upgraded to compensate for the additional work. That way, they would need fewer people and would save money while still getting all the work done. They found the win–win for her group and her department's leaders, and Melissa and her colleagues got the title and salary they so richly deserved.

With that success under her belt, she saw the power of setting specific goals. Thus emboldened, she turned her attention to her personal life. Melissa made a point of doing something every week where she might meet new people and she asked her brother to find another place to live. With a new focus and a bit of luck, it didn't take her long to meet and marry her husband. Their first child is due any day and she couldn't be happier.

Presence Leads to Pleasure

The hundreds of busy professionals I've taught and coached over the years share a common struggle: they try to do too much. High achievers think they can do it all. Often they can, but at a great cost to themselves.

A physician enrolled in the Business of Life course because she was feeling burned out from the emotional intensity of meeting her cancer patients' medical and personal needs while keeping up with the demands of her young family. She said of her experience:

> I came to this class feeling guilty trying to do it all and doing nothing well. Now I feel so empowered. You taught me to be present and fully commit to whatever it was I chose to do. Everything changed. I actually played trains with my son without folding laundry at the same time. And to my surprise, it was fun. Until recently, I haven't had much fun in my life.
>
> Even work has changed. I experience much more joy when I allow myself to be fully there for my patients and give them my undivided attention. It gives me great satisfaction to help my frightened patients face their disease with optimism. The tools you taught me allowed me to let go of worrying about all the trivial tasks that needed doing. Your advice to schedule time on the calendar to complete these tasks was so simple, yet so powerful.

All it took for this bright and talented woman to find some joy from all of the effort she was expending was setting a goal of doing so and shifting her focus enough to let it happen. She learned to let go of the unimportant to make room for what really mattered. And it took no time at all to accomplish that—just awareness.

Toolbox

Presence

Staying in the moment is a powerful tool for finding joy or at least fully experiencing whatever it is you choose to do. We miss out on a lot of pleasure when our minds are on anything but what we're doing in the moment. So when you choose to do something, commit to focusing on it and giving it your all—in that moment.

Choose and Commit

One thing that makes me exceptionally sad is hearing from new mothers who return to work after their maternity leave saying, "I didn't accomplish a thing." They had expected to paint the house, write the great American novel, or plant a new garden in their "time off." I ask them how many diapers they changed, how many times they fed and bathed their tiny new companion or kissed his sweet-smelling head. Their job was bonding with their baby and giving her a good start in life. And yet, they missed the fact that they had indeed accomplished what they'd really set out to do. Their wistful, in-retrospect smile breaks my heart every time. So please be conscious of what you've chosen to do and commit to it fully. Then savor the memory of those satisfying moments. Don't look back with regret.

I witnessed a poignant reminder of just how important committing to being present is to those around us during my son's seventh-grade soccer season. His teammate's father traveled routinely for business and seldom came to his games. He finally made it to the last game of the season and the boy triumphantly looked to the sidelines when he scored the winning goal. But he crumpled to the ground in a sobbing heap when his searching eyes found his father on the phone with his back to the field. It would have been better for him if his father hadn't come at all, since his expectations were raised and then his hopes dashed. If you choose to go to a soccer game, or your equivalent, commit to really *being* there and let other distractions wait. Especially if someone else is counting on you.

Claim Your Power

Once we determined that the main thing standing between Brenda and the management career she desired was the college degree she never pursued because she simply accepted her middle school teacher's inaccurate declaration that she had no aptitude for math, she was able to set specific goals that would set her up to fulfill her dream. "Earn a college degree" was her ultimate goal, but that was so large and lofty that Brenda was afraid to commit to it. So, we talked about what she felt she *could* tackle as a first step. She agreed to face her fear head-on and set an immediate goal of taking a math course at a local university the very next semester. She agreed that if she passed that course, she would commit to the longer-term goal of pursuing her bachelor's degree.

Success

Another compelling reason to commit your goals to paper is the simple fact that it works. A recent study by Dr. Gail Matthews at Dominican University of California confirmed that people who wrote down their goals and committed to giving regular updates to their friends were 33 percent more likely to accomplish them than people who simply thought about their objectives.[2] For years, I've been pairing participants in my workshops with a "buddy" when the course ends and instructing them to check in at regular intervals to see how the other is doing. The accountability and mutual support has really helped people stay committed to their goals, ensuring long-term dividends on the time they invested in creating their personal business plan.

Eliminate Anxiety

If you are like many people I work with, you carry a lot of details in your head and worry that you'll forget something critically important. By writing down your goals and referring to them frequently, you can let go of that concern. You can free up some valuable real estate in your brain for other important pursuits.

Clarity

Goal setting may also help to clarify how you can use your strengths to achieve your vision, sometimes in a most unexpected way. Remember Diane, the doctor who wanted to positively impact the practice of medicine nationally while maintaining her busy clinical practice and being available to her young children? How she would achieve this eluded her even as she listed her critical success factors. Conducting her SWOT analysis reminded her of the pleasure she got from thoroughly researching the issues related to prescribing narcotics in order to write a policy manual for her hospital's primary care department.

She enjoyed being an expert on the nuances of this delicate matter facing doctors across the nation, and she'd noted this as a major strength on her SWOT. She realized that her depth of knowledge and understanding was a strength that would be of value well beyond the walls of her own institution and which had the potential for widespread impact on her profession. She'd recorded the need for better prescribing guidelines as an opportunity to leverage her knowledge on the national stage and she set a goal of establishing herself as a recognized leader in this area within five years. She had the added goal of having family dinners at least five nights a week until her youngest child left for college in thirteen years. With her list of critical success factors and SWOT in hand, she set an immediate goal to turn a spare bedroom into her home office. She would use the laptop her husband had given her as her home computer. She made a priority of speaking to her division chief about rearranging her clinical schedule and she booked another coaching session to work on strategies to put the remaining two critical success factors in place: her communications platform and salary for the nonclinical time. You will see the strategies she developed in step 7.

SMART Goals

I'm often asked what makes a "good" goal. The goal that you'll work toward, the one you're committed to achieving and whose achievement is likely to bring you closer to fulfilling your vision is a good one. In management circles, the goals voted most likely to succeed are SMART:

- Specific
- Measureable
- Attainable
- Realistic
- Timely

So consider these attributes as you think about your own goals. A specific goal says "I will lose ten pounds by Christmas by exercising before work three times a week and cutting out sweets." This goal has a much higher likelihood of getting results than the more general "I want to lose weight," because it leads clearly to specific actions. Wishing doesn't make something so. And plenty of research bears this out. In her book *Succeed*,[3] Heidi Grant Halvorson describes an experiment conducted by German social psychologist Peter Gollwitzer that showed that students who planned the time and place that they would write their essays were more than twice as likely to complete them on time than those who simply agreed to write it over Christmas break.

Measurable goals can be tracked easily, and monitoring your progress can keep you motivated to keep moving forward. Watching those ten pounds melt away, one at a time, inspires continued vigilance.

Setting attainable and realistic goals is not the same as setting easy ones. You can still challenge yourself and aim high. Attainable means that you have the skills and capacities to make them happen—these are the strengths in your SWOT. Realistic means that you are willing and able to work toward it. If there's no way you'll give up your daily hot fudge sundae, losing ten pounds by giving up sweets is not a realistic goal for you.

Finally, time-bounded goals create a sense of urgency and get you moving. Losing those ten pounds by Christmas means you'd better get started with your exercise program now since that's right around the corner. Without that deadline, you can always start your regimen tomorrow. A tomorrow that never comes.

Melissa's goals were SMART. To meet her future husband, she set a goal of enrolling in an on-line dating service and meeting at least one new person a month (specific and measurable). She had plenty of friends who had done the same thing, so she knew this was attainable and realistic. She also planned to start immediately. It would be hard to be more timely than that.

Goal-Setting Guidelines

As you prepare to write down your own goals, here are a few points to consider.

- Remember that having it all is not the same as doing it all. So focus on what's most important. You will never be able to do everything, and accepting that simple fact can be liberating.
- Don't let fear inhibit your ambitions.
- Consider breaking large goals into smaller "mini goals." "Lose one hundred pounds" is such a big goal that it may seem undoable. "Join a gym" and "hire a nutrition coach" are actionable priorities that you can commit to and hold yourself accountable for achieving.
- Be sure to include "joy notes" and keep pleasure among your priorities. As Danielle, our soon-to-be-laid-off fashion buyer,

approached redefining her work life, she had a hard time knowing where to start. When she reviewed her self-assessment, she took note of how much she enjoyed cooking even though she hadn't done much of that while she was working and commuting such long hours. So, to prime her goal-setting pump, she put taking a cooking class on her list of short-term priorities just to inject some fun into her days. Little did she know where that decision would lead her a few months down the road.

EXERCISE

Set Your Goals and Priorities

Make your own version of a custom closet in your notebook or download one from joyofstrategy.com.

- Write down your goals and priorities across the four major areas: work/career, family/relationships, community, and mind/body/spirit. Check to see that you are happy with the distribution of your priorities and that they reflect your sense of a good balance among them.
- Consider your short-, medium-, and long-term goals. Those shelves are there for you if you find them helpful. You are under no obligation to fill them all with priorities. Recording long-term goals is especially helpful if you need to accomplish short-term goals to be ready when the time comes to fulfill the later objective. If you have the goal of flying around the world in ten years, you may want to set short-term goals that include getting your pilot's license and saving up to buy a plane.
- Be sure to include some health-related goals to make sure your body runs efficiently, so that you feel well and are capable of enjoying whatever it is you choose to do.
- Once you've recorded your priorities, color code each one as follows:

- ○ green = most important, highest priority
- ○ yellow = medium priority
- ○ red = least important, low priority

Consider why any low-priority items are on your list and think about eliminating them.

Your color-coded closet gives you a nice visual of how you want to spend your precious time and other resources. Take one more look at your priorities and goals. If you are able to accomplish everything, will you fulfill your mission and vision? Consider adding to your list until your answer to that question is a resounding "yes."

Toolbox

got joy?

As you set your goals and priorities, do a gut check and see how you feel about your choices. Do your goals excite you and inspire you to act? Do they tip your scale away from hassle toward joy? The goals that you are most likely to pursue fully are those that will bring you pleasure and fulfillment. Be sure to include a healthy dose of happiness among your priorities.

Step ❻

Perform a Time and Emotion Study

"How we spend our days, of course, is how we spend our lives."[1]
— Annie Dillard

Money can't buy me love and it can't buy more time either. Now that you have a closet full of goals, you may be wondering how you'll find time to do everything on your list. As I keep emphasizing, a strategic plan for your life requires being mindful about what you want to achieve in your heart of hearts and *deliberately* using your limited resources (time, money, energy, and attention) to get the results you want. For most of us, time is in especially short supply. No matter how wealthy you may be, you get the same twenty-four-hour days as everyone else, so you will need to manage this essential resource as carefully as possible.

In this step of the planning process, you will look at:

- How well your current use of time lines up with your newly stated goals
- What is contributing to any lack of alignment between your actions and priorities
- Tips and tools to clear the clutter and make room for what matters most to you

Diagnosis: Match Your Doings to Your Desires

You will start by conducting what I call a time and emotion study. It's as simple as taking a hard look at your calendar to see how you are currently investing your time compared to what you'd be doing if you were living in perfect harmony with the goals and priorities you just identified. Your emotions also give you valuable information about how well your actions are aligned with your mission, vision, and values, so you will pay attention to how you feel about what you see on your schedule.

This straightforward exercise will give you a great idea of what's working well for you and it will show you what you're doing that's robbing you of joy or standing in the way of your goals. Warning: your first look may be disheartening if you've fallen into some counterproductive habits. Remember that essential to fixing any problem is recognizing that it exists in the first place. Be gentle with yourself and view this as an opportunity to reclaim any time you are not using optimally and redirect it toward more worthy pursuits. While your calendar may feel like your enemy at the beginning of this step, you will turn it into a critical tool that serves your higher purpose in the end. So just be curious and see what possibilities present themselves. This simple exercise normally takes less than thirty minutes to complete, and many people I know have found several hours they could free up each week: not a bad return on investment.

EXERCISE

Time and Emotion Study: How Do You Spend Your Time?

Part One: Complete Your Calendar

For this exercise, you will recreate your calendar, formatted to line up with the section of your custom closet that contains your goals and priorities. Start by looking at how you spend a typical day. I know;

there rarely is a "typical" day. Just do your best. Usually, it makes the most sense to start by looking at a workday. Then you can use a weekly view and/or a monthly view to factor in weekends and occasional activities. For example, you buy groceries every Saturday and you volunteer at a soup kitchen the second Sunday of the month.

Record how you're using all of your time, and slot each activity into one of the four categories you assigned to your goals. Just choose the one that fits best. The more specifically and completely you record *all* of your actions, no matter how trivial, the more information you will have to work with. How you assign an activity may depend on why you do it and what you expect to get from it. For example, watching television may fit best into mind/body/spirit if you zone out in front of the tube by yourself every night. However, viewing a televised presidential debate may be a family/relationship activity if you're watching with your kids so you can discuss its impact on world events later.

After you've filled in your calendar, grab the same markers you used in assigning priority scores to your goals and do the same thing for your current activities. Highlight your most important actions in green, use yellow for moderately important activities, and use red for the least important ones. Then mark each with asterisks to denote its level of urgency: three stars go to the most urgent, two to the moderately urgent, and one for less urgent or long-term activities. In the TV example, tuning in for half an hour to decompress from the workday so you can transition to your evening activities may fit best in mind/body/spirit. It works well and gives you some "me" time, so you might color it yellow or even green and assign it two or three stars. But if you don't find that it actually refreshes you, or half an hour turns into an entire mindless evening, you may highlight it in red and give it one star. Alternatively, the presidential debate contributes to family time well spent and informs you all about community matters. That may earn it a green rating. And it's certainly urgent when preparing you to vote responsibly and discuss current events at work or school the next day. That earns it three stars. Here's an example of what your calendar shell might look like.

DAILY SCHEDULE

	Family/ Relationships	Career/Vocation	Community	Mind/Body/ Spirit
AM				
5:00				
6:00				
7:00				
8:00				
9:00				
10:00				
11:00				
PM				
12:00				
1:00				
2:00				
3:00				
4:00				
5:00				
6:00				
7:00				
8:00				
9:00				
10:00				
11:00				

Part Two: Analyze Your Agenda

To assess how you are using your time, hold your color-coded calendar next to your color-coded goals and priorities. How similar do they look? Are any glaring differences immediately apparent? Be careful not to judge yourself too harshly if the images do not line up as well as you might like. For one thing, you just did a lot of work to set your goals and order your priorities, so it would be surprising if they were already perfect reflections of one another.

To help zero in on where your issues are and where opportunities present themselves, answer the guiding questions below. Consider where you might be able to make some adjustments and write that down in your notebook.

TIME SPENT ON PRIORITIES
- How much time am I spending on my most important/urgent activities?
- Am I devoting enough attention to make progress on each of my important goals?
- Are any priorities missing from my calendar?
- Am I preparing to address longer-term priorities?
- What am I doing that isn't on my list of priorities? Does it merit my time?
- Do I have time to accommodate everything I want to do?

HARMONY: ALIGNMENT OF ACTIONS AND ASPIRATIONS
- How do I spend my time?
- Am I using my unique skills and talents?
- Are my actions in harmony with my core values? Mission? Vision?

MISSPENT TIME
- What am I spending time on that is *not* important to me?
- *Why* am I spending time on non-value-added activities?
- What am I not getting to because I'm spending time on unimportant matters?

How Do You Feel About Your Calendar?

It's about this time in my workshops that the business planning process gets very real for some people, especially those who tend to be more task-oriented. That's because the earlier steps were all about getting clear and about what you want and setting some goals to help you get it. At this point, people start to see very concretely how what they do day to day is either helping or hindering their progress. Some discover they are on the right track. They may need only minor tweaks to their schedules to be able to attend to everything they value. Others, not so much. If you feel a groan of your own rising in your throat, fear not. You are now going to look at why you do the things you do and how you can make some needed adjustments so your actions are more in harmony with your goals. Remember, this is not about passing judgment or berating yourself if you've made some subpar choices in the past. Consider this a simple diagnostic exercise that will lead you to some effective treatments. Here are some common discoveries people made during this exercise and what they did about them.

Scale Tilts Hard Toward the Left

It is quite common for professionals, particularly those who are raising young children, to see lots of activities in the career and family sections and precious little in community and mind/body/spirit. The daily demands placed on us by our families and employers often consume every waking moment. The first thing to give is often our own self-care—sufficient sleep, exercise, and leisure time. Yet neglecting our health in favor of investing more time in other areas can paradoxically lead us to be *less* effective in these pursuits. It's hard to be attentive in a meeting if you aren't feeling your best, for one example.

When Regina, the IT project manager who set some new goals in the last chapter, reviewed her calendar, it revealed what she already knew. She put all of her time into work and family and paid the price with her rising weight and falling spirits. While she liked her work and cherished her husband and young child, she was less and less able to enjoy them. Failing to get enough sleep day after day, she tried to boost her flagging energy with coffee and sweets. Not only did she not lose the weight she'd put on during her pregnancy, she'd gained another thirty pounds in the eighteen months since her daughter was born.

She was not surprised when her calendar revealed that she spent no time exercising and relied on fast food dinners far too often to be healthy. Her husband worked later hours and when he wasn't home for dinner, she grabbed whatever she could for dinner and ate while watching whatever was on television. She was embarrassed to realize when she filled out her calendar how many full evenings she spent snacking and zoning out in front of the TV until she finally dragged herself to bed. It was easy to see why she'd put on so much weight. She was just so tired at the end of the day there was no energy left for anything else.

However, she was especially troubled by the realization that she was teaching her daughter some very bad habits. She resolved in that moment to add exercise to her schedule and to do some of it with her daughter. She joined the gym at her company and planned to spend her lunch hour working out three days a week. By taking walks with her daughter on the days she didn't get to the gym, she was able to meet her goal of exercising daily without compromising family time. In fact, she was happy to be modeling healthy behavior for her daughter.

Regina was so motivated to improve her eating and exercise habits that she decided it was worth it to let her daughter eat a little later two evenings a week so they could go for a walk before they settled down for the evening. They also walked both days on weekends and Regina was surprised how much she enjoyed her exercise regime. Her daughter enjoyed being outside, and evenings were much more peaceful when they returned. Regina was also happily amazed that she had much more energy when she walked in the evenings. When she wasn't so tired, it was easier to make the effort to cook something healthy for dinner. As the pounds slowly dropped, she felt better and better. Eventually, she felt well enough in the evenings to do more than collapse in front of the TV. These small changes required very little tweaking to her calendar. Small changes created a huge shift in

REGINA'S DAILY SCHEDULE

	Relationships	Career/ Vocation	Mind/Body/ Spirit	Community
AM				
5:00			Sleep	
6:00	Feed baby, prepare for day			
7:00		Commute		
8:00		Work		
9:00		Work		
10:00		Work		
11:00		Work		
12:00		Work/Lunch		
PM				
1:00		Work		
2:00		Work		
3:00		Work		
4:00		Work		
5:00		Commute		
6:00	Feed baby			
7:00	Family time to play/read, put baby to bed			
8:00			Dinner/Watch TV	
9:00			Snack/Watch TV	
10:00			Watch TV Sleep	
11:00			Sleep	

her health and mood. She felt more equipped to start preparing for some of her longer-term goals.

With their schedules somewhat out of sync during the week, Regina and her husband had to make a special effort to spend time together on the weekends. She had set an immediate goal of having a date night every other Saturday. To her delight, her husband suggested they go out every Saturday. She felt that her improved moods made her better company, so he was more excited about spending time with her. She was even more thrilled when her niece agreed to babysit every week.

Regina was able to accomplish her community goals at church on the weekends. She reported back to me that she's been able to maintain and even improve on her new habits for the past several years and has just started a part-time MBA program and takes classes two evenings a week. She credits her improved eating and exercise habits for making that possible. And those big changes required only a slight shift on her schedule.

Not Having Such a Wonderful Time, Wish I Were Here

Thelma had a tougher challenge when she looked at her calendar next to her goals and priorities. She was nowhere to be found in either place. She had focused a great deal of effort on her career and she was thriving at work. It wasn't until she was discussing her goals and strategies in her Business of Life workshop that she realized just how absent she had been from her own priorities, let alone her agenda. She spent virtually no time attending to her personal needs that included exercise and some kind of spiritual practice.

She was seeking input from the class on her goal to stop yelling at her husband and son so much. She yearned to enjoy their family time, but found that what little they had was often filled with tension and discord. The men in her life continuously dropped their socks on the living room floor and left their clothes all over the house despite her constant (loud) requests that they put their things away. Her classmates were not impressed with her proposed strategy—rather than continuing to scold her husband and son, going forward, she intended to bite her tongue every time she saw the offending laundry and just pick it up and put it away. They told Thelma that not only would she have some nasty teeth marks, keeping her mouth shut would lead to simmering resentment that was likely to come to a boil over time. Her colleagues pointed out that her proposed approach would only continue to train her husband and son that it was okay with her that they disregarded her feelings and were as slovenly as they pleased.

What was so obvious to everyone else was a revelation to Thelma, who was used to being a highly regarded and effective leader at work. She was truly stunned to confront what she tolerated at home. One more look at her goals and calendar confirmed that she needed to make herself a priority.

Thelma's calendar revealed that she spent at least an hour each day on housework. Despite the fact that she had a husband and two able-bodied teens in the house, she carried most of this responsibility on her own shoulders. She put a load of wash in before work and dried and folded it in the evenings. It was no wonder that she was so angry with her husband and son when they dropped their socks on the floor even as she folded the laundry. Now that she confronted the reality of her situation while she discussed its implications with her classmates, she was even angrier with herself for letting it go on for so long. She also faced up to the fact that all her yelling wasn't changing their behavior. There had to be a better approach.

She had been intrigued and somewhat disquieted by the discussion in class about the importance of being present and decided to set some goals to cultivate awareness in that area. She realized she didn't feel as connected to her kids, especially her son, as she'd like to be. Upon reflection, she thought she could make more of an effort to focus on him, his schoolwork, his social life, and just having some fun with him. It would lighten the mood around the house and maybe open up an opportunity to talk about some things that mattered to her. She thought she'd have more success getting through to him if she could talk to him calmly when she wasn't angrily picking up his socks.

Thelma had long been frustrated by the time she felt was wasted in meetings and commuting, but it wasn't until she did her time and emotion study that she made a serious effort to make some changes. And those shifts were profound.

Thelma's staff worked in a few different locations. Once she established strong relationships, she held more of their regular meetings by phone, saving precious travel time in between. She also reduced the time she allotted to most meetings to thirty minutes rather than the hour she'd defaulted to in the past more out of habit than necessity. She also started to schedule conferences she could conduct by phone or remote meeting software at the beginning and end of the workday so she could participate from home. That allowed her to commute outside of rush hour, saving as much as ninety minutes in travel time and avoiding maddening frustration. As important, she was able to see her son off to school in the mornings and be home earlier in the evenings. A special bonus—she found she was much more patient and able to focus her full attention on him when she wasn't so worn out and stressed by her commute.

Now that she was close to home some mornings, she could get up early, go to a six a.m. yoga class (for exercise and meditation, a nice "twofer") and be back home to see her kids before starting her meetings. She has found that her days are more pleasant and productive when they start off that way.

By making these small shifts, her mornings and evenings went much more smoothly and efficiently. She got more done in less time and created precious space to think and plan. And she did so just in time since, little did she know, her home life was about to hit the fan. We'll see what happened and what she did about it later in the book.

We Just Keep Adding to the List

Bruce is the mid-level manager who, along with his wife, had a vision that included having a third child. This busy two-career couple couldn't see how they could possibly make time for more offspring. Until, that is, Bruce made an important discovery when reviewing his

time and emotion study. Bruce and Mara had worked long hours for
years as they established their careers and were quite satisfied with
their progress. Bruce's calendar revealed some inertia and a pattern
of working extraordinarily long hours that persisted longer than was
necessary. He and Mara had agreed when they were newly married
that they would work hard and advance professionally before having
kids. They had their children right on schedule, but they'd forgotten
an important part of their plan.

They'd never scaled back their work hours, though their careers
were long past the point when they needed to put in extra hours to
prove themselves on the job. Like many professionals, they excelled at
adding new activities to their calendars but were remiss in removing
old ones that no longer served an important purpose. Bruce knew in
the early years of his management career that he would have to put in
a lot of "face time" to establish his credibility, reputation, and relationships. That goal was accomplished years ago, but he had not made any
adjustments to reflect his evolving status. As he reviewed his time and
emotion study, he realized he no longer needed to serve on so many
committees. And since he worked with surgeons, most of those meetings were held before and after normal business hours. Using a critical eye to determine which meetings were still necessary for him to
attend, he determined that he could step down from three working
groups. Doing so would free up two evenings and one morning a week.

After Bruce stepped down from those extra committees, he was
able to have dinner with his family four nights a week. On the morning that was freed up, Bruce stayed home and made breakfast for the
kids. He also skipped the gym that day so Mara could get in a workout
for herself. Each week, Bruce whipped up French toast with a surprise
topping and the kids took bets on what it would be. Thursday's breakfast turned into a much-anticipated ritual. Bruce also realized that,
over time, he could adjust his work schedule further and start going
into the office later most mornings.

What are you doing just because it hasn't occurred to you that it's

BRUCE'S DAILY SCHEDULE

	Relationships	Career/Vocation	Mind/Body/Spirit	Community
AM				
5:00			Arise and travel	
6:00		Work (2-3 days/ week)	Exercise at gym 2-3 days	
7:00		Work		
8:00		Work		
9:00		Work		
10:00		Work		
11:00		Work		
12:00		Work		
PM				
1:00		Work		
2:00		Work		
3:00		Work		
4:00		Work		
5:00		Work		
6:00		Work		
7:00	Family dinner	Work (3 nights/wk)		
8:00	Bedtime routine			
9:00		Business reading, return e-mails		
10:00	Check in with Mara		Sleep	
11:00			Sleep	

no longer important for you to be doing it? For me, that was getting my eight-year-old son his milk every time he wanted a drink. For some reason, I hadn't noticed he'd long since been able to reach the milk and glasses just as well as I could. At some point, our children can switch from being a cost center to a revenue center and they can actually be some help around the house. We just have to remember to ask them.

I've Left Joy off My Agenda

Using our time well is essential to our sense of well-being. Feeling fulfilled requires putting our talents and passions to good use. As Aristotle said some 2,300 years ago, "we can't be truly happy unless and until we apply the fruits of our personal self-development to meeting the needs of others."[2]

Danielle, the fashion buyer who'd been stuck in a career she hated for twenty years, saw an opportunity to add more fun to her schedule immediately, even while she took time to find a new career direction. She'd set a goal of taking a cooking class because she enjoyed being in the kitchen so much. She also loved cooking for her husband, delighting him with artistically presented delicacies, so she set a goal of doing that at least once a week. She got such a boost from his obvious enjoyment of her cooking that she ended up preparing elaborate meals even more frequently. Between the delicious cuisine and the special time she had with her husband, every dinner felt like a celebration.

Get to the Heart of the Matter

If you find yourself relating to any of these dilemmas or have identified some other patterns of your own, there is plenty you can do about it. Take another look at your calendar and consider the following:

- What are you doing that doesn't serve you well?
- Why are you doing it?
- What can you do to change it?
- What are you not doing that you'd like to add into the mix?

Allow yourself to be present with whatever is happening. Aim for understanding why you're in this situation and try not to judge yourself harshly.

Why Am I Doing What I'm Doing?

It's important to recognize what's driving your behavior so you can address the source of the problem rather than just the symptoms. Toyota developed a simple approach to root cause analysis that has since become quite popular in health care and other industries: the five whys. I've often employed this technique myself when leading large projects. And it also works well with my students and clients. Manufacturing leaders at Toyota found that if they asked the question "Why?" five times, they could get to the root of just about any problem.

Here's how it worked for one of my coaching clients who had a goal of exercising daily, but was having trouble finding the time to do so:

Why don't I work out every day?
I don't have enough time.

Why (don't I have enough time)?
My commute is taking longer than it used to.

Why (is my commute taking longer than it used to)?
I am driving instead of taking the train. Traffic is lousy.

Why (am I driving instead of taking the train)?
So my car is with me at the end of the day.

Why (do I need my car at the end of the day)?
So I can drive to the gym to exercise.

This gentleman discovered that, ironically, his strategy for exercising was the very thing that was preventing him from doing so. He changed strategies and bought a treadmill and a set of free weights. The clincher was that he convinced his wife that he "needed" a new flat-screen television and a DVR so he could record his favorite sporting events so that he always had something to watch when it was time to exercise. It worked so well that they added an elliptical machine to their home gym and started recording movies so they could work out together while watching something they both enjoyed. Problem solved.

Toolbox

Root Cause Analysis: Five Whys

Seek to find the cause of your problem so you can address it at its root rather than just treating the symptom. This gives you insight into what's leading to your dilemma and will help you find solutions that will have a lasting impact.

Is Fear at the Root of Any Misalignment?

Go back to your SWOT analysis. Did you identify with any of the fear-based behavioral patterns described in that chapter? Several of these can lead to spending time doing things that divert you from your priorities. Let's examine how some of these can suck precious time from your days.

- **People pleasing:** Fear of disappointing others can often lead you to do whatever they ask of you, even when you'd rather not. People with this problem have a very hard time saying "no" to all kinds of requests. If you find yourself volunteering for every extra project at work or bake sale at your church, consider carefully what it is costing you to do so. Ask yourself what would happen if you said no to one request. You might be surprised that often the answer is "very little."

- **Perfectionism:** Do you find that you are never satisfied with your work to the point that you continue revising it long after you've crossed the point of diminishing returns? Believe me, this is something I can relate to very well. This book is partially a product of that tendency. In fact, there's a good chance I'll redraft this very section next time I reread it.

As the famous "they" say, don't let perfect be the enemy of good. Many times, good is good enough. Save the extra effort for those initiatives that truly call for excellence. In management circles, we often work by the Pareto Principle, which states that 80 percent of the work on any given project is completed with the first 20 percent of effort. The return on the investment of that last 80 percent is far lower than the initial 20. Consider that tenet next time you're grinding away on trying to get something "perfect." I just did.

- **Control issues:** Controlling people are sure that no one else can do anything as well as they can, so they end up doing most everything themselves. These people often make lousy bosses because they either refuse to delegate anything or they second-guess everything they assign to others. If you fall prey to this belief, once again, consider what it is costing you. Doing things that others can accomplish reasonably well takes you away from other activities—perhaps even those where you really *are* the best one for the job. If you are a manager, your job is to coach your people so they can learn to be as good as, if not better than, you are at performing their tasks. Try a new approach. See if coaching your staff pays dividends in freed-up time for you to invest elsewhere.

- **Procrastination:** Despite Mark Twain's advice, "Never put off till tomorrow what can be put off till day-after-tomorrow just as well,"[3] chronic procrastinators waste a lot of time. And it's getting easier than ever to procrastinate when, with the stroke of a computer key, you can peek at your e-mail, satisfy even the most frivolous curiosity by looking up the price of sugar in Siberia on the Internet, or play just one more game of.... The digital age is shortening our attention spans and along with our attention goes the ability to complete a task efficiently and effectively. Mr. Twain's wry observation may actually help determine the urgency of a given task and guide us to make a good decision about when to accomplish it. And taking scheduled breaks to clear your mind and refresh yourself may boost productivity. But protracted procrastination can prevent you from achieving a goal. Take an honest look at your calendar—make sure you've accurately filled in how you *really* spend your time. Do you find evidence of chronic procrastination?

Find Some Fixes

Now that you've examined what's driving your behavior, you can address any tendencies that are working against you. The following are a few more time management ideas. In the next chapter, you will learn a whole array of tools you can employ to choose those strategies that optimize your chances for success.

Tame the Electronic Beast

By far, the single thing that robs my clients, colleagues, and kids of precious time are the never-ending, ever-growing options for distracting ourselves with computer games, e-mail, texting, social media, podcasts, and on and on. The information age has many of us feeling like we are hopelessly behind in our knowledge because no human being can possibly keep up with the constant barrage of really cool stuff coming our way. And I mean that sincerely. There *is* great information to be consumed. There are awesome games to be played. There's nothing wrong with much of what's out there. It's the sheer amount that is constantly and readily available to us that threatens our productivity.

These distractions impact more than just how much we get done. Dr. Glenn Wilson, a psychiatrist at King's College London, found that the IQ of workers who tried to juggle phone, texts, and e-mail messages fell by ten points, which is equivalent to missing a whole night's sleep and more than twice the decline seen after smoking marijuana.[4]

The lure is seductive, so we need to impose some discipline. Here are some techniques that have helped my clients.

• **Be mindful about your electronics use:** Make deliberate decisions about how much time you will allocate to these activities. This may sound simplistic, but having a plan puts you in control of how you use your time and makes you less likely to get swept away for too long.

• **Schedule breaks:** Big projects like writing a book, for instance, require long stretches of intense concentration that can be very difficult to sustain. It's easy to convince yourself that you "need" to take a quick look at your e-mail just to keep up. The problem is that quick peek often turns into an hour or more and it breaks your focus. One way to deal with this is to divide your work time into chunks that are punctuated with refreshing breaks. It's good to get up and move around. There is evidence that students perform better at school when bouts of physical activity are sprinkled throughout the day. Schedule time to look at e-mail, play a game, or surf the web, and discipline yourself to limit your break to the allotted time. It may help to know another respite is only ninety minutes away.

• **Beat your e-mail addiction:** Are you, like many of my clients, addicted to e-mail? Do you drop whatever you're doing the instant you hear the ping announcing yet another not-so-special delivery? I was on a wilderness hike out West with a friend who stopped every few minutes to pull his smartphone out of his pocket to see what juicy nugget just arrived. Really? I'm not sure which is worse—that or the fact that nearly 40 percent of people admit to using their smartphones in the bathroom.

If your e-mail habit is distracting you, here is some advice:

○ Schedule two times a day to check and answer e-mail, and stay away from it at all other times.

○ Turn off alerts that let you know every time a message comes in.

○ Inform everyone that you will be checking your e-mails at the appointed times and will get back to them then. Putting a message on your out of office reply is a good way to do that. You can also let people know if they need a quicker response that they should contact you another way. Over time, people will learn what to expect from you and will adjust their behavior accordingly.

Put First Things First

Be mindful that your calendar reflects your priorities, and make conscious, well-considered choices about what is worthy of your time and attention. Use your mission, vision, and goals as filters that help you decide what you will do. Remember there are some things only you can do. Be sure to reserve time for the most essential items. For everything else, apply the "three D's" and ask yourself what can be:

• **Ditched:** Does each task need to be done? Ask yourself what would happen if it wasn't completed. If there isn't a serious consequence, consider dropping it from your list.

• **Delegated:** Okay, so it has to be done, but does it have to be done by you? Is there someone else who could handle this task?

• **Delayed:** How urgent is this task? When is the most appropriate time to tackle it, considering everything else on your list?

Put Last Things off the List

Many of us live by our to-do lists, but few of us have mastered the "not-to-do" list. This is not the same as not getting to something on the to-do list. This is about deliberately choosing *not* to do something that will not yield much value. If you have lots of red on your calendar, this may be an especially fruitful exercise for you. Ask yourself why you are doing things that have limited utility and consider eliminating them.

Toolbox

Not-To-Do List

Before you schedule every activity someone requests of you, take a moment to consider carefully whether it merits the time it would require. It's easier to be judicious before adding something to your load than it is to back out later once people are counting on you.

"There is more to life than simply increasing its speed."[5]

—Mahatma Gandhi

Remember that one reason for creating a business plan for your life is to be present and get the full value from whatever it is you choose to do. Trying to cram too much activity into a crowded schedule is not a great recipe for staying in the moment. So do give careful consideration to using the not-to-do list as another way to avoid letting unimportant things creep onto your calendar.

Once you've convinced yourself that everything on your calendar deserves its place, you will want to be sure you're as efficient as possible. There are many excellent books on time management that offer detailed approaches to improving productivity. David Allen's *Getting Things Done: The Art of Stress-Free Productivity*,[6] offers a thoughtful system that you may want to consider reviewing.

Toolbox

Calendar

If you are prone to distractions, use your calendar to schedule time to enjoy activities that might otherwise sidetrack you from the task at hand. Allow yourself a certain amount of time for breaks a few times a day when you can indulge these diversions. Be disciplined and stick within the allotted time. Then return to your task with new focus.

Frequently interrupted? Schedule office hours and tell your colleagues or students to come during the appointed time only.

If you struggle with perfectionism, schedule a specific amount of time for a given undertaking. Factor in a set number of inputs and revisions and then resolve to be satisfied with the result.

When your actions are guided by your core beliefs and you're focused on priorities that you've chosen consciously, you'll feel balanced. Purposeful. Joyful. And you'll keep heading steadily in the direction of fulfilling your vision. Hopefully you now have that wonderful sense of order and possibility that comes from cleaning all the old junk out of your closet. With room to breathe, you can contemplate how best to invest your newfound time to achieve your goals. In the next step, you will develop some strategies to do just that.

Step ⑦

Select Successful Strategies:
Tools to Set You on a Productive Path

"Action expresses priorities."

—Mahatma Gandhi

Designing a business plan for your life is all about setting you up to live with integrity—so that what you do is a true reflection of who you are and what you value. In this step, you will select the strategies that best serve your priorities and are most likely to bring your glowing vision to life. You will get very specific about *how* you will accomplish those objectives. Sometimes the approach is fairly obvious—it's almost a given. If your goal is to have Sunday brunch with the family every week, you probably don't have to create overwrought plans to do that. You all love pancakes and orange juice and sleeping in. So you decide to meet at the table by eleven, agree to rotate cooking and grocery shopping duties, and you're pretty much there. For more complex goals, however, such as switching careers or pursuing a promotion, you will need a more sophisticated plan. In this section, you will sift through your potential strategies and choose those that are most likely to get you the results you desire.

To make wise choices, you will need to size up the alternatives and select the strategy that is most feasible and likely to work. And if previous efforts you've made to accomplish a goal have fallen short, you'll want to examine those as well, so you learn from your experiences and pick a more rewarding path. Bringing a vision to life takes skill.

This chapter offers a collection of tools you can use to evaluate your options, whether you seek to embark on a major life change or to simply make each day joyful and productive.

Jargon Alert

Are you finding yourself questioning what's a goal and what's a strategy? Wondering about the difference between priorities and objectives? Strategies and tactics? Don't worry about the terminology. Some business types spend a lot of time arguing over the lingo used to describe the strategic planning process. The names are not important. What matters is that you know *what* you want to do and *how* you will do it. You set goals and priorities so you are clear about *what* is most important for you to accomplish. This chapter is devoted to figuring out how you will get it done.

Here's one example of how people get tied up in knots. Say you've set a goal to lose ten pounds. Your strategy—the way you're going to accomplish that goal—is to cut refined sugar out of your diet and start an exercise program. Your exercise program could be accomplished with any number of tactics: join a gym, go for daily walks, ride a bike, and on and on. This chapter will help you decide which approach to the exercise program is most likely to lead you to success with your goal of losing weight.

Another person, however, might call starting an exercise program her goal. Maybe that contributes to a larger goal, such as "getting healthy." Or maybe exercise *is* the goal. That person will still need to get specific about how she is going to initiate her fitness regimen. So, one person may consider exercising a goal while the other thinks of it as a strategy to achieve a different goal. For one, the different exercise options are tactics while the other considers them strategies. Does it really matter?

For our purposes, we will use the term "strategy" to describe how you will accomplish something. Generally speaking, strategies are the general approach you will take and tactics are the smaller steps that contribute to the execution of a given strategy. There, you have the definitions if that helps you.

Make Sure Your List Is Complete

Before launching into action, let's be sure you are looking at the whole picture. Pull out your notebook. Review your mission and vision statements, both for inspiration and to ensure you've covered all your bases. Do you have all your critical success factors in place or a strategy to secure them?

Reviewing your critical success factors can serve as a good starting point for developing a winning strategy. Dr. Vicki Jackson is the director of Palliative Care at Massachusetts General Hospital and she successfully employed this technique as we worked on her department's strategic plan. To zero in on their priorities, we started with a look at their critical success factors. Vicki knows that the quality of the service she can provide is entirely dependent on employing the best practitioners in this young field, and she's been extraordinarily successful in this regard. A quality staff is her most essential success factor, so recruiting, retaining, and developing the best of the best is one of her top goals.

Her SWOT (strengths, weaknesses, opportunities, and threats) analysis showed her what she already knew. One of her division's greatest strengths is her highly dedicated and skilled multidisciplinary team of professionals. She knows not to take this extraordinary asset for granted as her profession faces serious threats nationally. First, the intense nature of their work with gravely ill patients, while richly rewarding, can be emotionally draining. Burnout is a well-known occupational hazard. Furthermore, there is an undersupply of qualified practitioners because the field is so new, so replacing her staff would not be a simple undertaking. Vicki intuitively understands that nurturing her clinicians' career growth and general well-being is essential to meeting her retention goal. As director, it is her responsibility to steward her resources wisely. She considers paying attention to how her people think *and* feel to be essential to the team's collective responsibility for managing their energy and emotions. This isn't a luxury in the palliative care field. It's a pragmatic necessity.

She also knows from experience that there is no "one size fits all" prescription for keeping everyone on the staff energized, so it is essential for her to offer an array of choices to address everyone's needs. Her approach, fittingly, was to appoint a task force led by two clinicians to develop a menu of renewal options. She calls this their sustainability strategy. While she respects the personal nature of this undertaking and doesn't dictate a single approach, she does insist that everyone on her team engage in some form of self-care to stave off burnout.

As you can see from this example, a significant part of the MGH palliative care strategy emerged directly from a review of the department's critical success factors, taking into account their strengths and weakness and evaluating the opportunities and threats presented by the state of their profession on the national level. As you review your strategic options, you will benefit from doing a similar analysis for yourself.

So Much to Do, So Little Time

You have a full life and are busy, busy. Most of what you're doing may even be pretty rewarding. As if that's not enough, you've just written down a closetful of goals to do even more. Your cup runneth over, but so doth your plate. There is far more on your list than you can possibly do. So how do you choose? In the last chapter, you reviewed your calendar and did some work to clear out the clutter. Now you can employ some new tools to judiciously determine what you add back to your schedule so that everything on it serves your goals and priorities.

Since you want your efforts to be both efficient and effective, this would be a good time to review your SWOT analysis. You need to ensure that your strategies leverage your strengths and opportunities, and that you have plans to address any potential weaknesses or threats. Remember not to get down on yourself for anything you've identified as a weakness. We all have them. Simple acceptance of the facts will allow you to think calmly about how to fill in for what you lack. From a resource-management perspective, you are far better off leveraging your strengths than trying to get up to speed to do everything yourself. If you happen to be lousy at math, all the math training in the world is likely to get you to adequate at best. And most of us are after excellent. So embrace your gifts and accept your limitations with grace and humility. Then go about finding other ways to fill in for your weaknesses if those points are necessary to achieving your goals.

Peggy and Gail are the artists who were starting Our Space, an organization to provide art therapy and other support for children affected by cancer. When they evaluated their readiness to launch this initiative, their SWOT, presented in step 4, revealed a mixed picture. They had a lot going for them, but their list of weaknesses showed that several of their critical success factors were not exactly in their wheelhouse. Their gap analysis revealed a significant lack of business know-how. They are very bright women, and certainly could have compensated for this particular weakness with courses at a local university. However, that would have taken years, and increasing their business education played neither to their strengths nor their passions. In one of their coaching sessions, we determined that there was likely a more expedient way to acquire the business acumen they needed, so we generated a list of alternate possibilities. You will see how they met this objective in the final chapter.

Admittedly, launching an entire organization is a complicated undertaking. So let's look at someone who had more modest goals. Mark is an attorney I coached who saw mixed results when he looked at his time and emotion study. He'd recently made partner at his firm after a concerted campaign to accomplish this long-term goal. He felt great about his achievement. However, his singular focus on work over the years took its toll. He had stopped his already sporadic exercise "program" in order to put in additional time on the job and had given up any semblance of a social life. His last physical revealed that his weight and blood pressure had started to creep up. He was interested in getting married and starting a family, but had not made much effort to go on dates or participate in any activities where he might meet his future bride. He had not contributed to any community service initiatives in recent memory and didn't feel so great about that.

A natural list maker, Mark started by brainstorming all of the ways he could fill in the gaps. Work was on a positive track, so focusing on the other three areas, he came up with something that looked like this:

Exercise	Social Life	Community Service
Run before work	Run with friends/family	Participate in events sponsored by his law firm
Join a gym	Invite someone to dinner out two nights a week	Raise money for children with autism
Trek the Himalayas	Join a hiking club	
Play tennis	Play tennis with friends	
Build a home gym	Ask friends to set him up on dates	

Even though Mark's time was still in pretty short supply, he decided to make daily exercise and reconnecting with friends and family immediate priorities. Being naturally very efficient in his actions, he looked for activities that could address one or more of his objectives at the same time. Running and playing tennis were two ways to improve his fitness that he could do with friends. That would help his social life as well. He'd always wanted to go trekking in Nepal. He thought joining a local hiking club might be a way to get in shape for a big trip and meet health-conscious women. He thought joining a gym might be another way to get fit and meet women. While he felt slightly less urgency to be active in community service, he looked for a convenient way to contribute to a cause that was personally meaningful and important to him. His nephew's struggles with autism touched him deeply and he hoped to find a way to make a difference for other families coping with this condition.

Despite the efficiencies he built into his list, he was still over-whelmed at the thought of adding more to his already crowded sched-ule. He just didn't know where to begin. So we used one of his coaching sessions to run his options through a series of tools and filters to zero in on the few things he *could* do that were most likely to achieve his larger goals of gaining better balance in his life and getting back into decent physical shape. As you will see illustrated below, when Mark used a series of tools to rank his priorities and multiply efficiencies, he began to reshape his schedule and take control of his life.

First Things First: Prioritization Tools

When the demands for your time and attention are relentless and more than you can possibly accomplish, it is very useful to impose some dis-cipline and carefully evaluate which initiatives merit a spot at the top of your to-do list. That is a lot easier than it sounds and the time these tech-niques can save you by preventing you from taking on unworthy tasks is an impressive return on this investment. You will find that once you've used them for a while, they just become part of the way you think.

Big Rocks

My mentor, Dr. James Cash, professor and former chairman of the MBA program at Harvard Business School, shared a metaphor years ago that has stayed with me ever since. He talked about filling a jar with rocks until they brim over the top. He asked if the jar appeared full, but then pointed out that there was still space between the rocks to fit in pebbles. Again, he asked if the jar was full, but now mentioned how sand could still fill in the small spaces between the pebbles. Finally, he noted that water could fill in the micro-gaps between the grains of sand. His point became quite clear: you could fit quite a lot into a jar if you start with the big stuff first.

If you put the trivial matters, the metaphorical sand, in your jar (schedule) first and then try to layer on the big rocks, you'll find that you have less room for the more important matters. What sand are you allowing to keep you from getting to some of your big rocks? Make a point from now on to consciously focus on the things that matter most to you. Give them the priority they deserve when allocating your time, resources, and attention.

Importance/Urgency Matrix

One of the most powerful and commonly used prioritization tools is a very simple importance/urgency matrix. First, it can be used to triage your "inbox" and help you decide whether a given task is worth doing and how quickly it should be addressed. It looks like this:

	Urgent	*Not Urgent*
Important	Immediate Priority	Planning and Preparation/ Renewal Activities
Not Important	Interruptions	Busywork

If something is urgent and important, it zooms to the top of your to-do list. If something is not important and not time sensitive, it's likely to be busywork and doesn't merit your time. This item should populate your not-to-do-list.

The other two quadrants require judgment. If something is urgent, but not important, you need to decide if it is worth the effort. These are likely to be interruptions. Sometimes, it is almost as quick to address them as it is to dismiss them, and it can be worth the brief effort to satisfy someone else. Other times, what someone else is asking of you would take you away from something more pressing, so you're better off passing on it.

Important items that are not time sensitive require your attention. Often, these are activities like taking care of your health or doing some long-range planning—maybe even what you are doing right now. They often allow you to be more efficient and effective over the long term, but there's usually no burning need to address these items immediately. Because urgency isn't forcing you to address these matters, it's important to proactively make time on your calendar for them. If you don't make a point of finding the time, they will likely continue to be pushed to the back burner until they fall off the stove altogether. They may never get your attention, or worse, they will hang over your head as a nagging undone chore. Vacations and spiritual renewal activities fall into this category as well. Taking breaks to refresh and renew often does not feel urgent, but it is essential.

As a visually oriented thinker, I like to use this grid to look at how the many potential projects compare to one another as they compete for limited time. To show you how this looks, let's go back to Mark's list of activities. I've altered the grid slightly to show relative importance and urgency so that it now presents more of a continuum than absolute values.

MARK'S GOALS AND PRIORITIES

	More Urgent	*Less Urgent*
High Importance	Autism Run Exercise	Dinner Dates
Low Importance		Community Service Firm Events

Mark assigned exercise the highest level of importance and it was very urgent as well. And while finding a wife was at least as important to him, it didn't feel quite as urgent as getting his blood pressure under control. He found he was not terribly motivated to participate in community service activities sponsored by his law firm. Initially, he thought that would be an easy way to fulfill the obligation he felt to contribute to worthy causes. However, when he looked at that activity relative to the other things on his list, the programs his firm supported just didn't move him. That came off his list. Just before he came to our coaching session, his sister told him about a ten-kilometer road race to raise money for an agency that provides services and advocacy for children with autism. Because training for that race would contribute to both his fitness and community service goals, that rocketed to the highest importance quadrant. And because he had to be ready to run by the predetermined date just a few weeks away, this effort took on the highest urgency.

Mark also confessed that he hoped he'd meet some single, community-minded women at the race as well, making that a potential "three-fer." So he went right to work training for that race. He also committed to setting up some dinner dates. While not as urgent, reconnecting with friends and family was important to adding some joy back into his days. He was able to accomplish this by scheduling dinners with family and friends a little later in the evening without competing with his other priorities.

Will This Work? Feasibility Filters

Once you have prioritized your initiatives in terms of importance and time sensitivity, you'll want to look at which strategies are most likely to help you achieve a given goal. In business, we're trained to look at return on investment. This is usually expressed in financial terms. If you invest a hundred dollars in X, you'll make a thousand dollars profit. For your life plan, you will look at how to invest your time and attention to get the biggest payoff for the least effort, leaving as much time as possible to invest on other endeavors. Also, you'll need to address the fact that the more difficult something is to accomplish, the higher the risk that it might not work at all.

Risk/Reward Matrix

I've developed a tool I call the Risk/Reward Matrix to evaluate the difficulty of implementing certain strategies relative to their potential benefit. If something is easy to do and is going to pay huge dividends, pursuing it is a no brainer. Likewise, if something is difficult to achieve and won't yield much benefit, it's clear that you'd cross that off your list. Judgment again becomes a factor where something is easy to do but produces relatively little benefit. You'll also need to decide if it's worth investing in something that may be difficult to carry out, but comes with huge rewards if achieved.

		Reward/Payoff	
		High	*Low*
Risk/Difficulty/ Resource Requirement	*Low*	Must do	Quick hits—fine if you have the time
	High	The impact may be huge, but not guaranteed; evaluate the effort required against the likelihood of achievement	Add to *not-to-do* list

You can use this grid to evaluate each strategy you are contemplating on its own merits or in relation to other items on your list. To maximize your chances for success, strive to choose the actions that will give you the biggest payoff for your efforts and that will play to your strengths. Remember to balance the portfolio of strategies you select to reflect the mix of priorities you set for yourself.

This grid can also be used to evaluate the relative cost/benefit of the many strategies you're considering. Let's look at how Mark used it to guide his thinking about developing his exercise program. You will consider the risks and benefits on a continuum and create a picture of how the initiatives rate relative to one another.

MARK'S EXERCISE PROGRAM STRATEGIES

		Reward/Payoff	
		Higher	*Lower*
Risk/Difficulty/ Resource Requirement	**Higher**	Hike the Himalayas / Play tennis	Build home gym / Join hiking club
	Lower	Join gym / Running	

Mark's matrix led him to decide to start running before breakfast several days a week. It was not only great exercise, all he needed was a decent weather forecast and the discipline to put on his sneakers and go. To top it off, several of his friends were runners and he had a natural gift for organizing groups. He set up a system so they could notify each other when they were heading out; that way, group members could easily meet up for company and encouragement. That met his social and health goals. Joining a gym also rose to the top of his strategies list, since it allowed him to exercise in bad weather. While there was a cost to gym membership that running did not have, and Mark had to drive to the health club, the benefit of membership was well worth the expense because it rounded out his fitness routine. Tennis also made the list because he enjoyed it so much. However, when it came to adding tennis to his schedule, Mark viewed it as a complement to running and his gym routine, because court time was expensive and required more intricate scheduling to meet friends at the club.

He took things off his list, starting with building a home gym. The ease of rolling out of bed to work out in his PJs wasn't worth the expense of the equipment and it offered no social opportunity. He also crossed the Himalayan trekking expedition off his list. While it would be a very cool trip, the fitness benefits would be short lived and the logistics were extremely complicated. Last, Mark removed joining a hiking club from his list. His SWOT reflected that he is not a good "joiner." He likes being in charge rather than following someone else's itinerary. He also knew that finding the time for group outings would be difficult at best. Besides, his health club membership satisfied the physical and social benefits he would realize from joining a hiking club, and it therefore offered minimal incremental value.

Personal Power Grid

Organization consultants and psychologists Dennis Jaffe and Cynthia Scott created the final matrix I present here, called a Personal Power Grid.[1] This is another excellent filter to evaluate whether your efforts will have the impact you seek. It can also help you see how your own behavior either propels you toward fulfilling your vision, stalls your progress, or pulls you off course altogether.

	Can Control Outcome	Cannot Control Outcome
Take Action	Mastery	Ceaseless Striving
Take No Action	Giving Up	Letting Go

In this instance, mastery means taking action when you know it is going to pay off. If Mark exercises regularly and follows his nutritionist's advice, he will lose weight. That's mastery, and what you should be aiming for whenever possible. If Mark decides to throw up his hands and not make the effort to work out, that's giving up. Copping out is another term for knowing what you need to do and choosing not to do it.

Taking action when you can't control the outcome is what the authors of this grid call ceaseless striving. People pleasers take note: one of the most insidious time wasters falls in this category if you're continually trying to win the approval of someone whom you've not been able to please in the past, no matter how extreme your efforts. Many of us spin our wheels at some point. How many people are yo-yo dieters? Every time they start a new regimen, they are convinced that *this* time it will be different. Is that really true? There's a popular definition of insanity—doing the same thing over and over but expecting a different result. If you find yourself in this situation, take some time to figure out what's driving your behavior and what it is costing you—especially in relation to what else you could be doing to achieve your goal.

On the other hand, if you cannot control the outcome of a situation and you choose not to act, there's grace in letting go. This is another way to populate your not-to-do list. I can't play foosball to save my life. Do you think I'm being modest? A four-year-old once refused to have me on his team because I'm so lousy at it. No matter how much I practice, I just can't get good at flipping plastic footballers on a metal rod. While my ego may not like conceding a lack of talent in any area, spending any more time on that worthless pursuit would be wasted effort. Now I just play Ping-Pong with that kid. I can even beat him on that table, thank you very much.

Toolbox

Serenity Prayer

If you have a hard time letting go, try reciting this prayer that is a common fixture in the recovery movement:

Grant me the serenity to accept the things I cannot change; the courage to change the things I can; and the wisdom to know the difference.

But beware of giving up and calling it letting go. When my daughter moved up to high school, she was the only kid in her eighth grade class to be recommended for Advanced Placement Math, the highest level available. My daughter's teacher cautioned her that she'd be mixed in with the best math students in town and that she'd have to work hard to earn a "C" grade. She agreed, and took on the challenge. Sure enough, it was a real struggle. Her new teacher sent her several notes suggesting she see him for extra help. Accustomed to breezing through her lessons unaided, she opted to keep trying on her own—until she'd had enough and told me she wanted to drop down into Honors Math. Fortunately, her teacher had told me that one of the goals of AP Math was teaching students how to learn when learning is hard. That's something these kids had not yet experienced.

I told my daughter that if she gave AP Math everything she had and it was still too hard for her, it would be just fine for her to drop to a level where she might learn more. However, I knew she could still accept the extra help her teacher offered and there may have been other available avenues for help that she hadn't pursued. I explained that she was learning to use new intellectual muscles, and like lifting weights for the first time, the effort can leave you feeling sore. But with perseverance, the pain goes away and eventually you can lift more and more weight. So she hung in there, got the help she needed, and did just fine. That effort moved her into the mastery quadrant on the personal power grid. Had she given up without making that extra effort, she never would have discovered the true limits of her abilities. However, if she made the effort and the math was still too hard, she could have let go of the notion she belonged in AP Math and gracefully moved into a class that was a better match for her abilities.

It is worth the effort to be sure you're not giving up too soon or hanging on too long. That's not always clear before you've given something a try. So, you can also use this grid after you've implemented a strategy to help you evaluate whether it's worth continuing or whether you'd be better off trying something new.

Joy Meter

Remember that your emotions give you important information about how well something is aligned with your values and your purpose. This is actually a very practical statement. You are much more likely to stick with something you enjoy doing. I always find visual reminders helpful for decision making, particularly because our heads often have a tendency to overrule our hearts. That's why I created the joy meter and presented it in a toolbox for goal setting. And because we're trying to maximize joy along with optimizing outcomes, we need to keep our joy quotient front and center in our calculus of which activities merit our attention.

Diane, the physician who was looking to raise her professional profile, kept a clear focus on her joy quotient at work. She had so thoroughly researched the issues related to prescribing narcotics in order to write a policy manual that her knowledge on the subject was on a par with any leading authority. And she so thoroughly enjoyed being a subject matter expert that she had set a goal to contribute to the national discourse on this important topic. So she came to her coaching session to explore strategies to create a platform to share her expertise on a broader stage. She also had to address the practical necessity of finding funding to support this endeavor if it meant giving up clinical time to do it.

We reviewed the options open to her. The traditional course in her discipline would be to present at national and international conferences. However, that would require a great deal of travel and would be in direct conflict with her goal of being home as much as possible for her young family. I asked her if she'd considered blogging on the topic and establishing herself as an online thought leader. This was so far out of the norm in medicine that it hadn't even ocurred to her. But it appealed in many ways. First, she loved writing and could do it from home. Second, she'd be blazing new trails and it looked like a niche she could claim for her own.

We then turned our attention to how she would replace the salary she would lose by giving up a clinical session to free up time for this new endeavor. It was clear that the traditional funding sources were unlikely to pay her to blog. But she had come across a few resources during her research that she thought might support her if she turned some of her posts into white papers that could be used by other health-care leaders. We also discussed some foundations that might give her a grant for this worthy endeavor. Finally, she agreed to check into the feasibility of setting up a proprietary website and charging a subscription fee to access her policy suggestions. Alternatively, we discussed her posting the information free of charge, but charging for phone consultations to help hospitals and clinics with writing their own policy manuals. The consulting idea especially appealed to her as it would add significantly to her joy quotient, pushing that strategy up high in her rankings.

EXERCISE

Rank and Select Your Strategies

Grab your notebook and closet. Review your checklist, goals, and priorities. Start with the immediate-term items and record your plan for addressing each one. For those without an obvious approach, brainstorm all of the possible strategies you can think of to accomplish your goals. It's often useful to ask a close friend, family member, or mentor to help you with this exercise. Use the tools presented in this chapter to rank your immediate-term items according to their ease of accomplishment and likelihood to produce the desired result. Select the top candidates. (Make sure to keep the whole list so you can revisit your options if the selected approach proves less effective than predicted.) Then look at your medium- and long-range goals and make sure you have strategies in place to address those at the appropriate times. Rank your strategies and record them in your notebook.

Once you've selected your top strategies, put them on a shelf in your closet. Create a recurring appointment on your calendar to check your closet at regular intervals to monitor your progress and revise your approach as needed. Remember to take a moment to celebrate your successes, no matter how small. There's great joy in making progress, so be sure to soak it all in and give yourself the credit you deserve.

Make Every Day Count

All of these tools can be adapted for everyday use. Each morning, I set aside time to set an intention for the day. I think about what I want to accomplish, how I want to feel, and anything else of importance. I use this time to zero in on my two or three "big rocks" and commit to accomplishing them before allowing any sand to distract me. This is a good time to think about your priorities in a balanced way—whatever balance means for you.

Step ❽ Get Going

Your Simplementation Plan™

"A journey of a thousand miles begins with a single step."[1]

—Lao-Tzu

The time to act has arrived. If you're the "let's just get in the car and start driving" type, this comes as welcome news. For others, it's not easy to embark on a new adventure, no matter how exciting the destination. You've completed all the preliminaries, so grab your compass, map, and walking stick (or your vision, goals, and strategies) and set out on the path toward fulfilling your dreams. There's no time like the present.

Start Simply, but Simply Start

How will you begin executing the strategies for achieving your most pressing priorities? At this point in the Business of Life workshops, I have people pair up and talk to their partners about what they will do in the next *day* to move forward, start a new venture, work on restoring balance, or simply grace their days with more joy notes. With a room full of witnesses, they commit to making it happen. Now it is your turn.

I know. The idea of starting to "live the life of my dreams" may be so daunting that it paralyzes you and nestles you even more firmly into the well-worn rut you've occupied for some time. So how do you suddenly burst into action? By starting small and creating what I call your "simplementation plan."

Neuroscientists know that the human brain is wired to resist change. It's a dilemma that stops a lot of people dead in their tracks. Contemplating any shift that requires a significant departure from your normal routine can be frightening. Your brain senses your fear and triggers the "fight or flight" reaction that floods your body with chemicals to prepare you to cope with dangerous situations. Because your brain can't always distinguish between the types of threats you face, this primitive response can actually send you running away from the idea of initiating a job search just as fast as if you were being chased down by a saber-toothed tiger. Early in our evolution, such an extreme response made sense. But now that most of us don't have to worry about being someone's lunch, it can be a bit much. In order to deal with the immediate and potentially fatal threat of a snarling predator, your brain actually shuts down other functions so you can channel all of your energy into running for cover. When the "threat" is emotional stress, it can shut down your ability to tackle the very issue you need to focus on most.

So what's the answer? Persuade your brain that the change is something it can handle. The trick is to keep taking small steps and let all those little things add up to something big. By asking your brain to accept small, incremental changes, you bypass the fight-or-flight response. That's the premise behind kaizen, the Japanese term for "change for the better." It's about taking small steps to achieve a goal and pursue continuous improvement.[2]

The great news is that your brain is plastic, meaning that it reshapes itself throughout your life. As you learn new skills or acquire new habits, connections between brain cells called neurons are established or strengthened. If you do take those small steps and keep at it, those connections become stronger until the new routines become second nature. Alternatively, your brain prunes away connections that aren't used over time.[3] This is a use-it-or-lose-it system. The key is to get started and persevere until your brain adapts to help you make the new habit stick.

Break It Down

You don't eat a watermelon by trying to sink your teeth into the uncut whole. You can't get your mouth around the rind and it isn't particularly tasty either. But if you cut it open, there are soft, sweet chunks that are easy—and delicious—to eat. You will take one small step at a time until you build up some momentum and become an unstoppable force moving toward your vision. Nothing begets success like success. So to get you started and keep you motivated, this chapter will focus on how to keep your vision quest simple while you master the art of breaking a big journey down into walkable steps.

You Are Just a First Step Away

Peggy and Gail, the artists who wanted to start an art therapy program for kids with cancer, were overwhelmed with the idea of launching a nonprofit organization, creating a business plan, establishing a fundraising program, and on and on. In fact, when we finished mapping out the steps they'd have to go through to carry out their plan, they were pretty much convinced they'd bitten off more than they could chew. My job, however, is to leave my clients feeling empowered to act, so we couldn't finish our session until that was accomplished. I looked for ways to work with their natural wiring so they could find something in their wheelhouse that they could accomplish that would give them a sense of progress and possibility. Because they are both visual artists, the assignment I designed appealed to that sensibility. I sent them to a nearby art supply store to buy the most beautiful file folders they could find. The next day, they gathered all their loose papers and organized them into those pretty folders. They popped them into a file cabinet and, voilà! Our Space, Inc. had an office. It can be that simple to begin.

Creating a base of operations for Our Space was clearly an important and urgent goal. Choosing attractive folders—the very act of taking such a concrete step—registered a decidedly positive "joy-to-hassle ratio" on their joy meter. On the Risk/Reward Matrix, buying office supplies was a very low-risk effort and the reward was also relatively small when viewed against the goal of launching a whole organization. But it had an enormous payoff in that doing something so tangible had the critical effect of moving Peggy and Gail from being dreamers to doers. That simple act changed their whole perception of their ability to achieve their vision because it set them on a path where each step led to the next small, doable task.

Setting up the file system also convinced them that they could organize themselves even further. They pulled out their SWOT and decided to focus on their strengths first. They needed to build a base of support for Our Space, Inc. both for program development and for fundraising. They noted that they had an inspiring mission and vision and, as cancer survivors themselves, had a compelling message. They decided the next logical step was to develop some printed materials that would help them communicate their mission to people who could help them get the effort up and running. They also had some aptitude for writing, so this played to their strengths. Next, they used their artistic skills to design a logo, create some stationery, and print some business cards. Day by day, Our Space was closer to becoming a reality. Each successful step energized Gail and Peggy and led them to the next logical task.

Just Do It

The journey toward a new career can begin with a single phone call, followed by a commitment to make another one every day, asking for an informational interview. Just do something on your list related to your dream, no matter how trivial it seems. Accomplishing the first small thing is incentive to take the next step, then the next. And soon it's a quick jog toward your destination.

EXERCISE

Take Action—Create Your Simplementation Plan

Go through your rank-ordered list of strategies and choose one or more that you can initiate *today* that will set you on your way to achieving one of your goals. What concrete action will you take to get started? What is the next task you will undertake to keep moving forward? Commit to taking at least one small action each day until you achieve that goal. Because you are far more likely to do something if you plan a specific time and place to tackle it, make an appointment on your calendar each day to attend to whatever task you've selected. Then honor that commitment as you would any other appointment. You are worth it.

When Simplementing Doesn't Seem So Simple

Most of us can find the equivalent of Peggy and Gail's file folders—that one small step we can take to get started implementing our strategies. But what do you do if a good first step for each part of your action plan isn't so clear or if you face other obstacles that make it hard to get started? The following sections address some of the common challenges that can stand in the way of progress. We will look at some examples of how people got over (or around) their blocks and on their way. However, please note that the recommendations presented here are not a substitute for clinical care. If you are experiencing serious distress, please consider seeing a trained professional to help identify the root of your difficulties and prescribe the appropriate treatment.

> *"Almost all quality improvement comes via simplification of design, manufacturing…layout, processes, and procedures."*[4]
>
> —Tom Peters

As you've no doubt noticed by now, keeping your tasks simple and doable is one of the greatest keys to successful implementation of your well-crafted plans. If you've completed all the steps in the planning process, you have carefully considered what you want to do and how you want to do it. People tend to make matters much more complicated than they need to be. That tendency makes it hard to do things and even harder to do them well. So let's take a look at how you can cut through the complexity and get going when the going seems tough.

Implementing When Inertia Overwhelms Your Resolve

Change is hard, even when it's good. And it's especially hard when your current pattern is as well worn and cozy as your favorite pair of furry slippers. When you're stuck in a rut, any shift can seem so overwhelming that finding the energy to make such a major move seems truly impossible.

My coaching clients frequently find it helpful to get geared up to take that first step by reviewing what it's costing them to stay put. Reminding yourself what motivated you to start this process in the first place is often enough to nudge you in a new direction.

Danielle got her wake-up call that day in her Business of Life workshop when she discovered that she had not employed most of her creative talents nor pursued any of her passions in her twenty-year career as a fashion buyer. But staying in an industry where she was so well established was her path of least resistance. She'd been so comfortably uncomfortable there for so long, it was daunting to even contemplate doing anything else. That day in her workshop, she confronted for the first time what staying put would cost her. It would continue to rob her of experiencing the joy she knew she could find doing something else.

What that something else was wasn't entirely clear just yet, but one fact was evident. As long as she stayed where she was, nothing was going to change. Her first step was to leave her current company even as they offered her a promotion and ever-bigger bonuses. Simple enough. Easy? Not at all. Danielle needed to acknowledge that disentangling herself from her current situation was indeed taking action toward her new future. It was a critically important first step. Doing so would actually create the space she needed to consider her next steps.

Sure enough, contemplating so much free time was truly frightening to this high-powered executive who was so used to getting up at dawn to exercise before her marathon days at work. But she'd finally had enough and was ready to accept that the risk of not finding and pursuing her passion was greater than taking the leap.

After finally leaving her job, Danielle gave herself a few weeks to clean out her closets and play with her puppy. She took some time to take long walks on the beach near her house that she'd not been around to fully enjoy. Those walks gave her time and space to think about what she wanted to do next. She also had a shocking revelation: from the day she left her office, she'd not missed being there for a single moment. That realization made her feel like she was finally free to contemplate the future without looking back.

Danielle wasn't ready to make big decisions about her next job, but she was ready for a little fun. She went back to her closet and zeroed in on her short-term goal of taking a cooking class. Her husband had recently given her a gift certificate for just such a class, so she signed up right away. Stepping into the school's kitchen felt so great to Danielle that she had a strong feeling that she was exactly where she was meant to be. She felt so happy there, like she was finally in her element. This newfound joy was something she could get used to.

Implementing When the Task Seems Too Big

When the prospect of starting a new project seems too daunting because of its sheer size or just its newness, it's natural to feel overwhelmed and let your nervous neurons get the better of you. This is especially true for the chronic procrastinator. If this rings a bell with you, a simplementation plan may be just what you need to get going. Martin was a corporate vice president who procrastinated by heeding the call to solve his colleague's crisis du jour to the detriment of his own projects. He actually got a little rush of adrenaline every time he helped put out a fire and he enjoyed the sense of accomplishment. He finally conquered his penchant for putting off his own projects by igniting a little drama for himself.

Martin needed to present a report on the state of his industry to his company's board of directors in three months' time and had put off starting this enormous undertaking for several weeks already. The looming deadline made him nervous enough that he enlisted the help of one of his fellow vice presidents and asked her to hold him accountable for turning in the various analyses he needed to complete his white paper.

To raise the stakes, she invited him to share his findings at her weekly department head meetings. He ended each presentation with a promise of what he would discuss at the following meeting. By giving himself a deadline and a roomful of colleagues whose own work depended on his completing these tasks, he suddenly had a burning platform. While the idea of writing the magnum opus on the entire industry overwhelmed him and drove him to keep putting it off, each individual analysis was something he could wrap his brain around and accomplish. Having an audience for the individual components appealed to his desire to feel appreciated and created the sense of urgency that he needed to swing into action mode. It took advantage of his wiring and it worked like a charm. Martin finished his report with two weeks to spare.

Implementing When Fear Stands in the Way

Brenda's math phobia had kept her from pursuing the college degree that was necessary for fulfilling her dream to have a career in management. A root cause analysis helped her identify the source of that problem—the middle school teacher who humiliated her in front of her classmates and told her she had no talent for math. It didn't even take five whys to get to the core of her problem.

Why have I been unable to obtain a management position?
I don't have the college degree most require.

Why don't I have a college degree?
I'm afraid I can't pass the math courses.

Why am I afraid of failing math?
My middle school teacher told me I have no aptitude for math.

Now that we knew the root of her problem, we could address it. In our coaching sessions, Brenda acknowledged that, in fact, she used mathematics every day in her job and that her teacher was simply wrong. But letting go of that long-held belief wasn't as simple as it sounds. She had so fully identified with the label of math failure that accepting that the opposite was true required a leap of faith that was hard to take.

She was filled with dread as she prepared to register for her first college math course at age forty. Taking that initial step was so hard for her that we had to review her options. If she didn't conquer her fear, it was highly unlikely she'd ever have the management career she so dearly desired. The opportunity cost of not taking that first step was high indeed. When asked what's the worst that could happen if she did take the course, she said she might flunk out. She had to admit, however, that while it would be another blow to her self-esteem, she'd be no worse off than she already was. And if she conquered her fear, she just might have a shot at her dream. That was enough to drive her into action. She registered for her first class that very day.

If fear is holding you back, try asking yourself the same questions Brenda considered. Then determine for yourself what is more frightening—never reaching your full potential or facing down a worry that's been limiting your prospects all along.

Implementing When Your Plan Isn't Perfect Yet

Perfectionists often have trouble starting and finishing projects. Starting because the plan isn't watertight. Finishing because it's never 100 percent "right." Well, I've got news for you. No matter how "right" you get your plan, you are most likely going to have to work with other people to make it all happen. People are messy creatures who seem to like doing things their own way. Try as you might, you will never be able to control everything and everyone. So you need to prepare as well as you can and then find the courage to let go.

If it helps, remind yourself you don't have to be perfect to be helpful. In fact, showing your vulnerability just might be a gift that you can give to others. I once gave a talk at a high-stakes conference and was mortified when I couldn't recall a word and stumbled through a short section of my speech. I was beside myself that these leaders of industry caught me in a moment of imperfection. So imagine my surprise—and delight—when the line of people coming up to talk to me at the end of the program snaked all the way out of the ballroom. One after another, the attendees thanked me for inspiring them and making the material so "relatable." Those mumbling moments ended up being an important ingredient in the cement that created such a powerful bond with the audience. I won't go so far as to recommend tripping over your words just to seem "real," but do just take a deep breath and know that often "really good" is as close to perfect as you need to be.

Implementing When There Are Not Enough Hours in the Day

"I don't have enough time to…" is the common refrain of people with the yeah-but habit. There are so many things you'd like to be doing, *but* you just don't have the time. *But,* there are too many other things competing for your attention. The *but*s never end. The fact is you have the same twenty-four hours a day that everyone else has. How you spend that time is an expression of your priorities. Without a doubt, there are many things you must do. But it's unlikely that you can't free up *any* time to accommodate a new priority. If that *is* the case, the new thing isn't truly your highest priority.

If you find yourself in this position and you didn't free up enough space on your schedule in the time and emotion exercise, there's one more thing you can try.

You can perform something called a paired comparison test to assess whether everything that is currently on your calendar is more important and urgent than the new task you are having trouble accommodating.

To accomplish this, take out your notebook and your calendar. For each item on your schedule, assign an importance score from one (least important) to five (most important). Then do the same for each of the activities you'd like to accommodate that don't currently fit. Create a grid like the one below and record the relative scores. The first number in each box is the importance of the item on the left side of the grid. The second number corresponds to the item along the top. This grid allows you to look at the relative importance of each entry in comparison with everything else on your schedule.

PAIRED COMPARISON TEST

	Exercise	Work	Family Dinners	Watch TV	Read Novels	Read Trade Journals	Sleep
Exercise	5/5	5/5	5/5	5/2	5/4	5/5	5/5
Work	5/5	5/5	5/5	5/2	5/4	5/5	5/5
Family Dinners	5/5	5/5	5/5	5/2	5/4	5/5	5/5
Watch TV	2/5	2/5	2/5	2/2	5/4	2/5	2/5
Read Novels	4/5	4/5	4/5	4/2	4/4	4/5	4/5
Read Trade Journals	5/5	5/5	5/5	5/2	5/4	5/5	5/5
Sleep	5/5	5/5	5/5	5/2	5/4	5/5	5/5

In this example, the new activity I want to add is reading trade journals. I believe this will add to my knowledge base and prepare me to achieve my goal of getting a promotion at work. It's a top priority. When I look at everything else currently on my schedule, there's not much there that isn't a high priority. The only two things that don't rank a five are my downtime activities of reading novels (which rates a four) and watching television (which rates a two). I need a little breathing time, so I'm not willing to give up both. But I see when I look at it this way that I generally prefer reading novels to watching TV. Because reading trade journals rates a five, I need to make time for that. So, reluctantly, I decide to give up television. Then I challenge my own all-or-nothing thinking and realize I don't have to go cold turkey. If I read trade journals three days a week, I can probably keep up on the latest industry trends. That allows me to watch my favorite programs the other four days a week. Whew.

Try this exercise for yourself. If everything rates a tie, that tells you something already. Is everything you're doing *really* as important as you think? If yes, go ahead and rank each item with an urgency score and repeat the comparison. What can wait and be done once you've accomplished something that is more time sensitive?

Take a critical look at your chart. Make some decisions; then make a switch. Or make peace with your assessment if you decide you're already doing everything that is most urgent and important.

Just Get Moving

If creating your simplementation plan was simple for you, you're ready to act. If it was less so, use all the tools in your kit and make your plan now. Then look at what you've committed to doing within the next day and do it. You are only a small first step away from making your dreams come true.

I know how frightening this can be. If I'd given in to my own fears, I wouldn't have sung in public after my third-grade music teacher silenced me for decades. But I faced my deepest insecurity and here I am, stronger than ever, to tell the tale.

Whatever is holding you back, consider carefully whether you're better off staying put or forging ahead. If you choose moving forward, realize that it's unlikely to get easier, so you might as well hold your nose and jump. And once you've done it, you can jump for joy.

How Is It Going?

The hardest part is over. You've set out on your path and are on your way toward fulfilling your vision. If all is going well, you have added the grace notes that make each day a pleasure and fill your reservoirs of joy. You're making steady progress and enjoying the journey.

But how do you know if it's going well or not? Remember the importance of cultivating presence and awareness. Pay attention to how you feel and whether or not you are advancing toward the accomplishment of your goals. In keeping with your newly formed habits, you will not leave this to chance. You will schedule appointments on your calendar to check in at regular intervals to see how you're doing.

EXERCISE

Evaluate Your Progress

Where are you relative to where you want to be? Now that you've taken some strategic steps forward, have you:

- Maintained a focus on your priorities?
- Used your gifts and talents?
- Achieved some goals?
- Made progress toward others?
- Kept joy in the picture?

Are your strategies working well?

- Yes? Keep going.
- No? Make some adjustments to your current approach or try something else on your list of potential strategies. Reviewing

the Personal Power Grid in step 7 may be useful to help you be sure you're not giving up too soon. But if, after giving your strategy your best shot, it's still not working, there is grace in letting go. As W.C. Fields once said, "If at first you don't succeed, try, try again. Then quit. No use being a damn fool about it."[5]

Are you enjoying the process?
Are your strategies fueling you or leaving you feeling drained?

- Fueling? Keep going.
- Draining? Is there a more pleasant way to approach the goal?

Do you have SMART (specific, measurable, attainable, realistic, timely) goals? If so, determine the appropriate metrics to evaluate those particular goals. Be specific about measuring your progress. For example, the metrics for your exercise program could be the number of times you made it to the gym each week over the past month. You may have a fitness measure you'd like to track such as the duration and intensity of your workouts over time and your endurance levels. If your exercise is meant to contribute to a weight loss goal, you might want to get on the scale weekly and track that as well.

Toolbox

Gut Check

Your emotions provide you with important information about how well your actions are aligned with your sense of joy and purpose. As you review your progress, how do you *feel* about the way it's going? Respect what your feelings are telling you.

Set Your Check-In Schedule

How often should you track your progress? The appropriate interval is determined by what you are trying to accomplish. Depending on what is on your list, you may want to track your initiatives separately. If one goal is to get in shape by exercising regularly, weekly reviews of your success in getting to the gym might be fitting. If you are working on the cure for cancer, you'll have to give yourself a much longer time frame. While you'll want to track your progress toward that overall goal, you are likely to have broken it down into several initiatives. Perhaps you are a scientist and you set goals of:

- Getting a job at an academic medical center
- Establishing a research laboratory
- Hiring a staff
- Securing funding

You will need to evaluate each of these goals on its own as well as in relation to one another. You'll need the appointment at the medical school before you can establish a laboratory. You may get start-up funding when you land your job, but then you'll have to demonstrate some results in order to get federal grants to continue your research.

Whatever your goals, give careful consideration to the appropriate time frame to measure your success. Choose a window that will give your strategy a sufficient opportunity to prove its worth, but not so much that you lose precious time if it isn't effective. Be sure to do a careful assessment so you don't continue to pursue activities that prevent your forward motion.

Once again, put a recurring appointment on your calendar to review your closet to ensure you are making good progress toward your goals. Many Business of Life graduates tell me that years after taking their class, they're still looking in their closets to stay focused on their priorities. They make adjustments as necessary and enjoy seeing their successes. It simply works.

Enjoy the Ride

You are on your way. If you've completed all eight steps, you are well prepared to move toward the vision that sets you aglow. Stay present and alert to what you're doing so you will continually make conscious choices about how you spend your precious time.

You can repeat any of the assessment and alignment exercises in this book periodically to make sure you stay the course or alter your approach if your evolving circumstances call for a change in direction. You will want to stick with your plans as long as they serve you, but you don't want to be so rigid that you become stuck in a new rut. Be open to new possibilities. You now have a powerful framework for evaluating how well they fit into your plans.

As you saw with Martin's experience, being accountable to someone else is a great way to ensure you make regular progress. Knowing that you will have to tell someone else what you've accomplished greatly increases the odds that you will have something significant to report. At the end of my Business of Life programs, everyone is assigned a buddy and I encourage them to schedule regular dates to check in with one another. I recommend you do the same. Find a friend or colleague who is interested in your undertaking. Schedule regular check-ins, whether by e-mail, phone, or in person, and take a few moments to update your "buddy" on your progress. Beyond giving you an incentive to keep moving, this serves as an opportunity to discuss any challenges you may be facing and brainstorm potential solutions.

One last thing: remember to celebrate your triumphs. Share your success stories. Honor your efforts and inspire someone else. That will add to your joy quotient—which in turn will fuel you to keep on keeping on.

Step Back: Tips and Tools to Get Back on Track and Stay the Course

"No matter how far you have gone on a wrong road, turn back."
—Turkish proverb

Strategic planning is a neat, methodical, and dependable process that, in a perfect world, would give us neat, methodical, and dependable results. Though wondrous, the world is far from perfect and life can be messy. History, habits, and happenstance can conspire to pull our best-laid plans off course. Did you run into difficulty as you set your priorities and made your plans? What's been getting in your way? I have yet to encounter anyone who doesn't have something that causes them to make suboptimal choices from time to time. Often it's something as straightforward as watching too much television or constantly succumbing to digital distractions. For others, more ingrained behaviors pull them off course.

Strategies to Get Back on Track

Becoming aware of what is pulling you off track from making steady progress is a great first step toward recalibrating the way you make decisions going forward. The techniques presented in this section may also be helpful if you found yourself back in step 4 identifying with one or more of the descriptions of people with an inclination toward:

- People pleasing
- Perfectionism
- Inertia
- Ego identification and control issues
- Listening to naysayers
- Succumbing to the yeah-but habit
- Procrastination

Cultivate Conscious Awareness

As obvious as this may sound, it's important to pay attention to the reasons you make decisions that create situations you consider less than optimal. What compels you to cede your power to someone else or just react to whatever comes your way rather than steering your own ship? If you are prone to inertia, staying the course even when it no longer suits you, be alert to any nagging sensations of vague dissatisfaction. It may behoove you to perform regular gut checks to see how you're feeling about your current lot. Use the joy meter to keep tabs.

Remember that you will never get "there." As soon as you bag one peak, you'll be off looking for the next hill to conquer. That is part of the human condition, especially for high achievers. Just remember to enjoy the climb. Be aware of what is enough for *you*. Avoid mindlessly going after more just for the sake of more.

Strive for Acceptance;
Set Reasonable Expectations

Many of us spin our wheels because we think we can or should change the essential nature of things. This is a common pitfall for people who have control issues. They want things the way they want them, even when that's an unreasonable expectation. I'm always bemused by people who buy hunting dogs and then get angry with them for behaving like hunters. Retrievers roll in smelly things when given a chance. That's what they do. It's unreasonable for humans to put this kind of canine in a house and then be upset with them for doing what is part of their essential nature, even though that behavior is not compatible with pristine housekeeping.

Likewise, a young mother was talking to me at work one day about how frustrated she was when her eight-year-old son put holes in the knees of an expensive suit she bought for him the first time he wore it. I asked her what she was thinking when she bought an eight-year-old boy fancy pants knowing full well he was tough on his clothing. She blushed with recognition at her mistake and vowed to buy him clothing one step up from disposable next time they had a formal event to attend. It's much easier to accept that some kids crawl on floors than to curse the holey knees.

You Are the Expert on You

There is no shortage of experts touting their point of view and exhorting you to embrace their wisdom. And you can learn a lot from them. However, no one knows you as well as you know yourself, so you need to be a critical consumer of advice and make decisions that make the most sense for you given your current circumstances.

This point was brought home to me when I had a stubborn hamstring injury that took years to heal. I'd been practicing yoga for years, all the while listening to several instructors touting the virtues of a vegetarian diet. Then my doctor referred me for acupuncture to try to improve the circulation near my injury to speed up healing. On my first visit, the acupuncturist did an assessment and declared that I didn't have enough meat in my diet. Both were giving sound dietary advice backed up with long history and good evidence for their perspective. And it's even possible that both are right—for some people at some time. My goal is to be healthy. How I achieve that health is up to me. Only I can decide what works best for me at any given time. Maybe more meat will be important when I get older and need more iron. I'll put that idea on a shelf in my closet and refer back to it in a few years if I feel the need for a change in my diet.

Humor Can Help

Armed with your mission and vision, you have some great tools to serve as filters that will help you define *your* priorities and what is most important to you. With these in your arsenal (and a sense of humor doesn't hurt either), you can stand firm in the face of others' suggestions and judgments. Not that I hold a grudge or anything, but about eighteen years ago, I met with a new colleague, an older and much more senior executive. He was of the strong opinion that women with young children (I had a two-year-old at the time) should stay at home to take care of them. He told me that his wife was a homemaker and you could "eat off his floors." I replied that you could eat off my floors too—and on a good day, you could find a whole meal. We moved on to the next topic.

It would have been easy to be intimidated by this man who outranked me, was significantly older, and was at least twice my size. However, I knew that my life's mission included a career and I had a clear set of priorities that achieved a balance of career, family, mind/body/spirit, and community activities that worked for me. Having examined my own priorities for myself before this conversation took place allowed me to laugh at the absurdity of what he was suggesting. Had I not known so clearly who I was as a well-rounded person who plays several different roles, I may have been vulnerable to his criticisms and likely to pack for the guilt trip he was trying to send me on. Instead, I bought a busy rug that hid the Cheerios.

Toolbox

Humor

Consider a witty retort when someone gives you unsolicited advice about what he thinks is right for you. With your mission and vision well articulated, *you* are the expert. Find a firm but lighthearted way to hold your ground.

Don't Let Yourself Be Shouldwinked

Who among us hasn't done something out of a sense of obligation, misplaced or not? We often say yes to something when we'd rather say no because we feel we should. This is especially common among pleasers and perfectionists, and it can be a real problem. My friend calls it "shoulding all over yourself." When you put it that way, it sounds especially unappealing.

I've been plenty guilty of this myself. One morning, my then ten-year-old daughter saw me eating my usual luscious breakfast of fat-free cottage cheese and bran nuggets. She asked me why I ate that and I told her that it was good for me. She asked if I liked it and I had to admit, not so much. That simple question was enough to bust me out of my inertia. That was the last day I ate "cottage cheese and crunchies" for breakfast just because I thought I should be eating something healthy. Lo and behold, there are tastier options. It was a great reminder that there's no dishonor in enjoying the journey.

Toolbox

Shed the Shoulds

What are your "cottage cheese and crunchies"—those things you do only because you feel you should? Is that really necessary? What would happen if you didn't do it or looked for a more pleasant way to accomplish the same objective?

Sharon, the vice president of a prestigious financial operation, signed up for my Business of Life course. A highly disciplined professional, she held such a stringent work ethic that she always felt she should eat her metaphorical vegetables before she could have dessert. During the session when people were recording their priorities, she was visibly upset. A couple of weeks later, as we were working on action plans, she broke down in tears. She had set spending more time with her daughter as a priority. Even as she did so, she felt the tug of the notion that always gnawed at her—that she *should* be attending to work matters instead of indulging in play with her child. The memory of a recent exchange with her six-year-old was what had her in tears. Sharon had promised to play a game one evening and asked if she could just make a quick business call before they started. Her daughter said no. Her business calls were never quick. Kids have a way of humbling us with the truth.

She came for a private coaching session to develop some strategies that would allow her to spend some guilt-free time with her child. Appealing to her strong sense of obligation, I asked her whose responsibility it was to nurture her child and model healthy behavior. She blanched at the realization that she was teaching her child to be a one-dimensional workaholic and admitted it was her job to spend quality time with her daughter. I recommended that she make playing with her kid a task that went right on her to-do list, alongside financial analyses and the laundry. If it made her feel any better, I conceded it could be an educational game, as long as she gave her child her undivided attention while they played. She needed to start thinking of time with her child as eating her spinach and not a chocolate éclair. That time was truly nourishing her child and their relationship. Showing Sharon that playing with her daughter was an item that merited a coveted spot on her to-do list worked with her wiring and helped her accept that it was at least as important and urgent as any business matter that threatened to invade her family time.

Step Back Before You React

Before saying yes to something you'd really rather not do, take a moment to assess what's really happening, what you're feeling and why you're feeling it. A good strategy for dealing with an unwelcome request is to say you'll need to think about it and get back to the person asking. Here are some good questions to ask when you see yourself slipping into some fear-driven behaviors:

- Why am I even considering this request/demand/expectation? Alternatively, why am I even considering *not* doing something about which I am passionately interested?
- What am I afraid of?
- Is my fear based on something real? If it is, so what?
- What if I don't do what someone's asking of me (or do what I want that someone else disapproves of)?
- What will it cost me to comply with their wishes?
- What's the worst thing that can happen? How bad is it really? What strategies can I employ to make the worst case not so bad?

Consider the Opportunity Cost

If you choose to do one thing, it likely means not being able to do another. What comes off the list to accommodate what you are contemplating taking on? Is it worthy or is it less important than the new activity? It's popular to advise a people pleaser to "learn to say no." Try flipping that around and discover what you want to say yes to. Then make conscious decisions that are in line with your own priorities.

It can also be helpful to remember that while those conversations in which you are saying no to someone's request can be uncomfortable, the discomfort dissipates shortly afterward. The tools and techniques in this book can help those talks go more smoothly. Remember that the discomfort of being "stuck" with a task that you've taken on reluctantly can cause you much more discomfort in the long run than the brief act of declining.

Toolbox

NO

There may be more power in the word "no" than any other two letters in the alphabet. I often assign my clients the task of saying no to five requests just to flex those muscles and see what happens. Often, people are surprised by how little resistance they actually meet. The filters in this chapter provide you with a vocabulary to explain your choices in a rational, objective, unemotional way that often helps your assertion to be accepted.

Use Compassion as a Tool

It's hard to feel intimidated by someone while you are feeling genuine compassion for her. As you can imagine, in my years as a senior executive in a large organization, I engaged in some pretty tense conversations, often when the stakes were very high. I happen to be petite and soft spoken and I like to think of myself as a kind person. But I couldn't be effective in my position if I were a pushover, so some confrontations were inevitable.

As a student of meditation techniques, I learned about compassion meditation, in which the practitioner focuses on a sincere desire for all suffering to cease. So I reasoned that if someone was acting in an aggressive manner, he must be suffering in some way. When I approached the encounter seeking to find out what was at the root of the negativity and to address it in a productive manner, I found I could confront the issue and the behavior without needing to attack the person in any way. In fact, the would-be confrontations often turned into cathartic conversations that cleared the way for productive problem solving. In some cases, we even emerged from these meetings with a stronger appreciation for one another.

Compassion

When you are facing a conversation where you fear the other person will respond in an angry or aggressive manner, try to be aware that pain of some sort is likely driving his behavior. Seek to address the cause of this discomfort and see if you can find a solution that satisfies the needs of the other person without sacrificing your own. Or, at the very least, to stand your ground without being intimidated.

The Tool Kit in Action

Let's take a look at how you might use a collection of these tools to change the outcome of a situation where you might be inclined to bend to another's wishes at the expense of your own priorities or desires.

Reframing a Bake Sale

I'd like to say no to making my hundredth batch of Rice Krispies Treats for the PTO, but there's Patsy, the cookie queen, looking like she's depending on me again. I always say yes to her, but this time, I *really* don't have time. Taking on the task this time is a threat to the work/life/health balance that's so important to my vision. What do I do? Asking the questions mentioned above can help evaluate and reframe the situation.

Why am I even considering this request? I'm afraid Patsy will be angry. Maybe she'll hate me and tell all the other mothers at the school that I'm a selfish so-and-so and they should have nothing to do with me. That'll hurt my feelings and I'm very sensitive.

Is it really true that she'll be angry? Well, I don't know Patsy that well, but she once looked at me funny. I've been trying to make sure I'm not on her bad side ever since.

Can I be sure? I guess I really don't know if she'll be angry or tell anyone else about my brazen refusal because I don't know her that well and I don't even know who she knows.

How can I find out? I could ask her if she'd be very upset with me if I demurred and explain that I'd love to comply with her wishes, but it would come at a great cost to me.

Okay, say it's true that she'd get mad. So what? I hate the feeling that someone doesn't like me or I've let her down.

What will it cost me to comply (i.e., what is the opportunity cost)? I guess I'd have to weigh whether it is worse to let a near stranger be disappointed or to miss two hours of sleep on a night when I can only get six because I've already agreed to build the sets for my daughter's play, which is scheduled for the very next night.

Bottom line: When I look at it that way, it doesn't make a lot of sense to skip my sleep because I'm scared of Patsy.

Closer—break the news to Patsy: Using compassion and my own, well-justified reasons to refuse, I break it to her gently. I tell Patsy that I fully identify with her need for volunteers and under most circumstances, I'd be delighted to turn out a batch of gooey goodies. Unfortunately, I've already committed to be at the school all evening building sets and won't be able to make it to the grocery store before it closes. But I'd be glad to volunteer for the next time if she can give me a little more notice. To my surprise, Patsy tells me she appreciates that. She was actually surprised by the outpouring of volunteers for this sale and has been worried that no one will step up for the next one scheduled for two weeks from now. I agree to bring a double batch and we're both relieved at the outcome.

If you are a people pleaser, you might benefit from trying your own version of this example, starting with some low-stakes situation. Think of it as a gym where you can try exercising a new "no" muscle. It might also help to do a root cause analysis. Why are you a people pleaser? Try asking yourself "why?" five times and see what comes up. Pleasers need to understand that they have no control over other peoples' opinions. Strive for cheerful indifference. As Terry Cole-

Whitaker says in her book of the same name, what you think of me is none of my business.[6]

Yeah-But—Compared to What?

You've got your dreams and desires, but everywhere you turn, there's an obstacle or problem. Everything looks like a reason you can't get what you want. The yeah-but habit can put you in a continuous inertia loop where eventually you give up altogether and hibernate in the comfortably unsatisfying rut you burrowed into long ago.

If you've made it this far, I hope that means you have crafted a vision that sets you so vibrantly aglow that it is enough to rouse you from your slumber. That picture of what your life could be represents what you are giving up on in order to stay stuck for any number of reasons that may seem quite valid to you. If your buts are getting the better of you, take a page out of Stella's playbook. Her willingness to be alert to different ways of reaching her goals led her to find an unexpected opportunity to open a religious bookstore in her church building. Focus on what you *can* do and do that. Also challenge your buts and see if you can find a way to reframe your situation and make it work for you even in the most unexpected ways. Perhaps, like Stella, you'll find the answer was there all along. Awake to new possibilities.

I'll Get to It Just As Soon As...

Martin looks like anything but a procrastinator. He's the senior vice president in charge of several operational units in a large corporation. He is a vision of perpetual motion, in constant demand and always on the go. He is busy from dawn to dusk. The only problem is, he rarely gets anything on *his* list done. He is a bit of a pleaser and does relish the fact that he's the "go-to" guy for many of his colleagues. He loves being in on the action. But as I coached him through an analysis, the root cause of his problem revealed itself to be his proclivity toward procrastination.

Martin is a live-in-the-moment kind of guy, so he really enjoys responding to urgent matters, no matter how unimportant. He likes the drama and feeling needed. As we looked at what was on his list of priorities and how he spent his days, there was a huge disconnect. He was responsible for a number of large initiatives, several of which he'd not even started. All of his activities fit onto the urgent side of his importance/urgency matrix. The good news was that he wasn't wasting any time on unimportant/nonurgent matters. The bad news was that he wasn't spending any time on nonurgent important matters either. Every time a colleague knocked on his door with an urgent request, he reasoned he could get to his own work "tomorrow." Well, his boss referred him to me for coaching when a year full of tomorrows never came and Martin fell significantly behind on his own workload.

If you share Martin's inability to discipline yourself to dig into a large project and keep saying, I'll get to that just as soon as…any number of excuses will do…you need a strategy to get focused. Martin is so social and in the moment that I suggested he seek out one of his colleagues that he keeps helping and ask her to help him put a plan in place to tackle his own projects. Since he loves to respond to a crisis, I recommended he ask his colleague to set several "burning" deadlines and to put regular progress reports on the agenda of his boss's staff meetings so he'd be accountable for meeting them.

Perfectionists

Martin was not the only one in his office whose habits kept him from producing stellar results. When his boss, Richard, interviewed me as a potential executive coach for Martin, I asked him a few questions of my own, only to discover that Richard was a bit of a perfectionist and was rarely satisfied with any work product on its first pass. Without intending to, he was actually contributing to Martin's procrastination. By setting standards that were practically impossible to satisfy, he unwittingly added to Martin's resistance to starting difficult new projects that he knew were likely to fall short of Richard's expectations.

Throughout the time I coached Martin, I checked in regularly with Richard. During this time, Richard did some self-analysis of his own, which revealed a fear of failure at the root of his perfectionism. Always afraid that he wasn't on top of all the emerging trends in his industry, Richard felt that every quarterly board meeting was an oral exam he could fail at any time. His board included some of the greats in his industry, and he worried he couldn't keep up with them, each with his own team of top-tier analysts. He passed his anxiety on to his staff to the point that he undercut their self-confidence and made them fearful of turning in work that he was likely to reject.

Richard's fears were contagious and, ironically, were perpetuating the conditions he feared the most. So we worked on reframing the situation and finding another approach that would work and *feel* better for him and his staff. I pointed out that he and the board of directors were actually on the same team and wanted the same thing, namely for the company to perform well. Their incentives were well aligned. Richard needed to stop looking at the directors as a board of examiners he needed to dazzle with perfect presentations and start looking at them as the rich resource they were.

I suggested he start reaching out to the directors one at a time to see what he could learn from each of them and how they could help his staff design and research their analyses. This strategy accomplished a few important objectives. First, by spending time getting to know the directors, he was building important relationships. As he got better acquainted with each board member, he started to feel more confident that they wanted to help him succeed rather than catch him falling short of expectations. Second, he learned valuable information about his industry that improved the quality of his work. Finally, and perhaps most importantly, he was able to shift the tenor of the board meetings into more of a collaborative discussion of key issues rather than a show and tell that left the directors bored and feeling underutilized by the company. Within a few short months, he felt much more confident in his standing with the board and, over time, he was able to ease up the pressure on his staff, making the workplace much more pleasant and productive.

If you are a perfectionist, you need to accept that you cannot control every outcome and you will never know everything. Remember the serenity prayer and put your efforts where you can have a positive impact.

I'm reminded of a moment of clarity on my yoga mat when I realized that strength is the ability to hold on, but power is the ability to let go. The best any of us can do is to prepare as thoroughly as possible and then find the courage to jump in with both feet.

Conclusion

How They Got Their Glow

"Little by little, one walks far."

—Peruvian proverb

One of the most popular sessions in my longer workshops is the reunion we hold about six weeks after the course ends. Participants come together to report on their successes and struggles. They celebrate one another's achievements and share strategies to overcome obstacles.

The people whose stories fill these pages came to me for courses or coaching with similar goals: to fill their days with more satisfaction, fulfillment, and joy. They wanted to improve their experience at work and at home. They all went through the same process, defining their purpose and creating visions that set them aglow. They lit up at different points and in their own unique way. They made changes, large, medium, and small. They came to improve how they managed the business of their lives and that they did.

Has everyone who has ever taken my courses made improvements? I really can't say. I do everything possible to set people up for long-term success. Life happens and it is entirely possible that some people go back to business as usual. Hopefully, they pull a technique out of their new tool kit when faced with a decision to make or a dilemma to solve, whenever the time is right. The people who come to see me in the months and years following their workshops or coaching do so because they're excited to tell me how they've used what they learned to do something that was meaningful for them.

As I've mentioned before, the framework presented in this book is tidy and structured, but the world we live in can be chaotic and messy. These tools can't always compensate for tough circumstances, but they can help you do the best you can with the cards you've been dealt. Sometimes, they can help you see how to reshuffle the deck and even find some new cards to play. As one example, in this economy, many people feel happy to have any job (if they even have one), let alone one they find gratifying. They have bills to pay and can't afford to take time off to contemplate a more satisfying career. So the workshop provided them with tools and ideas to make their current job more enjoyable. Beyond that, they were able to find ways to incorporate their passions and talents in other aspects of their lives, like Regina, who found so much joy singing in her church choir.

This program can help you find the resilience you need and a new, more productive approach when you have tried something that didn't work out the way you'd hoped. As the Chinese proverb says, if you get up one more time than you fall, you will make it through. You can always go back to the list of potential strategies you developed in step 7 if the first one you tried didn't produce the results you expected.

Consider this your reunion. People take from the experience what they need, when they need it. Some come hoping to make minor adjustments to a life that's already going pretty well. Others are looking for a complete change in direction because they're unhappy with the status quo or their circumstances shift. In a moment, we will take a look at how the people whose stories you've been reading have fared thus far. But your story doesn't end here.

You have just learned a framework and tools that you can use at any time to achieve whatever it is you want or need to do. At this point, are you wondering if you've done enough? Done it right? Pshaw. Right, shmite. Let me remind you that YOU are the expert on you. Only you can answer those questions for yourself. This is not a course that comes with a final exam and a grade on a report card. The program presented in this book is meant to serve you. It is *not* meant to be one more set of expectations for you to fulfill. No "shoulds" here.

This book can serve as a resource for years to come. I hope you have found it useful to think about things in a new way and learned some tricks that help you be more productive and effective—in whatever way benefits you. Only you can be the judge of that.

Tweaks and Transformations

The people in this book have selected the techniques that work for them and have assembled their own custom toolkits to serve their specific needs. I am always delighted to hear some of the interesting ways they have applied the tools to fix their own unique circumstances.

Using Their Tools to Build a Better Situation

One last time, allow me to emphasize just how important it is to write down the elements of this program that mean the most to you somewhere it will be easy for you to access at any time. Your custom closet can serve that purpose, or you are most welcome to use whatever application or technique works for you. Just be sure to find one that does. Then, so you won't forget, schedule time to review it at regular intervals. Telling someone about your plans and committing to keeping them updated on your progress is another excellent way to stay on track. Also, the more you make a practice of using the tools presented here, the more likely they will just become a part of the way you think.

Setting Priorities and Staying on Point

Brandon is the busy executive who used his vision statement to decide if he should accept the invitation to serve on a prestigious corporate board. His picture of success had him available to attend his children's soccer games and special events, so it was clear that joining that board at that particular time was in conflict with his immediate priorities. He found the clarity his vision provided so powerful that he continues to use his tools and filters to maintain awareness and make good decisions. He reasoned that he will likely have another opportunity to serve on a corporate board, but his son would never be eleven again.

He has used the importance/urgency matrix to prioritize projects at work and at home. He has shared his tool kit with his family and colleagues and encourages them to give careful thought to the choices they make. Brandon is a fan of the "big rock" concept presented in step 7 and uses that thinking each morning to determine what he wants to achieve. Then he sticks to the plan as much as circumstances allow.

He had been particularly concerned that his colleagues would look at him askance if he left work during the day to go to an event at his kids' school, so he worked out an ironclad plan to make sure he consistently delivered high-quality work on time and on budget. That plan worked well. He is thriving at work and is home when needed. But something unexpected happened. Far from being looked down upon for making family a priority, he has become a leader in his company and a champion of work–life balance. His colleagues look to him as a role model. Something he feared has actually boosted his career and improved retention and morale in his company. In turn, his personal goals are much easier to achieve.

Keeping Joy on the Agenda

As you saw, the visioning and goal-setting steps provided a powerful framework for Sandra. Her vision statement helped focus her prodigious energy on those initiatives that mattered most to her. Setting priorities helped her see that launching her nonprofit organization, Fertility Within Reach, was an urgent desire. So much so that she launched it in one year, not the five years she had initially envisioned.

Sandra also became more disciplined about managing the projects she and her team took on at work. She developed a full-blown project plan for each initiative, figuring that if it was worth doing, it was worth doing right. The structured approach helped her hold her staff accountable, which was especially important because they were scattered across a few different locations.

Sandra told me that her Business of Life tools helped her do something else that completely transformed her personal life. She now runs every decision through a "joy-to-hassle ratio" analysis. Before agreeing to a request from her family, community, whomever, she asks herself, "Am I going to get any joy out of this?" If the answer is no, she feels no guilt from declining. She wouldn't do anything that wouldn't benefit her business, so why would she do that in her personal life? Her vision statement and a few simple questions help her keep joy on the agenda.

Small Shifts Can Yield Big Dividends

Richard also found that, paradoxically, easing up a bit can make a huge difference in the workplace. He is the corporate executive whose impossibly high standards were inhibiting his staff, who were reluctant to turn in assignments because he was so likely to find fault with them. Richard did a "five whys" analysis to get to the root of his paranoia-driven perfectionism.

Why do I demand perfection from my staff and myself?

I am afraid our analyses fall short of board members' high expectations.

Why (do I fear our analyses will fall short of expectations)?

The board members are industry leaders with access to the most cutting-edge intelligence and economic forecasts and they will expect the same of us.

Why (would they expect that of us)?

I'm not sure, but I assume they would expect me to know what they know.

Why (do I assume they would expect me to know what they know)?

I am afraid to ask them what they expect.

Why (am I afraid to ask them)?

I might look weak since they probably expect me to know what they expect.

When we reviewed his answers, Richard appreciated the irony of his own lack of thoroughness in preparing himself to produce a stellar product. He wasn't holding himself to the same high standard to which he was holding his staff. All out of fear of looking "bad" to his board. He created a great deal of angst for himself and everyone else by managing according to what he imagined might be expected of him. Leadership 101 calls for setting explicit expectations and managing to objective, measurable outcomes. Richard wasn't even managing himself well, since he failed to establish expectations with his board.

I also pointed out to him that his board members were there to be a resource for him and his company, not to trip him up at meetings. Richard needed to create relationships with the directors so he could make the most of this valuable resource and establish an agreement on the best approach to their collective work. Not only had his paranoia stifled his staff's creativity, it deprived the board members of the satisfaction of fully contributing their expertise to benefit the company.

We agreed that Richard would invite one locally based director to lunch each week or set up a phone call if the director was located at a distance. Most board members were pleased to be engaged in this way and were eager to share their advice. Once Richard realized that he had allies and even mentors on the board, he was able to relax in the knowledge that they wanted to see him succeed, not fail.

This simple shift in the way he looked at his board was a game changer. With the knowledge that he could ask for help and advice, he was able to ease up on his staff, letting them be more creative and take some risks. Their performance and morale increased immeasurably. As an added benefit, Richard's intake of ulcer medication went down proportionately. Probably more than anyone, his wife was delighted that he managed to be home for dinner and was in a good mood much more frequently.

Freedom from Fear

Brenda, the would-be manager whose middle school teacher told her she had no ability with numbers, faced down her phobia and enrolled in a college math course en route to pursuing the management career to which she aspired. During the semester, she worked hard, took advantage of every bit of extra help she could get, and joined a study group. During this time, we also looked for ways she could bring more elements of management into her current job. She asked for a project to lead so she could build up her track record and beef up her résumé. Her manager was pleased to see her take the initiative and gratefully put her in charge of overseeing their department's renovations and the process of moving all the faculty and staff to their new space.

The day Brenda showed up in my office to show me her final grade—an A—she was positively beaming. She had shed the shackles that had held her back for years and truly believed there was nothing she couldn't do. After acing the one thing she was sure was beyond her abilities, her confidence soared and she enrolled in a degree program. She loved college life and immersed herself fully in that experience. Rather than exhausting her, school *gave* her energy and she sailed through her program, working day and night to complete it. Tragically, just a few months shy of graduating, she was diagnosed with an aggressive form of cancer. With every ounce of strength and determination she possessed, she earned her bachelor's degree before succumbing to her disease.

At her memorial service, I was filled with grief and gratitude. Brenda faced her fate with grace. She had finally discovered what she was capable of achieving. What's more, she was able to teach her nieces to question anyone who told them there was something they couldn't do. As Brenda learned more about management at school, she had several opportunities to put that knowledge to use at work. Her efforts were appreciated and she found that enormously satisfying right up until the time she was too ill to work any longer. Brenda unchained her melody. She did not die with her song still inside her. And that was enough for her.

Total Reboots

The pain of not pursuing their dreams or making a difference was enough to compel several people to seek wholesale change. They wanted to use their considerable talents more fully and to make their days matter. Despite their professional accomplishments, they were unfulfilled and curious why that was. So I showed them that to achieve *soul-satisfying* success, they needed a plan.

Passion Pushes Past Inertia

Danielle found the courage to leave her lucrative yet soul-sucking career in fashion to pursue her passions when she was laid off from her job. She was able to resist taking another position in the same industry once she realized that her work hadn't incorporated any of the things she truly enjoyed. While she was very nervous about making a living, she finally had the time and mental space to contemplate her options. She started by injecting the free days that stretched before her with some pleasure. Having set goals to take a cooking class and to start preparing home-cooked meals, she got right to it. When she stepped into the cooking school's kitchen, she had that wonderful feeling that she was finally home.

As soon as that course ended, she immediately searched for her next gastronomic adventure and enrolled in a class to learn how to make artisanal chocolates. From the moment she plunged her hands into the warm liquid confection, she knew she was literally dipping into her dreams. This was *it*. Danielle had stumbled on a way to combine her artistic skills, business acumen, and love of all things culinary. She took the entrepreneurial plunge. She has never looked back. Her website states the principles that fueled the goals she set for her enterprise: "Our passion for recapturing small production, sane business practices, and quality of life and product defines us."

Her story doesn't end there. With what she considers a kind of cosmic confirmation that all is right with her world, she received an e-mail from a woman who had lost her job and wanted to strike out on her own. Danielle recounted the tale:

> I called her and we chatted for a while. She was in New York and her dad had forwarded an article written about me from

South Shore Magazine. Two weeks later I received an e-mail from my college roommate thanking me for being so kind to her best friend. Her friend told her she had spoken with a woman in Massachusetts who had started a chocolate business. She knew it had to be me. It was a crazy small world moment that I just loved. It makes me feel that I am doing exactly what I should be doing and we are connected to certain people for a reason.

Danielle is having the time of her life and business couldn't be better. In fact, I recently logged on to her website to find a picture of a chocolate man wearing a Santa Claus hat and waving a white flag. It said, "We surrender! We can't make it fast enough…(to guarantee delivery on new orders) before Christmas." This statement is evidence of her adhering to the principles that define her business.

She has also hung onto her razor-sharp wit as she relayed her adventures with a photo shoot for yet another magazine feature: "They sent Manolo Blahniks but my bunioned feet would not fit in them so I had to wear my real chocolate shoes, which are cork-soled clogs. Hmmm…could I dip in Manolos? Anyway, it was fabulous to be fawned over by hair and makeup stylists for the day. I felt like a princess. A princess in clogs."

Danielle's renaissance began when she took her first cooking class. If you are looking for a change, consider following your heart and doing something you love—just because you love doing it. You're practically guaranteed to have a good time and you just never know where it might lead you.

Time to Please Me

Like Danielle, spending time considering his passions convinced our people-pleasing lawyer, Jim, to re-chart his course and get off the path he'd embarked on to please his parents. While a law career wasn't what he'd envisioned for himself, he thought that he would be able to find a niche in that field where he could fulfill his desire to connect with his clients and have a meaningful impact on their lives. But the reality of legal practice did not fit his idealistic notions of how he could make a difference while making a living.

When Jim looked at what he liked about his legal work, he realized that it was counseling his clients, mastering an extensive body of information, and writing complex legal briefs that brought him pleasure. But he found that working in a corporate environment and focusing so much attention on billable hours left him feeling spiritually bankrupt. He didn't mind the tasks he had to perform, but he felt like a fish out of water in that setting.

Jim found a new direction when he focused on his mission. He had no trouble identifying where his talents and passions intersected with the needs of individuals and the world.[1] He loved counseling people, reading and writing on spiritual topics, and working with nonprofit organizations. Somewhere deep inside him, he knew what he felt called to do. He wanted to be a rabbi, trading in torts for Torah. And he's in good company. Jim called to tell me that he knew of at least six other attorneys who were pursuing the rabbinate at his seminary. Each day he's in school, he feels sure he is in the right place. And while he's finally following his own heart, his parents couldn't be more pleased. Who knew?

Who AM I Anyway?

Truth be told, I take the time in my courses to teach about guiding principles mostly as an affirmation of peoples' good intentions. This exercise is usually just a quick listing of the core values that fuel our behavior. It doesn't usually prompt major changes. It just makes everyone conscious of what drives them so they feel good about their motivations before they move on to the next step. That is, until I met Miranda.

Miranda, the corporate CEO we first encountered in the mission step, was in her late fifties when her beloved, elderly Chihuahua, Carmen, died. As time went on, Miranda's grief deepened and she felt seriously depressed. She wasn't in the habit of allowing herself time to notice, let alone indulge, her feelings. Now, however, she was so overwhelmed with sorrow that she did the unthinkable: she cancelled her attendance at a board meeting and spent a few unscheduled days at home for the first time in recent memory.

On a long, solitary walk on the beach, she made a major discovery about herself: she was an addict. While some people turn to alcohol or cocaine, Miranda's drug of choice was activity. Now, with three days on her hands with little to do but think, she couldn't avoid her emotions. She realized that Carmen's death was so devastating because not only did she lose her constant companion, she lost the only friend who ever loved her unconditionally. She felt angry, alone in the company of others, and afraid she would die a bitter, bejeweled old woman. The vision of where she was headed frightened her so intensely she did something else she would have found unthinkable a few short weeks earlier. She asked for help.

Miranda knew that a colleague on one of her boards was coming to me for coaching and she decided to give it a try herself. She was still quite upset when she arrived for her first session. We decided to start by examining the source of her distress so her plans could address the root cause rather than the symptoms. Once she started paying attention, her insights flowed freely.

Her parents were very traditional and very well off. Her father was a prominent businessman and her mother was very active in civic affairs as a volunteer. They lavished Miranda with gifts and her brother with attention. When she was a young girl, her parents expected Miranda to have impeccable manners and to marry well some day. They invested most of their parenting energy on her brother, whom they groomed to take over his father's company—something Miranda would have liked very much for herself. She rebelled by getting an education and working her way up the corporate ladder. She was determined to show her parents what a girl could do and hoped to gain their admiration in the process. Her behavior didn't meet their expectations of what was becoming for their precious jewel, and they were rarely impressed by her accomplishments. She was promoted, won awards, and commanded a huge salary, and still her parents never offered their approval. Frustrated, she became a shrill, demanding taskmaster prone to legendary outbursts of temper.

Before we got going in earnest on developing her personal strategic plan, Miranda required more data. An exacting executive, she wanted a full dossier before she was ready to tackle the project of her life. So, we performed a 360-degree evaluation in which I confidentially interviewed those all around her at work and in the community. The results were sobering. She wasn't surprised that many of the professionals I interviewed thought she was tough and highly competitive. However, she was truly pained to find out the administrative staff secretly referred to her as "Cruella Deville" because she would "bite their heads off" if she didn't like the way they carried out an assignment. Miranda was quite fond of these young women and had no idea that they felt that way about her.

This revelation haunted her as she began the planning process. Her "ahas" started right from the beginning as we reviewed her life's purpose. She'd never given much thought to her mission other than showing her parents how wrong they were about what a girl could do. She'd long ago proven that she could succeed in the male-dominated business world, but that never filled the void. Yet she kept on going after promotions and honors—all sorts of outward validation of her worth. Like an addict, she was seeking to fill a hole in her soul with awards and accolades. It didn't work. She needed to make a difference.

Her experiences, coupled with the pain of learning that her young colleagues disliked her so intensely, led her to believe her life's mission had something to do with creating opportunities for other women to develop their full potential and thrive in the workplace. Working on her vision statement and looking at her strengths helped her flesh out how she might approach that mission.

For Miranda, who did whatever it took to whomever was in her path on the way to the corner office, stopping to contemplate the principles that would guide her actions going forward was a transformational exercise. She committed to fostering empowerment, excellence, opportunity, honesty, integrity, and generosity in herself and others. Her newly espoused values clearly lit the path she would follow to the end of her career.

With this important groundwork completed, setting priorities was fairly simple for such a consummate businesswoman, as was developing strategies to achieve her new goals. She knew how to mobilize resources to get results. She created a plan and started a program to help disadvantaged young women prepare to enter the workplace. She held them to exacting standards, but most were able to rise to her high expectations. Miranda worked directly with several of the girls and found that watching them gain confidence, skills, and, ultimately, jobs was extremely satisfying. While I can't say Miranda turned into a marshmallow, her edges have softened a great deal. Her face looks more serene and far less pinched. And she's held on to a secretary for several years, after having gone through more assistants than Murphy Brown.

Now Miranda finds much more satisfaction giving out scholarships and awards than she ever experienced in receiving them. She finds fulfillment in giving what she never received from her own parents—the gift of listening to what these girls really want and helping them to achieve their dreams. In turn, with each young woman she helps, she is healing her own wounds.

Miranda called me recently to tell me she had just received the most meaningful award of her career. A few of the young women she had helped along the way chipped in to buy her a pewter bowl to thank her for seeing their potential and insisting they stick with the rigorous program until they graduated and secured employment. She was particularly touched that a young woman whom she helped to land her first job presented the gift. Miranda had a first of her own that day: she shed her very first tears of joy.

Built a Better Balance

Countless people come for classes or coaching when they feel like their lives are out of balance. For many, that means spending so much time on work that there is little time left over for other priorities. The administrative and time management skills they learn help them become more efficient. But often it is the act of committing those other priorities to paper and making a plan to address them that allows the real shifts to take place. There is something about the visual experience of seeing your priorities mapped out that snaps that vague sense of imbalance into sharp relief. Once you can see where your issues lie, you can make choices that serve you better.

He Finally Fit in Some Fun

Paul is the finance manager who took my Business of Life course after relocating for his new position. In class, he had a very serious demeanor, dour almost, and made a point of emphasizing that he was taking the course to sharpen his planning skills so he could dazzle his new boss. He never participated in discussions about the "softer" issues that engaged his classmates. So he surprised us all when it came time to talk about goal setting. He realized when he looked at his custom life closet that he had put all of his eggs in the career basket and had not made a priority of his relationships, health, or place in the community. This hit him especially hard as he thought about what it meant to live in a new city where he didn't know anyone. Frankly, he found it rather depressing.

He immediately set some goals to get more exercise and to meet new people. And he wanted to have some fun. Paul had always liked volleyball, so when his local adult education center organized a team, he joined. After their first game, a rousing victory, he invited his teammates out for a celebratory drink. In the weeks that followed, the team often went out after games and he made a few new friends whom he met for meals and movies. Paul's newly balanced life paid dividends for him on the job as well.

With a life outside of work, Paul had something to talk about with his colleagues besides budgets and balance sheets. His colleagues found him more likable. Once he loosened up, his colleagues started to include him in their social activities. They were also more willing to collaborate with him on projects. The quality of his work life *and* work products improved when he focused on leading a more balanced existence.

Metabolic Multitasking

Mark is the attorney who sought out coaching once he made partner in his law firm. Years of a singular focus on getting promoted had taken its toll on his health and social life. He was ready to get back into shape and back in the game. He used all of the prioritization matrices to establish an exercise program that would also serve his goal to be more social. He had settled on jogging a few days a week with friends as part of his routine. When his sister invited him to participate in a ten-kilometer race to raise money for kids with autism, he readily agreed. It served a cause that mattered to him and was a catalyst to get him off the couch and on the road.

Using his natural ability to organize groups, he put together an e-mail distribution list and invited several friends to meet him at the appointed time and place for his planned runs. He encouraged everyone to invite their friends and post their plans as well. Before long, there were more than thirty people on the e-mail list and a dozen or more showed up for most of the morning runs. Several signed up to participate in the autism race as well. At our last meeting, Mark told me he had just met an intriguing woman on one of his morning runs. With a twinkle in his eye he said, "I'm thinking of running a few extra days a week. You know, to get in shape faster."

Starting with Their Strengths

When they first set out to start Our Space, Inc. to provide art therapy programs for children affected by cancer, Peggy and Gail were overwhelmed by the myriad steps required to launch their new organization. They started small, with tasks that appealed to their artistic sensibilities and drew on their strengths. But they well knew they lacked the business skills and other things they needed to make Our

Space a reality. Their SWOT analysis (strengths, weaknesses, opportunities, and threats) defined the gulf that stood between them and fulfilling their vision.

Just when they needed it most, Lee Ann appeared, ready to bridge the gap. She was the talented program manager who told me of her desire to use her artistic and planning skills to help people with cancer. As you saw in the SWOT step, her skills and Peggy and Gail's vision were the missing pieces in each other's puzzles. I was delighted to make an introduction and witness the impressive results of this collaboration. Lee Ann guided Gail and Peggy through the process of creating a business plan, setting up an advisory board, and incorporating Our Space. She provided the structure that was essential to harnessing their creative energy and channeling it into practical action that produced tangible results. In turn, Lee Ann found a worthy outlet for her organizational gifts. Clearly, her talents and passions collided with a real need in the world.

All the while, Gail and Peggy continue to draw on their strengths to grow the program and work toward building a permanent space. With Lee Ann's help, they've hosted several successful fundraisers showcasing Gail's comedic talents and artwork they and their many friends created. They offer their art therapy programs in numerous hospitals and other settings while they continue to march toward their vision of opening a dedicated space. Connecting with patients and supporting their families in these challenging moments brings them great satisfaction, infusing their path with joy and inspiration.

Do you think they were just lucky to find each other? As the saying goes, luck is what happens when preparation meets opportunity. Peggy and Gail were so passionately committed to finding meaning in their own struggles with cancer that they kept looking for ways to make it happen, even when their dream seemed impossibly beyond their reach. They told everyone they knew about their vision. Their friends connected them with others who could help bring it to life. And, as we've seen in other examples, a compelling vision makes others want to be a part of it.

As for Lee Ann, corralling these artistic types could be a challenge at times, but it was enormously exciting to guide them and see their vision take shape. Helping kids with their art projects in those early days gave beautiful expression to her desire to work with cancer patients. Not long after Our Space hit its stride, Lee Ann landed a great job in risk management, the field she missed after leaving her previous position to care for her aunt. Her employer allows enough flexibility for volunteer work. Now she's happily engaging her heart *and* head, using her gifts to make a difference.

Steadying the Boat in Stormy Seas

Thelma is the hospital department head whose goal was to stop yelling at her family. Her Business of Life classmates wouldn't let her get away with her proposed strategy: trying to pretend she wasn't angry when her husband and son left their dirty socks on the floor. She was grateful to her colleagues for pushing her to be honest with herself and confront what was really causing her such distress. And to value herself enough to put herself on her list of priorities. She shared her powerful story when I interviewed her some three years after her course ended:

> Your class couldn't have come at a better time in my life. It was about a year before my world fell apart, and if I hadn't learned those skills and had time to practice them and make them my own, I don't know how I would have managed. Really.

Thelma recalled her class project and how touched she was when her classmates challenged her with so much compassion. Her closet and calendar exercises showed her how she'd left herself out of every equation, putting everyone and everything ahead of her own needs. She was exhausted. Her goal for that group exercise was to stop yelling at her family. Her strategy was to just forget how angry it made her when her son and husband took off their socks in the living room and just left them on the floor. For such a strategic thinker, that wasn't much of a strategy, so I instructed her do a root cause analysis on why this situation upset her so much.

This exercise showed Thelma that the socks bothered her so much because they were a symptom of a much larger issue.

With her new knowledge, the class encouraged Thelma to talk to her son, who was thirteen at the time, and she put up a chart that rewarded him for every day the living room was free of his socks. He lost a point for every day the socks (or hats or whatever) were there. It took him close to a year, but he earned enough points to get the game system he wanted.

But Thelma discovered her challenges went much deeper as she recounted in her interview. "My husband was another story. It turns out he was having an affair and my son found out about it. My husband insisted he keep it to himself. My son (who knew the socks were the least of his worries) became seriously depressed because he felt powerless to do anything about it. To make a long story short, he ended up in the hospital to get treated for his anger and depression. It was there he found the courage to tell me about my husband's affair...I threw my husband out that very day."

Thelma took responsibility for her part in this family drama and set out immediately to chart a more productive course for herself and her children. She recalled that she could have fallen apart, but found that the Business of Life tools showed her there was another way out of this situation. She knew her kids needed her to be strong and steady. Work was her safe place where she was in charge, respected, and successful. She needed for that to remain the case so she revised her personal strategic plan. When Thelma got to the SWOT, she realized that she'd contributed to her son's depression by not being stronger about holding him to higher standards of respectful behavior. She felt that contributed to his poor self-esteem. She realized, thanks to her classmates, the sock chart was the first time she'd really held him accountable for his behavior. "He needed me to do more of that. I knew I couldn't do that without building my own sense of self-worth."

Thelma re-read her class notes and what I'd said about being present. That led her to a yoga class that is all about cultivating awareness. She reported that she learned how to be present, aware, and able to cope with life as a single mother and so many transitions. And she learned to put taking care of her own wellbeing on the to do list.

Maybe most of all, the planning tools you taught me helped me to be viewed as a strong leader in the hospital. I know I have the respect and support of the doctors I work with and that's crucial to my sense of self-worth. Work was the one constant positive thing during the year from hell. The strategic planning structure made it easy to evaluate even the most complicated project and to break it down into doable steps.

Now, everything feels doable.

Slow, Steady Success

Stella, who broke her "yeah-but" habit when she established the religious bookstore and cafe she'd always dreamed of, provided an update a few years after taking her class. She came to her workshop assuming her goal was beyond her reach because she couldn't afford to quit her day job and lose her benefits. So how would she ever realize this ambition? Stella learned to question her limiting beliefs and look beyond the "buts" to find what's possible. As soon as she opened herself up to seeing novel opportunities to fulfill her aspiration, she found a way to do it. "Your course was a catalyst for me…Thank you. The bookstore and cafe is my joy. Although open on weekends only, I expanded to a larger space and increased my product line."

She is working on a new website where she plans to sell T-shirt designs that her graphic designer son is creating exclusively for her shop. He is helping her with marketing to boost sales. Stella considers her bookstore a work in progress that is "moving in the right direction (ever so slowly). In the meantime the café is holding its own … The fellowship is amazing."

And They Lived ... Ever After

The people featured in the sections that follow make a regular practice of reviewing their closets to ensure they stay on track. It reminds them to continue with their productive strategies or take on new priorities as they achieve goals or their circumstances shift.

Gratefully Ever After

You met Regina in the goal-setting step. She's the IT project manager who had fallen into some unhealthy habits, such as dining on fast food, after having her first child. Despite having a satisfying job and a family she adored, Regina was exhausted and prone to bouts of depression. Among others, her goals included starting an exercise regimen and setting a good example for her young daughter.

Regina has ditched the fast-food drive-through in favor of stopping at the salad bar on nights she doesn't have time to cook. She set modest fitness goals and, as a result, has had no difficulty meeting them. In fact, she looks forward to her evening walks with her daughter, who is now four years old. Steadily, her weight has dropped and her moods have lifted.

With more energy and more confidence in her ability to manage, she had a second daughter (whom she straps into her baby carrier for those walks) and is taking a graduate-level course one day a week. Regina continues to sing in her church choir and loves everything about it—the music, friendships, and spending time in the building that always makes her feel divinely inspired. Despite the ups and downs that go with being a working mother, Regina has always been appreciative of her many gifts. Now she has added a practice of a gratitude meditation during her morning commute on the train so she never loses sight of her great fortune.

Consciously Ever After

Angie is the bank vice president who left her prestigious job to raise her children and, ironically, busied herself with volunteer work to the point where she didn't have the time she wanted to be able to spend with her children. Her identity was so caught up with being respected for her business know-how that she had a hard time embracing her role as full-time mother. However, that's just what she longed to be—for now.

The key for Angie was becoming conscious of what was driving her decisions. For some time, she'd convinced herself she was taking on so many volunteer assignments because she was the only one who could do them well enough. She was, after all, a bank vice president. Once she did her time and emotion study, she could see she was spending more of her time nurturing her ego than her children. Her goals and the way she invested her time were not in harmony. She very much wanted to help her kids with their homework and to see them excel academically. In addition, she wanted to be the one to drive them to their extracurricular activities. Family dinners were also a priority for her.

Once she confronted the reality of what she was doing, it was simple for her to realign her calendar with her priorities. She wanted to remain active in her community, but she became far more selective about the work she accepted. She still checks her custom closet now and then and limits herself to no more than one meeting per day with rare exception. Hoping to return to work when her kids are older, Angie gives priority to serving on boards that will help keep her professional network active. Until then, she is present and fully committed to her current position: mom.

Joyfully Ever After

As you saw in the vision step, Bruce's career was going well and he adored his wife and two little girls. Still, he felt a vague dissatisfaction when he came to his Business of Life course to sharpen his business skills and get to the bottom of his discontent. When he struggled to write his vision statement, he made some important discoveries. He knew that he and his wife, Mara, wanted to have a third child, though they didn't know how that could fit into their already crowded schedules. As he envisioned his ideal life, it was full of the love, laughter, and silliness he and Mara had enjoyed as a young couple. But as their days filled with more and more responsibility at work and logistics at home, their focus had shifted away from simply having fun with each other. Bruce worried that his circumstances made his vision infeasible to realize, so he was reluctant to write it down. I instructed him not to worry about *how* he would fulfill his vision or to limit his ambitions at that point. Cultivating some awareness was key to his ability to make some adjustments.

First, Bruce noted that he had yet to cut back on the extra "face time" he had started putting in years ago to establish his career, even though his star had already risen. Second, just writing his vision statement clarified for him the source of his other main issue. He and Mara had settled into a routine that did not make time for them to connect romantically and just enjoy each other. He didn't even need the five whys to tell him that they didn't giggle nearly as often as they used to.

With that kind of clarity, the fixes weren't hard to identify. His time and emotion exercise gave him the opportunity to reshuffle his work schedule now that he no longer needed to attend all the committee meetings that had helped establish his leadership position. He would reinvest that newly liberated time toward his family goals. Mara was overjoyed when Bruce proposed hiring a babysitter so they could go out every Saturday night with the simple goal of having fun and remembering to love each other.

One of the sweetest moments of my career came when Bruce dropped by for a surprise visit about a year after his course ended. He stuck his head in the door, a goofy grin stretching from one ear to the other. Then he stepped all the way in and revealed the bundle in his arms. With as much pride and joy as can fit on a single face, Bruce said, "Meet Zoe." Then we both laughed until we cried.

Epilogue

Be on Your Merry Way

Like all these people, you can use your closet and tools for years to come. You can use these strategic planning steps to structure any undertaking and optimize its chances for success. With regular practice, this just becomes part of how you think. There is no need to leave your dreams to chance. If you haven't already, this is a good time to put monthly reminders on your calendar to keep your priorities up to date and track your progress.

Life is a wild, wondrous adventure and you never know what awaits you around the next bend. Stick to your plans as long as they continue to guide you toward the results you desire, but don't get so attached to them that they constrain you. Stay alert to changes around you and adapt as needed. Be open to new possibilities.

My mission is to help you to use your gifts and make your dreams come true. You have defined your destination, selected a route, and figured out what you need to fill your days with pleasure. You are well prepared for your journey, ready to step onto your path with confidence. Have a great trip and keep in touch. It will be my true joy to hear about your triumphs. You are about to change your own little corner of the world.

Endnotes

Introduction

1. *U.S. News and World Report,* 2012–2013, accessed December 14, 2012, http://health.usnews.com/best-hospitals/area/ma/massachusetts-general-hospital-6140430

2. Lester R. Bittel, *The Nine Master Keys of Management* (New York: McGraw-Hill, 1972), 123.

3. Henry David Thoreau, *Walden* (New York: Thomas Y. Crowell and Company, 1910), 118.

4. Abigail Klein Leichman, "Supportive Bosses Help Reduce Employee Sick Days," Israel 21C, March 18, 2012, accessed December 14, 2012, http://israel21c.org/health/research/supportive-bosses-help-reduce-employee-sick-days/.

5. *Merriam-Webster Dictionary,* accessed February 9, 2013, http://www.merriam-webster.com/dictionary/organize.

Step 1

1. Benjamin Franklin, *Benjamin Franklin, Wit and Wisdom* (White Plains, NY: Peter Pauper Press, 1998), 19.

2. Matthew Kelly, *Perfectly Yourself—9 Lessons for Enduring Happiness* (New York: Ballantine, 2006), 180.

3. Abraham. H. Maslow, *Motivation and Personality, Second Edition* (New York: Harper and Row, 1970), 46.

4. Dick Richards, *Is Your Genius at Work? Four Key Questions to Ask Before Your Next Career Move* (Mountain View, CA: Davies-Black Publishing, 2005), 122.

Step 2

1. Lewis Carroll, *The Annotated Alice: The Definitive Version* (New York: W.W. Norton and Company, 2000), 66.

2. Mike Robbins, *Be Yourself, Everyone Else Is Already Taken* (San Francisco: Jossey Bass, 2009).

3. Image can be found at http://web.mit.edu/persci/gaz/gaz-teaching/flash/koffka-movie.swf. Reproduced with permission from Edward H. Adelson.

Step 3

1. Michael P. Wright, *The Coaches' Chalkboard* (Lincoln, NE: Writers Club Press, 2003), 39.

Step 4

1. Laurence Chang, *Wisdom of the Soul: Five Millennia of Prescriptions for Spiritual Healing* (Washington, DC: Gnosophia Publishers, 2006), 565.

2. Jimmy Dean, *Thirty Years of Sausage, Fifty Years of Ham: Jimmy Dean's Own Story* (New York: Penguin Books, 2004), 7.

Step 5

1. Jim Collins, *Good to Great* (New York, HarperCollins, 2001).

2. Gail Matthews, Goals Research Summary, http://www.dominican.edu/academics/ahss/undergraduate-programs-1/psych/faculty/fulltime/gailmatthews/researchsummary2.pdf, accessed November 4, 2012.

3. Heidi Grant Halvorson, Ph.D., *Succeed* (New York: Hudson Street Press, 2010).

Step 6

1. Annie Dillard, *The Writing Life* (New York: Harper and Row, 1989), 32.

2. James O'Toole, *Creating the Good Life: Applying Aristotle's Wisdom to Find Meaning and Happiness* (Emmaus, PA: Rodale, 2005), 194.

3. Mark Twain, *The Wit and Wisdom of Mark Twain: A Book of Quotations* (Mineola, NY: Dover Publications, 1999), 47.

4. "E-mails 'Hurt IQ More Than Pot'," CNN.com, accessed November 15, 2012, http://www.cnn.com/2005/WORLD/europe/04/22/text.iq/.

5. Mahatma Gandhi, *Inspiring Thoughts* (Delhi: Rajpal & Sons, 2009), 65.

6. David Allen, *Getting Things Done* (New York: Penguin Group, 2003).

Step 7

1. Dennis T. Jaffe and Cynthia D. Scott, *Take This Job and Love It* (New York: Simon and Schuster, 1988), 161. Reproduced with permission.

Step 8

1. Lao-Tzu, *Tao Te Ching: The New Translation from Tao Te Ching: The Definitive Edition,* translated by Jonathan Star (New York: Penguin Group, 2001), 83.

2. Robert Maurer, Ph.D., *One Small Step Can Change Your Life the Kaizen Way* (New York: Workman Publishing Company, 2004).

3. "Mind Trip: Journey into the Brain," from the film, *Wired to Win: Surviving the Tour de France,* accessed on December 6, 2012, http://www.wiredtowinthe movie.com/mindtrip_xml.html.

4. Tom Peters, *Thriving on Chaos: Handbook for a Management Revolution* (New York: Excel/A California Limited Partnership, 1987), 97.

5. Anthony St. Peter, *The Greatest Quotations of All Time* (www.Xlibris.com: Xlibris, 2010), 598.

6. Terry Cole-Whitaker, *What You Think of Me Is None of My Business* (New York: Penguin, 1979).

Conclusion

1. Matthew Kelly, *Perfectly Yourself—9 Lessons for Enduring Happiness* (New York: Ballantine, 2006), 180.

References

Adelson, ELH. "Lightness Perception and Lightness Illusions." In the *New Cognitive Neurosciences,* Second Edition. Edited by M. Gazzanig. Cambridge, MA: MIT Press, 2009.

Allen, David. *Getting Things Done.* New York: Penguin Group, 2003.

Bittel, Lester R. *The Nine Master Keys of Management.* New York: McGraw-Hill, 1972.

Carroll, Lewis. *The Annotated Alice: The Definitive Version.* New York: W.W. Norton and Company, 2000.

Chang, Laurence. *Wisdom of the Soul: Five Millennia of Prescriptions for Spiritual Healing.* Washington, DC: Gnosophia Publishers, 2006.

CNN.com. "E-mails 'Hurt IQ More Than Pot'." Accessed November 15, 2012. http://www.cnn.com/2005/WORLD/europe/04/22/text.iq/.

Cole-Whitaker, Terry. *What You Think of Me Is None of My Business.* New York: Penguin, 1979.

Collins, Jim. *Good to Great.* New York, HarperCollins, 2001.

Dean, Jimmy. *Thirty Years of Sausage, Fifty Years of Ham: Jimmy Dean's Own Story.* New York: Penguin Books, 2004.

Dillard, Annie. *The Writing Life.* New York: Harper and Row, 1989.

Franklin, Benjamin. *Benjamin Franklin, Wit and Wisdom.* White Plains, NY: Peter Pauper Press, 1998.

Gandhi, Mahatma. *Inspiring Thoughts.* Delhi: Rajpal & Sons, 2009.

Halvorson Heidi Grant. *Succeed.* New York: Hudson Street Press, 2010.

Jaffe, Dennis T., and Cynthia D. Scott. *Take This Job and Love It.* New York: Simon and Schuster, 1988.

Kelly, Matthew. *Perfectly Yourself—9 Lessons for Enduring Happiness*. New York: Ballantine, 2006.

Lao-Tzu. *Tao Te Ching: The New Translation from Tao Te Ching: The Definitive Edition*. Translated by Jonathan Star. New York: Penguin Group, 2001, 83.

Leichman, Abigail Klein. "Supportive Bosses Help Reduce Employee Sick Days." Israel 21C, March 18, 2012. Accessed December 14, 2012. http://israel21c.org/health/research/supportive-bosses-help-reduce-employee-sick-days/.

Maslow, Abraham. H. *Motivation and Personality, Second Edition*. New York: Harper and Row, 1970.

Matthews, Gail. *Goals Research Summary*. Accessed November 4, 2012. http://www.dominican.edu/academics/ahss/undergraduate-programs-1/psych/faculty/fulltime/gailmatthews/researchsummary2.pdf.

Maurer, Robert. *One Small Step Can Change Your Life the Kaizen Way*. New York: Workman Publishing Company, 2004.

Menon, PK. *The Urgent/Important Matrix*. Accessed March 1, 2013. http://driven.pkmenon.com/the-urgent-important-matrix/.

Merriam-Webster Dictionary, online edition. Accessed February 9, 2013. http://www.merriam-webster.com/dictionary/organize.

O'Toole, James. *Creating the Good Life: Applying Aristotle's Wisdom to Find Meaning and Happiness*. Emmaus, PA: Rodale, 2005.

Peters, Tom. *Thriving on Chaos: Handbook for a Management Revolution*. New York: Excel/A California Limited Partnership, 1987.

Richards, Dick. *Is Your Genius at Work? Four Key Questions to Ask Before Your Next Career Move*. Mountain View, CA: Davies-Black Publishing, 2005.

Robbins, Mike. *Be Yourself, Everyone Else Is Already Taken*. San Francisco: Jossey Bass, 2009.

St. Peter, Anthony. *The Greatest Quotations of All Time*. Xlibris, 2010. Xlibris.com.

Thoreau, Henry David. *Walden*. New York: Thomas Y. Crowell and Company, 1910.

Twain, Mark. *The Wit and Wisdom of Mark Twain: A Book of Quotations*. Mineola, NY: Dover Publications, 1999.

U.S. News and World Report, 2012–2013. "Massachusetts General Hospital." Accessed December 14, 2012. http://health.usnews.com/best-hospitals/area/ma/massachusetts-general-hospital-6140430.

Wired to Win: Surviving the Tour de France. "Mind Trip: Journey into the Brain." Accessed December 6, 2012. http://www.wiredtowinthemovie.com/mindtrip_xml.html.

Wright, Michael P. *The Coaches' Chalkboard.* Lincoln, NE: Writers Club Press, 2003.

Index

What's Next?

If you have enjoyed *The Joy of Strategy,* I invite you to connect personally so I can help you create a business plan and make it come to life. There are several ways to do this:

- Visit my website allisonrimm.com to:
  - Sign up for our newsletter filled with tips, tools, and inspiring stories of success and resilience
  - Connect with me on LinkedIn
  - Follow me on Twitter
- Participate in a workshop
- Sponsor any of our professional development programs in your workplace
- Work with one of our coaches for one-on-one guidance with your business plan for life
- Hire our team of consultants to help you develop and execute your organization's strategic plan
- Engage us to help you plan and facilitate your next management retreat
- Invite me to speak at an upcoming event

Go to allisonrimm.com to find out more about these and other offerings.

- Join me at JoyofStrategy.com, where you will find tips, tools, resources, and inspiration to stay on track in business and in life.

- Let me know about your triumphs and challenges. Write to me at allison@allisonrimm.com to ask a question, tell your story, or share a tip that helped you get around a roadblock or take advantage of an interesting opportunity. I will answer as many questions as I can and will feature selected stories and answer questions in upcoming blog posts and newsletters.

I sincerely hope that you have found the inspiration and practical advice you need to make your dreams come true. It will be my great joy to hear from you.